Führer, Folk
and Fatherland

Best wishes
Douglas Sagel

Albin Gagel

Führer, Folk and Fatherland

A Soldier's Story

Douglas Wolfgang Oskar Gagel

ISBN 978-0-9952091-0-7 (pbk.)
ISBN 978-0-9952091-1-4 (epub)
ISBN 978-0-9952091-2-1 (mobi)

Copyright © Douglas Wolfgang Oskar Gagel 2010

Cover, design, formatting: Magdalene Carson

The author and publisher have made every attempt to locate the sources of photographs and written excerpts. Should there be errors or omissions, please contact the author/publisher for correction in future publications.

Cataloguing in Publication data available from Library and Archives Canada

Contents

	Acknowledgements	vii
	Preface	vii
Chapter	July 4, 1943	1
1	"This Will Lead to War"	4
2	*Reichsarbeitsdienst*	21
3	Any Mother's Son Will Do	34
4	Blitzkrieg	46
5	Interlude	63
6	Cold War	73
7	Field Marshal Winter	86
8	The *Rasputiza*	94
9	*Sitzkrieg*	109
10	Prussians	122
11	Gisela Winkelsdorf	141
12	The Best Cabaret in Town	151
13	All Quiet on the Eastern Front	163
14	In the Jaws of the Bear	178
15	Hold Back the Tide	202
16	An Army Marches on Its Stomach	224
17	Night Moves	234
18	Sound and Fury	247
19	The Longest Day	267
20	The Lifesaver	279
21	Someone to Live For	301
22	Christmas Trees in the Sky	312
23	*Marsch Kompanie*	326
24	To Flee or Not To Flee	347
25	Between the Lines	350
26	Refugees	359
27	To the Rescue	362
28	The Last Ones Across the Elbe	368
29	POW	377
30	"The Russkies Are Coming"	390
31	*"Voiena Kaput"*	393
32	Gulag Hohengöhren	402
33	The Road Home	424
34	"The Peace Will Be Worse"	439
Epilogue	Never Again	464
Appendix	Glossary of German Terminology	467

Acknowledgements

A DEBT OF GRATITUDE is owed to the following:

My daughter Jennifer for inspirational guidance in constructing the story;

My brother, Ronald, for his uncompromising attention to detail in editing the book; and

My wife, Lynn, for her steadfast support and encouragement.

Preface

THIS IS A TRUE STORY. It is written in the first person, for that is how it was told by my father, Albin Gagel, recounting his experiences of the war years and their aftermath. There were surprisingly few lapses in his memory after more than half a century. As he put it, "I thought my memory would fade over time, but I can remember events from the war more clearly than what I did last week. Some things are unforgettable." Many wartime images must have been so dramatic that they left an indelible impression in his mind.

It took the family years to convince Father to set his story to print. He was initially reluctant, saying repeatedly that he only wanted to forget about the war, and that everyone who lived through it had their own story to tell. His experiences during those arduous times obviously left a profound psychological legacy, and only in his later years was he able to look back dispassionately and put his ordeal into words objectively, with some sense of purpose. Once convinced that we really were interested in his experiences, he bent to his task with characteristic vigour. It then took four years for his narrative to unfold and make it to the page.

"This book is for my grandchildren," Father said. "They must never know war. No one should ever again have to become a soldier, to go through what my generation experienced. I hope my grandchildren and future generations will learn from the mistakes of my generation. Perhaps my own story can help them understand the true nature of war and how it affected the lives of real people."

Most of our knowledge of World War II has been presented through the victor's eyes and often coloured by Hollywood, a propaganda machine just as powerful as the Third Reich. Father's story gives us an account of the German experience and a different perspective of events over which the average German had no control. It is probably representative of almost any soldier's perception of war—that it is instigated by a few ruthless industrialists and politicians who do not experience the horrors of warfare, but is fought by ordinary people who under the circumstances have more in common with the enemy than they have with their own leaders. Probably most soldiers' experiences in war are so terrible they just want to forget about them completely, leaving no legacy from which following generations could learn about what really happened. "Lest we forget" still has meaning.

Father's story provides insight into how it was even possible for such a thing as a world war to happen, for an entire nation to succumb to the leadership of a madman and endure living in a totalitarian state. It shows us that the Nazi government and the *Wehrmacht* military were not the same, that most Germans were not Nazis, that the Gestapo—secret police—were loathed and feared by every German, and that war crimes were committed by both sides, but only the losers were punished. The lessons to be learned about government, politics, the media, warfare, and human nature are as relevant today as they were then. The incentives that drove events in the 1930s and '40s are still operating in our world today.

"We never saw it coming until it was too late," Al said. "There were warning signs about the Nazis soon after the First World War, long before Hitler came to power, but the majority of people did not understand their importance. Do not assume it can't happen again, anywhere. My generation did not listen to the veterans from the First World War and did not learn from their mistakes."

Father's book is not so much a war story as it is one man's personal experience of the war years and their aftermath. It describes a foot soldier's perspective of events and their emotional impact during the most cataclysmic event in human history. In hindsight, what was considered normal during the war years seems completely alien to current ways of thinking in a country like Canada, where the horrors of warfare have not been experienced on Canadian soil.

Father lived a life of decency, diligence, and commitment to his family. He was gregarious, compassionate, generous, friendly, and patient. None of us ever knew him to tell a lie or break a promise, so the events described in this book are absolutely as true to his recollections as is possible after so many years. His story is a lesson in adaptability and tenacity, and an affirmation that the human spirit is able to overcome seemingly overwhelming adversity. Even with its dour observations and sometimes grim chronicle, in the end, his story is one of extraordinary optimism.

I knew Father to be interested in everything, to always see the good in people, and often to recognize opportunities where others saw only misfortune. For the rest of his life, he never lost his enthusiasm for simple pleasures, like dancing, playing cards with friends, tending his garden, building things with his sons, or watching his grandchildren play soccer or hockey. He appreciated the beauty and wonder in all of life's precious gifts. He cherished his family and friends, and never took anything for granted, from food on the table and a comfortable place to live, to health and love. He imparted in me an understanding of what is truly important in life, and an abiding feeling of gratitude for being alive.

Al died shortly before Christmas 1997 at the age of seventy-nine, leaving behind Gisela, his wife of fifty-three years, their two sons, and six grandchildren. On his deathbed he said, "Don't mourn my dying. Celebrate my life, for I have lived a full life. What more could I ask for?"

—Douglas Wolfgang Oskar Gagel
London, Ontario, Canada

July 4, 1943

THE INSECTS IN THE GRASS made a continuous scratching sound, as if the earth itself felt the itching, as if the field surrounding my little hole in the ground were alive. I was aware of that sound even over the distant detonations of the barrage.

The battle had begun before daybreak that morning, when we were awakened by the thudding reverberation of heavy weapons fire and explosions coming from the north. At first those dull popping sounds had been muffled and faint, too far away to affect us directly, but gradually and relentlessly that symphony of hostilities became louder and louder—the guttural voice of the terrifying monster closing in on me.

Very slowly I lifted my head, stretching my neck just enough to peek out over the edge of my foxhole, careful not to become a target for a sniper, and hoping to see some sign that the Russians had evacuated the top of the hill. There was no sign of enemy movement anywhere in front of our lines. Plumes of black smoke rose against the northern horizon, which flattened out into a continuous smoky haze. Eventually it covered the entire northern sky as it gradually drifted toward us. The pungent smell of smoke from the burning battlefield permeated the air. It had been faint at first, but now it had become an insidious presence.

The screaming howls of Stuka dive-bombers could be heard from the north as they dived and dropped their bombs, even though they were a long way away. The explosions could be heard and felt through the ground as the bombs hit, like ominous, thudding footsteps.

The previous night my company had been ordered to prepare to attack the hill the next morning, as part of a major German offensive. I knew what was expected of all of us. My military training had included how to execute an infantry attack, but no matter how much faith I had in my training, it was impossible to dispel the apprehension of the impending fight. I dreaded the thought of having to get out of my foxhole and charge into the face of an enemy dug into concealed positions.

The terrain between our lines was almost flat, with no holes, ditches, or even furrows in the ground deep enough to provide shielding from enemy fire. We would have to cross open ground with very little cover to hide behind and no opportunity to protect our bodies in the event the Russians stood their ground. Regardless, when the time came, I and everyone with me would have to go.

All that morning I expected the signal to attack, but we just waited and waited. By early afternoon we had still not received the signal to go. To say the waiting was nerve-wracking does not begin to convey the stress of that time. I prayed for some miracle that would preserve my life, knowing I had to get out of my little haven in the ground to charge at the enemy. "Dear God, let me survive this day!" my mind screamed.

I began to wonder if perhaps the attack had been called off. Command may have changed their mind? Perhaps the situation elsewhere at the front had altered and our attack would not be necessary? Whatever was going to happen, there was nothing any of us could do but continue to wait. It was pointless to speculate as to what might be going on.

I took a deep breath, dropped my shoulders, and slumped low into my foxhole. The insistent heat of the July sun permeated my body, dulling my senses, blurring reality and imagination. We waited, and waited. I spent time swatting flies away from my face as the relentless sun beat down. The scratching and buzzing of the bugs in the field diverted my thoughts. The insects were not concerned with our stupid military follies. Life goes on for the bugs regardless of the foolish machinations of mankind. They would be here long after we were gone.

Every few minutes I was reminded of the slowly approaching battle by the sound and tremor of each explosion—the violent convulsions of the monster. The very stark reality that this could be the last day of my life stared me in the face.

The wireless operator in the next foxhole signalled me. It was the captain. The attack would go at 1600 hours—in about half an hour. The tension level immediately went up another notch, and this time the knot in my stomach was not hunger. The order was passed down the line of foxholes in both directions. I slung my rifle across my back and checked the ammunition clip in my automatic. That short-barrelled, hand-held little machine gun would be more useful than my rifle when attacking, because it could be fired in quick bursts while on the move. The clip held thirty-two rounds. It was most effective at ranges of less than fifty metres, which is where I expected to be shortly.

It was impossible to alleviate the tension and terror I felt over the impending action. The pounding in my ears was my beating heart, drowning out the bugs and the distant sounds of battle. I noticed my uniform was wet with sweat. "Please let me survive this!" I implored again and again.

When the time came, the signal flare went up.

The knot in the pit of my stomach worsened instantly and a wave of intense heat flashed through my body. This was it! Nothing for it but to go. I yelled, "*Go!*" Everyone sprang out of their foxholes and headed toward the enemy at a steady run. All thoughts of salvation or even survival disappeared from my consciousness. I ran straight ahead. I could not turn back. I could not veer from my course. No clever tactics, no agile movements, no prayer, nothing could help me now. Nothing but luck.

1 "This Will Lead to War"

HOW HAD IT COME TO THIS? How was it possible that I had ended up here at the very edge of Hitler's Reich on the Russian Front, thousands of kilometres from home? How was it possible for an entire nation to have succumbed to the will of a madman? Why were we being consumed in the fires of another world war?

The seeds that helped bring forth the Second World War were planted by the nations that claimed victory over Germany at the end of First World War. The leaders of the former warring nations had signed the Peace Treaty of Versailles, formally ending the First World War, on June 28, 1919, almost eight months after the end of what they had called "the war to end all wars." The British and French navies had continued to blockade Germany long after the end of the fighting, preventing vital overseas supplies, including food and essential raw materials, from reaching Germany. It caused widespread famine, which made post-war living conditions extremely harsh for most Germans. That blockade was only lifted on condition that Germany admit blame for the war and pay exorbitant reparations for the cost of the war. Germany was compelled to sign the treaty even though the German army had not been defeated in the field.

The Treaty of Versailles required large parts of Germany, over 95,000 square kilometres, to be ceded to Poland, Czechoslovakia, France, and Denmark, reducing the country in size by almost a quarter. The homes of over 11 million Germans were suddenly under foreign occupation. The harsh terms of the treaty sowed seeds of animosity amongst the people of the German nation. The lingering legacy of hunger, humiliation, and discrimination had nurtured resentment against the victors, which helped Adolf Hitler eventually attain power in 1933.

Things did not improve in Germany during the 1920s like they did in other parts of the Western world. The economy continued to suffer, largely due to the staggering reparations Germany was forced to pay the victors of the First World War. From 1918 to 1933 the situation was characterized by high unemployment, rampant inflation, and persistent general discontent. German currency soon became practically worthless. In 1914, it took 4.2 Marks to purchase one American dollar; in December 1923, it took 250 billion Marks to buy one pound of sugar and 3 trillion Marks to buy one pound of meat. The economic chaos resulted in serious political instability that hampered the rebuilding of both the German economy and the nation.

Europe was still seized in the brutal grip of the First World War when, on January 13, 1918, I, Albin Alfons Gagel, was born. My father, Hartmann Lorenz Gagel, was not even at home to witness my birth. He was in the army serving his country. The cold of that winter was made all the more bleak by the desperate situation in Germany after four debilitating years of warfare. Even in my little home village of Michelau, Bavaria, which was far removed from the front, the years of strife had taken their toll.

Even though the fighting in the "Great War" had come to an end on November 11, 1918, substantial changes were slow in coming for postwar Germany. For years after the end of the war there was a scarcity of consumer goods and foodstuffs everywhere in Germany. Other than apples or plums in the fall, fruit was impossible to get. Meat was scarce and expensive. Even if you had money, there was not much available to buy. Clothing was expensive. I wore clothes and shoes that my older brother Hermann outgrew, then passed them on to my younger twin brothers, Edwin and Oskar, when I outgrew them. During most of my childhood I never had more than one pair of long pants, one pair of *Lederhosen*, which were short leather pants made from deerskin, two shirts at best, and one jacket. I usually had two pairs of socks and one pair of shoes. All of this seemed normal, so I did not miss the clothes I never had.

After leaving the army in 1923 my father found it difficult to make a decent living. Everyone worked hard to try to put the war behind them and rebuild their lives, but larger events were brewing in Germany, political events that would shape the country's destiny—and mine—for years to come.

People in small rural communities like Michelau were not affected as severely as the vast majority who lived in the large cities, so in spite of the austere post-war living conditions, growing up in Michelau was probably a blessing that I would only come to understand much later in life.

Michelau was a typical village of about 6,000 inhabitants in Oberfranken, a province of Bavaria. Few people had decent jobs. Barter on

Hartman Lorenz Gagel   *Anna Mathilde Gagel*

the *Schwarzmarkt*, the black market, was the only way to obtain most goods and services. Nevertheless, living in such a humble village within a farming community where everyone knew and helped each other went a long way to make life enjoyable, if not lavish, after the First World War.

As a schoolboy I really paid no attention to the economic situation in the country. I was preoccupied with my daily meals, playing soccer, playing cowboys and Indians or cops and robbers in the woods near our house with my friends, and with going to school. My memories of childhood are very happy, in spite of what I now realize were often very hard times. We were a working-class family, relatively poor by today's standards, but it seems I survived my early childhood intact.

My family planted a few vegetables in our front yard every spring. There were also gooseberry and raspberry plants in the backyard. In the fall my mother, Anna, made preserves to be eaten during the winter. We ate simple meals, including lots of heavy rye bread. One of my favourite treats was a slice of rye bread smeared with pig lard and sprinkled with a little sugar. If we were lucky enough to have some meat with dinner, I would sell my portion to Hermann for a few pennies, enough money to buy a *Krapfen*, a sweet donut-like pastry, at the bakery.

The most serious part of my childhood was my formal education. School in Michelau, and probably all of Germany, was very serious and strict. Teachers had absolute authority in the classroom and were respected professionals in society. The motto carved in stone above the doorway of the elementary school in Michelau read, *"OHN' FLEISS KEIN PREIS"* (without diligence no prize), which sums up the typical German attitude at the time, certainly toward education and by and large toward life in general. My most enduring memory from my academic career was of being hungry. All through grade school I rarely had enough to eat. Only occasionally was there food left over from breakfast or the previous night's dinner to provide me with a lunch.

The economic situation in Germany deteriorated even more after the stock market crash of 1929. In spite of the brief semblance of normality, which was portrayed by the media during what was called the Roaring Twenties, there was no prolonged recovery. That display of gaiety had been an illusion that things were going well with the world after the hardships of the First World War, masking the unstable German economy. Serious infighting persisted among various political groups in Germany, from communists to monarchists to fascists, all vying for control of the country. That internal struggle, combined with intrigues by foreign governments, and compounded by the reparations that Germany was forced to pay to the victors of the First World War, would eventually lead to the country's bankruptcy. The post-war *Rentenmark* became practically worthless. Unemployment became endemic until, by 1932, there were over six million Germans out of work. More and more the German people felt betrayed by their government, until they eventually lost confidence in the Weimar Republic's ability to solve any of Germany's woes. The nation was desperate for a leader to step up and take charge.

In January 1933, Adolf Hitler and the *Nazionalsozialistische Arbeiter Partei* (National Socialist Workers Party) were voted into power after a prolonged, bitter, and sometimes violent struggle with the communists for political control. They won that election by a very thin majority. The political programme and strategy that supported Hitler's rise to power had been deliberately designed to revive German nationalism and restore confidence and pride in the downtrodden German people. More significantly, it had been carefully orchestrated to convince Germans that National Socialism, and Hitler himself, was the answer to Germany's need for leadership. During the early thirties, radio broadcasts and newspapers were persuaded to keep up a constant media barrage that reinforced the impression that the National Socialists were the cure for whatever ailed the country.[1]

In August 1934, Hitler became Germany's *Reichskanzler* (chancellor). Most of the news media quickly became ardent government supporters, so that what was written in newspapers and magazines and heard on the radio, as well as shown on newsreels in the theatres, became unquestionable testimony that the National Socialist regime was turning Germany into the greatest state in the world. Newspaper articles and radio broadcasts critical of the government's actions became more and more rare. Eventually everything the average citizen was exposed to supported the government's actions.

What were heard more often than I think anyone wanted to hear were Hitler's speeches, which always contained glorifications of his recent achievements and promises of greater things to come. The newsreels showed him delivering his mesmerizing speeches before jubilant crowds. The elaborate and grandiose National Socialist Party rallies in the huge new stadium in Nürnberg were particularly impressive spectacles. German flags and National Socialist banners became popular signs of a growing national pride, and posters of Hitler adorned all public places.

Events actually fuelled the effect of the government's propaganda on German citizens. The economy improved dramatically after 1933. Reparations payments were finally stopped. Germany unilaterally went off the international gold standard, which for decades had been the foundation for most of Europe's and the rest of the Western world's currencies. Hitler declared that *Die Deutsche Arbeitskraft* (the power of the German workers) was now the government's guarantee for the Reichsmark. The government introduced measures designed to prime German industries into renewed productivity, and as industry boomed consumer goods became plentiful again. A sense of optimism about Germany's future swept the country under Hitler's leadership.

---

1   Germans did not refer to the government under Hitler as "Nazi," and did not call government officials Nazis. The term originated with the opposition parties during the 1933 election campaign as a derisive moniker for the National Socialists, in an attempt to belittle Hitler's political party. From 1933 to the end of World War II, Germans usually referred to their government simply as *Die Regierung* (the Regime). The Western allies adopted the term Nazi, and the occupation forces popularized it as a derogatory label for everything associated with Hitler's government.

Not surprisingly, my father supported Hitler during his rise to power, perhaps because the National Socialist Workers Party had such a powerful appeal for the average citizen through its determined efforts to get the country working again. From 1933 until the beginning of World War II the vast majority of Germans were very enthusiastic about Hitler's leadership and generally supportive of the direction the government was taking the nation. People were again able to work gainfully, buy goods, and feed their families. It was difficult to argue against success.

In 1933 I was in my second year at *Realschule* (high school). At the time I paid hardly any attention to political events. Political machinations and national events belonged in a realm outside my world. I was concerned with getting through school. After Hitler came to power the curriculum increased its emphasis on German history, especially on the heroic accomplishments of the German people. Those lessons were remembered only as long as it took to pass the next exam. One particularly noticeable change occurred soon after Hitler took power. In 1935 the government announced that everyone in Germany was to use the Latin (Roman) script, rather than the old Gothic script that had been in use in Germany for many generations. There was no debate or even discussion about this change, and nobody argued with it. It was probably a good idea, since the rest of the Western world was using the Latin script anyway. Perhaps Hitler reasoned it was time to conform to the ways of the modern world. So from one day to the next we were taught how to print and write the Latin script and used it exclusively from then on. It took me and my classmates a few days to adapt to the new way of forming letters, after which we never gave this passing of part of our cultural heritage another thought.

Growing up in a small community probably had a nurturing influence upon my personality, and I learned many important life lessons. The local Lutheran church was one of the cornerstones of Michelau society. Michelau and the neighbouring towns of Lichtenfels and Schnei were the only Lutheran enclaves in predominantly Catholic Bavaria. The personal interactions at church events helped foster a strong sense of community, of togetherness, and mutual support for Michelau's citizens, which was probably valuable for maintaining a peaceful and orderly social structure. Michelau society apparently worked well, for I never heard of any serious violence or crime. There was ever only one police officer serving the village's population of about 6,000.

My father taught me some useful and lasting lessons. One was that I should use my brain, act logically, and not make excuses. Behaving stupidly was probably the most contemptible thing I could ever have done in my father's eyes. I never heard any blatant moral judgement from my parents, but from the time I was old enough to understand anything, I knew that I was always expected to behave reasonably. That attitude, which is embodied in the Golden Rule, was characteristic of Michelauers. Displaying common sense was an attribute highly admired.

My father also taught me that no man should hit a woman or a child. He did not believe in physical punishment, and never hit us when we were growing up. I am grateful for that advice and have abided by it my whole life. It helped shape my attitude when raising my own two sons. Perhaps my father understood that punishment is a poor teaching technique, and that it was better to teach us responsibility, especially responsibility for our own actions.

My father instilled in his boys his optimistic nature. He taught that it was better to make the best of any situation that could not be changed than to complain about it. Complaining was something that he considered impolite. He told me to remember that, "no matter how bad you think things are, they can always get worse, so enjoy what you have while you can." Words to live by.

In 1934, shortly after turning sixteen, I joined the *Hitler Jugend* (Hitler Youth). The regime dictated that everyone from the ages of ten to eighteen join some kind of a Hitler Youth group, and there were a few fervent government types around who checked up on those who did not. At the time I thought it might be fun and exciting, and might even provide an opportunity to meet girls, which had become a keen interest.

At first the Hitler Youth was like joining the Boy Scouts; everyone participated in events such as hikes, sporting events, or performing theatre pageants. There were sharpshooting competitions for older teens, with prizes for the winners. I also knew of organized exchanges, which were usually three-week holidays for children from the big cities who were brought into small rural communities to learn about agrarian life, while the rural children were able to experience big city life. One of the more meaningful activities was collecting for charities, such as the *Winterhilfswerk* (Winter Help Works) fund. These charities were intended to augment the long-established government social assistance

Hitler Youth group

programs by helping the disadvantaged in times of need. In spite of their pension, widows were especially needy in the thirties, and the First World War had produced a great many widows in Germany.

Activities associated with Hitler Youth eventually included lectures by government officials on the virtues of the National Socialist Party and the state leadership. It was the first time I heard phrases like "patriotic duty" and "service for the Fatherland," which were meaningless to me. I soon grew disinterested in hearing about Hitler's heroic struggle to assume power and the great future that the Party would bring to Germany. At the time it was easy to disdain the Hitler Youth organizers, because they acted stuffy and patronizing. After attending a few such politically motivated events, I skipped as many as I could get away with, even though I knew that the local government representatives frowned upon truancy. They tried several times to pressure me to return, even telling my parents that my absence could have consequences. Happily for me, in a close-knit community like Michelau, there were enough understanding friends among those with influence that I was not forced to return.

Perhaps I disliked the Hitler Youth so much because all activities were segregated, boys with boys, girls with girls. That was a significant issue during my teenage years.

It was about this time that everyone started calling me "A." It was common in Michelau to give people nicknames. My father had been baptized Hartmann Lorenz Gagel, but everyone in the village knew

"Turkola"

him as *Turko*, probably because of his service with the German army in Turkey during the First World War. I was called *Turkola* as a small boy, which meant Little Turko. I was named after my god-father, Albin Werner, my mother's brother. Albin means "white one" in the old Teutonic language. Perhaps by a quirky family association, my younger twin brothers, Edwin and Oskar, were called "E" and "O." Those abbreviations stuck with Michelauers for the rest of our lives. A letter addressed simply to *O, Michelau, Oberfranken*, would reach my brother with no problem.

In 1938 I graduated from *Realschule*. Like many of my fellow graduates, I was fed up with school, but also had no clear ambition as to what career path I wanted to follow. Some of my friends volunteered for the military, hoping to get their two years of mandatory service over with as soon as possible. I was reluctant to volunteer, perhaps more out of procrastination than some insight into political trends. So, to earn some money and to help out the family business, I worked for my parents as a *Korbmacher* (basket maker), manufacturing mainly wicker bowls and other containers, until April 1939.

Michelau had long been the centre of the wicker furniture and ornamental basket industry in Germany, a fact that is acknowledged by the national *Korbmuseum* (Wicker Museum) located there. Konrad Gagel, probably a distant relative, established the first wicker factory in Michelau in 1850. August Gagel, probably another distant relative, owned the largest wicker factory in Michelau, and the name Gagel is synonymous with that industry to this day. That lucrative local industry produced wicker and cane furniture, all kinds of industrial and agricultural baskets, utilitarian and decorative containers, baby carriages, and other products for household use.

Taking advantage of a potential economic opportunity, in 1934 my parents had started a small part-time business making bowls and baskets out of fine wicker, cane, and coloured raffia. My father invented a novel pattern for a woven tray, which became very popular. That small venture gradually developed into a full-time cottage industry. Eventually they employed about eight people full time on contract, and sometimes more part-time people. My father was very pleased with his business, especially after the very lean times he had endured before Hitler came to power. He attributed much of his success to the improving national economy that Hitler and the National Socialists had engineered throughout Germany.

Those were prosperous times, especially compared to the desperately impoverished years that preceded Hitler's rise to power. After Hitler came to power, the public demonstrations and violence in the big cities that had repeatedly troubled post-war political life in Germany abated seemingly overnight. I, like most Germans, had grown up with the notion that criminal activity was impolite; but under Hitler, perhaps because of his strict government but more likely due to the healthy economy, the crime rate all but disappeared. I remember my mother saying that she could go alone into any part of Nürnberg or any other of Germany's big cities and feel safe. It certainly felt safe and secure living in my village, but that was the way it had always been.

From 1933 until 1939, I believe most Germans supported, or at least accepted, the National Socialist Party government. In retrospect it was easy to see that there was a dark side to the regime, which few people recognized at the time, or wanted to acknowledge if they did. It quickly became a brazen and unashamed dictatorship. Hitler turned from being a chancellor to being the "Führer."

There were warnings about Hitler and his brown-shirted followers right from the start of Hitler's quest to wrest power from the Weimar Republic. During the election campaign of 1933, in which members of the National Socialist Workers Party stood as candidates, someone in Michelau posted a large banner over the top of the bulletin board in the village square that read, "Who votes for Hitler votes for War." That was about as volatile as Michelauers got over political events. Apparently few people in Germany paid any attention to such warnings, and Hitler's National Socialists were elected. Considering the situation in the country, it was obvious that of all the political candidates running for election at the time, including communists and monarchists, the National Socialists held out the best hope for producing a positive change in Germany's fortunes.

One memory had a poignant warning about Germany's political fortunes. My mother and I were visiting an old friend of hers, Frau Guthseel, sometime shortly before Christmas 1937. During the conversation the two women discussed Hitler's public rhetoric and the sacrifices he asked the German people to make for the good of the country. I got the distinct impression that Frau Guthseel disliked the regime, and that she was suspicious and fearful of Hitler's ambition.

At the time I thought the regime was doing an excellent job managing the country's economy, by providing work and a decent standard of living for all Germans. Germany's status as a country to be respected among European nations had been restored. Earlier, in March 1936, Hitler had ordered the reoccupation by German troops of the Rhineland, which had been made a demilitarized zone, occupied by foreign French troops after the end of the First World War. That was an audacious gamble, considering that the German army at the time could not have defended the Rhineland from the French army if France had retaliated. Watching newsreel footage of our troops marching into Rhineland cities, I believe few people knew how weak the German military really was. It had been restricted by the Treaty of Versailles to one hundred thousand men in total, and they were equipped with very few weapons and insufficient ammunition to sustain any kind of fight. As it turned out, France did not retaliate, and Hitler's gamble succeeded. It was greeted with great enthusiasm by the German public, who thought Hitler was justified in reoccupying the Rhineland. It was German territory, populated mainly by Germans, so it was only fair that German troops should occupy it. It eliminated the imposed borders that had separated German families and friends.

Berlin had hosted the Olympics in 1936. It was a showcase event, well organized, staged in beautiful new facilities, and resplendent with impressive ceremonies. It turned out to be a magnificent success. The sporting events were closely followed by everyone in the country through newspaper reports, radio broadcasts, and newsreels. It was the first time I felt a sense that the whole world had been brought together in something grand and noble. That prestigious event provided a tremendous boost to the sense of pride in their own nation

Michelau Oberfranken, 1939

felt by all Germans. It elevated my opinion of the stature of Germany internationally. Hitler's government had resurrected Germany from the ashes of the First World War and the terrible conditions of the post-war era to a prosperous nation that was once again a First World country.

All of Hitler's successes notwithstanding, my mother's friend was not persuaded that what was going on in the country was a good thing. She bluntly said, "You watch out, this will lead to war."

I dismissed such talk as unnecessarily alarmist, the prattling of an old woman out of step with the times. Everything in Germany was obviously going great. By then Hitler's government was a dictatorship to be sure, but it was very popular. I believed he had no need to go to war, as he had accomplished more than anyone had expected. Germany was once again a great nation, so naturally Hitler should be satisfied with the state of the country. I thought that it must just be old people who were by nature fearful of change. What did they know? Could they not understand this was a new age?

At the time there was no reason in my mind to be overly concerned with the regime's management of affairs; still, if I had taken the time to think about it, there were indications of trouble long before the outbreak of war in 1939, portents that all was not well with Hitler's government. For one thing, there was obviously too much meddling in matters that should have had nothing to do with legislative policies or went beyond legitimate administrative regulations.

One such aspect was a deliberate campaign to discredit *Juden* (Jews), which had started out as subtle propaganda but had become increasingly explicit and blatant the longer Hitler's regime was in power. Eventually even the mention of *Juden* in the press or on the radio took on a derogatory connotation. We saw and heard so many reputable news articles about the "threat" of the Zionist plot for world domination that it was difficult not to believe it.

The film *Der Ewige Jude* (*The Eternal Jew*) was a blatantly bigoted piece of propaganda; however, it was cunningly crafted by the government's filmmakers to espouse its message—that German citizens should feel abhorrence for Jews. One scene was particularly appalling; it showed the slaughter of a cow according to Jewish kosher tradition, by slicing its throat and letting it bleed to death. I was young and impressionable at the time and found that depiction to be extremely gruesome and deeply disturbing. The film also portrayed Jewish people as a plague of rats, literally using special camera effects to morph images of bearded Jewish men into hundreds of scurrying rats. The film was a carefully crafted piece of propaganda, but was presented as if it was a documentary, and must have had a profound effect upon most viewers. The repugnant impression it left in people's minds was a calculated ploy to help the government implement Hitler's plans for persecuting Europe's Jews and confiscating Jewish property.

I personally never witnessed any mistreatment of anyone Jewish. There were no Jewish families living in Michelau. There were two Jewish boys in my class in the *Realschule* in the nearby town of Lichtenfels. I got to know one of them, Siegfried Kahn, quite well because we did schoolwork together. I visited his parents' house often. His mother was an amiable, generous woman, who always offered me food and drinks when I came to visit. During a visit, probably in 1936, I noticed a change in her. She seemed nervous and less happy than I had seen her before. Perhaps she realized how things were developing in Germany and how it would affect her and her family personally. She mentioned that their whole family might leave Germany. I did not pay much attention to that kind of talk, until sometime later when Siegfried told me his family really was moving away. Shortly after that he stopped coming to school. He did not tell me where they went, but I assumed his family left the country.

On November 9, 1938, we heard news on the radio of what was to become known as *Kristallnacht* (Crystal Night). The radio broadcasts and newspapers said that Jewish businesses had their storefront windows deliberately broken by "outraged citizens," allegedly as a warning to the Jewish proprietors to leave the country. The media picked up on the event to demonstrate the extent to which Germany's economy was controlled by "Zionists," as there were a great many downtown stores, businesses, and banks that had been attacked. The timing and scale of that act of vandalism seemed very suspicious.[2]

I found it bewildering that such a destructive crime could happen to German citizens, regardless of their religious or ethnic background. Evidently something was seriously wrong with the way the country was being run if the perpetrators could get away with that kind of lawlessness, but by then everyone had learned to be reluctant to openly criticize anything that may be sanctioned by the government. Even though the media had downplayed the actual events, most Germans were well aware of the suspicious deaths of many of Hitler's political adversaries. My father may have understood more than I gave him credit for at the time, when he had told me not to believe everything I heard on the radio or read in the newspapers.

That organized vandalism only happened in the big cities; absolutely nothing happened in Michelau, or Lichtenfels, or any of the other towns and villages in Oberfranken that I was familiar with. So, after a few manifestations of disbelief and outrage, most Michelauers just dismissed it as an isolated incident and soon put it out of their minds. Those types of political confrontations were only of passing interest, especially because they happened in big cities far away. Like most citizens, I just hoped for the best.

For many months after August 1938 I cared less about political events, as I had to deal with the first tragedy of my life. My mother had been found floating face down in the Main River about five kilometres downstream from our house. Her death was a grievous, traumatic shock. At

---

2   *Kristallnacht* had been deliberately planned and executed by elements of the *Gestapo* (Secret Police) and the *Sturm Abteilung* (Storm Unit), or SA for short, the brown-shirted paramilitary group that had become an agency of the ruling party. After the fall from grace of their leader, this agency was transformed into the *Schutzstaffel* (Guard Corps), or SS for short, the National Socialists' private army. Neither the SA nor the SS ever became part of the *Wehrmacht*, the regular German Army.

the funeral I met members from her side of the family that I hardly knew. Despite all the expressions of condolences and sympathy, I moved as if in a daze, my mind numbed by the tragedy of the occasion. I felt an oppressive sadness for a long time afterwards, like a physical thing, a pain felt throughout my body.

Home was never the same again. After her death I realized that my mother had held the family together. I had not really been aware of how much she did for us. Her personality and caring had made our house a home. Much of our family life had been devoted to events that were important to her and centred upon aspects of the household that were her responsibility.

My father tried to show a strong face, but he sometimes sat quietly in the living room holding her picture. At ten years old, my youngest brother Karl was absolutely devastated by her loss. We tried to support each other as best we could, but Karl acted strangely detached for a long time, as if refusing to accept or even acknowledge the reality that she was gone forever.

No matter what, life goes on. My Aunt Gustel, Turko's unmarried sister, took over much of the responsibility of raising Karl. As his god-mother, she more or less adopted Karl and considered him the son she never had. Afterwards she always called him "*my Karla.*" Shortly after mother's death my older brother Hermann married Anna, and the two of them moved into the second floor of Father's house. Anna took over many of the household duties, including cooking and caring for the rest of the family, while the rest of us pitched in wherever we could.

I continued to work in the family business. I spent many evenings and Sundays playing soccer. Two or three evenings a week a few friends would gather at the local pub to play cards or just socialize. I started attending dances, parties, and other festive events in the village. I met many young ladies and spent some time dating a few, but nothing serious developed. I was not sure what I wanted to do with my life, or what kind of career to pursue, or even just how to settle down. All I knew for sure was that my life in Michelau was no longer fulfilling; however, I did not feel motivated to strike out in any particular direction. That was a time in my life when I just sort of drifted along aimlessly, restlessly, passing time until the inevitable moment when I would be called up to serve my country for compulsory military service.

In hindsight, it is easy to see there was a long-term strategy in the government's actions. Since coming to power, Hitler's regime had brought about major political changes. In March 1938 Hitler had engineered the *Anschluss* (merger) with Austria. We saw newsreels of Austrian citizens chanting in the streets of Vienna, "We want to return home into the Reich." In October 1938, he had acquired the Sudetenland, the part of Czechoslovakia near the German border that had been taken from Germany at the end of World War I. It had been settled by Germans since the twelfth century. Those were very bold and enterprising ventures, which made Hitler look like a brilliant strategist and leader. In March 1939, he annexed the rest of Czechoslovakia, in spite of British prime minister Chamberlain's "peace in our time" speech on his return to England from his meeting with Hitler. The annexation of Czechoslovakia was the first overtly aggressive and politically inexcusable move on Germany's part, and many of us expected dire consequences to follow from the other European nations. But when nothing adverse happened, Hitler again looked like a genius.

Throughout the late 1930s, Hitler's initiatives to return lands wrested from Germany by the Treaty of Versailles—lands still populated predominantly by ethnic Germans—back to Germany were of course popular with the majority of Germans. By the summer of 1939, it became obvious that his next target was Poland. Before World War I, most of what was now western and northern Poland had been part of Prussia, and Berlin was more or less in the centre of Prussian-dominated Germany. Afterwards, the victors had given the German provinces of West Prussia, Posen, and part of Silesia to Poland, including the Danzig Corridor, which divided what was left of East Prussia from the rest of Germany. Hitler had been negotiating with Poland to acquire the port of Danzig, at the northern end of the Danzig Corridor, and to restore land access to East Prussia and its state capital of Königsberg. When the Polish government not only refused but formally annexed Silesia in October 1938, war became inevitable.

Eventually it became apparent that unless something drastic happened to curb Hitler's ambitions, the path our government was following would lead to military confrontation with France and England. It should have been obvious that the government propaganda media were relentlessly preparing the public for war. *Informations Minister* Josef Goebbels did a shrewd job to convince the masses that our great

Führer had only the best interests of his people in mind, and that he had no love for our enemies, which in 1939 had become the Poles.

At the cinemas, we saw newsreels of Polish soldiers harassing ethnic German civilians living in Polish towns and cities, including scenes of Polish soldiers kicking women and children out of their homes at gunpoint. It was easy to believe those news events; it never occurred to us that they were complete fabrications by our government, designed to enrage upstanding German citizens and garner support for retaliation against the Poles. By the time Hitler was ready to invade Poland his "news" reports had been so effective that he had the support of the majority of his people. I, too, had believed those reports.[3]

All the inflammatory media propaganda about the country's so-called enemies, all the political news about international tension, and especially all the rhetorical frenzy about German nationalism, rearmament, and returning Germany to the empire it had been before the World War could only mean that Hitler was planning and preparing for another war. The prophetic words spoken by my mother's friend two years earlier echoed in my mind . . . "This will lead to war."

Regardless, by 1939 there was nothing I nor any of my fellow citizens could do to change things. For a German citizen living under Hitler's dictatorship there was no choice but to comply with the rules set by the regime. The common and innocent-sounding slogan that Germans were then fond of spoofing took on a much more serious meaning, as we could actually be called upon to make sacrifices "for Führer, Folk, and Fatherland."

---

3   The newsreel footages were staged by the Nazi propaganda media, but they were based upon facts. Between the two world wars, Polish authorities forcibly removed thousands of ethnic Germans from their homes and confiscated their lands and property, resulting in the deaths of many of those that chose to resist. In 1939 all military-aged German men in the occupied lands were rounded up and sent east, perhaps in anticipation of a German military invasion, and many of those men never returned.

2 *Reichsarbeitsdienst*

EARLY IN 1939, ALL GERMAN MEN MY AGE had received official notice from the government that in October they would be drafted into the armed forces for two years of military service.

Full of youthful bravado, some forty young men from my village went to Lichtenfels by train for the physical examination. We were assembled in a large public gymnasium, along with many other young men from other nearby communities. We were told to strip and line up for examination. The room was cold and I felt quite uncomfortable, not only because I was standing naked with a bunch of men, most of them strangers, but because personal dignity was totally disregarded. Not that being naked in the company of men was abnormal, as everyone on the soccer team normally showered in the dressing room after a game. That experience in that gym somehow had a mechanical, surreal feel to it.

When I reached the front of the line I stood before a doctor who wore a white hospital coat and a stethoscope around his neck. He squinted through his wire-rimmed spectacles as he examined me. He asked if I had any permanent disabilities, about my history of childhood diseases, and whether or not I was on medication. He looked me over from top to bottom, listened to my breathing with his stethoscope, told me to turn around, lift one foot, turn around again, and then dismissed me. The doctor's assistants pointed to the door and told me to get dressed. The whole examination took less than a minute. It was probably intended to make sure everyone had all their parts, no flat feet, and no communicable diseases, especially tuberculosis.

Each of us was handed a letter informing us as to which branch of the armed services we would be assigned. Most of the men were assigned to an infantry regiment with its home base in nearby Coburg. I was assigned to a regiment with its home base in Passau, near the Austrian border, about 300 kilometres from my home.

On the way home we all made fun of the doctor and the examination. There were the mandatory jokes about parading around naked, and unanimous superficial unconcern about the whole thing. But it left me with a sullied feeling that stayed with me for a long time. I was not used to being treated like a commodity. But everyone accepted it as a normal part of life. No one questioned the righteousness or morality of mandatory military service or anything that went with it. The possibility of having to fight in a war was not brought up by anybody.

At the time, most Michelauers certainly did not take the National Socialists too seriously and considered Hitler's manifesto, *Mein Kampf* (My Struggle), more as *Mein Krampf* (My Nonsense) than the political bible that Hitler's supporters said it was.

On April 1, 1939, I had to report to the construction camp near the village of Irlbach for a six-month stint in the *Reichsarbeitsdienst*, the compulsory government labour service.

All young men born in 1918 had to serve six months in the *Arbeitsdienst* before joining the army. My father considered it reasonable for everyone to serve his country for half a year. The government had been responsible for the resurgence of economic health and national pride in Germany, so perhaps he considered it a small repayment of sorts. He may also have thought the regimented discipline would be good for me.

My father's attitude to compulsory state service could easily have been different. He had returned from "the World War," as Germans called World War I, with a bullet lodged in his body, next to his right lung near his heart, which was never removed. It could be that at the time surgical techniques were not sophisticated enough to remove such a foreign object so close to his heart without risking his life. Later he may have considered it too much trouble to undergo an operation.

My father rarely talked about his experiences in the World War. What I did learn was that he had been a *Feldwebel* (sergeant) in the infantry, and that he had served with the German army in the Balkans and in Turkey. He had been wounded while fighting in Turkey. He had joined the army in 1911 and had remained in the post-war German armed forces, the *Reichswehr*, until 1923. Those twelve years of service entitled him to receive a one-time military allowance of 12,000 Reichsmark, the German currency at the time. That lump sum was used to make a down payment on the purchase of a house for the family, a big three-storey stucco house with twelve rooms, including an indoor outhouse. It was a tangible status symbol in Michelau at the time, and probably helped make my father a man of respect in the village. For me, it was the foundation of the family—home—with all the benevolent and sentimental connotations of that word.

My father convinced me it was my patriotic duty to serve my country. I was twenty-one, and it seemed an opportunity to get out of the dull routine of village life in Michelau. Besides, there was no choice. I was actually the first of my parents' sons to be conscripted into the *Arbeitsdienst*. My brother Hermann was already too old, and the twins, Edwin and Oskar, and my youngest brother, Karl, were too young.

I was informed that uniforms and equipment would be supplied at the camp, so I packed only a few personal things—a toothbrush, a comb, and my shaving kit—and left with just the clothes on my back. Train tickets were supplied by the state. My father and younger brothers wished me luck, gave me the mandatory hugs, a quick goodbye, and off I went.

When the train halted at the station in Irlbach about a dozen other young men got off with me. I had expected to see an official welcoming us, but instead we had to ask the station attendant where the *Arbeitsdienst* camp was. We were told it was about a kilometre outside the village, near the river. It was a surprisingly casual and unceremonious beginning to what I had considered to be a relatively momentous event in my life.

Irlbach was like Michelau, only smaller. The three or four hundred houses were closely packed together along a maze of short and narrow streets. The village centre contained the town hall, the church, a pub, and some shops. The mandatory soccer field was located near the edge of the core area. The farmhouses were clustered together with their barns and sheds among the other residences. As with every other village in Bavaria, it was surrounded by cultivated farm fields within walking or oxcart distance from the farmer's home in the village.

At the labour camp we new recruits were assembled in front of the administration building and greeted by the camp's leader, the *Lagerführer*, with a speech. He said something about the privilege of serving the Fatherland and how we would be turned into men. It sounded like he had made that speech before.

One of the unit leaders, an *Abteilungsführer*, led us to our barrack. The camp consisted of rows of simple wooden barracks that all looked the same. Each barrack slept twenty men in two rows of bunk beds along the side walls. At the foot of each bunk was a small footlocker for our possessions. Hanging from the central beam was a row of light bulbs with white metal lampshades that looked like Chinese hats. There was a large, wood-burning stove in the middle of the floor and a table with a few chairs near the door. That was it. It was difficult not to be struck by the Spartan drabness of the place.

The camp contained a building reserved for staff, with an office and a first-aid station. Another had washrooms, toilets, and showers. The largest building contained the kitchen and a huge mess hall with long rows of tables and benches. There was also a residence for the camp commander.

At the camp storeroom we were each given three new uniforms. One was a short white outfit for sports and callisthenics. The next was a dull beige work uniform made of wool. It reminded me of outfits I had seen Mexican peasants wearing in Western movies. Mine fit poorly. None of the other guys looked comfortable in theirs, either. The last was a formal dress uniform that made us look almost like soldiers. The clerk made sure it fit better than my work clothes. It too was wool, beige-brown in colour, and ostensibly even stylish. The only uniforms I had worn previously were soccer team kits.

We were issued a pick, a shovel, and a spade. The shovel was a regular long-handled steel shovel, to be used for work. The spade was spotless and shiny, and looked like it had never touched dirt. When I asked what it was for, the clerk said it was to be used in place of a rifle for parade drill. He just grinned at my incredulous look.

And it was! At the first assembly we were informed that our spade was to be kept shiny and clean at all times. It was the symbol of our dedication to the *Arbeitsdienst*, to our *Führer*, and to our Fatherland. It took me a while to believe anyone could seriously think such tawdry symbolism should be inspiring.

We were assigned to the construction of a flood-control dyke along one side of a stretch of the Danube River. A large section had already been completed. The fill to build up the earthen dyke was mostly just dirt, containing everything from fine clay to small rocks. It was delivered by dump trucks and then loaded onto hopper cars waiting on railway tracks that extended onto the top of the dyke structure itself. The open-top cars were pushed by a small locomotive down to the head of the earthworks at the end of the track and then tipped over to dump the fill onto the end of the dyke. The fill was then shovelled into place and packed down by ramming it with hand-held piles. More track was added, and the process was repeated again and again, thereby extending the dyke. My task was to shovel the fill into place.

Building a dyke along the Danube River,
Reichsarbeitsdienst, summer 1939

Each day we were awakened at 6 a.m., had a quick breakfast in the barrack, then marched off to the work site. We worked until 11:30 a.m., then returned to camp for lunch. At 1 p.m. we marched back to work until 4:30 p.m., when we returned to the camp to clean up. Only noon meals were eaten in the main dining room. The food was not exactly gourmet, being mostly potato-based stew with some meat in it, but it was filling and reasonably tasty. We were so hungry we would have eaten almost anything. Supper consisted of sandwiches in the barracks at 6 p.m.—heavy rye bread with sausage, cheese, or jam. At first most of us were exhausted from the work and just went to sleep after supper, but after a few days we got accustomed to the pace of the routine and things became a little easier.

We were paid for our labour—a whole twenty-five pennies per day, the cost of half a litre of beer. "Paid" may be a misnomer, because soap was the only commodity supplied by the camp. Toothbrushes, toothpaste, shaving supplies, washcloths, and everything else had to be purchased from the camp store. Those purchases often amounted to every penny you had earned, so you really ended up working for free. Everyone was well aware it was in essence slave labour for the state, but nobody expressed any discontent. We understood it was our duty, our contribution to society, working for the good of the nation.

During the week we went nowhere other than to work and back. On Sundays we went into the village. Irlbach was a small rural community, and there was not much there to make the trip worthwhile, other than going to the one cinema or the pub, and certainly nothing that could be called a nightlife. None of us had much spending money to buy more than a beer, so a trip to the pub was just barely better than staying in camp.

We entertained ourselves as best we could after work, mainly by reading, playing cards, or telling stories or jokes. One of our barrack-mates could mimic Benito Mussolini very well, which we all thought was hilarious. We nicknamed him *Il Duce*, after the Italian dictator's nickname. He had the strut down perfectly, the fists on his hips, the forward-jutting jaw, and even the head-nodding, just like in the news-reels. He even pretended making speeches in what sounded like Italian. Mussolini's well-publicized antics lent themselves easily to ridicule.

We told stories about events from our homes, which were prob-ably embellished to make them sound like great adventures. We talked about women, which most of us knew absolutely nothing about, even if we never admitted it. Some discussions turned to our futures in Hitler's Germany; however, we avoided talking about politics in any meaning-ful way. Our illustrious *Führer* seemed to pervade every aspect of public life in Germany and was therefore too real and intimidating to be a suitable subject.

We often played soccer in the field at the camp with ad-hoc teams of shirts and skins. I was a good soccer player, so those games were fun diversions. I used the skills I had learned from Sunday afternoon soccer games in Michelau's *Sportplatz*, which were usually the highlight of the week. Skilful and decisive players were minor heroes in Michelau.

Even though I was with a group of what could be termed buddies, I did not form any strong bonds. All of us knew that the *Arbeitsdienst* was just time out from real life. The atmosphere of the place was not condu-cive to pleasantries. We knew that we would still have to serve another two years in the armed forces. It had not really sunk into my mind yet that the happy home life I had known in my youth was over forever.

After weeks of exactly the same routine, we were told to assemble the next morning in the compound's parade ground in full dress uniform and with our shiny spades. We were marched around the grounds in formation for hours. After lunch we were sent off to resume our regu-lar labours at the dyke. That happened every day for almost a month.

On each of those parade days we carried our shiny steel spades with us. Sometimes we went on long marches with the spades over our shoulders as if they were rifles. Another part of our exercises was the singing of songs. Some songs recounted heroic deeds performed by heroes of the Fatherland. I thought all that parading, marching, and singing was just senseless. Judging from the pained and bewildered expressions on their faces, most of the men with me felt as silly as I did.

One hot morning in July we were roused out of bed, assembled, and marched off to the meadow before I had a chance to have breakfast. We did our usual parading and then had to stand at attention for what seemed like hours more while the camp commandant babbled on and on about something to do with our glorious Fatherland. Apparently we were competing to attend the upcoming National Socialist rally in Nürnberg. Due to the merciless heat, the heavy dress uniform, the increasingly weighty spade, and because I had not fuelled up with food, I passed out while standing in the line. As my knees buckled I slumped against the man beside me. I recovered sufficiently to have been able to stand, but by that time I had enough of that nonsense and pretended to be incapacitated. As I had hoped, I was sent to the infirmary for the remainder of the day . . . to rest.

On one twenty-kilometre march I got tired of carrying my shiny spade and stuck it in my belt. That worked so well it even gave me a chance to rest my hand on it. Upon returning I hurriedly stored my gear and went right to bed, falling into an exhausted sleep. The next morning I discovered that the sweat from my hand had stained the spade's shiny surface. That could get me into trouble, as we had been expressly ordered to always keep our spade immaculate. Clean as I might, the stain would not come out completely. Afterwards I was apprehensive about being reprimanded for that damn stubborn stain if one of the group leaders were to examine the spade closely during inspection.

In addition to donating free labour to the state and learning to march in parades and sing songs, we were also required to take pre-military training. Starting in July, we were taught how to shoot a rifle and how to care for it. Learning to shoot a rifle was quite engaging. My mind had not yet made the conscious association between shooting a weapon and trying to kill someone.

At the rifle range we were lined up at the near edge of a large field, told to lie on the ground and aim at the bull's-eye targets at the far end of the field. The targets were paper sheets with concentric rings printed on them, the smallest at the centre being ten centimetres across, and the largest being about half a metre in diameter. They were mounted on the front of a large slope behind a deep wood-lined ditch, about a soccer field-length away from us. They looked impossibly far away to hit with a bullet. I had no clue how to accurately fire a rifle. When I was shown my target sheets, very few of my bullets had hit anywhere near the centre. I practised for hours, but never figured out why I kept missing the target, even though I could clearly see the centre circle of the target in the sights.

Eventually one of the *Truppenführers* (squad leader) explained the mechanics of firing a rifle so that you could hit exactly where you aimed. The secret was to relax and be patient. Breathe in, aim just above the target at first, then slowly breathe out as you lower the rifle sights slightly to the exact centre. At the end, hold your breath and gently squeeze the trigger as if you were gradually closing your hand. It was most important to keep your entire body absolutely still, your eye focused, and your hands steady until the moment the bullet was discharged, no matter what kind of distractions happen around you.

After that lesson I knew exactly where my bullets hit, every time. After a few more weeks of practice I could easily hit the centre ring of the target. That was also an object lesson—that concentration and patience could be very important aspects of a useful skill.

Most of my stint in the *Arbeitsdienst* was unpleasant and monotonous. Unbelievably, some of the *Truppenführers* and *Abteilungsführers* in charge actually made it worse. Most of them were about my age, some even younger. A few had the look and attitude of thugs. How those men had been assigned to their positions of authority was a mystery to me. Some of them tried deliberately to humiliate us at every opportunity. Bad enough that I was forced to work for free, but their attitude made it degrading. Their overt demonstrations of personal authority did nothing to enhance our military skills or to make us work harder. They probably received little training in how to be leaders, and most of them certainly did not have any natural talent for it. Perhaps they had been instructed to break us of any resistance to obeying orders?

Abteilungsführer Geiger was one such bully. On one training exercise we were ordered to crawl through a field full of cow shit while he watched. I had no idea what that was supposed to teach us. Needless to say, we detested it and we detested him. My guess is that types like him were probably too stupid for a productive career and would always be relegated to menial positions in semi-military settings like the *Arbeitsdienst*.

Our *Truppenführer* was only nineteen, two years younger than me. His name was Hager. I never did learn his first name. He was about my height, 172 cm (5' 8"), with a stocky, muscular build and a short military-style haircut. He was not well liked or respected by any of us in the squad. He often acted as if he needed to show us how tough he was. Worst of all, he seemed to need to show off his authority. The first time we met him he puffed up his chest and screeched out, "As long as I am your *Truppenführer*, you will obey me without question!" That struck me as strange. What was the big deal? We had all arrived well aware that we were here to work, so naturally we would follow someone's orders. He made it sound like it was his decision. I was not enthusiastic about being forced to play soldier for some petty dictator.

Regardless of my feelings, one thing was made clear very quickly: any display of personal initiative or non-conformity to the established rules was unacceptable. Individualism was relentlessly suppressed and replaced with strict obedience to authority. I was often reprimanded by our *Truppenführer* for some presumed misdemeanour, and most of those times wondered what the hell I had actually done wrong.

One day during regular inspection, Hager spotted that telltale stain on my spade. I knew right away that would be an excuse for him to try to embarrass me. "You are a disgrace!" he screamed in my face. "You will clean your spade until it sparkles and show it to me again tomorrow." Well, I had already tried to clean the damn thing, but tried again. Still no good. The same thing happened the next day. Hager made me clean it with a gritty cleaning compound, scrubbing until my fingertips were raw. Again no good. He centred me out three times before he finally gave up, or just got tired of the effort. The stain on the spade won that battle.

In spite of the strict regimen and the *Truppenführers'* tyranny, the temptation to buck the system was sometimes irresistible. One day Hager ordered me to clean the wood-burning stove in the centre of the barrack, an unpleasant task that may have been assigned as punishment for some unintentional or just imagined slight against the *Arbeitsdienst* or the integrity of my *Truppenführer*. I fetched a pail for the ashes, a scrub brush and a rag, and proceeded to do the best job I could. I scraped all the ashes out of the bottom of the stove into the pail, making sure there was none left, and cleaned up the soot and dirt on the floor under the stove. I then filled my pail with soapy water and carefully cleaned every inch of the stove. I even polished the flue and the steel sheet on which the stove stood. After satisfying myself that everything was as clean as I could make it, I confidently reported my task completed to Truppenführer Hager.

Naturally he had to inspect my work. He carefully checked the stove and seemed to find nothing amiss. Then he opened the door and ran his finger along the inside of the stove, turned toward me, and smeared his sooty finger across my cheek, announcing to everyone present that the stove was not clean and I had done a poor job. As I felt anger well up inside me I resisted my reaction to retaliate immediately, the consequences of which would surely have been grave. I endured that cretin's abuse in front of my barrack-mates, but resolved to get even.

As soon as he left I opened the flue, picked up my pail, and poured the rest of the soapy water into the stove. It sloshed down the flue and through the stove, and poured out onto the floor in a sudsy black mess. From the expressions on the faces of my barrack-mates, they must have thought I had lost my mind! When Hager returned a few minutes later and saw what I had done, he stood as if in shock for a moment, then ran out of the barrack, returning a few minutes later with the camp's *Lagerführer*. The other men in the barracks immediately moved away from the stove to avoid being considered guilty by association. The room went absolutely silent. Everyone stood at attention.

That was the first time I had been so close to the camp's commandant. He was probably in his mid-thirties, taller than I was, and slightly overweight. He exuded a professional and confident bearing. Right then I was more furious with Hager than scared of the *Lagerführer*, so it took a few moments to realize that being the centre of attention under those circumstances might not be good. He inspected the soapy black mess on the floor, checked the black streak on my cheek, and then looked me in the eye. "What happened?"

I explained how Truppenführer Hager had not been satisfied with my attempt to clean the stove. He kept remarkably calm, listening patiently to what I had to say. His expression remained dispassionate. Although I did not look him directly in the eye, I was sure a flash of understanding crossed his face. After I finished my account, he took one more look at the stove, and then left without saying another word, with Hager following close behind. Nobody moved for at least five minutes, probably expecting some swift reprisal. Then the wisecracks started—about how Hager was going to kill me, or how I would probably be shot, or at least spend the rest of my service cleaning latrines, or some other fate worse than death.

I never found out what the *Lagerführer* said to Truppenführer Hager, but neither of them returned that day.

Unfortunately we still had to clean up the mess on the floor. It took an hour of hard scrubbing, but this time my barrack-mates pitched in to help me, perhaps to show support, or perhaps just to make sure I did not do anything else overly dramatic. They had probably had enough excitement for one day, watching that "battle of wits."

My little ploy had been entertaining for my barrack-mates, but it had been a risky gamble. As it turned out, to my continued delight, from then on Hager avoided giving me any special attention and never bothered me again. It was one of the few gratifying events of my time in the *Arbeitsdienst*.

Late in July I was entitled to a week-long vacation. I looked forward to visiting my family and friends in Michelau. Upon arriving in Michelau, Turko's embrace felt unusually affectionate and generous, or was it that I had just not experienced such a commonplace thing as a hug for so long? Perhaps he had truly missed me. His face appeared full of pride and admiration, like his son had grown up fine and strong. "How is the *Arbeitsdienst*?" he asked. His hardy and forceful tone suggested that only one answer was appropriate.

"Fine," I replied, "a little boring." That was the correct thing to say, as there was no point in telling him I hated it. He seemed satisfied with my answer.

We talked over family dinner. I savoured the congenial warmth of my home, with people who cared about me. I now appreciated, perhaps for the first time, the amiable atmosphere and normality of "home."

*Michelau, July 1939. (BR) Hans Kessel (+), Fritz Bayer, Karl Knorr
(+), Albin Gagel, Andreas Rühr; (FR) Albert Pfaff, Wilfred Pfaff (+),
Martin Backaert (+). (+ denotes those who did not survive the war.
Andreas Rhür was still living when I visited Michelau in 1996.
He still had an excellent sense of humour.)*

Something else that felt good was being treated like a man, much more
so than ever before.

By coincidence, there were seven other lads on holiday from the
Arbeitsdienst in Michelau at that same time. We met in the local pub and
one got the idea to have us get together to have our picture taken by a
professional photographer, which we did.

When I stepped off the train on my return to Irlbach, I felt wretched.
Regardless, it was back to the routine. This time the dyke was being
extended into a forested area and we had to clear the trees from the
intended alignment. I learned how to properly swing an axe and use
a long double-handled saw to fell the trees and strip the branches. We
also sawed the logs into manageable lengths. Teams of horses dragged
the timbers out of the woods. We had no machinery to help clear and
prepare the ground, so it was back-breaking labour. My hands soon
became calloused and hard.

I eventually convinced myself that my contribution had actually
made an impact for the good of society. The flood-control dyke had
been extended by at least ten kilometres, thanks to our efforts. The
dyke would protect the neighbouring farmers' lands and villages from

the Danube's flood waters in future. That sense of accomplishment made the work and its conditions more bearable, but I was still counting the days until I could get out of there.

On September 1, 1939, we heard the news that the German army had invaded Poland. None of us at the camp seemed surprised. Some of the lads actually cheered. Whatever emotions were felt that fateful day, outwardly we asserted all kinds of bravado. Full of youthful bluster and confidence, we spouted enthusiastic rhetoric about our "righteous cause" to regain those parts of Germany that had been taken from us after World War I.

We heard radio broadcasts about British and French promises to aid Poland, and I hoped they would not declare war on Germany. When they did two days later, I was worried that events would develop into another monstrous world war. We talked in our barracks about the battle for Poland and its ramifications. The Polish army was just as large as Germany's, and there was no reason to believe it was any less powerful. Most of us were confident that Germany would defeat Poland.

"Man, that must be exciting!" one of the lads said. "I wish I could be there to help our troops. I would teach the Poles a lesson."

"Ya, you would make all the difference," one of the Austrians said in his characteristic southern drawl. "We are all surprised Hitler didn't wait for you."

Probably none of us had a realistic grasp on the implications of the situation. It may be inherent in human nature, or at least in the nature of young males, to be entertained by accounts of combat rather than appalled. Nobody expressed any concern over the many innocent lives that would be lost or shattered by war. We knew that World War I had lasted four years, and cost millions of lives, but that was then and this was now. We were convinced this war could not possibly last that long; after all, a lot had been learned since then. So I thought at the time.

We continued to hear impassioned news reports of German victories in decisive battles. By the middle of September, all reports indicated a German victory over Poland was imminent.

On September 22, 1939, after six months of hard labour and premilitary training in the *Arbeitsdienst*, I received my orders to report to München (Munich) to join the *Wehrmacht*, the armed forces of what Hitler had named the Third Reich.

3   *Any Mother's Son Will Do*

AT THE *MUSTERUNG* IN LICHTENFELS in early 1939, I had been told I would be sent to Passau to join an infantry division, so that was what I expected, but when I received my draft notice, the orders were to join an artillery battery in München. The artillery had a much more sanitary and elitist appeal than did the infantry. What little I had learned about warfare made me think that artillery units were usually stationed well back from the fighting front. It had been purely a matter of luck that placed me with the artillery instead of the infantry, as any mother's son who was fit and competent was assigned to some branch of the armed services when he reached draft age, probably at random.

I knew that the next two years of my life would belong to the army. There was no time to visit my family in Michelau before having to report to München on October 1, 1939. The orders to report included my train tickets and the name of my unit: 2nd Batterie, Leicht Artillerie, 1st Abteilung 157.

München had always been a big city for me, and now the maze of streets and buildings seemed to go on forever as I rode the streetcar from the train station to the garrison. The home base of my artillery battery was located in a residential district near the heart of the old city. It was a huge complex of solid stone buildings, some three storeys tall, extensive stone-walled stables, and a large parade ground in the centre. It had been a military base for more than a hundred years. Shortly after World War I it had been turned into a low-income housing project and continued as a residential complex until 1938, when Hitler decided to return it to its original military garrison function.

Shortly after arriving in München, we heard that Poland fell only five weeks after the start of the invasion. We also heard that Russia had invaded the eastern part of Poland. To my way of thinking that was a positive sign, as Russia was on Germany's side, rather than her enemy as had been the case in World War I. There might now be reason to believe that this new war would be a short war. I hoped so, but did not believe so. Each of Hitler's previous successes had served only to make him bolder. I surmised that, in Hitler's mind, Germany's defeat in France in 1918 still had to be avenged. However, at the time I did not think, and probably most people could not have imagined, that we would eventually have to fight against so many countries, and especially for so many years.

We soldiers-in-training were housed ten men to a room in large barracks. We were issued our gear, including a brand-new uniform. Unlike the uniforms at the *Arbeitsdienst*, which were merely the first one off the stack that looked like it might fit reasonably well, here we were carefully measured. It seemed important to the supply staff that we were dressed properly and looked good. We were also issued black leather boots, two pairs of socks, two white undershirts, and two pairs of underwear. The most novel item was a wide leather utility belt, onto which were fastened cartridge pouches for holding ammunition, grenade hooks, and a slot for a bayonet—truly formidable apparel.

Right from the start the training for the army was serious and purposeful business, not the mindless servitude that had characterized the *Arbeitsdienst*. Each training session began with an explanation of the nature and purpose of the lesson, and what was expected of us. We were trained how to handle and use various weapons, from pistols to cannons, how to care for them, clean them, store them, and use them. Much of the practice involved rifle drills. When practising in groups with our rifles, we used blanks, which would provide a loud and realistic-sounding report, but had no deadly bullets in the casings. Good thing, as some of the men were quite shaky at the beginning of our training.

What was surprisingly difficult was learning to shoot a pistol accurately. The first time I tried to hit a target with a handgun it was almost embarrassing. Anything smaller than a cabbage was practically impossible for me to hit beyond twenty metres. So much for Western movies, where the cowboy hero could hit any villain from a hundred yards away, even while riding a horse! A pistol could be useful only in close combat. A man armed with a pistol was no match for one armed with a rifle.

We were trained to use a machine gun, the Model 34. It was a thick, straight, black stick with a squared shaft and a slot in both sides comprising the centre section, a long perforated metal tube surrounding the barrel at one end, and a ridiculously flared wooden stock at the other end. There was a metal stand shaped like an inverted V near the end of the barrel to support the weight of the weapon. A leather strap handle around the centre made it easy to carry. It was about twice as heavy as my rifle. The bullets were fastened onto long belts that were stored in what looked like large metal tool boxes. One man aimed and fired while another fed the belt into the breech in the side of the gun. The whole machine gun appeared to be too skinny and fragile to justify its reputation as a deadly weapon—until the first time I actually fired one. It seemed to jump to life, like an animal with a fierce mind of its own, bending me to its will, not the other way around. It was quite intimidating. The rate of fire, the sheer volume of bullets that spewed out, was a revelation. It was truly a devastating instrument of carnage.

The first time I held a hand grenade it was difficult not to dwell on the scary fact that this lump of iron could kill you and everyone around you if you made a mistake. It looked like a soup can with a handle protruding from the base. The handle provided leverage to help propel the grenade farther than the can itself could be thrown. After yanking the detonator, you had about six seconds to get rid of it before it exploded, and you had to estimate the precise landing to prevent giving the enemy time to pick it up and throw it back at you.

We were taught to throw it accurately in a large arc from behind cover. Even thrown as far as possible, shrapnel from the exploding grenade could hit you if you remained standing, so it was important to duck behind an object that would shield you from the blast, some substantial object the shrapnel could not penetrate. A hole in the ground was best. If caught in level terrain you had to lie flat on the ground in the direction of where the grenade would land, relying on your helmet to protect your head from the shrapnel flying toward you. I did not dwell on what an exploding grenade would do to soldiers when it exploded in their midst.

Mortars were another infantry weapon we were trained to use. The projectile looked like a small bomb, a little larger than a grenade, weighing about ten pounds, with small fins at the tapered end. You dropped the shell backwards into the barrel, which was a metre-long hollow tube, turned your face away, plugged your ears, and waited two seconds. POP! The mortar shell was ejected by the explosion of the propellant charge in the base. It could fly anywhere from a few hundred to two thousand metres, depending on the angle at which the barrel was set. We quickly learned it was smart to have two men hold down the legs to prevent the projectile's kick from the making the mortar jump.

Each of us was issued a bayonet, which was a heavy, double-edged knife with a slot and pin in the handle. The blade edges were not particularly sharp, but there was a central spine that tapered to a deadly point. It was usually kept in a leather sheath attached to the utility belt. The hilt had a round ring in it, which, along with the notch in the handle, would fit exactly over the end of the rifle barrel. With the bayonet so affixed it could be used as a makeshift lance.

Bayonet drill included mounting the bayonet on the rifle, then charging at a straw-filled dummy, which was supposed to represent an enemy soldier, stabbing the dummy with as much force as possible, yanking the blade out, and then charging on to the next dummy. One of the instructors mentioned that if the bayonet got stuck in a body, we should put our foot on the chest beside the blade to help yank it out.

The thought that I might actually have to stab another human being to death with a bayonet was truly vile. All of the other practice sessions, such as learning to shoot rifles, pistols, machine guns, mortars, and cannons, or even learning to throw grenades, had a tidy and almost sanitary feel to them. They seemed to be a dispassionate and respectable means of waging war, with relatively long distances between yourself and your enemy. But using a bayonet, I could imagine having to get close enough to look a man in the eye, to physically touch him, to feel the blade pierce his body, and possibly to watch him bleed and die. Learning to kill someone with a knife was like rehearsing to be murderers, not soldiers.

Much of the training involved strenuous conditioning exercises, designed to make us physically fit and immune to hardships. It included long marches with full packs, running and climbing drills, and hours of callisthenics. We were taught to attack across various types of terrain with different ground conditions; sometimes crawling on our bellies through fields, over walls, across timbers, under or over barbed wire, across water, and around other obstacles. The sergeants in charge always pushed us to the limit.

As part of the artillery, we were organized into groups of nine and taught to man and service the cannons as a team. We were trained on 10.5cm cannons, probably the most common field artillery piece in the

German army at the time. I learned every aspect of loading, aiming, firing, cleaning, and moving those big weapons. It was a robust and easily transported howitzer with large steel wheels. Even though the cannon was extremely heavy, it was balanced on the axle so that the legs could be lifted by four men and swung around to aim in any direction. Each cannon was towed by a team of six horses. A four-wheeled wagon carried extra 10.5cm shells and supplies, which was usually towed by a team of two horses. Curiously, the 10.5cm cannons we were trained to use were made in Czechoslovakia, as were our rifles. Apparently the Czechs were manufacturing war materials for Germany after Czechoslovakia's forced unification with Germany. I suppose that made the Czechs our allies.

The cannon shells were heavy, much heavier than mortar grenades, and very intimidating until I got used to them. The fuse at the tip of the shell could be set with a key to vary the delay as to when it actually exploded. Without setting the timer fuse, the shells were just lumps of metal which could be handled and even dropped without fear of injury; unless you dropped one on your foot. Once armed, however, they became dangerous instruments of destruction. The safety aspects associated with the training of how to handle artillery shells properly was something I took very seriously.

From the start it was obvious that the intent of all this intensive military education was to make us into good soldiers as quickly as possible. The quality of leadership in the army was remarkable. Compared to some of the oafs who had barked orders at us in the *Arbeitsdienst*, the sergeants and corporals in the *Wehrmacht* were not only good instructors, but very reasonable people. Most were professional soldiers who knew their trade very well. They treated us firmly, but with courtesy and respect, as if each one of us were an important part of the army. I was very impressed with their competence and pleased with the camaraderie that was generated and encouraged among the troops.

The nine men in my squad were almost inseparable during the entire training period, and soon became buddies. Although we spent only two months together at the garrison, the fact that we toiled and sweated together did form a kinship among us. The uniform made us all feel part of a group and fostered a strong sense of loyalty to each other. The man in the next bunk, Reuss [pron. as in Rolls Royce], turned out to be one of the most sociable people I had ever met. He had a way of seeing the humour in situations or events that some-times left me in stitches. He was completely fearless, almost reckless, in his ability to expose that humorous side. He and I soon became close friends.

At the start of our training most of us slept at every opportunity, but we soon got used to it and then ventured out of the garrison at every opportunity. We were paid for our military service — not a lot, but enough that we could sometimes go to a local pub during the evenings and spend it on ladies or other entertainment.

The strict discipline was inescapable throughout every aspect of our training, and the absolute necessity of obedience to orders was con-stantly reinforced, but it was reasonably applied. Our trainers did not try to humiliate us; rather, they stressed the importance of our future role in a superb fighting force, and we believed it. An example of the difference in treatment between the army and the labour camp was the attitude toward curfew. In München the curfew for all soldiers was midnight. One evening Reuss and I returned to the barracks later than the time allowed, so we climbed over the fence to avoid the guard at the gate. Somehow the corporal in charge found out about it, but never re-ported us. He did insist that we be back before one a.m. in future, which made us feel like we had some control over our own lives.

In the München garrison one of my routine assignments was to tend to the army horses. Officers were allowed to own and ride their own horses, while we foot soldiers had to take care of them. I disliked the horses very much. They were big, smelly, temperamental animals that needed constant care, including grooming, feeding, watering and, worst of all, cleaning up after.

Of all my duties the most dangerous was feeding the horses. They were kept in long concrete barns, two to a stall on either side of a wide alleyway, with their back ends toward the alleyway to facilitate clean-ing out the manure. A wooden beam suspended on a chain at each end separated the two stall mates. To feed them you had to carry their fodder, which usually consisted of a bucket of oats or other grain, past one of the horses to the trough at the front of the stall. When they were approached with the feed the two stall mates would immediately start quarrelling like ravenous dogs over a bone. At that moment I realized just how big and powerful a horse really was. Sometimes I had to push the horse over with all my strength to get by, then dump the feed and beat a hasty retreat, all the while hoping the big beast did not crush me against the stall wall, or step on my foot, or kick me as I passed its back end. A few men were not lucky enough to escape unscathed from those feeding encounters. One young soldier trainee was kicked in the chest by one of the more ill-tempered horses. He suffered two broken ribs and had to be taken to the hospital.

One of the most unpleasant elements of all my military training was learning how to use a gas mask. Every soldier was issued one of those odious-looking devices. It was stowed in a cylindrical metal can and became part of our permanent gear. Just looking at a gas mask made me feel uncomfortable. The horror stories about chlorine gas attacks in World War I were common knowledge. The veterans called it mustard gas, due to its distinctive yellow colour. Knowing that breathing through the gas filter in one of those hideous contraptions could someday save my life did not make it any less repulsive. There was no reason to believe poison gas would not again be used as a weapon in this war.

For gas-mask training, we were put into a long enclosed trailer and shown how to don our masks without allowing any leaks. It was comical to watch some of the lads try to make the mask fit properly. Everyone laughed when Reuss commented that we looked like monsters in a second-rate horror movie, especially when he raised his hands like robotic claws and made growling noises. The comedic aspects quickly dissipated when the trailer filled with dense smoke and we had to breathe through our masks for our lives. We were told to breathe regularly and slowly, but my heart was racing and I was soon drenched in sweat, feeling like I was drowning. When the doors finally opened I was never so happy to gasp fresh air.

The two months of rigorous training in the München garrison had instilled in me a sense of order and purpose, which we surely all felt. I emerged with a subconscious conviction that the army's command structure worked efficiently, and that the military organization could be relied upon to take care of each individual in it. The training experience had also instilled a self-assured, almost smug, feeling that we new soldiers were part of a team that would function effectively in battle.

At the end of our military education, we were lined up and officially welcomed into the ranks of the *Wehrmacht*. Part of the ceremony required us to swear an oath of personal allegiance and obedience to Hitler. I remember feeling awkward, almost embarrassed, about that pretentious recital. We were also formally informed that as German soldiers we were not permitted to belong to any political party, including the ruling National Socialist Party.

Everyone in my battery was assigned to the 88th Infantry Division, which had been newly formed at the army's Grafenwöhr training area. As with the assignment to München, there was no chance to go home for a visit. On December 1, 1939, my artillery battery of about sixty men boarded the train for Grafenwöhr.

Grafenwöhr was a huge training area of dozens of square kilometres in the Oberpfalz region, east of Nürnberg and near the former German border with Czechoslovakia within an area of poor farmland and sandy soils. There were derelict farm fields interspersed with patches of forest and an abandoned farm village. The camp compound contained specially built military barracks, storage sheds, administration buildings, and huge stables. There were also rows of big tents behind the stables in which many hundreds of horses were kept, as there were not enough stables for all the horses in the camp at the time.

We arrived on a very cold day, and the grounds were covered with a blanket of snow. We were housed in long, narrow barracks. Our meals in the mess hall were reasonably good, if somewhat monotonous, and mostly potato or cabbage stew, with some form of meat, usually pork or chicken, along with bread and some type of pastry for dessert. I never complained about the food, as it was definitely more plentiful than what I had received during most of my early years of life.

The main purpose of the Grafenwöhr camp was to provide a training ground large enough to teach various branches of the armed services to coordinate their actions in battle. For example, the artillery would provide covering fire for the infantry, while armoured (*Panzer*) units would spearhead attacks at particular points. I was told that the *Luftwaffe* (air force) would provide air cover in a real battle, although there were no airplanes in Grafenwöhr. There were also no actual tanks in the camp, so the "panzers" were small trucks and automobiles that were made to look like tanks by covering them with a wooden framework, complete with a wooden gun barrel. The rest of the equipment was real enough, including cannons, anti-aircraft guns, machine guns, mortars, bicycles, motorcycles with sidecars, and wagons drawn by teams of draft horses, as well as some formidable-looking armoured cars.

I was impressed with how realistic the manoeuvres and field exercises were. Some were all too realistic, with plenty of shooting, explosions, and frenzied activity, sometimes under cold, wet, and excruciatingly uncomfortable circumstances. Crawling across rough and snow-covered ground while live rounds whizzed by overhead was particularly memorable. We had been told that live ammunition would be used, adding terror to the discomfort I already felt. Repeated drills taught us to react immediately and unquestioningly to orders, no matter what the circumstances and no matter how adverse the conditions. The end of a day often left me exhausted.

Some of the training exercises were quite massive undertakings, involving thousands of soldiers from many branches of the army with many different roles. We practised how to provide fire support for mock infantry assaults with carefully timed and placed shots. As a *Kanonier* (gunner) in an artillery unit, I was usually with our cannon at the rear of the offensive. During those training manoeuvres I was curious as to how the army masterminded and coordinated a large assault, but none of us ordinary soldiers ever received information about the larger picture. We were trained to do our part, which was of course an integral component of the overall operation.

Christmas 1939. I missed my home and my family. All the quaint affirmations of my youth, that Christmas is a time for family, for good cheer, for celebration, and for sharing and giving, flooded into my mind. Here in Grafenwöhr we were given the day off from regular duties. We cut down a spruce tree from the nearby woods and decorated it with cut-out paper figures and a few real candles. We tried to act merry and even sang Christmas carols. Everyone knew *"Heilige Nacht"* ("Silent Night") and *"O Tannenbaum"* ("Oh Christmas Tree"), and we good-naturedly tried to piece together the words of a few more. One of the men obtained an accordion from somewhere and could play it surprisingly well. He led the singing.

The cook prepared a special Christmas meal, with ham and goose, which was a welcome treat. After that it was drinks all around. Then a few more drinks, until late into the night. Then there was nothing left to do but get into my bunk to reminisce about Christmases past.

My family had been poor in post-war Germany before Hitler came to power, especially with so many mouths to feed and clothe. During most of my early childhood we boys received only one present each for Christmas. My earliest memory of a present was a brightly coloured rubber ball. It was given to me on Christmas Eve, and I could play with it until New Year's Day, when it was taken away and wrapped again to be saved until next Christmas. That did not seem unusual to me at the time. I never missed what I never knew. There were no presents here in the barracks, unless you considered extra cigarettes and chocolates as presents.

The training continued unabated for more than five months in Grafenwöhr. We were roused every morning at 6 a.m., made our bunks, which had to be absolutely perfect and wrinkle-free, washed, shaved, had a quick breakfast, and assembled for inspection. As in München, much of the training was strict physical conditioning to harden our bodies for the rigours of the battlefield and to numb our senses to pain. Initially the training was exciting and adventuresome, and much of it was an interesting new experience for me; but after months of army life, the novelty was wearing thin. I would have appreciated a break from the tedium and regimentation of military life.

One thing that became increasingly obvious as my service for my country lengthened was that the army was a society comprised exclusively of men. There were no women in Grafenwöhr. I never stopped to question why there were no women in the army, perhaps because the idea of female soldiers was alien to my way of thinking, which surely was shared by all the men with me.

On April 10, 1940, we heard that Germany had invaded Denmark and Norway. The news about the battle for Denmark was very brief, as the entire country was overrun in one day. That was a major escalation in the war. It was now evident that Hitler had far more grandiose ambitions than the reacquisition of former East Prussian territory. Norway was a foreign country very far away, which meant that this new war was rapidly escalating into a conflict that may become even more extensive than the First World War.

The next few weeks brought news reports about the English and French invasion of Norway and the tremendous battles fought by our troops, led by our General Dietl, against the Allied armies in Narvik. I expected the order to leave for Norway at any time.

Many of the men talked about those campaigns as if they were disappointed that they had not participated. There were other men who never said anything about the war. I got the impression they were there only because they had to be and wanted nothing to do with warfare. After hearing that Kurt Biesenecker from Michelau was killed in Poland, it occurred to me that Hitler's conquests carried a very real price. However, the news reports about the campaign in Norway were like hearing about some adventurers in a faraway land, with no mention of the personal tragedies that warfare invariably produces.

With our heads still spinning with reports from Norway, we heard that Germany had invaded France on May 10, 1940. Things were getting really ominous. Invading France while the fighting in Norway was not over seemed like a perilous gamble. Thinking about the situation, it was inevitable that Hitler would attack France. The French government had declared war on Germany after the invasion of Poland and was supposedly building up their forces to attack Germany. Sooner or later one country would have to invade and try to defeat the other.

The Treaty of Versailles came up in conversations. As a boy I had often listened to grumblings from veterans of World War I, that they had been betrayed by Germany's capitulation, as they had not been defeated by force of arms in the field. No one questioned the righteousness of attacking France. Hitler had promised to restore lands taken away from Germany by the Treaty of Versailles and that had included the German province of Elsass-Lothringen, which the French called Alsace and Lorraine. He had made good on his promises so far by having his armies recapture and restore German territory on Germany's eastern borders, so there was no reason to doubt he would do the same on Germany's western border.

All of that musing was just academic until the next day, when the sergeant told us to get our gear ready as we were leaving early the next morning for the front in France. There was a brief outburst of excited chatter in the barracks, after which there was surprisingly little emotion expressed by anyone. The attitude that this was something that had to be done and there was nothing any of us could do to change the situation was already ingrained in every soldier at Grafenwöhr.

I had ambivalent feelings regarding my upcoming participation in the attack on France. On the one hand, I understood it was my duty to serve my country and possibly even give my life for the greater good of my countrymen. On the other hand, I had not seriously thought about actually fighting in a real battle in a foreign country. Of course all our military training had to have a purpose, but it had not crossed my mind that I could be risking my life to serve Hitler's ambitions, and that there was a possibility I could be killed or wounded. Was I really prepared to sacrifice my life for Führer, Folk, and Fatherland?

I felt no real enthusiasm for warfare at this new Western Front, suspecting that Hitler may have bitten off more than we could chew. Images of the horrible trench warfare in Flanders from 1914 to 1918 had been vividly displayed on cinema screens and now played in my mind. There were many amputees around to remind us of the human cost of warfare, all victims of that protracted gruesome conflict.

Perhaps by way of rationalizing a potentially scary situation, I let myself believe that the news coverage I had seen of our swift victory over Poland was compelling evidence that the *Blitzkrieg* (lightning war) tactics developed by our military commanders were unbeatable. I was convinced that the gruesome and debilitating trench warfare that had characterized World War I would not be repeated this time. The use of highly mobile and technologically advanced panzer forces by well-trained troops and brilliant generals had fundamentally changed the nature of warfare. Perhaps such naivety is endemic in all young men. Not in my wildest dreams could I have imagined the extent of the conflict this war would produce.

There was another aspect to my attitude. Like most of the young men with me, I was convinced that bad things only happen to other people. It could not happen to me, not really. Full of youthful confidence, dying or being wounded were abstract concepts only.

Whatever our opinions and feelings were at the time, we soldiers were swept along in a swirling maelstrom of activity, preoccupied with preparations for the inevitable. There was little time to ponder any dire consequences of the upcoming foray into battle. I packed my belongings in my backpack, assembled my gear, and went to bed prepared for our morning departure.

That night my sleep was interrupted on a few occasions, and my mind conjured up dramatic images of the next day's trip and possible combat. Some of the other men also spent a restless night, judging by the number of times the toilet was flushed.

4 *Blitzkrieg*

VERY EARLY IN THE MORNING of May 12, 1940, we were roused from our bunks and assembled with our gear in preparation for being sent to the front. The entire division marched off to the railway station. In the dawn's early light there was tremendous activity in the train station. At first everything seemed completely chaotic, but I soon noticed that the whole operation was well organized and controlled. The cannons, limbers, wagons, horses, and tons of supplies were being loaded onto freight cars. The cannons were covered with tarpaulins and tied down with ropes and chains onto the flatcars. The wheels of the wagons were also fastened to the railway cars. There were other trains to be loaded, as it took a great many railway cars to move an entire division. Most of the freight cars on our train were for the horses, since they took up much more room than the men. All of us soldiers and support personnel with my battery, about sixty men, boarded the passenger cars, stowed our gear, and settled in for a long ride.

I contemplated that the upcoming battles were going to be truly tremendous to warrant such an impressive buildup of military might. We were not told where on the front we were being sent. Presumably we would soon be fighting the French army. The only strategic information I did have was that my battery was a part of the 88th Infantry Division.

As the train pulled out the excitement that had gripped the troops the previous night was still palpable, and that infectious enthusiasm swept me along with it. It was a "here we go" attitude. The soldiers talked blithely about their upcoming opportunity to "trounce the French," without any hint of pessimism or trepidation. The idea of going off to war seemed more interesting and exciting than frightening, offering an opportunity to test our youthful strength and newly acquired military skills. There were plenty of jokes about enjoying Paris's famous cabarets, and all the pretty French girls we were going to charm. You would have thought we were off to an international soccer match rather than to war.

I spent much of that trip looking out the window. The landscape gradually became less hilly, with fewer forests and more towns and

10.5cm artillery unit, 1940

villages. We travelled all day through countryside I had never seen before, stopping regularly at stations to service the engine and to stretch
our legs. By nightfall we were still moving, and I dozed in my seat.

The next day the train clattered on hour after hour, and we passed
many villages, towns, and cities, as well as countless farm fields. Eventually we were following the banks of the Mosel River, a tributary of
the Rhine. I was astounded by the grapevines that carpeted the sides
of the valley, arranged in neat rows on every patch of ground that was
not too steep to support plants. One of the other lads explained that
this was the heart of Germany's wine-growing country, the source of
the famous Mosel wines. Every third or fourth bend had an old castle
commanding the high ground. We passed through settlements nestled
into the narrow strip of relatively flat ground between the river and the
vine-covered valley slopes. Every community had ornamental flower
boxes and flower gardens along the streets. The picturesque scenery
looked straight out of a fairy tale, an idyllic example of the Fatherland
we were being sent to defend.

After travelling most of that day, we arrived in the German city of
Trier, near the border with Luxembourg. As we disembarked at the station I expected to hear gunfire in the distance, but there were no signs
of fighting anywhere.

The horses, guns, and supply wagons were unloaded in a frenzy of
activity. We rushed to get everything that belonged to our unit in order.

The battery was arranged in formation and we marched off—to the front, to meet the enemy. We probably arrived at the southerly edge of the Ardennes, a few days after the assault had been launched in that particular sector; so our 88th Infantry Division was not among the first units to cross into foreign territory.

Our artillery battery had four 10.5cm cannons, each of which was pulled by a team of six horses. Usually there would be riders on one row of horses. The front rider was responsible for guiding the team. Each soldier was allowed a turn in rotation to ride one of the wagons or ammunition carriages for about an hour, then he would walk again. The riders dismounted on hilly terrain to spare the horses.

Most of the ammunition for the cannons was carried in two-wheeled carts, or limbers, to which the horses were hitched. The cannons were hooked onto the backs of the limbers. Six men could ride the limber, facing forwards or backwards. The supplies for our battery were carried in wagons pulled by teams of two horses. One wagon of the battery was a mobile field kitchen, the most important wagon in the entire outfit as far as we soldiers were concerned.

There were three other artillery batteries like ours in the detachment, making a total of twelve 10.5cm cannons. Our battery was strung out along almost a kilometre of the road, and it was rarely possible to see from one end to the other because there are no straight roads in Europe, especially not in that hilly and mostly forested countryside. Sometimes we saw other columns like ours moving along nearby roads.

We were ordered not to bunch up because of the possibility of an enemy ambush or attack by airplanes.

We moved along as fast as we could go but did not get near any fighting front. I was surprised that no troops at all opposed our progress during that first day and I saw no evidence of combat along our route. Only the frequent sound of airplanes flying high overhead confirmed that it was wartime.

Near the end of the first day on the Western Front we may have crossed the border into Luxembourg. At the time I had no idea where we were, but by dusk of that very long day I felt like I had traversed half the world, most of it on foot. Finally we pulled off the road and made camp in a meadow. The cannons were arranged in line abreast and the horses were fed and watered. We lined up at the field kitchen wagon and had our evening meal of stew and bread. I was really hungry by then, and the food, as well as the rest, helped soothe my aching feet.

The battery commander gave us a quick briefing. We were told all was going well, the front was moving along ahead of schedule, and we would have to move quickly to achieve our next day's objective. We were not told what that objective was. Our anxiety about being on foreign soil as part of an invading army was not helped by the lack of information regarding the bigger picture. We had no choice but to trust our commanders.

Sentries were posted at the edge of camp all night. I laid my rain cape on the ground, covered myself with my jacket and blanket, and immediately fell asleep.

I woke up shivering in the night. Considering it was May, it was surprisingly cold at night. A clammy chill seeped through me and my blanket was wet from the dew. I shook off as much dew as I could and covered myself again. I had never slept in the open before, and it was impossible to get comfortable on the cold, hard ground.

At dawn we were roused and ate a quick breakfast from our packs. A canteen of hot *Malzkaffee* (a coffee substitute made from roasted barley malt) from the kitchen wagon helped warm my still shivering body. As soon as breakfast was over we were ordered to get moving. The horses were hitched, and we were back on the road just as the sun came over the horizon. All that day I marched along in a daze, not having rested sufficiently the night before. The stiffness in my bones did not trouble the army, so it was up to me to try to get used to it.

We soon saw the first signs of serious fighting along that sector. We marched past four mounds of fresh dirt along the side of the road, with small wooden crosses at one end and steel helmets on top of the crosses—German helmets. The dead had apparently been buried hastily, and the front had moved on. I noted with sadness and disappointment that the dead soldiers had been discarded and forgotten. Where was the admiration and respect that were surely due to men who had given their lives for their country?

The march continued at a headlong pace. The next night we again slept in the open. We spent the following night in abandoned houses and barns in a village along our route, which was a comfortable change. The villages we passed through were not completely deserted, as there were usually old men, women, and children remaining in their homes. Naturally there were few young men in any village, as most would all have been called up to serve in the military. We avoided contact with the inhabitants, and they avoided us. Even if I had wanted to talk to civilians, we would not have been able to understand each other because of the language difference.

At the time I thought we were in France right from the start, but our march may have initially went through Luxembourg and then Belgium. All I knew then was that we were in a foreign country. Everyone referred to the enemy as "the French," regardless of which troops were actually on the other side. Also at the time, we foot soldiers did not have any idea of the *Wehrmacht*'s larger campaign strategy to defeat France.

The unfortunate Belgian and Dutch people were inevitably caught in harm's way, living between two nations that had warred with each other for centuries, the French and the Germans. In the First World War the German armies had attacked France by going through Belgium, and now it was happening again. Both the French and German armies had constructed massive fortifications to defend their own sides of their common border. The French Maginot Line was the most intensive investiture of fortresses in the world, so it would have been foolish to launch the attack on France straight against that powerful edifice. So the path of least resistance was through the Low Countries, and their citizens were caught in a war they did not start and did not want.

I did not notice any border demarcation to indicate when we actually reached French territory. At evening briefings we were always told that the war was going well for our side. At the beginning some of the men had discussed the progress of the campaign and ventured guesses as to how it was really going, but after days of marching everyone's curiosity waned. Most of our waking time was preoccupied with just putting one foot in front of the other for hours and hours at a time. By the end of each day we were too exhausted to expend additional effort on speculative conversation. As soon as we could, and as long as we could, we slept.

One night while we were sleeping in a meadow, I was startled awake by the faint whistle of an incoming shell, followed by the loud clap of an explosive blast, which I estimated to have landed about two hundred metres away. It sounded like a relatively small artillery projectile. Alert for signs of danger, I expected to be ordered to move out or take some protective action, as it could have been the beginning of an enemy counterattack. But nobody moved, and no orders were shouted. I did not feel any fear, just curiosity as to what was happening. After seven months of intensive training I trusted our commanders and felt confident that if there had been any real danger we would have been ordered to move. I listened intently for about ten minutes, waiting for something else to happen, but everything remained quiet. I fell back asleep.

For over a week we did not encounter any resistance from enemy forces and were constantly advancing. From our initial train embarkation at Trier, we had at first moved through mostly rough and wooded countryside near the edge of the Ardennes region west of Luxembourg and were now somewhere in northern France, perhaps near St. Quentin. That area of France was densely populated, and we were never out of sight of a village or town.

I assumed the German assault was spearheaded by mechanized panzer units that could move much more swiftly than our marching feet. The reality of modern warfare for us was more monotonous and tiring than dangerous. Gunfire and detonations were often heard during those early days of the campaign, but always from far away. The only enemy soldiers we saw were columns of prisoners being marched off into captivity.

We eventually did see plenty of evidence of bloody and deadly combat. We passed remnants of what must have been a battle involving tanks. Burned and shattered hulks of trucks, tanks, armoured cars, half-track personnel carriers, motorcycles, and wagons littered the sides of the road and the fields, some still smouldering. There must have been furious fighting to create so much wreckage. Of those that I could identify by their markings or shapes, there were as many German panzers as enemy tanks among the wreckage. Some heaps of burning equipment were completely unrecognizable, as were some of the mangled and charred bodies. One particularly gruesome sight was the body of a tank soldier sticking half way out of the hatch in that scorched machine. His uniform and most of his flesh had been burned from his torso and face. There were only holes where his eyes had been. His still white teeth were exposed in his black charred face like a macabre grin. He had obviously been roasted alive trying to get out of his blazing tank. Seeing the fate of that poor soul gave me a knot in the pit of my stomach like I wanted to retch.

We were forced off the road a few times because of land mines, or at least I suspected it was mines. When that happened we advanced very slowly. Cannons and wagons could not easily be moved across open fields, as the wheels would sink into the soft soil, even if we could make a path for them across the ploughed furrows or ditches, or get them through hedgerows, so we just waited for the road to be cleared.

One morning we heard the roar of many fighter planes and saw dozens of them flying low overhead, accompanied by distinct changes in pitch as the planes descended or climbed. Our column was ordered to stop and quickly disperse along the sides of the road. That was unsettling, as we had never had to take cover before. If those were enemy planes, our battery would be a conspicuous target. As I crouched in the ditch beside the road I kept scanning the skies for approaching aircraft.

The distinctive popping rumble of heavy-weapons fire and explosions could be heard, followed by the unmistakable sound of Stuka dive-bombers. Stukas produced a dreadful howling scream when they dived steeply out of the sky toward their target. That sound leaves a lasting impression, even when hearing it from far away. I can only imagine the terror it must have induced in the victims of that diving attack. There must have been intense action ahead of us.

We started moving again a few hours after watching the skies and listening to that distant clamour of battle. After some kilometres our column was again delayed, this time because the road before us was completely blocked by the remnants of what might have been an entire division of the French army. As far as could be seen ahead, the roadsides, ditches, and adjoining fields, as well as the roadway itself, were littered with the broken and burning hulks of hundreds of wagons, two-wheeled carts, gun carriages, cannons, and bodies. Dead and injured horses were lying in the roadside ditches and in the nearby fields, some still hitched to their wagons and carts.

We were ordered to help clear the road of that detritus of battle as quickly as possible. The derelict wagons, carts, equipment, and dead bodies were unceremoniously dragged or pushed off the roadway into the ditches along both sides. There were dead and seriously wounded soldiers scattered among the debris, some being attended by medics and stretcher-bearers. Bedraggled-looking French prisoners were being shepherded into columns beside the road by German guards. That scene was made all the more dreadful and interminable because of the injured horses. Some shrieked pathetically as they struggled to get up, but could not. I knew the horses with broken bones would have to be shot to put them out of their misery. Even though I did not have any fond memories involving horses, their plight made me feel terrible. I felt more empathy for those wounded horses than for the wounded soldiers. Their grief was difficult to rationalize.

A catastrophe had overwhelmed that formerly powerful army. It must have been the aftermath of the fighting we had heard earlier from afar. They had been caught on the road by rapidly moving German panzer forces and warplanes, with no opportunity to establish useful defensive positions. The horror of that field of slaughter left a profound impression on me. After that I could not dispel the unsettling knowledge that death could easily engulf even a seemingly powerful army, ruthlessly and indiscriminately.

We were held up more than once because the road ahead was clogged with thousands of fleeing civilians. They lined the sides of the roads and stood about in bunches as we marched by. There were women, children, and old men pulling handcarts and little wagons, or pushing baby carriages loaded with personal belongings. Some rode two-wheeled carts pulled by a horse or oxen, others rode bicycles; most were just on foot. Many civilians had tried to flee in their automobiles, but they had been forced off the roads and were not going anywhere for a while. A calamity had descended upon those poor unfortunates, the terror of which had made them flee their homes and the lives they had built. I felt very sorry for them, and apologetic for being part of the invading war machine that had caused this turmoil in their lives.

Along one stretch of road the ditches and roadsides were littered with many hundreds of derelict wagons, oxcarts, carriages, handcarts, and broken-down or wrecked civilian cars, along with bags and suitcases, some of which had spilled the personal belongings of their owners like fallen leaves on the ground. There were also dead oxen, and what must have been hundreds of civilians sitting or lying by the sides of the road, some being attended to for wounds. Apparently the roads had become terribly dangerous places even for civilians. Airplanes must have attacked that throng of refugees. At first I thought they might have been fleeing with a column of soldiers, but there were no military uniforms among the casualties. Most likely airplanes had been trying to clear the roads for an advancing army. But whose airplanes? So many civilians clogging the roads would have been at least as much of a hindrance to Allied troops moving toward the front from the west as to German troops following from the east. Whether it was *Luftwaffe* or Allied planes that had attacked the throng of unfortunate refugees we passed, I suspected that both sides wanted the roads cleared to allow swift movements for their own troops. Civilians just got in the way.

We had heard that the Dutch army surrendered shortly after we arrived in France. Around the second week of our participation at the front, our commander told us that German forces had swept the Allied armies to the edge of the English Channel and trapped them near Dunkirk. Right afterwards there was a noticeable slowdown in our own advance. Our battery did not move for two or three days. I had no idea whether that meant the battle for France was going so well that Hitler believed he could slow down, or that the attack had ground to a halt. On May 28, 1940, we heard that Belgium had surrendered. So things must still be going well for us. Subsequently we heard that most of the British Army in Europe had fled to England.

We had set up in defensive formation facing south and were told to be prepared for an enemy attack. Then shortly after the beginning of June we were ordered to move out again.

That morning, before we had formed up along the road to move out, a German panzer unit went by. That was the first time I had seen such a mobile armoured force, and it was a very impressive sight. There were hundreds of motorcycles with sidecars, armoured cars, trucks, huge halftrack vehicles—some pulling cannons—as well as hundreds of tanks. The whole countryside seemed to reverberate with the rumble of motors, and the ground shook with the vibrations. The smell of oiled machinery, dust, and exhaust fumes was soon overwhelming, and I had to back away from the edge of the road to catch my breath. The halftracks and trucks were packed with infantry, and many more soldiers rode on the tanks. Some tank crew members sat with their torsos out the tops and sides of the turrets of their steel steeds. The panzer troops imparted a supremely self-confident attitude. That sight certainly impressed me as being a truly mighty congregation of motorized weapons. It took over an hour for the entire entourage to pass by. When they had moved out of sight and the dust had settled, we were left in a humbling, conspicuous silence.

In the late afternoon of that day's march we were ordered to pull off the road and set the cannons into firing positions in line abreast, about thirty metres apart, in the manner we had been trained. The limbers were parked next to the guns for quick access to the cannon shells. Hundreds of shells and charges were unloaded from the supply wagons and stacked near each gun in preparation for tomorrow's action. The horses were unhitched and moved a few hundred metres behind the firing lines, where they would remain while the cannons were in action. They had to be securely tied to trees or stakes in order to prevent them from running off when the shooting started, as the noise would be fearsome. We were set up in the middle of a large meadow. No attempt was made to hide the cannons or to camouflage our positions. It occurred to me that we would be very vulnerable to enemy attack, especially from the air. If that pile of projectiles near our cannons were to be hit we would surely all be killed.

Apparently we were going to support an assault that would begin the next morning before dawn. That was the first time we set up our cannons to actually shoot at the enemy, and it was almost a month after we had left Trier. We could have been somewhere east of Paris.

Up until then our own advance had been extremely tedious, so all of us expressed enthusiasm for tomorrow's action, as if eager for the chance to test our fighting prowess. There were plenty of comments making light of the upcoming events. "The French must have stopped running." "They will start again as soon as we shoot at them." To which Reuss wryly said, "You better watch out, hero, they might shoot back." One guy expressed what most of us probably felt: "Anything is better than this damn marching." I admit that I too welcomed the chance for some excitement, even if it meant real danger.

We were roused long before dawn, had a quick breakfast from our kit, and manned our guns. So this was it . . . battle!

As the sun brightened the eastern horizon the order was given to commence firing. My responsibilities included loading the shells into the breech and disposing of spent charge casings. We fired one round after another, as did the other guns of our battery, in a noisy frenzy. Our cannon shells could fly up to about twelve kilometres, depending on the trajectory set by the gunner. I assumed our targets were either the enemy's defensive lines or the enemy's artillery positions. Our firing orders came to the battery commander by wireless from artillery observers who were with the troops near the front lines. The range and traverse of the cannons were repeatedly adjusted to correct our aim or to hit new targets. We were handling the guns and shells with no more special consideration than if they had been farm machinery or construction equipment. The urgency of action gave us no time to ponder the destructive consequences of our shelling. I had no idea what our shells hit, as I could not see where they landed. It did not consciously occur to me that they actually struck and destroyed something, or possibly injured or killed people.

The 10.5cm shell had a timing fuse that could be adjusted so that it would explode on impact with the ground or, if the timer was set slightly earlier, the shell exploded in the air just before it hit the ground, throwing shrapnel all about. It could be set to detonate after the heavy shell penetrated the ground upon landing, wrecking whatever it landed near and creating a small crater. The timer could also be adjusted to detonate after the initial impact with the ground from a relatively flat trajectory, so that it would bounce or skip along the ground before exploding over the enemy positions.

After what seemed like an hour of almost constant shooting, one of the men tapped my shoulder and pointed toward the south, in the same direction we had been shooting. In the distance hundreds of armoured vehicles were moving across the landscape. "Our panzers!" he yelled during a pause in the din. They were a few kilometres away and moving steadily toward what I assumed was the enemy. Our barrage was probably covering their advance. I did not have time to study the situation, but repeatedly strained to catch a glimpse of that armoured armada moving into the distance.

Our guns produced quite a pile of spent shell casings. I wondered what would happen to them. Perhaps they were later collected by rear-guard troops and reused? Perhaps they just became part of the detritus of war? Warfare must be very expensive. It was certainly untidy.

An explosion a few hundred metres in front of us, quickly followed by more, startled me into realizing the enemy were returning fire. I had never before experienced being shelled. Perhaps I had not noticed the incoming barrage earlier because of the noise and activity at our own battery. Most of the enemy shells exploded far in front of us, but a few exploded uncomfortably close. No one took cover or even flinched; everyone was absorbed with carrying out his assigned tasks. The din and smoke of the artillery engagement made it difficult to grasp enough of what was happening to give me time to feel fear. We were letting off round after round—loading, firing, and ejecting the spent shell casings, in a tumult of activity that consumed my consciousness.

Suddenly there was an extraordinarily bright flash and loud explosion that came from my left side. At almost the same instant something flew through the air, knocking my cap off my head as I felt the concussion wave of the explosion hit me. I instinctively ducked to the ground to take cover, which I realized right afterwards was far too late to have saved me from anything. After the initial shock I regained my composure, looked around, and cautiously stood up, my heart pounding in my chest. I assumed an enemy shell had landed in our midst. One gunner remained lying face down on the ground beside the cannon, not moving. It was Reuss. I yelled really loud, "Reuss, let's go, get up!" but he did not respond. I sprang over to help him, assuming he had been knocked unconscious by the blast. He felt very heavy as I rolled him over. Pink froth was bubbling from his open mouth. His eyes were strangely half open. There were no noticeable marks on him or conspicuous holes in his uniform. I felt terribly helpless, not knowing what to do to revive him. Then his breathing stopped altogether.

He was dead!

With that realization a dreadful sickening feeling gripped me. I could not believe what was happening. Before I had time to think, the corporal in charge of our gun yelled for us to get back to our post on the double. He grabbed my shoulder and unceremoniously ordered me to take over Reuss's duties. I laid my dead comrade down. My head was spinning, my whole body ached, and my legs felt heavy as lead as I staggered back to my post.

The din of battle continued unabated for what seemed like an eternity, but was probably less than half an hour. It was difficult to concentrate on my duties of loading the shells and helping to swivel the base of the gun to change the direction of fire. Sickening feelings kept flashing through me. I could not dispel the image of my friend's face as he lay dead in my arms.

When the shooting was finally over we had a chance to investigate what had caused Reuss's death. We found a small hole in the side of his uniform, just under one arm. A piece of shrapnel must have pierced the side of his chest and punctured one of his lungs and possibly his heart. We snapped off his identification tag from the cord around his neck. The ghoul squad then came and took him away to be buried. He was from München. We had been together since joining the army and had become close friends. A pain stabbed my insides as I thought of his family receiving the terrible news.

The shock of realizing just how fast you could die drained the bravery from my body. Up until then the artillery battle had been much the same as I had expected, and was very similar to our training exercises in Grafenwöhr; but now things had suddenly become decidedly different. Death had not been part of the training. Afterwards warfare never again held any sense of adventure or excitement for me. Shells are completely indifferent to who gets in the way. That episode taught me that in order to survive, skill and courage could count for nothing. I would also need to be lucky.

After that artillery battle we quickly packed up and again headed off. Rumours spread that we were heading toward Paris. Once again we moved as fast as we could. Two days later our battery reached the Seine River; at least I thought it was the Seine, maybe because it was the most famous river in France. I knew that the Seine flowed through Paris, so we had to be near, but we could not see the city. We could have been almost anywhere east of Paris.

We stopped sometime during late morning and were again told to set up our cannons in firing positions facing the river. We could clearly see the river valley in the distance, demarcated by a continuous line of trees along the banks, but we could not see the river itself. Two villages were visible on the far side of the valley. The faint sounds of sporadic detonations and small-arms fire came from the direction of the river.

The other batteries also formed up facing the river. The amount of men and artillery massing beside and in front of our position gave the impression we were going to be involved in a major battle. We were assigned targets, which I assumed were the French forces dug in on the far bank of the river, judging by the range and trajectory. Once again we set up in a field, completely exposed. There were no woods or buildings nearby where we would be able to take cover if we came under enemy artillery fire or attack from the air.

From the first shot of the cannons there was an unremitting cacophony of noise from our cannons, which contributed to the fatigue

I soon began to feel. This time I could actually see some of the shells burst on our targets. Puffs of smoke and debris flew into the air as buildings at the edge of one of the villages on the other side of the river were repeatedly hit, and columns of dark smoke rose into the air. Eventually our fire became more sporadic but much more specific. Early in the afternoon the order came to cease fire and prepare to move out. The horses were quickly brought up and hitched to the guns and wagons. Equipment and supplies were loaded and gear stowed. It took about two hours before the entire battalion was ready to move. When the order came to advance everyone either climbed onto a wagon or limber, or just followed on foot. Sitting on an ammunition wagon gave me a chance to rest for the first time that day.

We moved forward until we became part of a long lineup in the midst of thousands of infantry soldiers with bicycles. We were waiting to take our turn to cross a pontoon bridge that our *Pionieres* (army engineers) had constructed. The engineers may have had to do their work under fire from enemy guns. They certainly worked under the shells that flew over their heads from our guns. I also saw dozens of small inflatable rubber boats that our *Sturmtruppen* (storm troopers) had used to make the initial river crossing.[4]

Our troops were pouring out onto the far bank from the newly won bridgehead. With their rifles slung across their backs, the soldiers riding bicycles looked like a group of hunters on an outing in the countryside.

Then it was our turn. The pontoon bridge swayed and rocked on the water as the heavy guns and wagons rolled across. As we reached the road on the other side I saw dozens of foxholes near the river bank, some still occupied by dead German soldiers slumped inside. One was still in a kneeling position, as if prepared to shoot. In a detached sort of way I noticed a hole in the front of his helmet. The entire scene swirled by like a hallucination . . . a hole? Could it be that the steel helmet we were told to wear in combat, which I had assumed was made of solid, hard, impenetrable metal, could be pierced by a bullet? That was a nasty surprise. It had not been part of our training.

There must have been French snipers in that village near the riverbank who had shot at the troops crossing the river and at those in

---

4   *Sturmtruppen* were regular *Wehrmacht* soldiers, specially trained to lead an
      assault under particularly difficult circumstances. They were not the politically
      constituted SS, who were not soldiers in the *Wehrmacht* and therefore not
      under regular army command.

the foxholes. Only a sniper armed with a telescope on his rifle could possibly have hit a man in the head at that range. It was unsettling to realize that you could be shot by someone you could not even see. I looked suspiciously at the windows of the houses in the next village we approached that day.

By the time my unit stopped at the end of the day we were very fatigued, but there was no time to rest yet. Like every other evening during the campaign, we had to unharness the horses and make sure they were watered, fed, groomed, and safely tethered for the night. Then we had to secure the guns, limbers and harnesses, and stow our own equipment. The cannons were wiped down and greased before being covered for the night. The supply wagons arrived and we replenished the carriages with artillery shells. Then the horse-drawn field kitchen arrived and we had our one hot meal of the day. Finally we could fall asleep on the ground. I wrapped myself in my blanket and promptly passed out.

After what seemed like only minutes, but which was probably six or seven hours, we were roused to prepare for the day's march. When I opened my eyes it was still twilight. Some of the men slept so soundly that it took considerable shaking and yelling to awaken them.

Much about the remainder of the campaign is lost in a fog of memories. We were constantly moving. We passed many groups of French prisoners of war. I did not want to let myself get too optimistic though, as it was still possible that the very hectic and aggressive German assault had only temporarily prevented the Allied forces from organizing and mounting a strong defence, as had happened in World War I. Perhaps this could still be an early stage of the war. I did not completely trust our commander's assurances at evening briefings that the campaign was going very well for us.

The march settled into a routine. Up, visit the latrine, a quick face wash and shave at the mobile kitchen wagon if you had time. We hurriedly ate whatever was in our packs for breakfast. Each morning we first had to water and feed the horses and get the equipment ready for the road. Then we hitched up the horses and headed back onto the road for the day's march. At noon we stopped to eat the rations we carried with us: rye bread, sausage spread, and cheese, along with a canteen full of *Malzkaffee*. Then we were off again. We marched as fast as we could for as long as the men and the horses could stand, from daybreak until sunset. We must have travelled twenty kilometres some days.

On June 10, 1940 we heard that the battle for Norway had been won. The Norwegian government had surrendered and the British and French forces had withdrawn.

Eventually I suspected that there was not much of a well-defined defensive line remaining. Briefings by our commander suggested the fighting had settled down to a series of minor mopping-up operations. I expected to see the Eiffel Tower looming in the distance at any time. There might have been good reason to suspect an enemy counterattack, but we were not engaged in any fighting at all during that part of the march southward through France. We also did not see any more remnants of battle as we had seen near the beginning of the campaign.

At this stage of the march we always stopped in a town or village to spend the night. They were not damaged, and the resident civilians were still in their homes. For a few nights we were able to sleep in a warm bed in an empty bedroom.

There was even a little windfall. We came upon abandoned buildings where we found racks and racks of wine bottles in the cellars. There must have been thousands of bottles of French wine. One cellar housed wooden casks a metre or so across, with spigots in the bottom for pouring out the wine. The basement was flooded knee-deep in red wine. The owner must have opened all the spigots and let the wine drain onto the floor. Perhaps he considered it his patriotic duty to deny the invaders his precious cache of the fruit of the vine. What a waste.

Before then I never imagined there could be so much wine in the whole world. I did not particularly like the taste of red wine, and probably could not have discerned the difference between a good and a bad wine, but most of us had to at least try some. We were sure no one would miss a bottle or two. The first bottle we opened, a dark red wine, tasted almost disgusting to me. Some of the men in our battery decided to try a few drinks. A few became a few more, until they were considerably drunk. It was comical to watch the guys with the hangovers try to keep up with the march in the aftermath of their immoderate imbibing. They wobbled and stumbled along, their sullen faces betraying obviously painful distress. As I had learned in the pubs in Michelau, a man cannot expect sympathy for self-inflicted wounds. We had opportunities to help ourselves to wine in other places, but after days of exposure to that deluge of fermented grape juice the novelty wore off and only a few drank much again.

When we heard Paris had been captured by German troops on June 14, I wished we would go into Paris, where there might have been an opportunity to partake of a little of its famous nightlife. We were installed in a small rural village where there was not even a decent cabaret in which to spend some merry moments. I would have liked to have been able to return from France with some fascinating stories to tell my family and friends, but it was not to be. We were soldiers on duty and not tourists on vacation.

My artillery battery had not been involved in any engagements since the battle at the river more than a week ago, and we never had to fire our cannons again. Even the sounds of distant combat, which had often accompanied us during much of the campaign, had completely ceased. By then we all assumed it would only be a matter of time before our sojourn into France would come to an end. Most of the men seemed as tired of warfare as I certainly was.

Our participation in the battle for France had consisted mostly of exhausting and surprisingly tedious marching, not the stuff of adventure that I had originally expected. My most poignant memory was the image of my friend Reuss lying dead in my arms. I felt the pain of that loss every time I thought of him.

On June 22, 1940, we were bivouacked in a small village, probably at least a hundred kilometres south of Paris. That evening we heard the news that France had surrendered. There was a brief celebration that our side had won. I felt relieved more than anything else, because it allayed my fears of a repeat of a drawn-out conflict like the First World War. This "second" world war would surely now be over. I admit I felt some smug satisfaction that the ignominy suffered by our fathers due to the Treaty of Versailles had been righted. For a moment I wondered how my father would have felt.

Everyone expressed the optimistic view that it would now be only a matter of time before we could all go home, after a job well done. Nobody expressed any misgivings about the war or any doubt that Germany had won it. Denmark, Holland, Belgium, Luxembourg, Norway, and now France, had fallen. When added to Austria, Czechoslovakia, half of Poland, and of course Germany itself, Hitler now had a vast empire. Surely that was enough, even for his huge ambition.

5 *Interlude*

THE FIGHTING IN FRANCE WAS OVER; now the occupation began. Each soldier in my battery was billeted in the home of a French family, one to four soldiers to a house, depending on the space available. I slept in a spare bed that belonged to a grown son who had been in the French army and was now probably a prisoner of war. The schoolhouse was converted into a temporary dormitory for soldiers who could not be accommodated in private homes.

We only slept in our billets; the rest of each day was spent attending to duties with our unit. Each of us had to take turns in pairs at sentry duty all night, the hardest part of which was trying to stay awake. We were supplied by the army with fresh clothes and fed from the mobile field kitchen. Time off usually meant just sitting around, telling stories, or playing cards. Sleeping was popular, especially if you had drawn guard duty the night before.

One of our officers spoke French fluently, and he spent hours at the family's kitchen table talking with the owners of the house where we were billeted. Although I did not speak French and understood very little of the conversation, it was often lively and animated. It became even more amiable after a bottle of the ubiquitous wine came out. The battle for France was now part of history, and life went on.

We soldiers were not allowed to take any of the French civilians' possessions. The senior officers from our division were stationed in a chateau just outside the village, on the grounds of the country estate of a wealthy Frenchman. One of the soldiers from our battalion had tried to catch a fish in a pond on the grounds of the estate. He was caught, hauled up in front of the military police, and reprimanded. We all thought his silly attempts to catch a fish had been hilarious, but army brass obviously had no sense of humour about such things. Private property was not to be taken. Other than drinking a few bottles of wine, I never witnessed any looting, nor did I ever witness or even hear of any mistreatment of civilians by German soldiers during the entire campaign in France or during my stay in that French village. That little fish-poaching incident exemplified the army's attitude as to what was expected in the exercise of responsibilities by the soldiers of the German occupation army.[5]

A few days after France surrendered, we assembled in the village square. Our commanding officer read out the names of those soldiers promoted to *Unteroffizier* (corporal), and I was one of them. My promotion was recorded in my *Soldbuch* (pay book), which every German soldier carried. The company tailor sewed corporal stripes onto the collar of my uniform, and that was it. From now on I was in charge of Cannon No. 1 and responsible for its gun crew, horses, and supply wagon. It pleased me to receive that promotion, perhaps because it flattered my ego to think that my superior officers had recognized some ability in me, whether that was true or not.

Now that the fighting in France had ended I expected to return to Germany. I wrote to my father and told him France had been interesting, that I had been promoted to corporal, that I was looking forward to going home and, what was probably most important to him, that I had survived the campaign without a scratch.

Two weeks after the fighting in France was over our battery was transferred back to Germany, to be stationed in various villages throughout Bavaria. I had a picture taken of me standing in front of a wall with the name Sedan in the background of the train station, so we obviously passed through Sedan. Each of us was assigned to a house in the town of Forchheim, which is located a few kilometres north of Nürnberg. Because it was wartime, the owners were told they would have to provide a temporary place to sleep for one German soldier who was serving his country. They did not have to provide our meals or care for us in any way. Each day we assembled in the town square, where we were fed from the mobile army field kitchen. We also brought our clothes to battery headquarters to be cleaned as needed.

I was assigned to stay with a couple who were probably in their late fifties, living in a farmhouse near the edge of the town. They were modest farmers, very nice people, who owned four cows and two pigs.

---

5   The occupying Nazis plundered gold, jewellery, and priceless art from the conquered countries, including France, while telling foot soldiers and everyone else to be good citizens. That was done by the administrators who came after the fighting, including political governors, occupation army generals, and government-appointed police, mainly by coercing the owners to "sell" their treasures at bargain prices. Much of the booty was sent back to private collections in Germany. Ironically, most of that, and more, was in turn stolen by the conquerors of Germany at war's end.

Their son, Karlheinz, was in the army, stationed somewhere else. They also had an older daughter who had a little boy. Her husband was also away serving in the military.

During my stay in Forchheim I learned to ride a horse. I was assigned an army horse, which had been purchased from a farmer while we were still in Grafenwöhr. At first I harboured some serious apprehension about keeping company with such a big animal, mainly due to my experiences tending horses at the garrison in München the previous year. Up until then the only time I felt positive about seeing a horse was when they arrived pulling a field kitchen. I had always assumed that horses were unintelligent beasts, especially when compared to dogs, but after a while I began to recognize that in his own way that animal understood his duties and his relationship with his master quite well. As we spent part of each day improving our riding skills, I was surprised to find myself forming a bond of trust with my steed. He was a dark brown gelding. I named him Toni, after American movie star cowboy Tom Mix's horse. I wondered why the army would spend so much on this equestrian training, as the days of mounted cavalry were surely long gone. Perhaps they figured mounted soldiers would look good at the head of a company of infantry in another monumental victory parade? Perhaps the old-timers in the military just loved the sight of mounted men in formation? Perhaps the military horsemanship tradition just dies hard? Whatever, it seemed pointless to me. Regardless of the army's motives, I actually enjoyed learning to ride.

After six weeks of training we were tested to demonstrate how well each of us could make our horse obey commands by navigating through an obstacle course of straw bales under control. I passed the riding test and received my *Reitersportabzeichen* (sport rider insignia).

My stay in the Forchheim area was relatively pleasant. We got to meet many of the locals. In the evenings and on Sundays we soldiers were free to go to a pub. Most Sunday evenings we went to dances, which were great fun. There were plenty of young women to dance with. Perhaps I flattered myself by thinking I was more popular than I really was, because most of the men from town were stationed in some distant outpost of the Third Reich. Anyway, I liked to dance and always had a date. The war quickly became an abstract concept, with little tangible evidence of it in that rural area of Germany.

By November I was entitled to another two-week vacation, so I went home to Michelau. Unlike the holiday from the *Arbeitsdienst*, this was not an escape from oppression, just a change of venue. I also did not dread the thought of returning to duty at the end of it. The re-union with my family was somewhat subdued this time. Hermann had been drafted and the latest Turko knew was that he was stationed in München. At seventeen years of age, the twins were still too young for military service. Karl was just eleven.

My father had continued his wicker-basket manufacturing business, but it had been scaled down considerably, as it was difficult to get good help and the market had slowed. Curiously, our neighbour, Tresko Held, who had his own wicker manufacturing business, had received a contract from the army to produce artillery shell-holders. These were square baskets with a wooden base and lid and four ribs up the sides interwoven with wicker strips. Each held one large cannon shell. I had handled many similar shell-holders myself in France.

By then Michelau's citizens were concerned with another aspect of the war. For months, radio broadcasts and newspaper articles had been preoccupied with accounts of the Battle of Britain, each report more ardent than the previous in recounting *Luftwaffe* victories. They made it sound like it was just a matter of time before the British air force would be wiped out and England would be defenceless against invasion. The battles in the skies over England had been going on for months, and must have been devastating. Two young men from Michelau served in the *Luftwaffe*, Georg Freitag and Georg Kessel, and neither of them returned home.

When my two-week holiday was over I returned to Forchheim, but my sojourn into rural Germany was too good to last for long.

In February 1941, another corporal, Heinz Wagner, and I were as-signed to join the 878th Artillery Battery in Küstrin, a small city on the Oder River in Prussia. My horse Toni would not be sent with me, so I assumed my stay in Kustrin would be temporary. I felt genuine sadness at having to leave my horse behind, and wondered what would happen to him.

Heinz and I had become good friends. We had known each other since military training in München. He had been promoted to corporal with me, and had also been transferred to Forchheim after the fall of France. Heinz was my age, a little taller than me, with dark hair and handsome features. He was from Saxony, where his family owned a small business. We had many interests in common, including women. I liked his character and personality. He was always in control of himself. He never acted shy, and it was impossible to embarrass him. He also had a subtle and dry sense of humour and was the master of the good-natured insult, especially when talking to women. Those attributes, combined with his good looks, made Heinz a skilful accomplice at sweet-talking the ladies in the pubs in Küstrin. We both knew that our evening outings could be curtailed at any time by a transfer to some other outpost of the Reich, so we were determined to have a good time at every opportunity.

On March 1, 1941, Heinz and I had to leave Küstrin. We were assigned to an artillery battery of four big 15cm guns that were transported by train to Ålborg, a port city near the northwest coast of Denmark.

We arrived in Ålborg late in the afternoon and had a few spare hours to wander around the city's downtown area near the waterfront to do some sightseeing. The city was truly an astounding sight at night. All the buildings downtown, especially the shops, were brightly lit. The business identification signs were almost gaudy-looking to a soldier who was used to seeing German cities dimly lit and colourless because of the regime's enforced measures to conserve electricity. German cities near the English Channel had an enforced blackout from dusk till dawn in an effort to hide them from enemy reconnaissance, as they were not immune to British bombing raids.

Denmark had been occupied by German forces since April 1940. Before that it had been neutral, which may explain why the residents were not afraid of air attacks.

It was extraordinary to see the shops in Ålborg filled with all kinds of consumer goods, especially food. There were meats, fish, breads, cakes, vegetables, and hundreds of different kinds of canned goods! After living with rationing for the past two years, it was astonishing to see such plenty. It struck me as ironic that, even though Germany's armies had been overwhelmingly victorious in this war, we Germans were living under relatively modest conditions while people in this conquered country were enjoying life with no visible hardships or even shortages.

In Hitler's Germany food was still rationed, consumer goods were scarce, and the standard of living had not improved since the war began. From all evidence, I discerned that life was certainly not better for the average citizen in Hitler's empire; in fact, conscription had forced all young men into protracted military service away from their homes, separated from their families, and rendered unable to build a normal life. Where were the benefits that Hitler had promised us so often? Hitler's military victories struck me as empty and meaningless.

Our entire battery boarded a small freighter of about 8,000 tons. Word got around that we were on our way to a place called Narvik, near the northern tip of Norway, more than two hundred kilometres north of the Arctic Circle! At that time all I knew about the situation in Norway was that the fighting had ended last summer. Norway was important to Hitler because of the valuable iron ore that was mined in Sweden and shipped out from Narvik. Also, the harbours and airfields in Norway were bases of operations for German navy ships and air squadrons.

The freighter left Ålborg and sailed east along the canal to the Kattegat, the strait that separates Denmark from Sweden. Once into open water, we headed north. I knew there were other transports going to places in Norway to supply German troops, but did not see any other ships accompanying us. I was aware that British submarines had sunk German warships and troop transports in the Skagerrak, the strait that separates Norway from Denmark. The thought that enemy submarines were skulking in those waters, searching for cargo ships like ours to ambush, was a bit disquieting. The first day out I scanned the surface of the sea intently, looking for traces of submarines or enemy ships on the horizon. But after a few hours of that sea hunt it became too wearisome and I spent my time just looking at the scenery. The ship docked briefly at Stavanger to unload supplies before continuing north.

About mid-afternoon of the third day at sea, there were a few of us leaning on the railing on deck, just idly chatting to pass the time. It was a cold but mostly clear day. The ship rocked back and forth with the swells of the North Sea, not enough to be bothersome, but certainly noticeable. Each time the ship pitched forward into a particularly large wave, it would throw up a white shower of spray from the bow. As the sunlight hit the spray a rainbow would be visible just for a moment, which was fascinating to watch. The Norwegian coast slowly drifting by to the east was rugged and beautiful, with tree-covered hills and many steep-sided arms of the sea jutting inland. Often we were close enough to discern houses and other buildings on the land. There were snow-covered mountains in the distance. One man had never seen mountains before. He had grown up in Prussia and that was his first trip so far from home. I thought to myself that this could have been a pleasure cruise, a sightseeing vacation to take in the scenic views of the Norwegian coast, the homeland of the old Vikings.

Suddenly, I heard poom-poom-poom-poom, and ducked. I immediately recognized the sound as the shooting of the ship's anti-aircraft guns. There were no targets visible from my side of the ship. We were about to run to better vantage points when the noise of an airplane engine suddenly burst overhead as it flew over the ship from west to east, only a few hundred metres high, again causing me to duck. The loud banging of both anti-aircraft pods continued, and the acrid smell of gunpowder came on the wind from the forward gun position.

Then two tremendous explosions in quick succession caused two huge plumes of water to burst out of the sea about fifty metres away from the side of the ship. The plane had dropped two bombs! Thankfully, both had missed. I watched to see if it would turn to launch another attack, but it kept on going, veered off to make a big circle, and eventually disappeared back into the horizon toward the west.

I wondered how many more planes of the British air force were patrolling the North Sea. Narvik was still a long way away, and perhaps we were in for a dangerous time trying to run the gauntlet of patrol planes all the way up the Norwegian coast. That one plane could have relayed our position to the British command and we might be attacked again, perhaps even by a warship.

We continued to search the sky for signs of enemy aircraft and listened intently for the wind to carry the telltale sound of aircraft engines. As evening approached we were on the port side of the ship, still scanning the horizon. Everything had been quiet for hours, so I was beginning to think we would escape undetected into the night. As the sun began to set toward the sea the intermittent clouds created brilliant rays of sunlight, piercing through holes in the clouds, so that the play of light and shadows made it difficult to distinguish what you were seeing. One or another of the men would occasionally point at some shape in the sky near the horizon and ask for confirmation as to what it was. Each time that happened I anticipated another air attack, but they were birds or just false alarms and I began to relax.

"Airplanes! Airplanes coming out of the sun!" one of the men on the upper deck shouted. Sure enough, we could make out the shapes of three airplanes heading for the ship. The first plane must have reported our position. Now we really were in for it.

I immediately felt very exposed and vulnerable, sitting on a floating target in the middle of the ocean with no place to hide. Thoughts of the ship being hit and sinking surged through my mind. The Atlantic Ocean, which a few hours earlier had appeared so tranquil and fascinating, now took on a totally different, and sinister, countenance. There were no signs of civilization on the adjacent coast, which now looked very distant, no signs of anyone who could rescue us if we were to be dumped into the icy black water.

We had not been given any instructions about what to do in the event we were hit and the ship started to sink. We were not even issued life jackets. There were lifeboats hanging from hooks along the sides of the superstructure, and I supposed they could save our lives if the ship were to be sunk from under us, provided there was enough time to launch them and get inside, and provided they were not destroyed by bombs or by fire.

When the three bombers approached to within range the anti-aircraft guns on our ship opened fire again. In the failing light of the late evening the dashed orange lines of the tracers could be seen as they flew toward the planes. I hoped that the stream of bullets from our guns would bring them down before they could release their bombs and blow us out of the water. "Why the hell can't those useless gunners hit anything?" the man beside me screamed. My sentiments exactly.

As the planes got closer I expected to see them dive and release torpedoes toward our ship, but they stayed at their altitude. Then we could clearly make out three bombs being dropped. Whether I felt terror or fascination as my eyes followed those missiles in their descent toward the ship was now irrelevant. This was it! I held my breath, expecting to be flying through the air and dumped into the sea in the next moment.

An enormous geyser of water erupted out of the sea with a tremendous reverberation that sounded like a thunderclap right in front of us, shortly followed by another, and another. The last bomb struck close enough that I felt the shower of seawater spray on my face. The entire ship shuddered, but we had not been hit. Lucky for us. The planes flew over the ship, banked steeply and continued in a large circle until they were headed back toward the west. Our anti-aircraft fire had been just as ineffectual as their bombing. Lucky for them. We continued to watch the planes until they disappeared into the sunset.

We kept scanning the sky until it was too dark to see. The night brought some relief, as hopefully it would hide us. No lights were permitted on board that might be seen. The next day I expected another attack and kept a nervous watch all day long. But no more planes came that day or the following, when we stopped at the port of Trondheim to unload more supplies. We may simply have moved out of range of the airfields in England. Other than waiting for another air attack, the rest of the trip was uneventful, which was all right by me. Better to be bored than shipwrecked.

After a week on board ship we finally arrived at our destination. Narvik is situated on the southern side of a large inlet of the Norwegian Sea, a fjord. Both sides of the fjord are rugged wilderness, with steep, rocky faces, and covered with small coniferous trees. In the distance, high, snow-covered hills could be seen. The long narrow entrance to Narvik is a perfect sheltered harbour. One of the men leaning on the railing mentioned that the warm ocean current (the Gulf Stream) flowing north along the coast kept the harbour ice-free, so that it could be used as a shipping port all year round. That was astounding, considering that Narvik is so far north.

A small motor launch came alongside and a pilot came aboard. His job was to guide us through the dozens of sunken ships in the water. The wrecks included warships and ore carriers, some of which showed only their tall masts protruding above the surface. They must have been sunk during the fighting last spring. How untidy of the military not to have removed those wrecks from the harbour by now.

We passed German destroyer escorts that had been sunk near the edge of the fjord. The clear calm water allowed the swastika on the deck near the front of one of those boats to be clearly seen from our vantage point on the bow of our ship. It looked at least thirty metres long and had been equipped with torpedoes. The sunken boat showed no signs of damage and looked in good enough condition that I thought it might have been possible to raise it. I later learned that those small warships had been scuttled by their captains when the British overran that part of Norway and the British navy blocked their escape out of the fjord.

The town and port itself were situated near the end of a promontory of land jutting into the fjord, with few signs of civilization outside the town. As the ship docked, work crews and large machinery were repairing the loading and unloading facilities in a bustle of activity. A steam locomotive moved along railway tracks on another dock farther away. Huge stockpiles of dark purple rock, which must have been iron ore, could be seen near the water in the background. There were long warehouse buildings along the docks.

Our four cannons were unloaded by cranes and towed away by trucks. We soldiers disembarked and were assembled in formation. After ensuring everyone was accounted for, we were marched along the main road through the town to our garrison, about a kilometre from the harbour. It was obvious that there had been intense fighting in Narvik before we arrived, as there were bomb craters, burned-out buildings, and piles of debris in the street.

The place was surprisingly built up, with many industrial areas and warehouse districts, and crisscrossed by many railways. There were small apartment buildings, as well as neat rows of residential houses. There was no farmland visible around the town, but there did appear to be farm fields on the other side of the harbour. I wondered how it was possible to grow any kind of crops so far north.

There were few civilians in the streets, certainly not like the throngs I had seen in France. Those we passed barely acknowledged our presence, and when anyone did it was with a look that was not welcoming. I felt strangely conspicuous, as if embarrassed to be here. The mood among the men was sombre. I was painfully aware that we were here as a part of the military occupation forces in a foreign country.

6   *Cold War*

THE MILITARY BASE THAT BECAME our new home was located just inland from the four gun positions along the coast. The garrison consisted of some wooden barracks, officers' quarters, and a large building with a kitchen, a mess hall, and a storage shed for military materials and supplies. Each barrack had a wood-burning stove in the middle of the floor, exactly the same as the barracks at the *Arbeitsdienst* in Irlbach.

The guns we brought with us were huge 15cm artillery pieces. The gun emplacements had been constructed and prepared before our arrival, and were partly sunk into the rock for protection. Each site had been chosen to provide a good field of view down the fjord. There was a position for each of the four guns, set about a hundred metres apart. Those fortifications looked old enough that they could have been constructed before the German forces arrived.

We started training on how to operate our big weapons. I soon learned that there was not much difference between these big 15cm guns and the 10.5cm field guns we had used in France, other than they weighed considerably more and were therefore more difficult to manoeuvre. The 15cm shells were much heavier than the 10.5cm shells. There was a separate shell and explosive charge to make them easier to handle.

The cannons had their two large steel wheels set on the ringed edge of a large steel ring in the ground, on which the entire gun assembly could be balanced and swivelled in a circle. It took four men to lift the back of each of the legs in order to point the barrel in the desired direction. We had a wide and unobstructed view of the fjord, so any ship approaching the harbour would have been an easy target. To counter possible air attacks there were also anti-aircraft emplacements nearby, one of which could be seen in the distance. They were manned by troops from a different battery, stationed at barracks far from ours.

We prepared for another venture by the British to recapture Narvik. I knew the Allies had attempted to dislodge the German troops from Norway shortly after the German invasion, and they may try

74 FÜHRER, FOLK AND FATHERLAND

again. We were there to defend the port, but I had no delusions that our small garrison of a few hundred men, even with those four cannons, could defeat a determined assault by strong Allied forces supported by airplanes or warships.

We soon settled into a routine. The cannons were manned on a rotating basis twenty-four hours a day, seven days a week, with each of us taking a four-hour shift every day. Two guards were posted at each gun position at all times. Guard duty during daylight was just tedious, with most of the time being spent watching the fjord, or the sky, or birds flying overhead. While on duty we were not permitted to sit down, so we just paced up and down beside the gun.

That first night on guard duty was unnerving. My imagination made every noise in the dark hold potential danger—perhaps Norwegian partisans trying to sabotage the gun, or British commandos on a search-and-destroy mission? After a week or so those imaginings diminished and eventually the night shifts became as boring as the day shifts. It was cold during the long nights, and the wind bit right through my skin as it blew down the fjord. The cold seeped up through my boots as I stood on the frigid cement. Even casual conversation with my fellow guard became an effort, as it required raising my head and exposing my face to the wind. I cared less about the importance of defending the gun position than about keeping from freezing.

The first snowstorm I experienced was unbelievable. The wind blew fiercely up the fjord, blowing the snow about so it was sometimes impossible to see more than a few metres. It felt like the elements were trying to punish us for being here. Such blizzards were unknown in Bavaria. Being so far north, the sun did not rise more than a few degrees above the horizon, with seemingly interminable periods of twilight. What an alien place, desolate and forlorn, absolutely at the end of the known world.

Life in Narvik was not all rigorous and disagreeable. On the rare occasions that the night was clear of clouds and moonless, I was astounded at how bright the stars were and how many I could see. Gazing up made me feel very small, like I could fall off the planet. One night I was startled by what appeared to be luminous curtains of light dancing in the sky—the aurora borealis. I had heard of those northern lights, but to actually see them was well beyond anything I could have imagined. They shimmered and waved across an impossibly huge portion of the sky, as if stirred by an unseen hand. I was mesmerized for hours by the dazzling display.

When not manning the gun positions we were put through weapons drills and other military exercises. Training included scrambling out to our gun positions, followed by repeated drills on gun-loading and firing, even though no shells were actually fired. We also practised rifle drills and underwent daily calisthenics. Regular maintenance of the guns and the barracks, including kitchen and cleaning duties, was also part of the routine. The purpose of the exercises was of course to keep everyone physically and mentally prepared for any emergency.

The routine soon became so tedious that some of the men began grumbling, even expressing the desire to get into some action just to relieve the boredom. I had no desire to get involved in any kind of battle, but have to admit I often felt absolutely miserable after a four-hour stint at my post in the cold darkness. I wondered if it was to become my fate to serve the rest of my life at some forsaken outpost of Hitler's Third Reich.

Even though there was no shooting during my stint in Narvik, I experienced another form of belligerence, a psychological and emotional cold war. Not only was the winter cold, but the people were cold toward us. Of course I could understand why. Norway had been neutral at the start of the war, but that neutrality had been violated by both Allied and German armies leading up to the occupation. I could imagine the Norwegians resented foreign domination.

There was no open or organized hostility, but there were isolated incidents. Late one night somebody fired a shot at one of the guards on duty at one of the cannons, hitting him in the arm. He was not seriously wounded, but it was bad enough that he had to be treated in hospital. There was no retaliation on the part of the German troops. The army commanders must have realized that such an isolated event, possibly perpetrated by one disgruntled or drunken person, was not the start of a partisan insurrection.

I went into the town some evenings with a few of the men. We had nothing other than our uniforms to wear, so we definitely stuck out. The local Norwegians did not do anything hostile or even say anything derogatory, but they very deliberately ignored us. On the bus into town I sat down beside a middle-aged lady. She did not look at me, but promptly got up and moved to another seat farther away. Even though I had no choice about being in Narvik, that very personal disdain by the locals made me feel uncomfortable. We soldiers kept mainly to ourselves and had little contact with the local residents. There was not much to do in downtown Narvik anyway. There were a few pubs and restaurants, but nothing that could be considered an attraction.

On a visit to a pub we met one of the soldiers who had lived through the battle for Narvik. His account of the fighting was an eye-opener. The fighting had been very fierce under difficult conditions and in exceptionally rough terrain. British, French, and Polish forces had attacked the Narvik peninsula and, after fierce fighting, captured Narvik near the end of May. The German forces, led by General Dietl, consisted of about 2,000 Austrian *Gebirgsjäger* (mountain infantry) and about another 3,000 German seamen who were survivors from the German warships that had been sunk or scuttled in Narvik harbour. They were forced to retreat farther and farther into the wooded and snow-covered mountains, where they were completely cut off from the rest of the German forces in Norway. The veteran said his training in the Austrian Alps was a picnic compared to the conditions in Norway's mountains. His account of huddling in a freezing foxhole on the mountainside, exhausted and nearly starving, was particularly graphic. The *Luftwaffe* had dropped supplies by parachute, but it had been barely enough to keep them alive. It was not until June that German reinforcements moving north from Trondheim turned the battle in Dietl's favour. One day the masses of Allied troops just left. "A miracle," as he described it.

During his narrative the veteran made light of the hardships he had endured. He said the aerial battles between *Luftwaffe* and Allied airplanes were "entertainment." He spoke with the confident optimism that all German soldiers felt in those days; however, his reflective countenance disclosed how arduous and brutal that month-long battle had been. Having survived it gave him the luxury of making fun of it. That recounting was a lesson for me. The stories told by a participant were certainly different from the official versions in the media last spring, which had downplayed the extent of the fighting and made it sound much easier than it was.

General Dietl was glorified as a hero in the German media, and perhaps rightly so. The veteran verified that the men who had served under his command adored him. He proudly relayed the heartening story of the eventual Norwegian surrender. When the British and French abandoned Norway in June 1940, taking King Haakon and his ministers with them, the Norwegian troops led by General Ruge were permitted to return to their homes. That may have helped make our own stay in Norway less hazardous than it could have been, since there was no reason for subsequent wholesale partisan vengeance on the part of the Norwegians.

We heard about Germany's invasion of the Balkans to help Mussolini's Fascist armies defeat Albania and Greece. From what I learned in history classes at the *Realschule*, there was little reason to have any faith in the Italian army's ability to help Germany's war efforts. The Italian army had had a difficult time subduing Ethiopia, and the fiasco in the Balkans only reinforced my image of Mussolini as an incompetent military commander.

We often heard news reports about the fighting in the North African desert, which were filled with General Rommel's daring deeds. Rommel's *Afrika Korps* had been sent to help our Italian allies fight the British. News accounts of tremendous tank battles sounded more like sporting events than the bloody conflicts I knew they must have been. I suspected that Rommel's assignment was to capture the Middle East oil fields in order to secure a source of petroleum for Germany's industries and motorized weapons, as Germany suffered a desperate shortage of oil. The British navy's blockade was common knowledge. No supplies of oil or other raw materials had been able to reach Germany from across the seas since the beginning of the war.

We continued to hear occasional reports about the Battle of Britain. Our media tried to make it sound like it was only a matter of time before the British sued for peace. When the astonishing news reached us that the British air force had bombed Berlin, I began to have doubts that the *Luftwaffe* actually was winning the air war. Our illustrious leader of the *Luftwaffe*, Hermann Goering, had previously boasted that Berlin would never be bombed, going so far as to announce that, "If they could, you can call me Maier."[6] After that we heard that the *Luftwaffe* bombed London and other cities in England in reprisal.

The bombing of cities, ostensibly to destroy military installations

---

6   Meaning, you could call him a peasant.

and industries, struck me as very repugnant, as there were always civilians in those cities under those bombs. The bombing of civilians was something I had never heard of happening before in history. Even if, like during the First World War, soldiers had to endure the brutal and dangerous conditions of the trenches, I could not think of any justification for attacking civilians in their own homes far from the front.

On June 23, 1941, we heard the news that Germany had invaded Russia the day before. The magnitude of that event immediately gave me an uneasy sense of foreboding. Napoleon had met disaster in Russia, when the Russian winter had swallowed up his supposedly invincible Grande Armée. Curiously, Hitler invaded Russia on the anniversary of Napoleon's invasion, in June 1812. I hoped that was not a portentous omen.

Why would Hitler want to tempt fate and venture into Russia anyway? Newsreels had depicted the Russian Ukraine as the breadbasket of Europe, and Germany needed the raw materials of that region to survive, especially with the continuing British blockade. In one of his pompous speeches Hitler had made reference to the German nation's need for *Lebensraum* (living space), so that invasion may have been inevitable. But why not just trade with Russia instead of trying to take their resources by force? Besides, I knew that Germany had signed a peace treaty with Russia, and it was disconcerting to me that the leader of our country would have so little regard for his own promises.

I eventually convinced myself that the invasion of Russia, although a dangerous gamble, was not necessarily fatal to Germany. It might be possible to topple Stalin's Bolshevik regime and set up new governments in the former Soviet states. The communist system under Stalin could not be popular with people in subjugated nations, such as the Ukraine and the Baltic countries. I also believed the situation in the west would eventually stabilize; after all, France had been defeated and England might make peace. The German armies had been very successful so far, and there was no reason to think they would not be just as successful in Russia.

Hitler's ambition was one thing; actually accomplishing his objectives was another. It was the individual men of the German armed forces who were assigned the task of conquering the lands Hitler coveted. We soldiers would be the ones risking our lives at the front lines, not our leaders. I wondered how long it would be before some of the men in my unit, including me, were going to be called to Russia.

Talking about the Russian war, one of the men was of the opinion that war with Russia had been unavoidable, as Stalin would have attacked Germany once his armies had grown strong and modern enough to make him confident of victory. Everyone knew that Stalin had built up a vast army with millions of troops and tens of thousands of armoured units positioned along the border with German-held territory. My personal suspicion, which I kept to myself, was that Hitler had no interest in peace; he was a delusional megalomaniac (the German word is *grösenwahnsinig*), and infatuated with the idea of conquest.

Throughout the summer of 1941, reports of events from the Russian front continued to reach us regularly in Narvik. Those reports consistently described the campaign as proceeding even better than had been predicted. A few of the men with us, however, had received letters from home that a brother had been killed or wounded in Russia. That drove home the personal consequences of a long war in the east.

When spring turned to summer the daylight hours became noticeably longer. It had begun with a gradually diminishing twilight darkness as the sun dipped less and less below the horizon each night, until there was constant daylight from the middle of May to the end of July. Although less depressing than the long darkness had been, the constant daylight was just as alien to me. The daily routine was set strictly by the clock, as the lack of any darkness was disorienting, including knowing when to sleep. The night shift at the cannon lost its meaning. On the bright side, the longer daylight hours seemed to provide more free time and encouraged us to venture into town more often.

In the summer of 1941, Heinz and I discovered that a local entrepreneur had opened a pleasant little outdoor café in Narvik, which offered an agreeable diversion from the drudgery of military life. There were a few dozen patrons in the café on one particular day. Sitting at the table next to us were two young Norwegian women. One of them was especially pretty. She looked about nineteen, with blonde hair tied into two long braids. We four struck up a faltering conversation. The pretty one spoke a little German, and although I spoke no Norwegian, there were similarities in the two languages which permitted me to grasp the meaning and intent of many Norwegian words. When she smiled I noticed she wore braces. Her name was Ingrid.

I tried to think of some activity that would give us an excuse to spend some time together. Because of the language barrier I could not express myself in the usually charming phraseology that I considered to be one of my most endearing qualities, so we gestured and smiled a lot. I bought her a cup of coffee and some cakes, which she accepted gracefully. I asked if she could give me a guided tour of the town, and she agreed to do so.

Even though we had not been forbidden to fraternize with the local civilians, it was discouraged by the army. It felt awkward trying to become personal with a Norwegian civilian, and only partly due to the language differences. The Norwegians surely discouraged members of their community from fraternizing with the occupation troops. Notwithstanding whatever cultural barriers there were operating in Narvik, biology still had a powerful influence, so I longed for some female company.

We left Heinz and Ingrid's girlfriend in the café and set off on a leisurely walk. Ingrid and I managed to spend the rest of that day together, sightseeing through Narvik, and continued our walk out of town along the road that led to the garrison. Eventually we stopped and sat down on a large boulder facing the fjord. Sitting in the sunshine with Ingrid, among the evergreens and blueberry bushes, I saw this rugged northern landscape with new eyes. The lichens and mosses made multi-coloured patterns on the rocks. The sunlight sparkling off the myriad tiny waves in the fjord made it look like a million diamonds had been strewn onto the water. It was quite beautiful.

It felt pleasant to spend time with someone other than my barrack-mates, especially someone with such a lovely face. I kept noticing the braces on her teeth and wondered what it would be like to kiss a girl with braces; but before my wandering imagination got the better of me I thought about the consequences of any rash action. I felt a strong urge to get close to her, but it also felt clumsy and peculiarly unreal. This situation was suddenly very personal and surprisingly intimidating. Spending time together in the days to come may have been nice, but she belonged to another world, with her own family, friends, home life, dreams, and ambitions. I could not be a part of that world. I belonged to an artificial world, one that was observable and tangible, but not permanent, like a shadow that would pass away as soon as it was no longer needed here. My life was not my own, as I was merely property of the state, and a foreign state at that, so there was no chance for me to give her anything of value, anything stable or meaningful. Besides, what was I to do, bring her back to the barracks? She was surely not going to bring me home to meet Mom and Dad. Whatever the reason, I knew nothing worthwhile would come of this.

We walked back to town, and after saying, "So long," I headed back to my barracks and never saw Ingrid again.

During our spare time we soldiers usually just stayed in the barracks or gathered in the mess hall, telling stories and playing cards or chess. I spent a lot of time reading books and old magazines. We ate in the mess hall every day. The food was almost always the same: potato stew with canned vegetables, usually accompanied by sausages, chicken, or pork, and the usual dark rye bread. Fresh fish provided some variety to our diet. We also had tea, *malzkaffee,* and sometimes milk or canned apple juice. Nothing fancy, but it was filling and nourishing.

The army supplied a daily cigarette ration. Since I did not smoke, I sometimes traded my cigarettes for items such as chocolate. Usually I just gave them away. Beer and liquor were also cheap and plentiful. The liquor came from the army supply store. Some of the more enterprising fellows in the garrison sold liquor, cigarettes, or other army supply items to the local Norwegian civilians. The Norwegians prized those items very much, and would trade any sort of goods or personal services they thought we soldiers might like. It appeared that commerce disdained political protocol and was able to overcome whatever sociological barriers the authorities put in place.

Drinking was one of the more common means of passing the time. Sometimes alcohol would help compensate for the boredom and the loneliness. One evening we were celebrating the birthday of one of our buddies in the barracks. Because it was a birthday party I could not refuse to drink with the other men. So we drank schnapps, told stories, drank some more, sang songs, and drank some more. After the first few drinks I stopped noticing the disagreeable taste. As the empties piled up, the stories became funnier and the songs became louder and lustier. Considering where we were, we might have convinced ourselves that we were having fun. The next day a wretched hangover made me feel so bad I never wanted to repeat it for the rest of my life.

By the end of October the sun again rose only a few degrees above the horizon and periods of bright daylight were brief. Real sunshine became almost nonexistent as the nights grew inexorably longer. During that fall the sky was mostly overcast, so that the passing of each day was marked with only a dull twilight that gradually increased from morning until noon and then gradually waned until it was dark again. Thick fog often rolled in from the Atlantic, a damp, cold presence, enveloping and smothering everything. Even sounds were muffled in the fog, producing a sensation of total isolation, as if all signs of life in the rest of the world had been extinguished. Foggy conditions could last for days, leaving me feeling gloomy and sometimes chilled to the bone. Those foggy nights on guard duty were interminably long.

The army had decided that during the polar night we must be exposed to artificial sunlight for one hour a week by lying under an ultraviolet lamp in a room at the garrison. That gave me the sensation of being a laboratory rat in a science experiment. I still wonder if the radiation from those lamps was more harmful than helpful. We also had to take a spoonful of cod-liver oil every day, as the only source of vitamin D. It was impossible to get used to its absolutely horrible flavour and texture. We also took vitamin C pills every day to combat scurvy, since there was no way to get fresh citrus fruit. At least the army was trying to keep us healthy.

On December 8, 1941, an announcement came over the loudspeakers that Japan had attacked Pearl Harbor the day before. The next day we heard that Hitler had declared war on America. Any hopes that this war could be confined to a limited European contest were now dashed. America had entered the war, not only against Japan, but against Germany as well. That momentous news had a profound influence on my attitude. It made no sense for Hitler to declare war on the United States. For the first time I realized it may actually be possible that Germany would lose the war, this Second World War. The huge population and the enormous industrial capacity of the United States had helped to decide the outcome of the First World War. I became convinced that Hitler's quest to attain domination over all of Europe was doomed to failure. All my enforced efforts to help that cause would be for nothing. Devotion to duty, personal sacrifice in the service of my country, and my former willingness to die for the greater good of the German nation became meaningless notions. Any sense of patriotic purpose I may have felt toward my military service was extinguished forever that day and replaced with a resolve to try to save my own skin.

Late in the fall of 1941, my two years of service entitled me to another two-week holiday. I decided to go home for Christmas. So in mid-December I boarded a passenger train in Narvik for the long trip home, along with a few other soldiers on leave, including my friend Heinz. We were required to travel in a passenger car reserved exclusively for German soldiers. It was pitch-dark out when we left, even though it was the middle of the morning. The train first went eastward through the mountains and into Sweden, after which we travelled south through the length of the country. After a few hours it became twilight and eventually the sun broke above the horizon, making it possible to see something of the countryside. Much of the trip was through absolute wilderness, rough country, often hilly, and beautiful in a wild and rugged way. The blanket of snow made the landscape look like a scene from a Christmas card. Identical trees passed by the window in unbroken succession for hours. There were villages, but signs of civilization were scarce for what seemed like hundreds of kilometres. The persistent thudding rhythm of the train eventually lulled me to sleep.

We were not permitted to get off the train in Sweden, even though the train stopped at its regular stations along the way. The army supplied us with a box lunch for the train ride. I was careful to keep my *Soldbuch* with me, as well as my train tickets. When in uniform, soldiers had to show their *Soldbuch,* with the vacation time stamped in it, to the conductor on the trains or to the stewards on the ships.

In Malmo we boarded a ferry to cross the Skagerrak to Kopenhagen, in Denmark, where we took another train to the port of Hamburg, Germany. We arrived in Hamburg very late at night, so there was no opportunity to see any of the sights. Heinz and I parted company in the Hamburg train station. I boarded a passenger train for Nürnberg. As the train travelled southward through Germany there were fewer soldiers in the train stations and fewer military vehicles along the roads. The tumult of warfare was apparently confined mainly to the borders of the Reich.

When I arrived in Michelau only my father and my youngest brother Karl were at home. At thirteen, Karl was still too young for military service. The last news my father had heard from Hermann was that he was at the Russian front. The twins, Edwin and Oskar, had just received their draft notices. Hermann's wife, Anna, was there, along with their two young sons, Richard and Adolf. Adolf may have been named after our illustrious leader, perhaps because Anna was a supporter of the regime. Her older brother was a big shot *Gauleiter* (district leader) in one of the administrative districts in Bavaria.

It was not much of a Christmas in the traditional sense that year. There were no presents. It may just have felt different because I had grown up. Still, the cooked goose and Anna's potato dumplings were wonderful. After the meal we had a few glasses of wine and talked about Christmases past. We wished my brother well, wherever he was.

I visited the local pubs and met a few old friends who were also on leave. The war did not seem to have affected life much in Michelau, other than the lack of military-age men. People naturally talked about the war and expressed their concerns. The 95th Infantry Regiment, which was stationed in Coburg, about fifteen kilometres north of Michelau, had taken part in the initial assault into Russia. Many Michelauers were in that regiment. The official news reports from the Russian front were resplendent with impressive victories by Hitler's armies, but I met people who had received notice that their son or brother or husband had been killed in Russia. I wondered how the news of Hitler's victories would have felt for them.

Shortly before my arrival in Michelau, the government made announcements asking all men and women in Germany who owned a fur coat to give them up to be sent to the soldiers at the Russian front. Reports of the severely cold winter in Russia made that seem like a small, patriotic sacrifice to make. It would have been selfish and imprudent for anyone to be caught wearing a fur coat after that request. Train-loads of fur coats were supposedly sent east. That enterprise was surely grandstanding on the part of our leaders. How could a few fur coats make any difference to the poor bastards in the middle of a snowstorm in Russia? And how would a small woman's coat be made to fit a man, especially over his uniform and gear? I wondered what really happened to those fur coats.

During the return trip to Narvik there was a brief stopover in Hamburg. We Norway-bound soldiers took the opportunity to visit Hamburg's famous *Reeperbahn*, a district in the heart of the old city devoted to revelry and entertainment. A few city blocks on either side of the main street near the harbour contained restaurants, theatres, pubs, night-clubs, strip joints, and brothels. Unfortunately, our few hours' stopover was during the day, so again we had no chance to sample the district's famous night life at night.

We stayed overnight in Flensburg, close to the Danish border in the German province of Schleswig–Holstein, where we had a meal of flounder. That was the best fish I had ever tasted in my life. I noted with some irony that this simple experience encapsulated the essence of the reality of my soldier lifestyle so far. Mealtimes were the vital events of my days. That a decent meal could make such a memorable impression on me was food for thought indeed.

The rest of the return trip to Narvik was uneventful, reversing my route home. All the trees were still there. When we arrived in Narvik it was pitch-black outside. Thinking that the last leg had taken a very long time because it was so dark at night, I looked at my watch. It was 3 p.m.! I had already forgotten that Narvik gets no sun at all during December and January.

When I returned to my post at the gun for the first time in 1942, it appeared almost like a familiar friend. Even the cold was more re-freshing than inhospitable, and the northern lights were downright de-lightful. But after a few weeks the military routine and especially the constant gloom again became depressing. Once again I lived with the oppressive feeling of segregation, as if cut off from the rest of the world. On a very personal level, I was annoyed with Hitler for starting this war, as my continued enforced military service was spoiling the best years of my young adulthood. Opportunities to live a regular life—to launch a career, to start a family, and to build a home of my own—were now on hold.

The tedium of my stint in Narvik made me forget my father's ad-monition, that no matter how bad you think things are, they can always get worse. I expected the rest of my stint in Narvik to be just as unevent-ful as it had been before the holiday. I had more or less assumed that the Eastern Front could get along without me. But my luck was soon to change.

On January 18, 1942, I received notice from the army to report to Küstrin, in East Prussia. I knew that would be the first leg of my journey to the Russian front.

7   *Field Marshal Winter*

NEAR THE END OF JANUARY 1942, four of us boarded the train from Narvik and took the same trip through Sweden I had taken at Christmas. This time my friend Heinz Wagner did not come with me; he stayed in Narvik. It was disappointing parting company. When I wished him good luck as I left the barracks, he replied wryly, "You may need it more than me where you're going." It crossed my mind that we might never see each other again.

After three days on the train we arrived in Küstrin and stayed at the same barracks I had spent a few weeks in before going to Narvik in February 1941. A few days later I received orders to report to the 2nd Battery of the 293rd Artillery Regiment, which was stationed in the field somewhere on the Eastern Front. Dozens of other soldiers boarded the train with me.

It was cold and damp near the Baltic coast at that time of year. The sky was overcast. A faint frost haze hung in the air. The weather seemed as miserable as my spirits. We travelled through the night.

I had been away from home a long time, and my adventures as a soldier in France and Norway had become enough for me. I was not looking forward to seeing Russia. The high casualties suffered at the Eastern Front were common knowledge. Still, at the time it was not as fearful as it perhaps should have been, since I had little concept of what to expect. Up until then our forces had been very successful. The recent setback where the German armies were thrown back at the gates of Moscow was publicized as just a temporary reversal, a brief delay before the inevitable victory. I had my doubts that we would be as easily successful in overrunning Russia. A simple geography lesson held obvious clues. Russia is fifty times the size of Germany, with over 250 million inhabitants, compared to about 80 million Germans. It seemed inconceivable that Germany could provide enough soldiers to conquer and garrison such a huge country.

During that trip east we passed through the Baltic countries of Lithuania and Latvia. We stopped overnight in the Latvian capital of Riga.

As we walked back to the train station from our hotel the next morning, there were some men wearing dark coats sweeping the streets as part of what appeared to be a work gang. Each wore the Star of David on his coat, meaning they were Jewish. That struck me as curious, so I stopped to speak with one of them. He appeared despondent, hunched over his broom. He was obviously not doing that street-sweeping chore by choice. I had seen that stoic expression before, on prisoners of war in France. He spoke German very well, which surprised me since it was a foreign country. I asked him if he was being paid to work in the streets. He said no. I then asked how he had been ordered to do that labour, since he was a civilian and it made no sense to me for civilians to have to follow orders for work detail against their will. He said that he had been pressed into that labour gang by the local city government. He repeatedly looked over his shoulder; perhaps he feared being reprimanded for spending time talking with me. Before walking away I wished him luck, and truly meant it.

Latvia and the other two Baltic countries were now under the domination of Germany; however, the German media had depicted the takeover of the Baltic countries as liberation from their Stalinist oppressors. There was nothing liberating about seeing that enforced labour. Not that everyone in Hitler's Reich did not have to work; however, this was deliberately demeaning work, not productive work. It made me uncomfortable that my government could have such control over civilians, and that it could arbitrarily designate any minority for mistreatment. If such discrimination could happen to Jewish people could the state not turn against anyone else whom the persons in power considered appropriate targets? At the time I never dreamed that the government leaders would expend such enormous efforts to persecute "undesirables" in the Third Reich. Those poor wretches sweeping the streets of Riga certainly did not look like they posed any threat to Latvia or Germany. I just hoped that incident was not a harbinger of what was in store for all of the German-occupied lands. What I understood very well was that my personal thoughts and feelings did not matter one bit to the government. I too was a prisoner of the state.

Most of the civilians we met during the remainder of our trip through the Baltic countries were very friendly. The majority of Latvians actually might have considered German occupation better than Russian communist occupation. After all, Stalin had annexed them to his empire only three years before. It appeared to me that we were being treated as soldiers of an allied nation, just passing through as if it were a normal event, part of the daily routine. What was considered normal was dictated by circumstances as they were perceived at the time, and it was wartime.

We spent two more days travelling by train through countryside that seemed to be nothing but trees, frozen swamps, and snow-covered stubble fields. Villages appeared to get smaller and less numerous the farther east we went. There was frost on the glass and it felt freezing cold to the touch. I imagined that there would be precious few comforts for us soldiers in this very foreign land.

The railway tracks in Russia are a wider gauge than the rest of Europe, so the German engineers had narrowed the tracks in occupied territory by moving the rail on one side a little closer to the other. That industrious task permitted rolling stock loaded in Germany to travel into Russia, at least part of the way.

When we reached our destination and I stepped off the train the cold hit my face like a brick. Our uniforms were regular wool, with a woollen cap and a large, heavy greatcoat, which I had always considered warm, even in Narvik. But here it quickly became obvious that my military clothes did not provide enough insulation to keep me warm. My rifle felt painfully frigid through my gloves. The cold gradually seeped upward through the soles of my leather boots as I stood on the frozen ground. I should have put on my spare set of socks and underwear, and not kept them in my kit bag.

A huge staff sergeant came up to our line of men. "Gentlemen, heartfelt welcome to the East Front!" We were ordered to assemble where he pointed as he called out the unit numbers of each of the batteries. "Two-hundred-ninety-third Regiment, Second Battery." That was me. About half a dozen of us stepped up. A corporal then led us away.

We climbed into the back of a truck and headed off. The truck ride was noisy, bumpy, chilly, and thoroughly uncomfortable. No wonder; what passed for roads in this country were very rough indeed, covered in frozen ruts that caused the truck to bump and sway, or lurch sideways as it skidded on ice. Gusts of wind blew whirling snow in through gaps in the canvas cover over the rear of the truck. We huddled together on the benches of the truck and said nothing. At least we did not have to walk.

After hours in the truck we disembarked. Looking around in the late evening light, I could see a line of cannons in the snow-covered distance, all facing away, along with a few tents and wagons—my new home.

The corporal led us down a trench and into a rudimentary underground bunker. It was about three metres wide and ten metres long, and just high enough to permit a man to stand upright. The walls and ceiling were held up by rough-cut wooden planks. A double-layered canvas tarpaulin hung across the entrance as a door. Just inside was a wood-burning stove made from an old steel drum. Bunks had been fashioned out of planks along the sides and covered with conifer branches and pieces of canvas. There was room enough for about a dozen men to sleep. Not exactly first-class accommodations, but at least we were out of the biting wind and the snow.

The other men in the bunker looked really rough. A gunnery mate introduced himself and welcomed me to the battery. He looked like he had been sleeping in his clothes in that hovel for weeks, which of course he had. He was a very good-natured chap, in spite of the way he looked. I found a spot on the planks by the wall and claimed it for my new berth. That night I scraped some spruce boughs together and tried to make myself a bed. Needless to say, it was a long and very uncomfortable night.

The next morning I woke up with ice frozen onto the stubble hairs under my nose. I had no idea any place on earth could get so cold. Even in Narvik, north of the Arctic Circle, it had never felt so cold. I warmed myself by the steel drum fire. When we assembled at our gun position the wind felt like it was cutting right through my skin. Duties were accomplished in a mindless daze, my mind preoccupied with trying to keep from freezing. The temperature fell so low that the grease in our cannons froze solid. The guns could not be fired and nothing motorized could move. Some soldiers lit a wood fire under the motor of the truck that brought me here, to thaw out the oil enough to allow the motor to start. It took a few tries, but after about an hour the truck started and drove off.

The gunnery mate was from *Köln* (Cologne), a big city on the Rhine River in the far western part of Germany. I learned that we new arrivals were indeed replacements for losses suffered during the winter. The battery had lost dozens of men due to frostbite. I also found out we were near Leningrad. The trenches and bunkers we were occupying had originally been the outermost Russian defences for the city. That explained the wide anti-tank ditches that crossed the site, the sides of which had partly collapsed and eroded. The bottoms were now filled with deep snow. Our artillery battery was situated far from the city itself. Even though the terrain was almost flat, the view was obscured by forests. There were dozens of cannons to the left and right of our battery, all pointed at the city. There were slit trenches connecting the cannon positions, as well as trenches leading to supply bunkers behind the cannons, all deep enough that a man could walk upright without exposing his head. Here and there were stockpiles of materiel in wooden crates, some covered with tarpaulins. By the look of the place, especially by the amount of debris and spent shell casings littering the ground, the artillery batteries had been there for some time. I assumed there were infantry dug in closer to the actual fighting front, although I never saw any.

I did not know to which division my artillery battery belonged, but was sure we were at the northern end of the Eastern Front, so we must have been part of Army Group North. The organization and logistics for our battery were accomplished by personnel who were probably far removed from the fighting. There was no mention of what our objectives were.

Conditions at the Eastern Front near Leningrad were appalling. We were ill-equipped to battle the elements, let alone the enemy. My uniform was woefully inadequate. The steel nails in my boots conducted the cold through the soles to my feet. I heard of men that had suffered frostbite and had to have toes amputated. I was lucky; only the little toe of my left foot turned blue, but I managed to revive the circulation before it turned black, otherwise I could have lost the toe. Good thing my boots were slightly large for my feet, so that I was able to wear two pairs of wool socks and a paper liner in the soles.

The cold weather not only made it difficult to stay warm, it also lowered resistance to diseases. A simple cold that would have been easily overcome back home could prove deadly here in Russia. Many German soldiers died of diseases or froze to death during that brutal winter of 1941–42. Some men had died because they had not covered their heads with warm clothing before putting on their steel helmets. The cold was so numbing that it gradually lowered the senses and prevented the body from noticing death approaching. In such conditions just falling asleep could be fatal. The Russians had a truly formidable ally—Field Marshal Winter, as some veterans called it.

In those brutally cold conditions I learned how to have a shit very quickly. The latrine was a small trench in the ground with two planks laid from one side to the other spanning the top. You timed everything carefully, because the cold gripped your butt like a vice as soon as you exposed it. With nothing but newspaper or other coarse material available, wiping my ass could be painful.

If Narvik had been somewhat primitive, this was downright primeval. However bad Narvik had seemed to me at the time, I appreciated that I had been extremely lucky to have been stationed in the relative luxury of that far-off outpost during much of that terrible first winter.

I was assigned to Cannon No. 1, which meant I had to make sure everything was kept in working order, including the gun itself, the supply wagon, and the ammunition stores, and that the gun crew performed their assigned duties correctly. Being in charge was more or less meaningless, as every man knew his responsibilities perfectly and performed his duties without any guidance from me. The horses for our battery were kept in a village a few kilometres behind the line of cannons. It was also my responsibility to ensure that the soldiers assigned to their care and feeding did so. By the time I arrived everyone had already settled into a routine, if routine is the right term under those conditions.

On the morning of the third or fourth day we were ordered to commence firing. It was still cold enough that the detonators from the cannon shells had to be kept in our pockets until it was time to fire, otherwise the shells would be sent to the target as nothing more than cold lumps of metal. It was hard work to aim the gun because the grease in the moving parts was thick from the cold. We fitted the detonator onto the shell, set the fuse, loaded the breech, and the gunner fired. The cold made handling the shells cumbersome. Setting the timing fuse on the tip was especially awkward when wearing big mitts. Once the timer was set the shell was live and we took great care ramming it into the breech. Ice on the palms of my mitts made me look and feel downright clumsy. Exposed skin could freeze onto the metal, so nobody took off his mitts.

For most of that day we were engaged in a sometimes raucous but mostly haphazard bombardment. It was an almost surreal experience—the deafening retorts, the smoke, the acrid stink of cordite, the exertion of lifting and loading shells. In the cold the smoke hung in the air like a dense fog and we had to wait a while for the smoke to clear. I assumed that our bombardment was the beginning of another lightning offensive by our troops; but at the end of the day we did not move. We stacked the spent shell casings, greased the gun, had our evening meal, and went to sleep in our underground bunker. I had a terrible headache, along with a continuous ringing in my ears.

For another week we fired shells off and on toward the city, at targets we could not see, targets that were given to us by radio from the battery commanders, expending many hundreds of rounds. I kept thinking that sooner or later we would be ordered to advance because the city had been captured. If it was not to support an assault, then to me all that shelling seemed completely senseless. But we did not move. Such apparently futile behaviour on the part of our forces was a new experience for me. In France we had been constantly advancing, and the fighting was always over quickly after furious but decisive battles. Here we were part of a huge siege, a sordid and ineffectual battle of attrition. I soon had visions of the campaign in the east turning into a repeat of the debilitating trench warfare of the First World War. Surely the army commanders would have learned not to repeat those mistakes, especially after the favourable victories the German forces had experienced at the start of the war? Still, I kept wondering why something decisive did not happen. Nobody with me had the slightest idea whether or not our cannon fire had any effect at all on the enemy.

One day the sound of incoming shells caught us in the open, so we raced for the shelter of our underground bunkers. Shells burst all around our positions. The enemy shells made a coarse sound like the tearing of heavy cloth. That caused a feeling of real terror. Once inside our bunkers we were relatively safe. The only thing I was afraid of then was having the bunker collapse on top of us, and that could only happen with a direct hit. The odds of that kind of hit were very long. The enemy's shelling produced no casualties that I ever witnessed.

While near Leningrad we heard an announcement about some battle for some other city at the front. That meant that the war had not deteriorated into a dreary stalemate, at least not at other sectors of the Eastern Front, and that there was still movement. It also meant that German forces could still be on the offensive.

Other conditions in Russia were terrible. The food was the worst I had experienced until then. The only cooked meal of the day was a bowl of thin potato soup, which was served after dark and was never hot by the time I got back from the field kitchen. If you waited too long to eat it would start to freeze. The bread was stale and as hard as wood. We received cans that contained some kind of processed meat. We heated the cans on the steel drum stove to thaw out the contents and ate them right out of the can. It tasted greasy and salty. Our tea smelled and tasted like it was made from conifer branches and motor oil. The best food, and the only variety in our rations, was an occasional serving of stringy boiled meat in the stew, which I ate with no thought to where it came from until one of the veterans pointed out that many horses had not survived the winter. In that frozen wilderness there was no problem preserving the meat.

It must have been increasingly difficult for our supply convoys to get through as the winter dragged on. That could also explain why our shelling was not more consistent, as there was a repeated shortage of ammunition. Either that or army command had relegated the siege of Leningrad to a low priority and diverted supplies to other more important sectors of the front.

The prospect of a speedy resolution near Leningrad eventually became remote. I feared having to spend the rest of the war in those miserable trenches. Still, I convinced myself that things could have been worse. Our guns were located a few kilometres behind the front lines, far enough away from any fighting that I never saw a single Russian soldier during my entire time near Leningrad with the 2nd Battery of the 293rd Regiment. We had to endure the cold, the crummy food, the uncomfortable sleeping accommodations, and the miserable living conditions; but my life was not in imminent danger from enemy activity.

After about three weeks near Leningrad our battery received orders that we were to be transferred to another part of the Eastern Front. There was no buildup to that order and no indication that something had changed. I asked the sergeant where we were going. He said, "I figure the army does not want to waste a lot of men and equipment fighting for Leningrad. Maybe it does not need to be captured."

With what seemed to me like hundreds of guns, a fair part of the might of the German *Wehrmacht*, pounding Leningrad, I never understood why Leningrad could not be taken. I also could not figure out why Leningrad had not been captured by the mighty panzer divisions that had been in the forefront of the assault last summer and fall.

8 *The Rasputiza*

MY ARTILLERY UNIT WAS PART of a large group of troops being prepared to move out. We gathered at our assembly point behind the rear of the battery position shortly after dawn and waited. It was not snowing, but very cold. It took most of the morning to amass the men and horse-drawn wagons and cannons in the staging area. I tucked my head down inside the collar of my greatcoat. A dirty scarf, which I had wrapped over my head and neck, was held down by my cap. I was wearing huge mittens, Russian mittens that had been given to me by one of the veterans in the trenches. They were much warmer than the gloves issued by the German army The winter had taught me quickly to take measures to keep from freezing any of my parts.

Laden with my gear, I looked out from behind the collar of my greatcoat. Everything looked grey. The sky was overcast, giving the snow a dull grey hue. Even the countless evergreen trees appeared more black than green. Just having been sent this far east was depressing enough, now we were going even deeper into this dismal country.

It was probably around ten a.m. when we started moving. Our battery had been joined by other artillery units from other sectors of the siege line. A large contingent of infantry had also joined our ranks. It may have been that there were enough troops in our congregation to form at least a battalion. It was hard to tell because it was possible to see only so far up and down the line before the view was blocked by woods or by frost haze.

Our moving column was not motorized, so we walked. The cannons and supply wagons were all horse-drawn. Some of the wagons were probably requisitioned farm wagons, which had formerly been used to transport farm materials, including manure, before they had become part of the *Wehrmacht*.

To move along Russia's so-called *Rollbahn* (the German euphemism for road) was often arduous for both men and horses. The roads were mostly covered with ice and grooved with deep ruts made by passing wheels. In open areas the wind blew fiercely across the road, forming extensive drifts. We had a difficult time making headway.

The second day on the road, it started snowing. At first it was just a steady snowfall with occasional gusts of wind, but after a few hours the wind picked up and blew the snow in sheets across the road. Ice crystals stung like hordes of needles against my face. The wind bit my skin right through my clothes, as it was impossible to keep my cape wrapped tightly around my torso.

The column came upon a village a few hours after the snowstorm began, where we took shelter. We put as many of the horses as would fit into sheds and the stable halves of the farmhouses, and quickly erected canvas lean-tos against the leeward sides of buildings for the rest. Every available room in every house, stable, and shed was crammed full with horses and soldiers. The rest of the men were forced to huddle in covered wagons, arranged to provide some shelter from the wind. Needless to say, it was very uncomfortable.

The storm lasted the rest of the day, all that night, and most of the following morning. I could only imagine how we would have fared if we had not found shelter. We had to dig ourselves out of the snowdrifts, some of which blocked entrances to houses and covered the tents and shelters, and many of the wagons and guns. The packed snow may actually have acted as insulation for the men huddling underneath. My recollection is that the village was uninhabited at the time, but I am not sure. I was focused on surviving the storm.

The march continued, every day, all day, day after day after day. Whenever the road was relatively level we took turns riding on a wagon to give our feet a rest, but those times were rare because we had to spare the horses. Mostly we walked, and walked, and walked.

The countryside was so monotonous that it eventually all looked the same to me. Here in northern Russia we marched through long stretches of forests that contained mostly homogeneous conifer trees along both sides of the road, completely uninterrupted by any signs of civilization, except for the road itself. It happened often that we were out of sight of any inhabited settlements for many hours at a time, which was completely foreign to me. Germany, Belgium, France, and Denmark were so populated that it was virtually impossible to be completely out of sight of a city, town, or village, or at least some man-made structure. Between the areas of forest there were sometimes vast open expanses, containing nothing but dead, brown reeds in frozen marshes as far as the eye could see. The sheer size of the natural features was overwhelming. Mankind's mark in that part of Russia was utterly insignificant.

For the first two weeks of the march the terrain was unrelentingly flat, with no hills, even in the distance. We crossed many rivers and streams, usually on old wooden bridges that looked very suspect. At some river crossings there was a new wooden bridge, possibly constructed by German army engineers. One curious piece of engineering we encountered was a wooden road. Two parallel rows of upright timbers had been driven into the ground and split logs were fastened across the tops to create a travelled surface. That was quite ingenious. The wagon wheels made a clattering rumble as they passed over the spaces between the boards, which was probably the loudest noise I heard during those days of marching.

Gradually the seemingly interminable forests and frozen marshlands gave way to a more familiar landscape, with snow-covered meadows and fields interspersed with settlements. Most of the terrain was still generally flat or gently rolling. We occasionally passed through villages and towns, or huge building complexes surrounded by very large fields. These were probably collective farms created by the communist state. One night many of us slept in a big storage shed on one of those agricultural collectives. That particular farm was inhabited by civilians, as were most others we passed during our march through that section of Russia.

We passed military outposts manned by German occupation troops, particularly in urban areas, and were resupplied with provisions, but the manifestations of German occupation forces were few and far between in this vast country. The most common reminders of the war were the airplanes that frequently flew overhead, sometimes low enough to attract attention. We occasionally stayed in one place for a few days, where we suspected we would head straight to the front to take part in some battle.

The equipment we carried increasingly became a burden. The steel helmet was heavy and uncomfortable to wear, as the straps that lined the inside would chafe my head, especially my forehead, so it was hung onto my belt. The helmet was not warm anyway. After a while the constant bumping of the helmet on my hip became aggravating. I wished I could just throw it away. Same with the spade, which also hung from the belt and bumped on my hip with every step. The rifle strap slung

Russian Rollbahn, *February 1942*

over the shoulder also became heavier with each passing hour. When the canteen, tin mess kit, food ration bag, gas-mask canister, toiletries kit, bayonet, and ammunition pouches were added to the parapher-nalia hanging on my person, they became a very clumsy, clanking as-semblage. Try as I might, there was no way to make all that baggage comfortable to carry, or even just to get used to. When combined with the cold wind and occasional snow flurries, and the rough roads, most of that long march was a constant series of small tortures.

Regardless of the countryside, the forced pace was a constant re-minder that we were not here on a sightseeing tour. There was no choice but to hunker down inside my greatcoat and trudge along. After weeks on the road the relentless monotony of putting one foot in front of the other for hours at a time, combined with the aches in my muscles and the pain in my feet, began to overwhelm my senses. My thoughts would wander, as if my brain were bewildered by the effort asked of my body. Abstract images of being elsewhere under different circumstances, or recollections of events from my past, would take over my thoughts, blocking out reality for hours at a time. All I knew was there were sol-diers walking ahead of me and there were others following behind me. We marched, stopped to eat, marched some more, and stopped to sleep for the night. Thankfully we were able to spend most nights in some kind of village.

At least nobody was shooting at us. Although not always secure in the knowledge, we were told by our commanders that the fighting front was farther east and that it had been more or less stabilized for months. I reckoned we had been heading in a southerly direction, which meant we were marching far behind and roughly parallel to where I assumed the front to be. I never saw or even heard any fighting, not even distant artillery fire. I never saw any Russian soldiers, other than once when we passed a column of what I estimated to be a thousand prisoners being herded through a town on some work detail. There was at least one occasion where we were ordered to set up our cannons and prepare for battle. We did so and waited. After a few days of suspense but no action, we moved on again. I suspected we were outside Moscow, but really had no idea where we were.

Sometime in mid-March, in the late afternoon of another typically dull day, we were marching along a road beside open fields. My mind was in its usual state of stupor when something unusual caught my eye a few metres off the side of the road, protruding from the frozen ground. The shape reminded me of something familiar . . . an arm! Immediately my mind snapped to. I could not believe what I was seeing. Arms, legs, and other pieces of uniform-covered corpses mixed grotesquely with the patches of snow, ice, surface dirt, and clumps of dead vegetation. We were crossing land that must have been the site of a terrible battle. Some of the snow had blown away, exposing hundreds and hundreds of frozen soldiers' bodies. Some of the corpses were hardly recognizable as human. All the ones I could identify wore German uniforms. Those unfortunate souls must have been killed and buried by snow before they could be buried by their comrades, perhaps late last fall. They had been preserved by the deep freeze of winter and were now resurfacing.

That field of death made me acutely aware of my own mortality. My imagination conjured up images of finding myself lying in that abhorrent foreign dirt like one of those corpses. A similar fate could easily overtake us. When we stopped to spend the night I could not dispel those haunting images of death from my mind's eye. We had marched through that gruesome scene as if it were just another part of the landscape. Was that experience perceived as ordinary by our commanders? What other horrors could the war have in store?

Russia was a huge and backward country, at least all of what I saw. None of the small villages we passed through even had running water. Instead, the community relied upon a communal well that was almost always near the centre of the village. Only towns and larger collectives had electricity, and then only the main buildings near the centre had electrical wires running from poles to provide service. There were no paved roads leading into or even inside most settlements. Very rarely did we see any kind of modern machinery, including farm machinery. Automobiles were nowhere to be seen and, as far as I was concerned, did not exist in Russia. It was as if we had passed backwards in time. The countryside we travelled through appeared the way I imagined Western Europe would have looked during the Middle Ages.

The water in the wells of deserted villages was sometimes putrid, which could have resulted simply from a dead animal being thrown into the well. In some places it appeared that the retreating Russian armies had implemented a deliberate scorched-earth policy. If what I had learned from history lessons in school was true, that deliberate destruction was eerily reminiscent of the Russians' reaction to Napoleon's invasion more than a century earlier.

Mostly we passed through towns and villages where nothing had been destroyed. They had obviously been spared the devastation often associated with the aftermath of a moving front. German forces had advanced so quickly in some sectors that whole Russian armies and countless inhabitants had been encircled by fast-moving armoured units. Vast province-sized districts had been captured, and the inhabited areas inside those districts appeared completely untouched by the war, full of civilians carrying on normal activities. Families were still living in their homes as if nothing unusual had happened.

I presumed that all of the able-bodied men had been conscripted into the Russian armed forces, and that most of the able-bodied women had been inducted into Russia's industrial structure, to work in factories, collective farms, public institutions, or transportation facilities, just like in Germany. The people in the towns we passed through were left alone by our troops. It was not permitted for us to harm civilians or to take or to damage their property. The one exception was horses and their feed, which were requisitioned by the army to replenish draft animals lost during the campaign. Horses were essential for our own survival.

There was never any opportunity for us to take even a brief pleasant diversion from our march. We never stopped at any kind of restaurant or pub, at least I never saw one. After a few weeks on the road I began to suspect that there was no such thing as a public establishment for socializing in all of rural Russia. Perhaps we just never encountered a large enough town to have any social amenities when the time came to stop for the night.

During that long march we always tried to overnight in houses within a village, rather than sleep on the ground in tents. The Russian villages typically contained a few dozen to a few hundred houses clustered on either side of the main road, or along several dirt side streets. Every rural house was generally the same design, with walls made of wood and with wood-slat or thatched roofs. Each house usually had two rooms, one for the family and one for the cattle. A heavy wooden door separated the living quarters from the stable. The Russian word for those characteristic rural houses was *isbas*.

The residential suite invariably had one big wooden table in the middle, a few wooden chairs, one or two cupboards at the sides, and an oven. The floor was usually wooden planks. The inside walls were sometimes papered with newspaper. There were no separate bedrooms or a bathroom. There was usually a pit privy out the back of each house, although in some villages a group of houses would share an outhouse. If there was any, lighting was accomplished with kerosene lamps in the more luxurious homes and paraffin candles in the poorer ones. Most dishes were simple iron or earthenware pots and bowls, with wooden tubs and utensils. Sometimes a tool shed or storage shed would be attached to the side or rear of the main house.

The dominant feature inside each *isba* was a massive, ceramic-tiled oven, which usually extended the entire length of the rear wall and sometimes continued in an "L" shape along part of one side wall. There were openings for stoking the fire and for putting bread into the oven for baking, as well as lids for cooking. The oven was long and wide enough that at least four persons could sleep on top of it during the night, a practical solution to the severe cold of the Russian winters. More could sleep on the floor next to the oven. Some houses contained separate beds, simple wooden cots or bunk beds that could be moved close to the oven. Strangely, all of the *isbas* in many of the smaller villages had obviously been abandoned for a long time.[7]

---

7   Stalin's Bolsheviks had reorganized most of Russian society during the 1930s by forcibly expelling the inhabitants of entire districts from their own lands and putting them into huge collective farms and forced labour camps (*gulags*), or newly established factories behind the Ural Mountains in Siberia. That is why many of the small towns and villages were deserted by the time the German forces arrived.

Spending the night in those rural houses was usually a mixed blessing. Almost every *isba* was infested with flies, cockroaches, lice, and especially bedbugs. Bedbugs were about three millimetres long, oval-shaped, and a dirty reddish-brown colour. They had a disagreeable odour and stunk terribly if you squished them. They would hide in the cracks and crevices of the floor, the walls, and bed boards during the day. At night they would creep out of their hiding places and crawl inside your clothes to attack any exposed skin. They would puncture your skin and suck out blood, leaving round red welts that itched terribly for hours. The only good thing about bedbugs was that they would return to their hiding places after feeding, so they were left behind when you departed for the next day's march. Some of the men were allergic to bedbug bites and developed large blisters which sometimes became infected after being scratched, leaving lasting, ugly scars. I wondered if the Russians had developed any immunity to bedbugs, since those tiny pests were obviously permanent residents.

Because every bed in the *isbas* had bugs, the most comfortable place to sleep often turned out to be on a pile of straw in the half of the *isba* that was used as a stable, as long as the night was not too cold. Those accommodations were sometimes shared with the cattle, the occasional cat, and rats. The first time I was awoken by a rat scrounging around in my pack I recoiled with a momentary fear that may have its origins in our primeval past. I was astonished at how brazen that rodent was, as if I were the intruder in his rightful territory. I learned to wrap my cape tight around my body to keep the repulsive pests from crawling right into my uniform, but never quite got used to their presence.

By the end of March the ceramic ovens were not always necessary to keep warm during the night. The ovens would continue to allow us to start a fire and heat some water in a kettle or pan so we could wash and shave. Sometimes there was time enough to wash our hair. Not being able to bathe properly for many weeks at a time meant you eventually got used to the smell, your own as well as others.

There was never the opportunity to thoroughly wash our clothes. Consequently every soldier eventually suffered from lice. Unlike bedbugs, which were nighttime companions only, lice were constant and intimate fellow sojourners that accompanied us wherever we went. They were body lice, which are larger than head lice, and lived inside our clothes, particularly in the seams of uniforms. Lice often produced a burning sensation on the skin, especially in the armpits and around the waist, which was almost impossible to calm. Sometimes it was so bad it made me scratch until my skin was raw and bleeding. They are very tough, impossible to squash inside the seams. During that long march there was no way for me to get rid of them.

The Russian winter eventually turned to spring. But much to our dismay the warmer weather brought along its own set of woes. Snow turned to rain. The oiled canvas cape each soldier carried would keep your upper body dry for a while, and the helmet would keep your hair dry, but after hours of marching through rain, practically everything eventually became wet. When we stopped in a village for the night after it had rained our first task would be to start a fire in the oven and try to warm up and dry our uniforms, which often resulted in petty squabbles over access to the best drying places.

As the snow and ice melted, the meltwater, along with heavy spring rains, caused what I remember the most from that interminable march—mud. What the Russians called roads were usually simple dirt trails from which the vegetation had been removed. During the winter the roads were frozen solid and mostly covered in snow or ice. The first signs of trouble came when melting snow turned the surface of the roads into a dangerously slippery covering layer of wet mud over the still-frozen ground. That was sticky and dirty, but more inconvenient than anything menacing, at first. As the frozen ground thawed the roads rapidly turned into horrible troughs of knee-deep mud, which gripped your feet so firmly that it would suck your boots off if you tried to move too quickly. The effort required just to keep moving made every step a painful struggle that soon left us exhausted.

Walking through mud was bad enough on its own, but often we had to help push vehicles ahead. Wagons and guns would bog down, their wheels completely clogged with sticky mud as they sank into the earth, sometimes right to their axles, and we could go no further until we dug them out. There were times when the mud was absolutely bottomless. On particularly bad days our column managed to make only two or three kilometres' progress, after back-breaking, mind-numbing, energy-sapping effort. I had never experienced anything so miserable. Sometimes Command even gave up, and we did not move from a settlement for days.

Our uniforms, especially the trousers, became so dirty and matted with mud that the cloth began to deteriorate. Trying to clean them only made them disintegrate more rapidly. It was also impossible to keep our

General Mud, April 1942

boots clean. The mud caused the leather to become rough and brittle, until it was impossible to keep our feet dry during the march. That created the added danger of developing trench foot, which is a smelly fungal ailment that rots the skin of the feet.

If the Russians had attacked our column under those wet, muddy conditions, we would have been trapped like sitting ducks. The only saving grace was that the Russian troops could not move through that endless morass any better than we could.

Mud was an adversary the like of which we had never before encountered—a relentless, tireless, insistent foe, the stuff of nightmares, made all the worse because it was completely mindless and impossible to overcome by way of brilliant military tactics or daring personal initiatives. Mud made a mockery of the vaunted fighting abilities of a modern army. We had now come up against what could be called Russia's second-best soldier—General Mud.

The Russians themselves referred to their roads as the *Rasputiza* when they turned into impassable mud-ways, after the notorious monk Rasputin of the old tsarist regime. The ordeal of battling mud left a lasting impression. Even more than fifty years later, the first smell of wet mud causes a momentary twinge in my gut and floods my mind with stressful memories.

The horses also suffered horribly in the mud. Their hooves would quickly become clogged. If they sank particularly deep into the mud they could break a leg. The repeated soaking by wet mud caused sores on the skin of their lower legs. To keep our horses in as good a condition as possible, most of us soldiers walked most of the time; even the driver got off his wagon and pulled on the halter to move and guide the horses. Everyone else helped push the wagons and the cannons every time they slowed.

I felt a genuine empathy for the horses, since they shared the same fate as the men. To this day I have an abiding respect for their forbearance and service to their human masters who had dragged them into that absurd predicament. They were an essential part of our forces, so much so that considerably more attention was lavished on the horses than the men. Even medical treatment was administered more urgently to ailing horses than to ailing men.

Usually there was enough room in stables or house-barns in each Russian village to keep the horses overnight. Sometimes we stayed in a village where all the stables were occupied by the farmers' cattle, leaving no extra room. Our horses then had to spend the night outdoors, tied to posts, each covered with a blanket. Guards were posted all night to ensure they were not harmed and that the blankets stayed on.

In that muddy spring our rations became increasingly sparse, and the quality of what we were fed became downright terrible. Supplies could not get through quickly enough to keep up with our demand for food. The daily evening meal of stew from the field kitchen soon deteriorated into a thin soup of potatoes or sauerkraut, sometimes with stringy and tough horsemeat. That was hardly enough to fill my belly and I was hungry again within an hour of eating. More often than not there were no bread rations.

Although we were not supposed to take anything from civilians, it was impossible for the army to prevent individual soldiers from scavenging food. We were forced to forage for food for ourselves during those times and soon learned not to be shy about confiscating anything edible from civilians. That did not make us popular with the local residents; however, it had come down to a matter of survival. After weeks on very thin rations we were almost always ravenously hungry, and that hunger overpowered our sense of propriety. Finding any kind of hidden food in civilian homes meant staving off starvation, so it was unceremoniously commandeered and devoured. Found food was rare and precious, and amounted to little more than small caches of smoked meat or sausages, or canned or preserved vegetables. Underground lockers, if discovered, were searched first. Sometimes we found bottled spirits, especially vodka, which never interested me, but was a big hit with some of the other men. Even with such occasional windfalls, I noticed myself becoming progressively thinner as the march went on.

It was just as bad for the horses, as they also suffered from malnutrition. By late spring many of them showed protruding ribs, just as we soldiers did. There was nothing for them to eat in the thawing fields, some of which were covered in dead grasses, crushed flat by winter snows. Grazing in green meadows would have to wait for the new growth. The best source of feed was usually the granary of a collective farm. Most other storage lofts had been stripped bare of fodder, some a long time ago.

Eventually the rains stopped and the roads began to dry. Conditions changed rapidly, becoming warmer and less hostile. There were a few nice, dry, and relatively warm days, which my aching bones welcomed very much. It was astonishing how quickly the weather turned warm, and the days eventually became downright hot. It was as if the three weeks of muddy conditions were all there was of a spring season.

I was just beginning to think things would get better for us when we were assailed by another foe—flies and mosquitoes, which brought their own form of torment. Most of the men soon had their faces and necks covered in small red spots where blood-gorged mosquitoes and tiny blackflies had been squished against their skins. Luckily, after the weather became truly hot, mosquitoes no longer came out during the bright sunshine of the days. The tiny blackflies, however, continued to plague us constantly.

By May the countryside had generally dried out. As the roads became firm and dry we were assaulted by another nuisance—dust. The bare roads and the soil of farm fields provided fine dirt that was picked up by the blowing wind, which would whip the dust into streamers that hurt the eyes and sometimes reduced visibility to a few hundred metres. It made us filthy, absolutely covered in dirt. The fine dust caked hair, permeated clothes, seeped down inside the collars of our necks, encrusted the edges of the eyes and mouth, and coated the insides of nostrils. It became so bad I tied a rag around my face to keep the dust out. That helped, but perhaps just psychologically, because at the end of the day I still had to wash caked-on dust from my face and blow dirty brown snot from my nose. I could only imagine the dirt in my lungs.

Regardless of conditions, the march continued, day after day. There were several occasions during our march when we were ordered to set up our cannons in formation and prepare for battle—which we did—and wait, sometimes for days.

Nothing I had imagined previously could match the reality of how immense the country was. The Russian armies had suffered tremendous defeats at the hands of our forces, had lost millions of soldiers as prisoners of war, and had been swept eastward deep into their own country, yet Russia had not been defeated and there were no signs that Stalin was going to surrender. In France I had experienced the euphoria of a victorious campaign, of being part of an army that had appeared to be invincible. Now I felt like part of an army that appeared forlorn and almost pathetic, abandoned and forgotten by my homeland.

Around midday of yet another endless day's march, I was again in that semi-conscious state when the soldier next to me pointed toward the front of the column. I looked up to see what at first appeared to be a herd of dark animals in the distance. As we drew nearer the herd grew larger and larger. Eventually it became clear that they were men! We marched past a vast area of former pasture that had been trampled into a dirty brown mess, enclosed by a high barbed-wire fence, filled with a truly sorrowful looking multitude—Russian prisoners of war. Most of them were just milling about along the fence as we marched past, staring at us with a hollow, forlorn look in their eyes. There must have been tens of thousands of prisoners, if not hundreds of thousands, in those barbed-wire enclosures.

But why were they still here? Was this an enforced labour camp? If so, why were they not working? I could not see any activity in the compounds, other than men walking around. How were they being cared for? There were only a few barns in sight for shelters, along with some wagons. There were no guard towers around the enclosures, just a machine-gun crew in sandbag-surrounded pits every few hundred metres along the edges of the enclosures and at every corner.

I speculated that it may have been that the German army command did not know what to do with so many prisoners all at once. Perhaps they were waiting for space on trains to ship them westward. There may already have been enough labourers to work the farms and factories back in Germany from the millions of Russian soldiers captured during the initial invasion of Russia last year. So what was to become of those poor souls? They could not be set free to rejoin the Russian army. These men could not just be left there to die? That terrible thought gave me a nauseatingly heavy feeling inside. I wondered how many other such prisoner-of-war compounds there might be in German-occupied Russia.

"Poor guys," the soldier marching beside me said as he too appraised that pitiful scene.

"Poor guys," I repeated. Regardless of what we felt inside, that was as much emotion as we showed.

After what seemed like an eternity but was probably about ten to twelve weeks of marching, we eventually ended up somewhere east of the city of Orel, about 300 kilometres south of Moscow. After we were roused that morning there was a sense of urgency in our departure that I had not experienced for months. We assembled on the main road of the village and marched smartly out as soon as everything was ready to move. I figured we would soon be at the front, because we had turned due east. I expected to hear gunfire coming from the east, or notice other signs of a fighting front. We passed a deserted village as evening approached, but did not stop. Contrary to every other evening during the past weeks of our trek, we kept marching well into the night.

An hour or so after sunset we approached a collection of military tents and some wagons at the side of the road. The light of burning kerosene lanterns lit a scene with German infantry milling about what looked like small bunkers. I could just distinguish officers in the midst, so it was probably a command post. We kept moving, passing some big tents where hundreds of wounded soldiers were sitting or lying on the ground outside, some being attended by medics. Judging by the repugnant smell of the place, it was a field hospital. We must now be very close to the front.

Shortly after passing the field hospital we were ordered to halt, get off the road, set up our cannons in formation facing east, and get ready for combat. After the past two months of almost uninterrupted drudgery, that sudden call to action was startling. We all knew the drill and could set up for firing even in the dark. I imagined the enemy lurking in the darkness toward the east.

I was directed to set up my No. 1 Cannon in firing position a few hundred metres off the side of the road. The horses were unhitched, taken back behind the line of cannons, and tethered to a long rope secured by stout stakes driven into the ground. The supply wagon was parked behind the cannon, and the shells were unloaded and placed beside the cannon for easy access. Everything else was quickly stowed away. Then we waited. The possibility of battle had replaced my feelings of exhaustion with apprehension.

All I could make out in the dark was that our column had stopped in a hayfield. The tension that precedes imminent action felt like a knot had been tied in the pit of my stomach. I also thought I could hear the faint sounds of small-arms fire in the distance, but since we were not ordered to start shooting, those sounds were probably just in my imagination. Perhaps we would be faced with an enemy attack in the morning. After a while I passed out in fitful and restless periods of sleep.

Before it was even fully light we were roused and ordered to assemble behind our cannons. I was in a daze and expected orders to commence firing right away. As our gun crew stood in the pre-dawn light I noticed sleeping soldiers all over the place. At first I thought it odd that they did not get up right away. A closer look at the man nearest me gave me a start. He looked absolutely filthy, worse even than what I had become accustomed to on our long trek; but what really caught my eye was an ugly black hole in his uniform at the back of his chest. It was a Russian uniform, and he was dead!

Surveying the scene I was staggered to see what must have been hundreds of bodies lying on the ground all around us. There were also dozens of shell craters scarring the ground, as well as rows of barbed wire strung onto pointed stakes protruding upward from the ground, and a series of foxholes and slit trenches running generally in a north-south alignment—the front.

We had arrived.

9   *Sitzkrieg*

BEFORE I HAD TIME FOR ANY SPECULATION about our situation, we were ordered to dig in and construct secure gun positions as quickly as possible. The battalion commander pointed out the exact location where he wanted our cannons to be set up and hidden. Expecting an attack any moment, we worked feverishly to move enough dirt to make shallow excavations, just deep enough to hide the cannons from enemy view and wide enough to accommodate the entire gun crew. That exhausting task took most of the morning and was so strenuous that I had no time to think about the corpses that littered the area. After hours of unrelenting work some of the tension subsided. We might not be faced with an attack, at least not right away, by either side. Before I had a chance to be grateful for that good fortune we were ordered to form squads, each of which was assigned to a different sector of the battlefield, for burial detail.

The terrible reality of the slaughter field became absolutely bewildering. I could only imagine the horrendous fighting that had taken place here just before our battalion arrived. Dead bodies were practically everywhere. In some spots they were piled on top of each other, and those piles turned out to be Russian dead. There were tank track marks crisscrossing the ground, although there were no tanks or other motorized vehicles anywhere. Numerous foxholes and slit trenches pockmarked the ground, most of which held corpses. There were also long rows of coiled barbed wire, as well as thousands of sharpened stakes protruding about a metre out of the ground, all pointing westward. The Russians had abandoned the battlefield and left the gruesome job of cleaning up to us.

I thought I could stomach just about anything by now, since I had already seen dead bodies during the fighting in France as well as frozen corpses on the march from Leningrad, but nothing could have prepared me for this task. We had to bury the corpses quickly as they would rot in the hot sun. Some had probably been dead for two or three days, and had begun to reek dreadfully, with hordes of flies swarming over their bloating corpses. Many of the Russian dead smelled strongly of the

distinctly pungent odour of army tobacco, even over the smell of pu-
trefaction. Eventually the sickening stench of decaying flesh pervaded
every part of the battlefield, overpowering everything else.

An officer ordered us to clear out a large open area within a low
point in the field. Explosive charges were placed, and after everyone was
out of range, the charges were set off and a tremendous boom ripped a
hole in the ground. That hole was not very deep, but had softened up an
area of soil, so we dug it and some other holes wide enough to accommodate dozens of bodies, making the walls steep. The dead were carried
or dragged to the excavated pits and thrown inside, lain like cordwood.
After a pit was almost full, quicklime was sprinkled over the bodies and
dirt was shovelled overtop, leaving a large, metre-high mound.

At first the individuality of each dead soldier made a profound impression on me and I noticed evidence of how they may have died.
A bullet usually makes a relatively small, neat hole where it enters,
and entry wounds were hardly noticeable, but it often makes a large
and messy hole if it exits the body. Some corpses were horribly mutilated with gaping holes filled with blackened blood. Some had pieces
of arms and legs missing. One body still in his foxhole had half a dozen
obvious stab wounds. The worst sights were the head wounds. Some
smashed faces looked absolutely macabre, grotesquely swollen and distorted, covered in blackened blood mixed with dirt. One body had been
crushed into the ground, apparently run over by a tank. When two of
us tried to lift the body his entrails fell out from under his uniform. Pu-
trefaction had turned his intestines into a mass of stinking yellow and
purple sausages. The uniform had held his guts in until we tried to lift
him. I had to turn away and catch my breath before we could shovel his
remains onto a cape and drag them to the pit.

After hours of unrelenting toil the former humanity of those dead
bodies eventually lost their emotional impact on my consciousness.
German or Russian, they were just repulsive corpses that had to be put
into the ground as fast as possible. The gruelling labour eventually replaced my feelings of sorrow for those dead people with a blurry numb-
ness, almost loathing, and a grim determination to get that gruesome
task over with. That feeling may have been shared by many of the men.
No one spoke any more. Talking, even exchanging a glance, would have
meant communication, and that was completely inappropriate under
the circumstances.

I moved like a robot, doing what had to be done—hack and dig into the ground with picks and spades; grab the boots, or lift the shoulders; drag, lift, carry, shove, and heave the remains into a pit; then shovel dirt over the rotting mass. I blocked out the terrible reality of what had happened on that killing field. The same outwardly dispassionate attitude that I had noticed among the more seasoned veterans, but had never thought I too would acquire, took over.

Even though necessity fostered an outward callousness toward death, some emotions were impossible to suppress. The dog tags around the necks of dead German soldiers were snapped off and handed to the officers in charge. Those tags were all that we retrieved, all that was considered of worth from the young men that had worn them, all that would be returned to their homeland.

The Russians were buried without removing their identification tags, with no regard for their records of casualties. They would be considered "missing in action" by their commanders.

Late afternoon the field kitchen arrived and squads were ordered to stop work in turns. We were absolutely filthy, covered in bloody grime and sweat. Still, I had not eaten since the day before and assumed that the sight and smell of food would renew the hunger pangs in my belly. When I joined the other men from our squad at our cannon with my mess tin I tried to eat, but the nauseating smell of death that pervaded the area made it impossible to get the food past my nose. I had to throw it out.

As soon as our break was over it was back to our task. We worked long into the evening. When it became too dark to see we worked by kerosene lanterns. Some men were so tired they just passed out on the ground. When the sun came up the dead had all been buried.

I felt an intense loathing for the government leaders who had started and directed this war. They were sitting back at home in their warm chambers, giving orders that caused the deaths of thousands of young men. They did not have to experience the cold, the mud, the bugs, the bullets, the dysentery and other diseases, the terror, the images of atrocities, the death of their friends, the pain and trauma that is part of the front-line soldier's lot. I hoped that some day those villains would suffer a justly deserved retribution. War is insanity, instigated by rich and powerful leaders who sell hollow promises to feed their ambitions. It is a pity that they cannot be made to experience first-hand the very personal tragedies and hardships that they force upon common people.

The following day I carried out my assigned duties in a daze, my mind numb from the trauma and lack of sleep, with every muscle aching. We cleaned up battlefield detritus, unloaded and stored supplies, cleaned and maintained the guns, and dug more bunkers. That night I slept in exhausted fits, accosted by the indelible stench that seemed to linger everywhere, long after the bodies had been buried. It was as if everything around us had been fouled by the putrid smell of death, including our uniforms, equipment, and stores. Whether that smell actually emanated from the ground or was just a persistent memory kept vivid by the impression it had made on my senses, it was inescapable for weeks. Eventually the memory faded from my consciousness, but ghostly corpses continued to haunt my dreams.

We were very busy the next few days digging extensive, interconnected trenches and earthen bunkers around the gun emplacements. Our forces occupied the top of a gently sloped rise in the ground, facing a broad, shallow valley toward the east. Lines of trees and shrubs marked the bottoms of hollows and gullies in the lowest parts of the valley. There were no villages nearby. Old wooden slat fences separated the hay and pasture fields from the roads.

The four cannons from our battery were positioned in the hollows we had excavated, with a good view of the entire valley. The other batteries from our battalion had set up to the north and south of our position, also facing the valley. Looking east, I could make out another series of defensive positions in a line roughly parallel to ours, four or five kilometres away—the enemy. They occupied the top of the gentle rise on the other side of the creek valley, facing west. They were quite visible in places, moving about among their own trenches, along with occasional horses and wagons.

Our section of the Eastern Front was defined by two stationary lines separated by what could be called a no-man's land. Although it was not a line of continuous trenches, such as those of the First World War, there were extensive earthworks, some fortified with sandbags, logs, plank retaining walls, sharpened stakes (abatis), and barbed wire. We dug deep trenches connecting rudimentary underground bunkers large enough to stand up inside. Rows of barbwire coils were strung along stakes in the ground in an almost continuous line that stretched as far as the eye could see in either direction. Even though our own infantry positions were not visible from where we were, I assumed they were dug in closer to the enemy lines. Occasionally German soldiers could be seen moving across open areas along the slope of the valley.

We posted two sentries in shifts all night and every night for each cannon. Guard duty at night was scary, much more so than it had ever been in Narvik, where there had not been any enemy soldiers in the whole country. During my first night on guard duty it did not require much imagination to visualize Russian soldiers creeping up on us in the darkness.

One evening an infantry squad stopped in for some vodka and smokes on their way to pick up supplies. They had been in the midst of the fighting that had established our lines. In response to our queries, one of those veterans told us about the battle. A tremendous German attack supported by armoured vehicles had initially captured the positions our troops were now occupying. The attacking troops had encountered extensive and thorough defences, with deep trenches, anti-tank ditches, barbed wire, mines, and abatis. The battlefield had then been left to the infantry after the armoured vehicles moved on.

"God only knows where our panzers went the next day, but they were nowhere to be seen when Ivan counterattacked. Maybe they were in a hurry to get to Moscow," the veteran said. He was quite graphic in his description of thousands of Russian soldiers charging across the space in front of the defended German lines, yelling and screaming at the top of their lungs. "The Russians were crazy to run at us like that. They must have been full of vodka when they attacked. Our machine guns just cut them down like wheat by a scythe."

His contemptuous tone may have been his trying to reassure himself that we Germans held a decisive superiority in weapons and tactics over our Russian adversaries.

Another veteran quietly said, "They were fearless, but now they are dead." I was taken aback by his obviously sad reflection, and that he would describe our enemies as "fearless." There was no contempt or even animosity in his voice; it was more like sympathy. His reaction was an insight into the true nature of modern warfare. It did not matter how courageously they had charged. Machine guns made a mockery of valour on the battlefield.

The Russian attack had continued into the night, when they crawled

up close to the German defences. Flares fired into the sky suddenly illuminated hordes of enemy soldiers in the open, rushing forward in a
frenzied charge. In the darkness it was difficult to see well enough to
shoot accurately, especially when confronted with an enemy who suddenly jumps out at you.

"One of our machine-gunners must have run out of bullets, or his
weapon overheated, because they ran right up to our line."

"Then my spade became my best friend," the veteran said as he
made a cutting motion with his hand across his neck. A wry smile
crossed his face as he noted the horrified reactions of some of the young
men listening to his narrative. "You artillery types should be all right
back here in the Bolshoi Hotel; you don't usually get that close to the
Russians." Comedy had taken on a new face at the Eastern Front.

The battle had raged for two days and nights. Only a determined
German counterattack had recaptured the lines. It had ended the day before our battalion arrived, when the Russians finally withdrew to the line
of entrenchments we could see on the other side of no-man's land. There
had been no opportunity to safely bury the dead before that withdrawal,
which explained the state of some of the bodies we had buried.

The veterans telling the story described the fighting in a detached,
impassive manner, recounting the events with a deadpan delivery and
laced with black humour that was somehow appropriate. However, the
expression on one veteran's face, and especially the long pauses while
he reflected on what had happened, betrayed the fact that his experiences had left permanent scars on his soul.

Life at the front settled into a routine for us, which included daily callisthenics, as well as digging earthworks, laying coils of barbed wire,
maintaining the guns, digging and maintaining latrines, helping prepare food, and periodically replenishing supplies. We enlarged and
excavated our primitive bunkers down in the firm, sandy soil, deep
enough to keep us safe from exploding artillery shells or bombs. The
in-ground bunkers became our living quarters. They were large enough
for a man to stand up inside, with about two metres of dirt overhead.
The walls and ceiling were shored up with timbers and planks to prevent the dirt from collapsing inward. Along the walls were bed frames
built with rough planks, raised above the floor to keep from getting wet
if it rained. Sacks filled with straw served as mattresses. The wood was

cut from trees felled in the woodlots near our positions.

At first there were intermittent periods of shelling by both sides, lasting a few minutes almost every day for weeks. At the first whine of an incoming shell everyone immediately dove into the nearest opening in the ground. The force of an exploding shell would burst more upwards than sideways, and unless the shell landed right inside your trench, you would probably survive the hit. I did not see any casualties from shelling during those first few weeks at the front. Eventually the shelling became infrequent, until weeks would pass without an incident. Shelling was never accompanied by an infantry assault, so it lost its original sense of danger.

The cannon I was in charge of was about forty metres away from our bunker. The gun itself was mainly hidden from enemy view by being depressed below the surrounding ground surface in a metre-deep excavation. It was surrounded on three sides by a wide wall of sandbags and dirt that had been taken out of the excavation. Only the tip of the barrel was visible above the dirt wall when viewed from the front. Loose camouflage netting was strung between poles across most of the gun position, and shrubs and branches were placed around the perimeter in an effort to hide it from enemy reconnaissance.

To oblige hygienic needs, a large hole in the ground with two planks laid across it served as a latrine. To help avoid the smell it was strategically placed far enough away from the rest of our accommodations. To indulge modesty, and to keep us from getting shot by snipers, it was enclosed by a sandbag wall and some camouflage netting hung on stakes. Eventually all our facilities and positions were interconnected by trenches.

I had disliked living in barracks during my stints in the *Arbeitsdienst*, Narvik, and Küstrin, but those places seemed like the lap of luxury now. Our accommodations here were like animal dens in the ground.

By the end of July 1942, our section of the Eastern Front had not moved since we arrived, but what I actually knew about the front was limited to what I could see. Except for sporadic artillery fire and occasionally airplanes flying overhead, our sector was predominantly quiet. We had not engaged in any kind of hostile action for over a month. We had been ordered not to waste ammunition, so shooting was allowed only when there was a good reason. There was little activity visible on the other side of the no-man's land. Still, we were always on alert. The guns had to be manned and cared for to ensure they were always ready for action. Sentry duty became more routine than scary.

Those of us at the very edge of the Eastern Front relied upon another army of workers to keep us supplied with food and materials. I am sure none of us in our bunker, including myself, thought much about how our rations got to us before we saw them in the pots of the field kitchens. Amazing how it was possible to provide millions of soldiers with enough food and equipment to keep them functioning, especially in this isolated location so far from Germany.

The field kitchen wagon pulled up to the same place each evening, and we lined up to have our dishes filled with hot food and our canteens filled with *Maltzkafee* or some other hot liquid that tasted a bit like tea. We also received our breakfast rations of bread, cheese, and sausage. We never went without food during those stalemate conditions in the summer of 1942, and the quality of what we had to eat was mostly satisfactory. Although it was never abundant, it was just filling enough to satisfy our hunger and obviously kept us reasonably healthy. Sometimes our rations included apples or plums, sweets, cigarettes, and alcohol, which was usually vodka. As in Narvik, I traded my cigarettes and alcohol for sweets.

German magazines and newspapers also reached us at the front. They were read over and over again until they were quite worn. There was nothing in those publications that was ever considered important or meaningful; they were just mindless entertainment to help pass the time. After attending to the needs of our minds, newspapers served other needs as well—as toilet paper. The hole in the ground that served as a latrine was littered with reading material. Considering all the times my asshole was wiped with printed paper, it should have learned to read.

Potable water was brought in by the field kitchen wagon every day, until about mid-July, when an army truck with a drilling rig on its back came and drilled a well for us. After that we had enough water for washing. A steel drum cut in half formed a washtub. Bathing was not a high priority. We just washed ourselves down whenever we thought it necessary. There was nobody around I wanted to impress anyway. One enterprising squad had rigged up a makeshift shower by setting a steel drum on a platform high enough to stand underneath. The drum was half-filled with water and set on a pivot. When the end of the drum was tipped up with an attached stick, the water poured out of holes that had been punched into the other end. The men of our unit were apparently not so enterprising.

The army supply wagon provided clean underwear and socks about every three or four weeks, which helped personal hygiene and controlled body lice. Spare time gave us a chance to battle the lice in our uniforms. We would heat a bayonet and meticulously press it against a section of seam on the uniform until a tiny pop from under the blade signalled the explosive death of another of the little fiends. That helped keep them in check; but they were relentless, and we never completely got rid of them.

So we were sheltered, clothed, and fed during the stalemate conditions at the front in the summer of 1942; at the Bolshoi Hotel, as the infantry veteran had put it.

In spite of the lack of serious fighting at our sector, there were surprisingly few opportunities for socializing among the men. We were kept occupied with regular duties almost every waking hour of the day, in a strictly controlled routine. By the time the sun went down I was usually tired. Our humble accommodations allowed precious little for us to do other than sleep. A deck of cards allowed us to play skat. The army may have deliberately kept us busy in an attempt to keep us from getting bored or homesick, but nothing could divert my thoughts from the tedium and the isolation.

We rarely visited other batteries or troops along the rest of our sector. They might as well have been in another country for all we saw of them. Our commanders were sequestered within their own bunker a few hundred metres from ours, and there had to be a very good reason—a military reason—to want to talk to any of them. In spite of the almost constant proximity and interaction with the soldiers of our own battery, it was a very lonely time. We were just there, and that was it.

In the middle of the summer the days were long and hot, so we seemed to have more spare time to sit around. If the battle for France could be called *Blitzkrieg*, my stint at the Eastern Front was more aptly termed *Sitzkrieg* (sitting war). After months in our earthwork bunkers, we were desperate for some relief from the monotony.

During one hot day late in August, after weeks of inactivity, one of the men pointed eastward, drawing our attention to a column of about a dozen horse-drawn wagons slowly heading northward along the Russian lines. We inspected the column through field glasses. Our enthusiastic comrade sprinted off to see our commander and convinced him to radio headquarters that a Russian supply column had arrived to resupply the enemy and that it was therefore a valuable target. We were granted permission to attack the supply column. So we loaded our cannons, calculated the range, and opened fire. As shells burst in their midst, the wagons scattered and quickly vanished. We probably fired fifty rounds, but I doubt we hit anything.

The Russians obviously realized the game was on and returned fire. The whine of incoming shells made us beat a hasty retreat to our bunkers. A few shells crashed into the ground around our position, but nothing significant was hit and nobody was injured. Even though nothing much had been accomplished, we could now brag that we had been in a "battle" on the Eastern Front. That action was about the most exciting event that happened to me during the entire summer of 1942. It was an example of what passed for entertaining the troops.

Sometime late in August, three other men from my unit and I were assigned the task of accompanying two wagons to Orel to pick up supplies for the battery. Orel was the main supply depot for the German army in our sector of the front. Periodically a detail had to travel the fifty or so kilometres round trip to fetch supplies. That was the first time I was assigned that task and I looked forward to a change of venue.

Very early in the morning we hopped onto the wagons and headed off. The sergeant made sure we brought our rifles. As we moved along the dirt road we passed through a few villages. We saw dozens of older women working in a potato field, hoeing weeds among the maturing crop. They were just shapeless forms in their long, loose-fitting dresses. *Babushkas* I had heard them called. Some were sitting at the edge of the field near the side of the road eating their lunch. None of them bothered even to look up at us as we passed by, as if they had seen it all before.

A few hours into the trip we approached a column of soldiers marching toward the front. As we passed by I suddenly recognized one young infantryman! There was Rudi Kober, a friend from Michelau. I yelled for joy and jumped off the wagon to greet him. After a hasty emotional exchange of questions and affirmations of good health, we had to move on. We wished each other good luck. It felt good to reaffirm personal bonds, even briefly.

The road eventually became paved as we approached the outskirts of Orel. Apartment houses flanked the road and there were more and more civilians about. Passing by the shell of a factory we got off the wagon to look around. It was a huge complex of empty concrete, steel, and glass buildings. Part of the roof on the largest building was gone. Evidently T–34 tanks had been produced there for the Russian army, as tank parts still littered the floor. The factory had been dismantled and the machinery and equipment had probably been taken eastward before it could fall into the hands of the advancing German armies. Seeing that deserted industrial edifice picked clean of anything useful meant that the absent machinery and equipment were now probably inside another factory, busy producing more tanks that would eventually be used against us.

Upon arriving at our destination in Orel we reported to the army quartermaster in an industrial area near the train station. First we had to water, feed, and stable the horses. After being fed in the army mess we were assigned rooms for the night in a house that had been requisitioned by the army. Orel was a surprisingly big city. Most of the inhabitants were probably still living there. There were hardly any signs that there had been fighting in the city, at least in the district we saw.

The two-storey building we spent the night in was built completely of wood. It had wide wooden planks on the floors, heavy and solid wooden doors, and few windows. The inside walls and fixtures were painted in a dazzling variety of colours. Each room had been painted a different colour, one bright yellow, another blue, another dark green. Some of the wooden furniture pieces were also brightly painted, producing a kaleidoscope of colours inside the house. Quantity of paint may have been more important than stylishness. There was a genuine bathroom on the main floor, with a bathtub and a water pump to fill it with. The water was cold, but we could not resist the temptation to have a bath. It was the first time I had felt clean in months. I silently thanked my absent Russian hosts for allowing me the luxury of using their home. After sleeping on boards for almost four months I had difficulty falling asleep on the soft bed. Imagine that. There were no bedbugs, which was a gift from heaven.

The next morning we lined the wagons up at the warehouse and loaded supplies, most of which were sacks of potatoes, various canned goods, and other boxes of foodstuffs. Both wagons were soon filled. Our sergeant confirmed the shipment with the quartermaster, and we were ready to head back to the front.

Just as we were about to leave I heard someone yell, "A!" A sound from home! No one here would call me that. To my amazement, there was my friend, Teffe Gick, a Michelauer, sitting on a supply wagon that was just arriving, waving.

"Teffe!" I yelled and jumped off my wagon to greet him. Another joyful reunion! I told him about meeting Rudi Kober. Teffe had left Michelau a few weeks before and gave me the latest news from home. As far as he knew, my father was fine. Karl was still at home. There was no news about my three other brothers. No news was good news. We wished each other luck and hoped we would see each other back home after the war. It felt great to have met Teffe and Rudi. How amazing that three friends from one village in Oberfranken could meet so far from home and in such a short space of time. For a while this foreign country did not seem quite so huge.

The trip to Orel was a nice break from the routine at the front, so much so that my travelling companion and I discussed possible ways to avoid having to return to our battery right away. The sergeant would have none of it, so we returned to our battery with our precious supplies late in the evening and unloaded them. Upon returning to my berth in our underground bunker, I was struck by the squalid and malodorous conditions in which we were forced to live, as if seeing them for the first time. Comfort and luxury were still part of life in other parts of the world, but not at the front. That two-day trip turned out to be the most pleasant event of my entire sojourn at the Eastern Front in 1942.

Early in October I was told to report to battery headquarters, along with another corporal from my battery. We were sent to a collection point behind the lines, where we joined a dozen other men already there, mostly corporals and sergeants from the infantry, as well as corporals from the artillery. We all boarded a truck and were driven to Orel. That afternoon we were assembled in a square near the train station, where we were joined by more soldiers that had been taken from other units. Apparently the army had scoured a large portion of the front, because eventually there were at least forty of us lined up. An officer walked along the ranks and selected about half of us to step out and go left, the others to stay.

Those that stayed, I among them, were told that we were to be sent to Potsdam, to an officer training school. We were given orders where and when to report, along with train tickets for the ride all the way to our destination. I was excited about the prospect of such a new adventure and thrilled to leave the front, so I happily boarded the train in Orel. Officers carried a great deal of authority in the German army. My experience so far in the war had taught me enough to perceive artillery officers as leading relatively sheltered lives. I could see myself stationed far behind the front lines, overseeing the action from the lap of luxury.

I have no idea whether any of the men chosen for officer training had displayed any kind of leadership qualities to their superior officers. They may have been chosen because all of them had completed at least high school education. I figured that was the reason I had been picked. Whatever the selection process, no one explained it to me.

Sometime during that train trip I learned that the Potsdam military school was for infantry officers, not artillery! At hearing that news it seemed to me that my good luck had run out. I felt disheartened about having to join the infantry, where I believed I stood a much greater chance of becoming a casualty than with the artillery. The men I spoke with all shared the same opinion. One fellow glumly stated that he would much rather have stayed a corporal in the artillery than become a lieutenant in the infantry. Being assigned to become an infantry officer was not considered a promotion; it was more like a sentence.

During the long train ride back to Germany I had time to ponder my fate. Even though my assignment to the infantry appeared to be a stroke of misfortune at the time, there just might be a bright side to it. When I contemplated the alternative of staying in Russia, my assignment to officer school could be lucky after all. Instead of feeling trapped at the Eastern Front, it felt good to be on my way back to the relative safety of Germany. Besides, there was nothing I could do about my situation, so I might as well make the best of it.

In retrospect it was a very lucky break to be sent back to Germany. The first Russian counter-offensives of the fall of 1942 were launched against the German and Axis forces in November, which resulted in heavy losses for our troops. If I had stayed at the front I could easily have been one of those losses.

10 *Prussians*

POTSDAM IS ABOUT THIRTY KILOMETRES west of Berlin. About twenty other young soldiers also got off the train, and we boarded the streetcar that would take us to the *Kriegsschule* (military academy). From the gate of the academy I looked upon a complex of stately buildings and manicured grounds, all surrounded by a wrought-iron fence on a concrete base. There were thirty-six new officer candidates with me. They would be my classmates for the next two months.

The barracks and school buildings were solid brick structures, mostly two storeys high. Some of the buildings looked newer than others, so apparently the school had been expanded and renovated recently. The grounds were landscaped with well-kept lawns and many trees. Wide sandy areas in the centre of the complex were used as drill grounds. The place exuded a formal and aristocratic atmosphere. This was the same officer training school where thousands of Prussian officers had graduated in the past, steeped in Prussian military tradition. It was one of the oldest military academies in Germany. Rumour had it that it had been established by Frederick the Great, King of Prussia, early in the last century. Perhaps I should have been more impressed with having been chosen to learn the trade of military leadership among such illustrious company; however, I was well aware that I was here because the army needed to fill the ranks of former infantry officers who had been lost at the Eastern Front, and that my duty would inevitably be to again risk my life because of Hitler's folly.

Every officer candidate had some previous military experience. My classmates were mostly corporals from the infantry and the artillery, like myself. Some were sergeants. All had served in Russia. As far as I knew, only high school graduates were accepted as candidates for officer; however, sergeants with sufficient front-line experience and intelligence had also been sent here, regardless of their academic achievements. Ability was the primary consideration for officer candidacy, regardless of anyone's social status or family wealth. Unlike the British army, in the German army an officer's commission could not be bought.

Our instructors were all infantry officers and sergeants with considerable front-line experience. Most of them were decorated, some with the Iron Cross First Class. Men wearing the Iron Cross were treated with great respect. That little symbol of their country's recognition for their exploits in battle afforded instant status to the bearer for the rest of us. It was silent testimony as to the veteran's courage and skill. Some instructors may have been here because they had been wounded and were not able to return to the fighting front, but could function well as instructors. One instructor likely had an artificial leg, because he walked with a pronounced and awkward limp. Another had an artificial right arm. He always wore black leather gloves. These men were all excellent instructors who knew more than academic theories of warfare; they had had actual first-hand experience in combat.

Some of my classmates were also casualties, and a few injuries were still evident. One man had a deep, wide scar on his cheek just below his eye. Another had a dark-coloured skin graft across the side of his forehead, where a section of hair was missing. He dismissed it as nothing serious, although he admitted he was lucky not to have been killed.

One of the most unusual injuries had happened to a quiet and easy-going sergeant in our group. He was probably in his early twenties, but his demeanour and manner of speaking suggested he had lived much longer. He told us he had "a little trouble" with his vision ever since he had been shot in the head at the Eastern Front. The bullet had passed right through his skull, just behind the top of his ears, and the two scars were still visible. The bullet had pierced one side of his helmet and lodged inside the other. He could not explain why he was still alive. The most noticeable legacy of that wound was a restriction in his peripheral vision. He could see clearly directly in front of him, but could not see anything to his sides. He was remarkably good-natured about his visual limitations, saying it much improved his chances with women. "They now find me irresistible, because I always look like I am seriously paying attention to everything they have to say. Actually, I have to turn my head and focus just to keep a woman in sight."

The fact that a man with such a serious disability was there revealed how desperate the need for infantry officers was at the time.

Notwithstanding the fact that we were housed in decent accommodations, far from the front, and there was a certain prestige associated with becoming an officer, I still despised the whole army thing. I had been drafted in October 1939 for what was supposed to have been a two-year stint, yet here I was still in the army three years later. Worst of all, it seemed as if there was no end in sight to my enforced servitude.

Officer training was intense and demanding. The waking hours were crammed with instruction, field exercises, and exams. Most evenings were committed to studying for the next exam. By the end of each day I was usually tired and ready for bed, as we had to be up at 6 a.m. to begin the next day's training. There was a constant sense of urgency about everything we did. It was clear that the army was trying to turn us into capable officers in as short a time as possible, and we were never permitted to lose sight of our reason for being here.

Training was also very practical. First of all, the operation of the chain of command and the absolute necessity of unwavering obedience to orders were drilled into us. It was repeatedly emphasized that as their commanding officer, each of us would be responsible for the lives of our men, and that responsibility could not be taken lightly.

We were trained how to use the terrain to maximize the efficiency of an assault while minimizing losses, and how to pick defensive sites with good opportunities for cover and a wide field of view toward the enemy. We were shown how to attack across open ground with little protective cover, using flanking and diversionary movements along with covering fire. We were taught to coordinate various elements of a company of soldiers in order to outmanoeuvre or outflank enemy positions, and how to cut off an enemy retreat. We were taught how to set up a defensive perimeter and the most effective ways of defending a position, including the use of slit trenches, barbed wire, stakes, camouflage, and land mines. We were instructed to choose ground that would allow the terrain to fight for you, by providing strongpoints and fields of fire that would trap attackers, particularly in built-up areas.

One of the most complicated lessons dealt with how to stage a quick counterattack, to try to nullify the assault before the enemy had a chance to consolidate gains, and how to recognize the opportunity. On the battlefield we would be expected to improvise actions on our own initiative if the circumstances precluded following textbook strategies or previous orders that had become irrelevant, and to execute those actions boldly and quickly, particularly if we lost contact with our commander. One lesson about battle included organizing and covering an orderly evacuation of a position in the face of an overwhelming enemy onslaught. The instructor got a laugh when he made a sarcastic point of describing it as a "tactical withdrawal" and not a "retreat." Regardless of its potential effect on morale, I made careful mental notes of those retreat tactics anyway.

One of the largest classrooms contained a big table about two metres wide and four metres long and covered with sand that was contained by a wooden lip around the edge. Battlefield scenarios could be arranged on that table, complete with model buildings, vegetation patches, and miniature cannons and tanks. We were taught how to attack various types of enemy strongpoints, across different kinds of terrain, as well as how to defend against enemy attacks, including attacks supported by tanks. One of the most complicated assignments was learning how to capture a town. Another was how to protect defensive positions in inhabited areas against enemy attack. It did not take much imagination to figure out that house-to-house fighting in urban areas would be extremely difficult. The best way to attack a defended building was to blow a hole in the side of the basement wall and fill the adjoining room with grenades or flames, especially in large towns or cities with common walls between adjoining buildings. Going through a front door or a window was likely to prove suicidal.

We were taught how to read maps, use a compass, and employ various signals when wireless would not work. We were taught how we were supposed to coordinate actions with other units, where accurate communication was essential. We learned how to set charges that would blow up bridges or obstacles, and how to put up anti-tank obstacles. One of the more notable lessons taught us how to deal with land mines, how to spot them, and especially how to avoid them. Planting anti-personnel mines is a particularly nasty way of making war. A mine could blow your leg off if you stepped on one, and anyone could step on a mine after it was planted, friend or foe, soldier or civilian. It took a truly sadistic mind to have invented land mines and an equally demented mind to order their continued use.

One of the more senior instructors said that we were not likely to encounter minefields in Russia because the front was not stable for long enough periods to make planting mines particularly useful. The front would undoubtedly be moving again by the time we returned. Neither side would want to chance having to cross their own minefields when the front moved, so there was little tactical advantage to minefields. I was suspicious about that opinion, since it contradicted my own experience at the Eastern Front near Orel, where the lines did not move for almost seven months. He conveyed an extreme distaste for mines, so I wondered what he had experienced at the front.

One instructor impressed me as being particularly astute when it came to battlefield tactics. He taught us to always look for opportunities that took advantage of physical features of the landscape, or the weather, or the time of day, anything that could improve our situation compared to the enemy's. He made me aware that the land can be used to fight for you, that small folds in open ground or scattered clumps of grass or shrubs can provide enough cover to hide an entire company and protect your men from enemy fire. Not being seen could help you survive better than armour or firepower. Even the direction of the sunshine could make a difference, either blinding you or silhouetting the enemy. Knowledge was an important weapon.

The function and use of patrols and other forms of reconnaissance was explained, as well as the necessity of constant vigilance. It was wise to keep the enemy confused about our own strength and position, and avoid doing what the enemy might expect. Timing was also essential. A quick counterattack could be decisive in dissipating an enemy offensive, whereas the same counterattack a few hours later would have no hope of success, as the enemy would have had time to dig in.

We were given some insight into what the army had learned about the Russians, so that we would know what to expect from them in combat. Their favourite offensive tactic was a mass attack, where huge numbers of infantry would assemble along a relatively narrow front and charge forward in almost continuous waves to overwhelm our defenders by sheer weight of numbers. Such attacks could be preceded by long and concentrated artillery barrages and supported by tanks. The best defence under those circumstances would be to give ground to avoid being overrun, and then counterattack the flanks of the assault.

The Russians were very good at infiltration, moving large numbers of troops through narrow gaps in our defences, usually through forested areas or stream gullies. Such troops could remain undetected for weeks behind our lines, to suddenly attack from a completely unexpected direction. The importance of roads, railways, and inhabited places in Russia was also noted, as man-made features could be few and far between in the vastness of the countryside. Our instructors had an obvious if begrudging respect for the Russians' ability to do us harm. They left no doubt that it would be foolish to underestimate the enemy.

No time was wasted on parading or marching drills, as there had been during my training to become a soldier. That skill was completely irrelevant at the front. Also, no time was spent on academic lessons about our government's accomplishments, national ambitions, or political ideology, knowledge of which would also be useless in combat. Perhaps the reality of the Eastern Front had rendered former dissertations about the glorious deeds of our heroic leaders of the Fatherland to the same relevance as fairy tales.

Even though the training consumed most of our time, once we had become familiar with the facilities and comfortable with the school routine, we sometimes took time in the evening to have a beer or two in the lounge behind the mess hall. Among the men who were being trained with me were a few who had a great deal more front-line experience than I had, and I learned a lot from them. They told some gripping stories about conditions during the initial invasion of Russia and the first enemy counterattacks. One man described the extreme cold he had endured during the first winter in Russia. He sounded bitter as he recounted how the troops had been completely unprepared for the extreme weather. The army had obviously miscalculated the effect the cold would have on the soldiers' ability to fight. The German uniforms were practically useless against the cold. He had survived by wearing the boots and greatcoat he had taken from a dead Russian soldier. Apparently the Russian boots were made of rubber and insulated with a thick layer of felt, which kept the feet much warmer than the German leather boots. He sarcastically extolled the invincibility of the German soldier. "We were all right as long as no one was struck sharply enough to shatter his frozen frame like an icicle," he said. "We only survived because there was enough vodka in our veins for antifreeze."

A good story well told, perhaps embellished with humorous anecdotes, is highly prized at any male social gathering. Most war stories were never told. Soldiers who had lived through truly harrowing ordeals at the front rarely discussed them, perhaps because their experiences were so unpleasant they just wanted to forget about them. Nobody wanted to sound like he was complaining. At the time I considered my own stint at the Eastern Front as far too boring to make entertaining listening.

On Saturday evenings we went downtown to one of the local pubs. A fellow officer in training, Wolfgang Schwarz, and I soon became friends. Wolfgang was an excellent person, easygoing and amiable. He had a quick and dry sense of humour that, along with a broad and honest smile, made him instantly likable. He also struck me as steadfast and trustworthy.

An important part of our training was field exercises, where we were taken to an outdoor camp to practise manoeuvres that simulated realistic battlefield situations. Here we had the opportunity to put academic strategies and tactics learned in the classroom to the test. I quickly realized how difficult it really was to coordinate the actions of an entire company in combat, and especially to minimize risking the safety of the men under my command.

The first time we were in the field to practise tactics our assignment was to learn how to capture a hill from dug-in enemy soldiers, how to set up defensive positions, and how to defend a newly won position from enemy attack. Potsdam is situated in the heart of Prussia, a German province where the countryside is relatively flat; so flat in fact that when we were instructed on how to capture *Höhe Dreisig* (Hill 30), I looked around for the hill and could not see it. When I asked what hill the instructor was referring to, his indignant reply was "The one you are standing on!" Well, to a boy who had grown up among the beautiful wooded hills of the Frankenwald and Juragebirge in Bavaria, the small bulge in the ground we were standing on hardly qualified as a hill. To the local Prussians it must have been a significant physical feature. Still, I did not take that lesson lightly, as it might happen that I would have to fight across similar terrain in Russia. It taught me that I should be more observant and aware of subtle changes in the terrain in order to take advantage of the ground, changes that I had not even noticed before.

Field training simulated battlefield conditions that required us to learn to coordinate the movements of all the individuals in the company who would actually be fighting together, including machine-gun crews, mortar crews, snipers, spotters, wireless operators, scouts, and riflemen. It was also necessary to synchronize actions with other companies, or even with support units such as engineers, artillery batteries, anti-tank gunners, ground-attack aircraft, and reconnaissance or other special-purpose units.

One of the most important tactics we learned was how to orchestrate an infantry attack across open ground. When attacking an enemy that is dug in, your machine-gunners would fire to try to keep the enemy soldiers pinned down while part of the company ran as fast as possible to the next piece of cover or onto the enemy positions. A part of the company always provided covering fire while other parts advanced. The best tactic would be to try to go around the flanks of the enemy positions, surround them, and force them to surrender. Still, no matter how skilfully such tactics were executed, it was apparent that attacking strongly defended enemy positions would be dreadful.

We were also taught how to survive a tank attack and how to destroy tanks with the proper use of anti-tank infantry weapons. We learned how to place magnetic mines onto moving vehicles and how to toss satchel bombs onto the engine's air inlet. Our instructor described how to set the timing fuse on the satchel bomb as a tank approached, jump onto the back of the moving tank, place the satchel under the rear overhang of the tank's turret, and jump off just before the bomb exploded. He said it was easy, that he had done it himself during a battle in Russia. He explained that tanks are practically blind, as the drivers close their viewing slits to keep from being shot in the head by rifle fire, so a tank is vulnerable as long as there are no infantry riding the tank or following closely behind. No matter how reasonable he made such tactics sound, it was apparent that a tank attack would also be dreadful.

The next day we were taken to an open field where we were given a practical lesson on what to do if we encountered armoured forces. The theory was to stay low inside holes in the ground, no matter what, until the tanks passed, and then to watch out for any following infantry. To drive home the lesson we were ordered into slit trenches, about one-and-a-half metres deep, and told to stay there until ordered to leave. About half a dozen obsolete tanks, probably old French machines, were parked along the side of the field. We were put into the trenches and shortly thereafter I heard the tank motors start up. Looking over the edge of the trench, I watched them crawl nearer and nearer.

"How do you feel about being buried alive?" I asked Wolfgang as he crouched beside me in the trench, joking but with escalating apprehension.

The tanks certainly looked fearsome enough, with their clanking treads crushing down everything in their path. As they approached to within a few metres one tank was heading straight at me, exactly at me! Surely it would stop before it crushed me to death. Surely there was no real danger. Surely our instructors knew what they were doing. Surely we were now too valuable for the army to let us be injured. Surely!

I looked around in desperation, but there was no signal for us to leave the trench and no sign for the tanks to stop. When the tank was almost on top of the trench it became absolutely terrifying! Wolfgang yelled, "They better dig us out in time!" as we ducked as deep into the trench as we could get, "or you will never get the ten marks I borrowed from you."

As the underside of the tank's leading edge came right overhead I pressed my back against the side of the trench to try to keep it from caving in under the treads and placed my hands over my face. I took a deep breath and held it as the thudding, clanking monster kept right on going, expecting the earth to swallow and crush me completely. Then I noticed the tank had continued onto the far side and realized the trench had held. With enormous relief I started breathing again. Just then I felt a tap on the top of my helmet and heard a voice from the edge of the trench, "You are dead." One of our instructors had been right behind the tank. In the terror of the moment I had forgotten the point of the lesson, that in a real battle the infantrymen following the tanks are more likely to kill you than the tank itself.

Regardless of what we learned during the lessons, I was impressed with the thorough professionalism of the officers and sergeants who were in charge of our training. We learned practical lessons regarding the necessity of absolute adherence to discipline, especially under fire. Following orders was essential to the functioning of an infantry company in battle. How faithfully orders were executed could determine your ultimate survival at the front. The constant emphasis that we officer candidates develop leadership skills made me understand that the main objective of officer school was not just to teach us tactics and battlefield skills, but to turn us into good leaders of men. Although I was not looking forward to putting my training to the test, I was convinced that my newly learned military skills would be instrumental in helping me and the soldiers with me survive at the front.

My impression was that we were about as ready as we could be to face whatever was to come in Russia. It is no wonder that the German armies had been so successful so far. Since the beginning of 1939, we were undoubtedly the best-trained soldiers in the world.

After ten weeks of training in Potsdam we took our final exam. When the results were printed we were informed that we were to receive our officer's commission in a formal ceremony. Admittedly, I felt a sense of accomplishment at having successfully completed my officer training.

We were sent to the supply room where each of us was outfitted with a splendid new dress uniform, which the staff made sure fit properly. We were also given new boots, an officer's cap, and an ivory-handled ceremonial dagger, which was ornate and quite impressive. The state must have a high regard for officers, since it had spent a considerable amount of money on each of us. Along with our lovely new officer's uniform we were also issued a regular combat-duty uniform, which I figured was the one I would really need at the front. It would be a shame to get my new dress uniform dirty.

That afternoon we stood at attention in neat rows while the commanding officer made a speech congratulating us on our achievement and sermonizing about our new duties and responsibilities in the service of our country. I received my officer's commission, along with all its privileges and obligations. I was now a lieutenant in the *Wehrmacht. Leutnant, Dezember 1942*, was marked in my *Soldbuch*. From then on I would receive a lieutenant's pay, which amounted to 300 Reichsmark per month. That was quite a sizable income at the time, certainly more money than I had ever earned before. I was looking forward to spending it.

The entire graduating class, along with our instructors, was arranged in the courtyard to have our picture taken. Every time I look at that picture it makes me sad, knowing that many of those young men did not survive the war.

Upon graduation I was assigned to the 68th Infantry Regiment, which had its home base in Brandenburg, a city in Prussia about thirty kilometres west of Potsdam. I was to report to the Brandenburg garrison on January 6, 1943.

After graduating from Officer School I was due another two-week vacation. The army owed every soldier a holiday once a year. Naturally I decided to visit my home again, and just in time for Christmas.

Graduating Class, Infantry Officer School, Potsdam, December 1942

Along with every service stint that I had attended for the army, vacations were registered in my *Soldbuch*. I went to the administration office at the Potsdam garrison and handed my book to the clerk to have my upcoming vacation recorded. I had spent so much time in the military and had been stationed at so many places that all the pages had been used up. So some genius in the office glued another page to the base of the last page inside the back cover. On that new page he stamped the requisite form and filled in the date and duration of the vacation. I had no idea why he did not give me another pay book, as the war was not over and there would surely be more entries. Maybe he assumed I did not warrant a new book as I would soon be dead anyway.

When I arrived in Michelau, Turko was the only one home. Big hugs and great expressions of joy at our reunion. He leaned back and took a long look at me in my new uniform. Although he did not say so, I sensed he was pleased and proud that his son had become an officer. That was an achievement for our family. Turko had served twelve years in the German army, including four years in the First World War, but had never been able to become an officer because he did not have enough formal education. He had eventually been promoted to *Oberfeldwebel* (sergeant major), which was as high a rank as a non-commissioned soldier could reach without attending Officer School.

After that initial acknowledgement of my achievement he returned to his usual dispassionate demeanour. He left me with the impression that it had almost been expected of me to become an officer; after all, I should have known that I had enough education and intelligence. That typified my father's attitude toward his sons, which was to do what is expected of you and not mess up. Whatever, I was just glad to be home for a while.

When Karl showed up he congratulated me on my promotion. He said he liked the uniform. My brother's wife, Anna, asserted that she was impressed, but also let me know that I should not be too smug about joining the ranks of the "military elite" as she termed it.

My Aunt Gustel gave me a big hug and told me I looked splendid, but she was very worried about me and hoped the army would not send me to fight in some awful place far away. "You be careful around those foreigners. You can never tell what they are up to, especially the women." She mentioned that last part with a deliberate nod of her head and closing of one eye that implied a serious message about feminine wiles that I may not have been aware of at my tender age. Dear old lady. I assured her that I could take care of myself, and that she need not worry, because German officers received special treatment in the army and were not allowed to go anywhere dangerous. I said that with a deliberate nod of my head and closing of one eye.

Anna did the cooking for us, assisted by Gustel. Gustel lived upstairs in Father's house, where she had her own bedroom and a tiny kitchen. She looked noticeably shorter since the last time I saw her. Turko commented on her shrinking frame by saying, "*Die wetzt sich ab*" (She is abrading herself down).

My father and I discussed the war only briefly, and only as far as it affected the family. We hoped my brother Hermann and the twins were safe. He was sure Hermann was still in Russia but had not heard from him for about half a year. Edwin and Oskar had recently left for military service and were probably still in training in München.

Turko invited me to accompany him to visit his friend Hermine, whom everyone called "Mini," on Christmas Day. In Michelau practically everyone knew each other. Mini's daughter Helga was not married, and I was suspicious that Turko considered her a perfect candidate as my wife. I was now a very eligible bachelor. Better keep my guard up, I thought to myself.

Mini's husband had been missing in action since January 1942, and Turko had struck up a close friendship with her. That was probably mutually beneficial, since Turko had been a widower since 1938. He was fifty-seven at the time, and beginning to show his age. He appeared to be in good spirits and content with his life. It was difficult to know what he really felt because he was never the type to flaunt his emotions.

I was happy to spend Christmas with these people, especially since Mini owned a bakery. I had never realized how much strenuous physical labour was involved in running a bakery and how hot working conditions can get. Regardless, I appreciated the delicious goodies. That Christmas dinner was the best memory I have of my two-week vacation. Helga let me know that she thought I looked just splendid in my new uniform.

At the local pub in Michelau it was noticeably interesting how well I was treated. Young women who had never shown any interest in me before were now very friendly. I must admit that I relished the attention. Perhaps I even played it up a bit, taking full advantage of my new status. Too bad the army had not made me an officer just to increase my popularity with women.

I discovered that as an officer I had suddenly become an authority on global politics and grand military strategies, and was expected to speak knowledgeably about the conduct of the war. The patrons in the pub asked my opinion as to how the war was going and what I expected to happen next. "You know, Hitler does not always keep me informed of his intentions," I replied. They wanted to know about my officer's commission, what Potsdam was like, and what it was like in Russia. Their queries were more than eagerness to learn about places and events outside their village; they were genuinely concerned about my welfare. They shared in my success at becoming an officer; after all, I was one of their own. It might have been dispiriting if I had told them how much I hated being in the military, so I just described some of the lands I had seen and people I had met. I also did not tell them that my officer's commission, which they seemed so impressed with, felt more like a penal conviction than an honourable promotion.

There had recently been disturbing rumours that all was not well with the German campaign in Russia. The fighting at Stalingrad was mentioned repeatedly in the news broadcasts, and although there was no mention of defeat, the encirclement of the German 6th Army had become common knowledge. Until then Hitler's armies had met overwhelming success wherever they had fought, and more news of that kind of success was what everyone in the pubs wanted and expected to hear. After almost two months in the Russian trap the plight of the 6th Army was becoming difficult for the media to conceal. Knowing that the Russian winter was a terrible adversary, I was sceptical about the media's optimistic attitude. However, the daily "Report from the Volga" broadcasts by 6th Army radio operators were so convincing that I had no reason to suspect they were actually a complete fabrication by our government.

On January 5, 1943, I left Michelau for Brandenburg to join my new infantry regiment.

Brandenburg is a very old city, which had been the capital of Prussia before Berlin became the capital of Germany. It was built in the middle of flat countryside, laced with rivers and canals. Brandenburg was also a garrison city. There were probably five military bases in Brandenburg, one each for the *Luftwaffe*, *Artillerie*, *Flak Abwehr* (Anti-Aircraft), *Pioniere* (Engineers), and at least one for the Infantry.

I was stationed at the home base of the 68th Infantry Regiment. The garrison was situated near the old core area of the city. There were old brick buildings, two or three storeys high, and a small square assembly area in the centre, covered with paving stones that formed an ornamental pattern. Many of the barracks were unoccupied.

When I first arrived in Brandenburg the only thing I knew about Prussians was that they were called *Sau-Preuss* in Michelau, mostly by the older women. That epithet denoted exactly what it sounds like. I remember from history classes in high school that Prussia had been a separate country before its prime minister, Otto Von Bismarck, united all the previously independent German states into one country. In fact it was Prussia, not Germany, that had defeated France in the Franco-Prussian War of 1870. Before the individual Germanic nations became the united country of Germany, there had been a historical rivalry between Prussia and Bavaria, probably going back centuries. That rivalry was still fashionably popular with many Bavarians, including people in my home village, many of whom considered Prussians to be as much foreigners as Frenchmen or Italians.

So here I was, a Bavarian lad amongst all those Prussians. Most Prussians, even though Germans, struck me as characteristically formal people, much more so than the people I had grown up with. When first meeting, it seemed as if they did not know how to relax or make me feel relaxed in their company. They could also be abrupt in conversation. I remembered my father telling me an anecdote that summed up his opinion of the difference between Prussians and Bavarians: "If there are eight tables in a pub in Prussia and eight patrons in the pub, each patron will be sitting at a different table. In Bavaria, all eight patrons would be sitting at the same table." After a few weeks in Brandenburg I understood the inference of that wry comparison perfectly.

All their proper and formal traits notwithstanding, there was one thing attributed to Prussians which I believed to be true—they had a reputation for being excellent soldiers. They had a very pragmatic attitude toward warfare, like it was a completely ordinary fact of life. The Prussians I met in the Brandenburg garrison left me with the impression that you could depend absolutely on their devotion to their comrades-in-arms. Their composed and self-confident manner, and especially their unequivocal pride in their military heritage, gave the impression that they could not be panicked, and even in the heat of battle they would not abandon you.

January 13, 1943. I told no one it was my birthday. There was no opportunity for any celebration anyway. Still, I was alive and healthy. As my father had often said, "No matter how bad you think things are, they can always get worse."

It could have been much worse. While not celebrating my birthday I kept up with news reports from Stalingrad, which repeatedly acknowledged that the 6th Army was still encircled, but maintained the charade that it would only be a matter of time before our eventual victory. The reports were particularly poignant for the families of the garrison here in Brandenburg because our 68th Infantry Regiment was a part of the 6th Army.

The 6th Army had been encircled during the huge Russian offensives that began early in November 1942. At first there had been hope that they could break out of their trap. Hermann Goering had promised that the 6th Army would be supplied by the *Luftwaffe* and it would still be in place by the spring, still holding Stalingrad. Hitler had made a bombastic speech about the invincibility of the German soldier: *"Wo der Deutsche Soldat steht kommt Kein anderer ran!"* ("Where the German soldier stands there comes no other near!") Political rhetoric notwithstanding, by mid-January 1943 it became obvious that something had gone seriously wrong at Stalingrad. On February 3 we heard that the entire 6th Army was lost. Field Marshal Von Paulus, its commander, had surrendered. Our devious media could not hide such a huge disaster. Even if the German media had not aired the story, people all over Germany listened clandestinely to the BBC radio broadcast news of the war. As a soldier, I knew an army had a complement of over 200,000 men! My heart went out to the unfortunate soldiers who were missing and to the families they left behind.

That was the first time in history that an entire German army had been captured. The official radio broadcasts used euphemistic words like *Front Begradigung* (front straightening) or *Front Bereinigung* (front cleaning) to try to explain that devastating disaster, but nobody could be fooled. Every soldier knew it would have dire consequences. The significance of those losses was inescapable. We now realized that Hitler's vaunted war machine was not invincible, and that our self-aggrandizing leader was an incompetent military commander to have masterminded such a catastrophe. On a more far-reaching scale, Germany's enemies now realized that Germany's armies could be beaten. With all able-bodied men already in uniform, the loss of all those trained soldiers would be impossible to replace. Anyone who could think at all must have known that the defeat at Stalingrad signalled the beginning of the end for Germany.

There was one small perk to my assignment at the garrison: during off-duty hours we were free to go out most evenings and try to have a good time. The Russian front was very far away, and unlike other big German cities, Brandenburg had not been bombed. Allied bombing raids were concentrated on Germany's industrial cities in the Ruhr region, on easily accessible northern cities like Hamburg, and on Berlin itself. The raid on the ball-bearing factories in Schweinfurt was a media event, mainly because the American bombers had attacked during daylight and suffered heavy losses before they could return to their base. So Brandenburg was a relatively congenial place in the winter of 1943.

Leutnants Kurt Raabe, Wolfgang Schwarz, Albin Gagel, January 1943.

Wolfgang and I often went to one or another of the local pubs in the evenings. Because Brandenburg had so many military garrisons there was always competition from other soldiers for the attention of the local ladies. Wolfgang had an uncanny ability to attract good-looking prospects by sweet talk. He was completely fearless, never intimidated by any woman's looks or demeanour, and never got flustered about anything. That talent, combined with his good looks, meant we were rarely without female companionship by the end of an evening in a pub.

There was sometimes an opportunity to dance in a hall or in the larger cafés, which were well attended by soldiers from the local garrisons. During the 6th Army's encirclement at Stalingrad, the government forbade dancing in public places completely. Perhaps Hitler's rationale was that the soldiers at the front did not want to think of their wives or girlfriends back home dancing in the arms of strangers while they were away.

The time I spent at the Brandenburg garrison was also an opportunity to make other friends, one of whom was another young officer, Kurt Raabe. Kurt was a typical Prussian, tall and thin, with a very fair complexion. He sometimes tried to manifest a haughty, almost arrogant, demeanour when in public. Perhaps only a Prussian could get away with such behaviour successfully. As I got to know him better, I suspected he was deliberately trying to cultivate an aristocratic image for himself. He insinuated that his family were landed gentry who owned a country estate, complete with resident workers. Perhaps he pretended to be an aristocrat to improve his social status. I later found out Kurt's parents were ordinary farmers who owned a small farm near Drossen, a little village outside of Brandenburg. He never invited us to join him on his trips home, so I suspected he might have been a bit ashamed of the fact that he came from a humble farm family. As farmers, capable of growing food on their own land, Kurt's family was quite wealthy in my eyes. It amazed me that Kurt, or anyone else, could think that personal prejudices about social status could possibly be important, especially during such times of adversity.

One of Kurt's more useful talents was that he could talk beautifully, even eloquently, utilizing sophisticated and ostentatious phrases, often accompanied by almost artistic gestures. Perhaps that was one of the reasons he was quite popular with the ladies. I had previously met a young woman on a streetcar in town, and we had gone out on a date, to a movie. After the movie we went to a café where we met Kurt. It soon became apparent that she was very impressed with Kurt. Her name was Margit, a pretty woman, but a little too pretentious for my liking. That obviously did not bother Kurt, or maybe he just understood her frame of mind better, since they were both Prussians. Kurt ended up dating Margit and actually became engaged to her a few weeks later.

While at the garrison Kurt received a package from his family about once a week. Those packages usually contained sausages, cheeses, baked goods, and other goodies. He usually shared those treasures with Wolfgang and me. That was until he met and fell in love with Margit, after which he must have thought it more sensible to share his goodies with her. That was capitulation, in my opinion.

One evening Kurt had arranged for us to meet some of the local ladies in Drossen, which he considered to be his hometown. That little accomplishment enhanced Kurt's reputation and stature in my eyes. At the restaurant Kurt introduced Wolfgang and me to two sisters and another young lady. During the "date," there was the usual small talk, telling of jokes and stories, and some innocent flirting, all accompanied by a few beers.

At the start of the evening the younger of the two sisters was sitting beside Wolfgang. She was very pretty, but it was soon evident that he had no interest in her. He obviously liked her older sister, who was sitting beside me. Her name was Trudchen. During the course of the evening Wolfgang made his move and sat down beside her, which was all right with me. As the evening continued the two of them became engrossed in what appeared to be an ardent and increasingly intimate conversation.

"What the devil are you doing?" I asked Wolfgang when we had a chance to speak without being overheard. "We have to be out of here in an hour."

"She is just so beautiful," he replied with a stupid grin on his face. Perhaps he had drunk more beers than I had noticed.

I knew my assignment to Brandenburg was just a stopover on my eventual return to Russia, so I did not take any social dating seriously. I certainly did not take that little outing to Drossen seriously, and considered it a brief interlude to be spent with some casual female company between military duties. We had to take the 11 o'clock train out of Drossen, back to the garrison in Brandenburg. That left precious little time to get to know anyone, let alone engender any romance. But Wolfgang seemed to have been smitten by the older sister.

On the way back to the garrison that night she was all he could talk about. I just listened patiently, assuming he would forget about her by morning. To my astonishment, the next day he still blathered on and on about this newfound wonder woman, telling me over and over, "I love this Trudchen."

"Love" had obviously addled his brains. The concept of love and all that it entailed struck me as completely meaningless during this time. We were soon to be shipped off to the front, from which we might never return. Falling in love was the last thing any of us needed.

11 *Gisela Winkelsdorf*

ONE EVENING IN FEBRUARY I went out to a local café with another officer, named Hans. He had assured me that this place, the Café Graf, was
absolutely the best place in all of Brandenburg to meet pretty young
ladies. When we arrived the place was packed, mostly with soldiers
and young women. There were at least forty tables inside, with four
to six chairs at each, as well as a dozen or so more on the patio, and
there were few empty chairs. Hans spotted three young ladies sitting
together at a table with two empty chairs. Perfect! We asked if we could
join them. They did not object, so we sat down. All three were drinking
coffee and eating cakes, so strategically we also ordered coffee and a
small piece of cake.

We struck up a conversation that at first was more formal than
friendly. Our attempts to be charming seemed to fall flat, and the atmosphere was soon stilted and awkward. I began to feel uncomfortable
and looked for a polite way out. There was a lot of whispering among
the ladies, and I assumed we had struck out. Then one of them said she
could use my help with a devious plan they had concocted. Apparently
an officer from the *Luftwaffe* had been dating one of the ladies at our
table, but this evening he was with another woman at a nearby restaurant, and our jilted lady wanted to get even. Their plan was to use me
to make him jealous, and they tried to convince me to go with her to
the other restaurant so that Mr. *Luftwaffe* playboy could see that other
men, especially another officer, were interested in her.

After the serious escapades I had endured during the past three
years as a soldier I had no interest in that trite little game; however, I
had ideas of my own. Beside me sat a beautiful young woman who had
caught my fancy. I was very interested in getting to know her. She acted
quiet, cool, and reserved. Typical Prussian, I thought.

I tried to impress her with my charm and wit, which strained my
mental resources, as she did not reply much. When she spoke it was
with a raspy voice, which she said was because of a sore throat. As she
appeared to show no interest in me I began to feel that our excursion to
the Café Graf would end up a disappointment. When she said she had

Gisela Winkelsdorf

better go home, my hopes of seeing her again dropped to near zero. Oh well, I thought, there are always other women. Wait a minute. I had faced the might of the French and Russian armies and come away unscathed, and now I felt intimidated by one young woman? I decided to take a chance and asked if I could walk her home. To my surprise she said yes. We said our goodbyes and left, leaving Hans to fend for himself with the other two ladies at the café.

We talked very little during our walk as her voice was not in good shape. She said her name was Gisela Winkelsdorf. What a lovely name. When we reached her apartment building I mustered my courage and asked if she would consent to accompany me on a date tomorrow. She looked me in the eye and, after a moment's hesitation, said, "Why not."

Yes! We agreed to meet the next day at the Café Graf after she finished work.

I left feeling elated, far better than I could ever remember feeling. After the isolation I had experienced throughout the war, I now basked in the warmth of ordinary personal contact with this beautiful person. But the sensation I was feeling was anything but ordinary! Amazing how she could make me feel so happy, so thrilled at being alive, especially after only spending such a short time with her. Lying in my bed in the barracks my mind replayed the evening's events over and over again, especially her consent to tomorrow's date.

The next evening we met at the Café Graf. She looked even better than she had the previous day. She introduced me to her friends, who now seemed an agreeable enough bunch. We talked, laughed, and drank cups of coffee and glasses of beer. They explained yesterday's jealousy-engendered plot, and all of us had a good laugh over it. Gisela's girlfriend seemed to be in good spirits in spite of her losing a skirmish in the battle of the sexes. I found out that Gisela was

apprenticing to become a window display decorator and her current job
was at the Kaufhaus Riedel, a large department store downtown.

Gisela suggested taking me on a tour of her neighbourhood, which
I thought was a splendid idea. So we walked along the streets and
looked at the shops, the sidewalk cafés, and the picturesque old houses.
Time stood still for me. She completely captivated my attention, carrying my spirits aloft simply with the inflections in her voice. She described landmarks as we walked by, and I acknowledged their social
importance, their marvellous architecture, and their cultural or historical significance, but I could hardly take my eyes off her.

Because Brandenburg had so many military garrisons we passed
many soldiers out on the town and every one of them saluted me, and
of course I had to salute back. After a while all that saluting drove me
to the point of distraction. Stupid army rules. I would have preferred
to hold Gisela's hand or put my arm around her, but the army frowned
on soldiers touching civilians at any time. So we just walked and talked
until it was time to escort her home again.

That night I could not get Gisela out of my thoughts. What a mar-
vellously wonderful person she was. I had never felt like this before.
Images of the two of us together consumed my mind. The contemplation of a relationship was absolutely intoxicating. I was so looking forward to seeing her again.

The following day was Sunday. We walked for hours through beautiful gardens and manicured lawns. Even though it was the end of February, the weather was mild and there was no snow on the ground.
Every sidewalk was adorned with planter boxes containing colourful
flowers. It seemed that Brandenburgers took great pride in the appearance of their city. I was amazed at how many parks there were in Brandenburg, especially along the waterways. Walking by the river we saw a
flock of swans swimming in the water under a bridge. I saw black swans
among the white ones, shiny black swans with bright red beaks that I
had never known existed. People were throwing bread into the water
to feed them. Gisela explained that they had been brought here from
Australia, as a gift from the city of Perth.

We spent a wonderful day together. She was articulate and charming, in a quiet and almost shy sort of way, conveying an innocence that
I found completely disarming. She also had an enchanting sense of humour, as she laughed at all my attempts at humour. The evening passed

too quickly. We kissed good night on the front steps to her apartment. As soon as I left I yearned to see her again.

After seeing each other every day for over a week, Gisela invited me in after walking her home. That was a pleasant surprise. She had impressed me as quite level-headed and would not bother to introduce every man she met to her family. I was flattered and encouraged that she chose to have me meet her mother.

Her mother, Margarete Winkelsdorf, immediately made me feel comfortable and welcome. She was a very agreeable person, completely unpretentious, with none of the standoffish characteristics I had come to expect from other Prussians. She had divorced her husband in 1936 and Gisela was her only child.

Gisela's father, Willie, lived a few blocks away, where he had started a new family with another woman. He had served in the German navy during World War I and shortly after that had signed on as a steward with Norddeutscher Lloyd, a big German international cruise line. That job paid him well enough to retire and purchase a restaurant, the Löwenhof, in the heart of Brandenburg, which he and Margarete ran for years. There were some exotic souvenirs in the apartment that had come from the far-off places he had visited in his travels, such as ornamental china, ivory carvings, and an ebony box. These were obviously artistic pieces and probably quite valuable. I sensed that Gisela and her mother did not want to talk much about her father, so did not ask any more questions about him or his souvenirs. After the separation her father continued to run the restaurant on his own. Whatever the circumstances of the separation, it seemed to me that her mother had done a fine job of raising Gisela.

Margarete worked at the Arado Flugzeugwerke, a factory located a few blocks away from their home, making light reconnaissance airplanes and seaplanes for the *Luftwaffe*. That factory had made small civilian pleasure craft before the war. She said most of her co-workers were also women, even though most of the work was labour-intensive and physically strenuous. That was of course because most of the men in Brandenburg, as well as in the rest of Germany, were away serving in the armed forces.

Gisela and her mother lived in a small two-bedroom apartment on the second floor of a three-storey building in a nice part of town. There was a small living room and a relatively large kitchen with a table and chairs in one corner for a dining area. It had a nice cosy feel to it.

Unlike my barracks, which was just a place to store men for the night, this was a home. There was a small yard behind the building, with a picnic table for sitting outside. Clotheslines had been strung across the yard from one building to the next for drying laundry.

When I left that evening to return to the garrison my soul was filled with music. I did not feel the cold in the winter air, I did not take notice of other people in the streets, and I heard nothing but the joyful beat of my heart. What a wonderful day this had been. I was completely unaware that the conviction to avoid falling in love, which had forged my opinion of Wolfgang's and Kurt's relationships with their girlfriends, had completely disappeared from my mind. I had fallen very much in love with Gisela Winkelsdorf.

After that night, Gisela and I saw each other as often as possible. We went for walks downtown or along the riverfront, or to the Café Graf, or some other restaurant. We always met friends to share some fun. We often met Wolfgang and Trudchen for some socializing. If we had the requisite ration stamps we could order a meal.

The coffeehouses usually played music, either records or the radio. We heard mostly traditional German music, including classical music by Mozart, Beethoven, Haydn, or Handel, or some other of our antique composers, although there were also popular modern songs by current German singing stars. Gisela knew the lyrics to almost every pop song. The government approved of the music of Germany's great classical composers, but absolutely forbade the playing of American jazz or swing, music that could "corrupt the morals of the people." Even though I appreciated and enjoyed classical music, it would have been fun to listen to modern swing music. One café had a band, three older men, one of whom played an accordion. The band tried their best to make the music sound delightful, and perhaps because I was with Gisela, it actually was delightful.

One evening we were walking by the cinema and Gisela mentioned that she would like to see the movie playing inside, entitled *Immensee*, as the female star, Christina Söderbaum, was one of her favourite actresses. So we stood in the ticket queue. When I asked for two tickets the attendant asked Gisela how old she was. Gisela looked sheepish for a moment, and then quietly said, "Seventeen."

Seventeen! It had not occurred to me that she was that young, although I had never stopped to think about it and had never asked her age. Somewhere in the back of my mind there was probably a voice telling me that she might be too young for a serious relationship. But those fleeting thoughts were overwhelmed by the feelings in my heart, which knew nothing of reason or caution. I loved her and loved being with her. Nothing else seemed important. As long as she wanted to be with me, I was hers.

"Well?" The ticket attendant's brusque query snapped at me. "She is underage. This movie is restricted to persons eighteen and older."

"It's all right, she is with me," I answered as if that would override the attendant's reservations; but she remained unmoved.

"I've come a long way," I added, leaning forward to make sure she could see I was an officer, "and we would really like to see this movie. I will take full responsibility." I put on my most polite and charming smile and tried to manifest an air of resolute determination to stand my ground.

"I'll be eighteen next week," Gisela added.

"Oh, very well, go on in."

Good! For a moment that was a victory more satisfying than any military conquest.

Movies were escapism. For one-and-a-half hours members of the audience were transported into a fantasy world where the harsh realities of life could be forgotten. I felt myself being drawn into the plot, vicariously caring about the characters on the screen, loathing the villain, and celebrating the happy ending. Gisela's reaction to the romantic aspects of the movie carried me along with her through the story, sharing the experience. She cried at the heartbreaking scenes and laughed at the comedic parts, completely enthralled. That innocent display of emotion further captivated my heart.

Something not so innocent was also part of movies at that time. Before every movie began they would show the weekly newsreel, the *Wochenschau*. They were capsules of recent events, including news from the fighting front. They would show moving pictures portraying war as a series of glorious victories won by our gallant soldiers. For example, we saw *Luftwaffe* planes blowing up enemy ships, *Wehrmacht* tanks pouring across meadows as they swept aside the hapless enemy, and endless lines of Russian prisoners being marched into captivity in the aftermath of mighty battles. Our officers and soldiers were depicted as infallible heroes. Enemy leaders were characterized as evil, incompetent oafs, and enemy soldiers were always losers. There was never any hint of a German military defeat on the screen. Even the undeniable disaster at Stalingrad was portrayed very briefly and only as a minor setback, as an "adjustment" in the campaign, and then ignored. Even scenes of wounded soldiers showed only nice, clean wounds, like an arm in a neat sling, or an immaculate white bandage wrapped around a soldier's forehead, his face still smiling as he was helped along by his comrade.

Newsreels never showed what I knew to be the true horrors of warfare, like the burned corpses I had witnessed in France, or the frozen bodies I had seen in Russia. There was never a hint of anything like the rotting remains I had helped bury in the fields near Orel. There was also never any mention of the countless personal tragedies caused by the loss of loved ones, or the emotional suffering that endures long after the battles are over. Instead, vividly portrayed were scenes from countries that had been overrun by German armies, some of them depicting civilians greeting our soldiers as liberators, with women throwing flowers at panzer troops driving by. Other scenes showed German soldiers building bridges or railways to help the local citizens. The newsreels made it appear as if being under German domination was the best thing that could have happened to the people in those "liberated" nations. They were very convincing at the time.[8]

After the movie I asked Gisela if she wanted to go to a restaurant. She said she did, even though it was almost 10 p.m. and there was a 9 p.m. curfew in effect throughout Germany for anyone under eighteen. Security patrols went around making sure the social rules were obeyed, including curfews. These were probably men rejected for military service because of some disability or they were too old. Gisela called them *Bonzen*[9] and ridiculed them more than feared them. They were osten-

---

8   Many of the newsreels that showed foreign civilians welcoming German troops in the Baltic states and Ukraine were accurate. Ukrainians especially despised the Russian occupation. Stalin had caused the deaths by starvation of millions of Ukrainian citizens shortly before the war, which Ukrainians still refer to as the *Holodomor*. Initially, they viewed the German forces as liberators from Stalin's tyranny.

9   *Bonzen* was the derogatory term most German civilians applied to local civil servants the regime had assigned to police the nation. It denotes the disdain they felt for the attitude many of these extremists had, that their cause was unquestionably righteous. Among themselves, Prussians referred to government dupes as *Bonzen*, and never as Nazis.

sibly appointed by the local government authorities to safeguard the public good. Those morality police types were more active in the large cities than the small towns and villages, presumably because, like Brandenburg, the larger cities contained military garrisons full of possibly incorrigible young men.

Those curfew enforcers were not *Feldgendarmerie*, the military police with authority to apprehend soldiers they suspected of misconduct. They were also not Gestapo, the feared secret police who had been assigned unequivocal authority over all German citizens. Still, it was smart to avoid confrontations with anyone representing authority, because they could denounce you to the Gestapo. No matter how inane they appeared to be, they were instruments by which control was exercised by our government.

Gisela probably reckoned that the *Bonzen* would not question an officer or his date, so she could ignore the curfew and stay out as long as she wanted, provided she was with me. Perhaps that was why she had neglected to tell me earlier she was underage.

Speculating on what life would be like in post-war Germany, Gisela left no doubt that Germany would lose the war and that conditions would be dreadful for German citizens after the war. She told me she hated the war and despised everything to do with the military. She was surprisingly passionate, candidly expressing those potentially dangerous opinions to me with very personal emotion. "The leaders play games," she said, "but the average people suffer the consequences. Because of Stalingrad, five of the girls that work with me at Kaufhaus Riedel are now widows."

Gisela's sincere compassion over those five very personal tragedies was poignant testimony that those left behind at the home front could be just as much casualties of the war as the lost soldiers.

Gisela asked what my plans were after the war was over, assuming I survived. I said I would very much like to marry her. I surprised myself, as I had not intended to be so bold so soon, but the reality of war imparted a sense of urgency to my thoughts. I might be called away to serve at some front from which I might not return. Time was a luxury I did not want to waste.

She did not react with enthusiasm as I had hoped, but seemed hesitant. She gave me a questioning, searching look, and then suggested we wait a bit. "I should at least be eighteen."

Although that could have been a serious setback, I convinced myself that she hesitated because she was very young and had never thought about getting married. She could meet lots of men in Brandenburg and I did not want someone else to steal her away from me. Undaunted, the thought of a life with Gisela was an inspiration, a reason for living and hoping for a happy future. I was sure we loved each other and, just like in the movies, love would triumph over everything else.

Before coming to Brandenburg I spent very little of the money the army paid me. Now I had an opportunity to spend it on Gisela, and was eager to do so. Gisela told me that she spent much of her efforts in her job at Kaufhaus Riedel to make sure the window displays looked marvellous; however, there was not much to buy in the store itself—or anywhere else throughout Germany—and what was available could only be purchased if you had sufficient government allocation stamps. War material production had almost drained the German industries of their ability to produce consumer goods. Even though decent food was becoming increasingly scarce, it was more of an inconvenience than a hardship. The government's allocation and distribution system actually worked remarkably well. While there was never any surplus and not much variety, everyone had enough to ensure that no one went hungry.

During our times together we talked about all manner of things: movies, movie stars, friends and the vagaries of their lives, Gisela's job and her workmates, clothing and shoe styles, and especially how much we would enjoy some good food or some fun if it were not for the war. They were mostly inconsequential topics that seemed interesting or even important at the time. Like most young people, we had no interest in discussing serious or potentially gloomy topics. Although it was always in the back of my mind, I avoided dwelling on the fact that I might soon be called away by the army.

It really did not matter to me what we did at the time. It felt wonderful being with Gisela, among congenial friends, and in civilized surroundings. Those were luxurious times. I was so happy that life contained such pleasant moments.

Unfortunately it ended all too soon. On March 10, 1943, after spending two all-too-short months in Brandenburg, I received orders that I was to be transferred to an outpost in France, to become part of a new infantry division. On our last double date I said a heartfelt farewell to Wolfgang. At the time I considered him my closest friend. He was from Stuttgart, and we exchanged home addresses and promised to write to each other. He joked about how we would all get together for some good times after the end of the war, just like old married couples. That was something to look forward to.

Gisela accompanied me to the train station to see me off. It felt so wonderful to hold her close to me in my arms. The train whistle blew its warning and we kissed one last kiss. It felt awful to tear myself away and get on the train.

As the train left the station I consoled myself with the knowledge that, instead of joining an infantry unit in Russia right away I was going to spend some time at an outpost garrison in Le Croisic, near Saint-Nazaire on the Atlantic coast of occupied France. With some good luck we might see each other again soon.

I fervently hoped so.

12 *The Best Cabaret in Town*

THE TRAIN RIDE FROM BRANDENBURG took three days as it travelled through most of northern Germany, the Low Countries, and all of northern France. I missed Gisela already. The train finally stopped in the city of Saint-Nazaire. Four of us got off the train at the station and were greeted by a sergeant. After a brief discussion with one of the other officers, the sergeant turned to the rest of us and asked with a grin, "You want to act like tourists? I can take you on a tour of the city." Sure, why not. So we piled into an army truck and went for a short ride through the downtown area to the harbour.

Saint-Nazaire is a port city on the Atlantic coast of France. It was being used by the *Kriegsmarine* (Navy) as the main base for all the *Untersee Boot* (U-boat) operations in the North Atlantic. Before the war it had been an attractive seaside port and shipbuilding centre with a fair-sized population. We passed few French civilians in the streets, but many German seamen and navy support personnel.

As we approached the harbour I noticed bomb craters and building debris in the streets, as well as shattered empty shells of buildings. We passed an anti-aircraft gun emplacement surrounded by remnants of a concrete wall and sandbags. It astounded me to learn that Allied bombers had wreaked this devastation on Saint-Nazaire, probably in their attempts to destroy the U-boat pens and their base. The U-boat pens themselves were quite impressive, built like a row of concrete caves at the edge of the harbour. They looked absolutely massive, with a nine-metre-thick roof that looked strong enough to withstand any amount of bombing.

After the tour through Saint-Nazaire we continued on to our destination, the small coastal town of Le Croisic, about twenty kilometres farther up the coast. The military complex was just a collection of row houses around a small plaza near the outskirts of the town. My room was a pleasant surprise, as it was far better than any of my previous quarters.

The next morning we four assembled in the mess hall for a briefing. Our senior officer introduced himself and explained the purpose of our being there, which was to form part of a new battalion that was being assembled and trained. His speech was strictly down to business. At the end we were reminded of the army's prohibition against fraternizing with the locals. "Consider yourselves guests in this country." He warned us about the Maquis (the French underground resistance fighters) and local civilians in general. "To the French girls in the cabarets, you soldiers are just an opportunity to fleece you out of your money or your goods. Venereal diseases are rife among the prostitutes. If any of you catch one, you will be useless to the army and will be punished severely."

I was to command one platoon of the new company. It would take about two months to train the men to become an effective force. Fine by me, as every day spent in the relative peace and quiet of France was another day not spent at the Eastern Front—a bonus.

Considerable organizational effort was required to turn a bunch of mostly new soldiers into cohesive fighting units. First they had to be trained in what was expected of them as a platoon, then three platoons had to be taught to operate as a company. Three companies then made up a battalion. The battalion would have to function as an integral part of an infantry division at the front. Most of the training dealt with practical tactics for an infantry company in the field. Most of my own training emphasized how orders were to be communicated between myself and the other platoon leaders, and the battalion commander.

For me things were decidedly different from any of my previous military service. As an officer I had a private room in one of the buildings, and was assigned a *Bursche* (batman), who served my meals, cleaned my uniform and boots, and generally took care of housekeeping duties for me. At first it felt awkward that someone else was taking care of my domestic obligations, but I eventually allowed myself to feel pleased at having what amounted to a personal butler. Another benefit of being an officer was that I could come and go as I pleased, without asking anyone's permission. I could eat in the officers' mess, which was more lavishly appointed than the dining hall for the enlisted men. The food was the same, but there were elegant glasses, china, and cutlery on the tables, which were covered with clean, white tablecloths. I could also have meals brought to me in my room if I wanted. Outstanding luxury.

There were few opportunities to have fun on our off-duty hours, as there had been in Brandenburg. I did not feel like frequenting the local bistros. It was very much a French town, and we were looked upon as interlopers. Other than sightseeing in the village and the occasional swim in the ocean, there was not much else to do. I felt more or less stranded on the base, still a prisoner of the *Wehrmacht*. My status as an officer did nothing to change that reality, it was just dressed in finer accoutrements.

Evenings were mainly devoted to reading military manuals on the system of command or about infantry support equipment. A few officers sometimes met in the mess hall after supper to share some conversation or play cards. Those of us who knew how to play skat taught the other men. After a while we played for money, usually a penny a point. Playing cards was better than reading military weapons manuals every night. I believe many of the enlisted men sometimes went downtown to patronize the cabarets.

Spending time in the officers' mess I noticed a subtle but unmistakable contempt among the majority of the senior officers for our Nazi government. Although there were never any blatant expressions of dissent, there were unmistakable undertones of disdain in the manner in which they spoke of the country's leaders. There was often implied and sometimes unambiguous disapproval of our Führer's military decisions. Hitler's self-appointed status as Supreme Commander was evidently not popular with the members of the army's high command.

The mood among the officers at Le Croisic was different in a fundamental way from what it had been among the officers who had trained us at the Potsdam Military Academy; it lacked the inspirational confidence that had been evident in Potsdam. The costly siege of Leningrad, the failure before Moscow, and especially the disaster at Stalingrad had shaken everyone's faith in an eventual German victory. No one in the officers' mess expressed any optimism about the conduct of the war. However, long military tradition demanded absolute loyalty to our nation and dictated obedience to our country's leaders. That included me.

After weeks of boring routine one of the other officers had arranged for a group to go into Saint-Nazaire for an evening on the town and asked if I wanted to go. I figured any opportunity for some entertainment was a good one. They had somehow commandeered a car. Four of us set off on our adventure. In Saint-Nazaire we rendezvoused with a guide who would take us to the cabaret. He turned out to be a German who had been living in France for years. He looked older than the rest of us, and sported a goatee-style beard. When he squeezed into the back seat beside me he smelled disagreeably of cheap cologne. But even that could not completely mask the other smells emanating from his body—tobacco, sweat, and alcohol. I had serious reservations about his trustworthiness. He directed us to what he called "the best cabaret in town."

A voice from the front seat asked if there were any women in this place.

"The only women you'll meet in this town are professionals, if that's your objective, soldier."

"Hey, we just want to have some fun," replied the voice.

"You young chaps tend to let your willie do your thinking," he said. "Around here that can be bad for you." He intimated that the Maquis were active in the city. "Never come into town alone," he said, "and do not sleep in town overnight. Keep your wits about you. I found a German sailor lying in the gutter one morning, knifed and robbed."

He was serious! So much for a good time. Apparently just getting drunk could get you killed in this town. Undeterred, we wanted to have a few drinks and see some entertainment.

It was dark when we eventually pulled up in front of a pub. As we piled out of the car I noticed that all the lights were out in the street, which I assumed was for fear of air raids.

"Gentlemen, fraternizing with civilians is forbidden by the army," said our guide, with a sarcastic tone in his voice. Human nature being what it is, the army's standing order was mostly interpreted loosely, and compliance was very much dependent upon circumstances. Anyway, it was only relevant if we were caught.

He further warned us that, "The local Frenchmen do not like to cater to foreigners, especially not Germans. They call us *Bosche*. So don't get rowdy. We don't want to attract the military police."

Still undeterred, we went into "the best cabaret in town." There were about five dozen patrons inside, which just about filled the place. Some of them were German sailors who ignored us. The French patrons also ignored us. We found an empty table and tried to get the waiter's attention, but he did not acknowledge our presence. When he finally came to our table he acted as if he spoke no German. Speaking French, our guide ordered a bottle of wine and some beers.

Two ladies approached the table and asked if we wanted some company. They spoke a few words of broken German, but conversation was not why they were there. The only words said distinctly in German, and which they both said over and over again, were, "buy me a Schnapps." One of them edged her way between the chairs and sat on my lap. Up close she was so tough looking she scared me half to death. Her frilly blouse was only loosely tied and she bent toward me to reveal her ample bosom. I did not want to appear aloof or uncongenial, but I felt decidedly uncomfortable. Perhaps she had a strategy: the only way to get her off me was to buy her a Schnapps.

Then, salvation. One of our guys signalled the waiter to come over and ordered her a Schnapps. She got off my lap, bent over in front of me and said something which was surely sarcastic, and then sat on my saviour's lap, which he seemed to relish. The waiter brought her a shot of some clear liquor. Apparently our smelly guide's assessment of my drinking buddy's thinking had been correct.

Then a three-man band started up, with a female singer. After a few more rounds of drinks and stilted, stupid attempts at communicating over the noise with our female company, I felt disgruntled dissatisfaction at being there. I repeatedly threw awkward glances around the room, feeling like I had to keep on my guard. The majority eventually agreed that the "best cabaret in town" was just too unfriendly a place, despite the entertainment and the ladies' attempts at winning our hearts. So we left, dragging our would-be Romeo out the door with us.

When we left it was pitch-black outside. During the short walk back to our car and the ride through the dark streets, I was more wary than I had ever been on any previous night at the front.

It crossed my mind that life for the average German soldier in occupied France would be confined to the least attractive parts of society. Perhaps some of the men, like our Romeo, could find opportunities for fun and excitement anywhere, but I felt thoroughly out of place. It was particularly disconcerting to encounter a situation where the proprietors, employees, and other patrons of a public establishment were so inhospitable. Afterwards, when others went on excursions into Saint-Nazaire and asked me to go, I always declined.

I wished it would have been possible for Gisela to visit me in Le Croisic. The town was quite pretty and the ocean gave it a romantic air. However, it was occupied France during wartime, so there was no way she would be allowed to take time off from her work to come here. I had written to her shortly after arriving, describing the trip, the town itself, and the sea. I wrote every week, mainly to tell her I missed her. And I did miss her terribly.

Gisela's letters contained nothing newsworthy or anything of special significance, just accountings of everyday events back home. The affable tone of her letters confirmed to me that life had not become dangerous for Brandenburg's citizens. I was very pleased that she took the time to write to me, as her letters kept my dreams alive that we would someday be able to build a normal life together.

One day in April 1943, I heard the unmistakable drone of heavy bombers coming from the direction of Saint-Nazaire. We watched more than a hundred four-engine bombers attack what I assumed was the harbour in Saint-Nazaire. Even though we were standing too far away to actually see the bombs exploding on the ground, we could feel the tremors under our feet from the impacts and heard the thunderous explosions for what must have been fifteen minutes. Smoke rose up over the city. The bombers made a wide turn and flew toward us after they dropped their bombs, slowly coming closer and closer.

Suddenly one of the bombers burst into flames and dived into the sea. The much smaller shapes of German Messerschmitt fighter planes could be seen attacking the bombers. I had not seen them approach. More bombers were hit as the aerial battle turned into a maelstrom of noisy action that came closer and closer until it was almost overhead. There were trails of small white puffs of smoke across the sky produced by the gunfire. When a bomber was hit the burning fuel left a thick trail of dark smoke. One bomber exploded with a huge blast when it hit the ground. The fighters looked like small, nimble sparrows, diving and circling around the big clumsy blackbirds that were the bombers. We cheered every time a bomber was hit and plunged from the sky.

I estimated that the Messerschmitts shot down fourteen bombers while we watched. I counted the German fighters at seven or eight, which was apparently not enough to shoot down more bombers. I saw no fighter planes shot down. I was completely engrossed in that display of air power. The entire air battle probably lasted less than five minutes.

Then the distinct whine of a crippled airplane could be distinguished over the general drone of all the other airplanes. A bomber was heading straight in our direction, descending rapidly, black smoke streaming from one of its wings. As the bomber came closer I started looking for shelter. It hit the ground in a field about two hundred metres from where we were standing, making a hard landing on its belly, throwing up a cloud of dust and smoke as it skidded to a stop. We ran over to investigate and to see if there were survivors. I had not seen anyone bail out of the bomber; in fact, I had not seen any parachutes appear from the stricken airplanes.

The wreck was an American B-17 four-engine bomber. Pieces of wreckage were strewn about. I had never seen a bomber close up before, and marvelled that such a huge and heavy piece of machinery could get off the ground and fly, especially with a heavy load of bombs. The crew compartment at the front had been crushed partway into the ground, and all the windows had been smashed. There was a gaping fissure in the side of the fuselage, just in front of the wing. One of the wheels had been bent backwards by the impact on the bottom of the wing. The wheel alone was almost as tall as I was.

The interior was full of equipment, probably radio and navigation instruments. Metal boxes were strewn about and wires hung all over the place. The centre section had metal racks attached from floor to ceiling. A huge machine gun was sticking awkwardly out of the open window in the side. There was a large opening in the floor. The interior smelled strongly of oil, gasoline, smoke, burnt metal, and the musty smell of freshly ploughed earth.

To our surprise, we counted ten dead bodies inside the wreckage, all black American airmen. The shock of the impact had probably killed them. Curiously, none of them was wearing parachutes, which may explain why no one had bailed out, even though they would have had time before the plane struck the ground. Another pile of junk had joined the wreckage of war, and another group of young men would not be returning home.

After that episode Allied bombers attacked Saint-Nazaire many more times, each time dropping tons of bombs on the U-boat pens and on the city. Eventually they destroyed the entire city. The Allied bombers destroyed the homes of many thousands of French civilians, their own allies. The heavily reinforced U-boat pens suffered hardly any damage and continued to operate throughout the German occupation of France. Perhaps they destroyed the city to deny the German occupation troops the easy use of the city.

After that demonstration of air power was over I wondered what might be in store for the German people if the Allied air forces achieved air superiority in the skies over Germany. The dwindling strength of the *Luftwaffe* would eventually permit bombers to rain destruction on German cities indiscriminately. I hoped that for the millions of civilians living in the cities such a horrible contemplation would never become reality. Bombing cities full of civilians struck me as a particularly malicious way to wage war. By now the Allied leaders should have learned it was also an ineffectual military strategy that would do nothing to hasten the end of the war. Hitler had ordered the bombing of London and other cities in England, and that such bombing had probably hardened the resolve of the English people to continue the fight. There was no doubt in my mind about the kind of ruthless and maniacal tyrant Hitler was, but surely the Allies knew better. So I thought in the spring of 1943.

By May the time of our departure for the Eastern Front was rapidly drawing near. I wished I could see Gisela before being sent to Russia. I had already used up my two weeks' vacation in Michelau just this past Christmas, so I would not be permitted to take any more time this year. Then I remembered the page-gluing incident in Potsdam.

I retrieved my *Soldbuch* and inspected the last page. It had been pasted to the last regular page of that chronicle of my military career, and contained the note recording my last holiday. There was no stamp to indicate it was attached to any other page. The glue line was relatively thin. Perhaps there was an opportunity here? If I removed the last page, the army might not be able to track down my last holiday. I knew if they caught me I would be punished, but I had already served three-and-half years of what was supposed to have been only a two-year stint in the army, so why not try to take advantage of administrative bungling on their part? I decided that the prospect of seeing Gisela again was worth the gamble.

I took a razor and carefully slit the back of the added page along the glue line and removed it from the book. Most of the glue came off with the extra page. I carefully scraped the last page with the razor until it looked just like it had before the extra page had been glued to it. Now there was no evidence to incriminate me.

Armed with that newly constituted documentation of my steadfast devotion to duty, I marched off to the administration office. When the adjutant asked what he could do for me, I informed him that I was due a holiday after almost seventeen months of continuous service in the army. I tried to display the polite demeanour of a righteous soldier doing his duty.

He took my *Soldbuch*, told me to wait, and disappeared into the next room. I became tense. Perhaps the army kept a duplicate record of my service and the adjutant would discover my ruse? After about ten nerve-wracking minutes the adjutant returned.

"Right you are, *Herr Leutnant*. The army owes you a vacation. You have two weeks as soon as I can arrange it."

Yes! Outwardly I tried to appear nonplussed, but inside I was elated.

"Where would you like to go?" he asked.

"To Brandenburg."

"I'll see to it that the trip is arranged."

"Many thanks." I sauntered out of the room feeling like I had just won the jackpot. The following day my *Soldbuch* was returned to me along with round-trip tickets to Brandenburg. I was scheduled to leave in four days. Incredibly, another page had again been glued to the last page of my *Soldbuch*, but this time it was stamped across the edge so that it could not be removed. No matter, I had purloined two extra weeks' vacation from the army. As soon as I got back to my room I wrote to Gisela to tell her I was coming to see her.

The ocean near my seaside village made me think it might be nice to bring Gisela something from France, so I went to a curio shop that had probably sold a lot of souvenirs to carefree tourists before the war. Now the tourists were mainly German occupation troops. A seashell with "Le Croisic" carved into it was just the thing, along with a post-card. I had no idea what the French franc was worth, so I handed the sales clerk ten German Reichsmark and politely waited for my change, which was a few French coins. With my souvenirs in hand I went back to my barracks to count the days until my departure.

When finally on my way to Brandenburg I was so looking forward to seeing my sweetheart again. I arrived at the Brandenburg train station late in the afternoon. Figuring Gisela would shortly be getting off work, I headed for her department store. I must have floated across the last few blocks to Kaufhaus Riedel.

When Gisela stepped out of the door my heart leapt for joy. I was almost in tears as we hugged each other. Walking her home I felt the loneliness of garrison life fall away, replaced by a wonderful feeling of togetherness. When we arrived at the apartment I even gave Gisela's mother a big hug and kiss on the cheek. She seemed genuinely pleased to see me. Gisela had not received my letter from Le Croisic, so my arrival in Brandenburg was a big surprise. I relished telling Gisela about altering my *Soldbuch* to allow me that extra holiday.

She said, "Good for you, the army owes you. I just hope you don't get caught."

"What are they going to do to me if they do catch me, send me to Russia?"

I spent ten wonderful days with Gisela. Rather than stay at the garrison, I slept on the couch in the living room of the apartment. The seashell was put on the side table in the living room. Her mother appeared quite taken with that little memento, and mentioned it was very thoughtful of me to bring something back for her from faraway France.

Both Gisela and her mother worked during the days until 5 p.m., so I had to content myself with doing chores around the apartment while they were away. In the afternoon I would bring up potatoes from the cellar for our evening meal. Sometimes I went sightseeing in town or to buy little things for them or the apartment. Some days I just lounged in the sunshine in the backyard, often talking to the neighbours. The landlord and his wife were an older retired couple. They were especially friendly and talkative. They called me *Unser Leutnant* (our lieutenant) and spent hours telling stories about friends or relatives I did not know, or relaying the latest gossip about people in the neighbourhood that I also did not know.

Most evenings Gisela and I went out to a café, or to a movie, or just window shopping. As before, we would go to the Café Graf or some other restaurant and order cups of that ubiquitous elixir made from roasted barley. We went for long walks in the nearby parks or along the Havel River, where we sometimes sat for hours watching the swans. The spring flowers in the many public gardens, flower beds, and planter boxes made the city look cheerful and beautiful. A friend of Gisela's owned a small box camera, which she lent us for the day. As film was a scarce luxury, it took us a while to find some in a department store. We took a few pictures on one of our walks along the Havel, not far from

Brandenburg

Gisela's home. The pictures turned out to be among the very rare and precious souvenirs we have of those joyful days of courtship.

As my two weeks of vacation were coming to an end, Gisela and I talked about how lucky I had been to avoid being sent back to Russia up until now. "I just hope your good luck does not run out."

"What will be will be," I replied, trying to sound unconcerned. What could anyone say anyway? I had to obey orders, no matter how we felt about it.

I asked Gisela if I could have a picture of her to carry with me while I was away at the front. She retrieved a picture of her in a pretty print dress and handed it to me.

"It's not the best," she said, with a hint of demure humility in her voice. I was bemused that such a pretty woman could have any modesty about her appearance.

"It will be a good luck charm," I heard myself say with more emotion than I had expected of myself.

At the train station I held her tight and kissed her gently. When I let her go my arms ached as if I had torn myself away. From my seat at the coach window, I watched her waving as the train pulled out of the station. I thought my heart would break as she gradually faded into the distance. Once again I felt anger and frustration at being separated from the love of my life.

When I arrived at the garrison in Le Croisic preparations were already underway for our departure to the Eastern Front, after two months of assembling and training the battalion. It was near the end of May 1943. As with every previous year, the schools had produced another crop of graduates to manhood, many of whom were now members of our battalion and who would be forced to grow old all too soon.

I had come to know personally each of the men I would command during our training. They were all too young. A few of them had already served some time in the army before joining our battalion, although I suspected most were new recruits who had only recently completed their military training. As far as I knew, none of the privates or corporals had yet seen combat.

The training sessions at the garrison in Le Croisic, as well as the time we spent together getting to know each other, were designed to make sure we would function well as a cohesive fighting unit. By the time we left for Russia a strong bond had been forged between them. They now considered themselves more than just a group of fellow soldiers; they were close friends, brothers in arms.

The entire battalion was assembled in the plaza in Le Croisic and marched off to the train station at Saint-Nazaire. In addition to the three regular infantry companies in our battalion, there were field kitchens, supply staff, an office and communications unit, and a collection of other assorted support personnel. Each company also had medics, ordnance handlers, wagon masters, a blacksmith, a shoemaker, a tailor, and a chaplain.

No matter what our assigned role was, we all boarded the train with the same hope—to survive the Russian front.

13 All Quiet on the Eastern Front

ALL TOO SOON THE ENTIRE BATTALION, including my infantry company, was on a train heading for the front in Russia. It was the beginning of June 1943. We had boarded regular passenger coaches in a long passenger train. Our weapons were put into freight cars on the train. I did not see any heavy weapons or horses on the train. We rode east for days, traversing France, then Germany, then Poland, and then the Russian Ukraine. The most memorable thing about that trip was that the countryside seemed unrelentingly monotonous. I was not in a sight-seeing mood anyway, feeling despair at having to return to the Eastern Front. I thought of Gisela. It felt as if a part of my being were being drained away with every kilometre that carried me deeper into an abyss from which I might never return. Night made it worse, as I pictured the train disappearing forever into a huge black void.

There must have been at least a thousand soldiers on the train. We travelled day and night, stopping frequently to feed the engine and the troops. The mood on the train was sombre, and became downright op-pressive as we entered Russia. Anxiety rode with us on that train. The news from Russia had not been encouraging. The state media repeat-edly continued using the euphemisms "front straightening" or "front cleansing" to portray the Russian offensives of the past winter that had pushed our armies westward. There was nothing to give me any hope that we might undergo a reversal of fortune. It was impossible for the media to hide the ever-increasing number of casualties at the Russian front. Too many people had lost sons, husbands, fathers, or brothers in Russia, or had them return home maimed for life. The devastating losses suffered at Stalingrad had just been the beginning of a series of disasters. Government propagandists tried their best to make the Ger-man people think the war was going well and that it would be just a matter of time before Russia collapsed; but I knew different, and prob-ably most of the men with me did, too—this was a war Germany could not win.

With America's participation in the war I knew things were going to become rapidly worse for Germany. America's industrial might would increasingly be brought to bear on Russia's side. I had no delusions that we were in for a very hard time on the Eastern Front. Unless they were very lucky, like the ones who were sent back for officer school, the only men that returned from the Eastern Front were casualties. I had already been through officer school, so the other alternative was not appealing. I fervently hoped that the good fortune that had accompanied me so far would not desert me.

After spending at least a week on the train we finally stopped in a small town in the middle of rolling countryside. The landscape was mainly vast wheat fields, hayfields, and meadows scattered about, occasionally separated by roads, gullies, and thin woodlots along shallow stream valleys. Some of the pastures looked like scrub wilderness.

We disembarked about mid-morning, and the tiny station quickly became a disorganized madhouse. There did not seem to be anyone in charge. Finally a whistle blew, and someone shouted orders to collect our weapons and gear from the freight cars near the front of the train and then assemble in the street that ran past the front of the station. A few army vehicles were parked in the street and there were other German troops about, as well as what I assumed were Russian civilians. I remembered the last time I had arrived in Russia, on my way to the siege at Leningrad, when it had been bitterly cold. This time at least the weather was pleasant. As I stood waiting in formation, a small group of officers gathered on the platform.

"Gentlemen, welcome to Russia!" a voice boomed. "You are here to help defeat the godless Russians. We are the righteous defenders of Christian values. The Bolsheviks and their Jewish supporters are plotting the takeover of the world. We courageous Christian soldiers must prevent that terrible fate. God is with us. He will guide our hands to vanquish the Russian menace. We expect every man to do his sacred duty." After shouting out his bombastic speech, the major turned and left with his entourage.

I just stood there bewildered. I had not experienced any of that fanatical rhetoric during the Battle for France, or any other previous military assignment, not even the first time I was sent to Russia, last year. That speech may have been dreamed up by someone far removed from the reality of the fighting men's lives, as an attempt to foster what should have been righteous indignation against the Russian people. Instead, it had the effect of making me feel like I was on the way to be sacrificed at a slaughterhouse. Unlike the campaign in France, which had felt like we were off to an international soccer match, this had the very disturbing feel of a religious crusade. I wondered if the pompous-sounding ass who had made the welcoming speech would come with us to the front.

A few horse-drawn supply wagons joined the assembly. We were issued food rations for our packs and then marched down the street of the town and out into the countryside, eastward. So much for formalities.

We marched for hours along dirt roads, the dust thrown up by our boots and the wagon wheels eventually covering everyone in a fine, grey film. The dust mixed with the sweat from my brow to cake onto my face and neck. My uniform, gear, and weapons, which had been spotlessly clean when we left Le Croisic, became covered in dirt. I remembered the dismal march last spring along these same types of roads. At least it was not raining, and it had not rained recently, so we did not have to slog through mud. In spite of the dust, this march was a walk in the park compared to that ordeal last year.

My initial interest in my surroundings waned as the monotony of the landscape overtook my senses. Once again I was struck by the vast-ness of this land. The almost flat horizon in all directions made it look absolutely endless. We passed through a village that was nothing more than a cluster of farmhouses at a crossroads. The villagers watched us march by with vacant expressions, devoid of even a hint of emotion. Once again I was struck by the feeling that we had just passed backwards in time, into a medieval world that was completely alien to what we had left behind in the rest of Europe.

After marching for hours we arrived late that afternoon at what I assumed was the front. The first signs of military activity were about two dozen supply wagons and their horses, along with a field kitchen, parked at the side of a dirt road at the outskirts of a village. We took the opportunity to shake the dust out of our clothes and wash off some of the grime at the water troughs. The field kitchen was a welcome sight.

Another kilometre or so and we reached the battalion headquarters, which consisted of a medical unit tent, a parked command truck, and a motorcycle. An officer and staff emerged from a trench in the ground. It was a very humble assembly indeed; nothing that would have been conspicuous to the enemy. The tents were set up beside the road that separated the post from a wheat field. The whole unit could probably be moved in a matter of minutes.

We were met by the *Hauptmann* (captain) in charge of that sector, who introduced himself to me and our *Oberleutnant* (first lieutenant) the company's commanding officer. He was a tall man, probably in his late twenties, with a demeanour suggesting he was not a professional soldier, since he lacked that brusque haughtiness that characterized many of the career officers I had met before. He seemed like a regular fellow who probably disliked being here as much as any of us.

The captain showed me and the other platoon commanders exactly where our defensive positions were to be set up. Each platoon was assigned to man a different piece of ground along a rough line facing east. The captain suggested we make a secure place to spend the night, as there was always the possibility of an enemy attack any morning, even though there had not been any fighting for weeks.

Looking around, I kept expecting to see a neatly organized series of trenches and bunkers in well-established defensive sites nearest the enemy, with artillery stationed farther back, similar to the situation that had existed last year during my *Sitzkrieg* days east of Orel. But all I could see was a huge meadow stretching off toward the east, north, and south, across a gently rolling landscape interspersed with lines of small trees and bushes, and the one road. Toward the south I could see our soldiers occupying the slope of a broad, shallow valley. There were no bunkers, no trenches, no coils or fences of barbed wire, no sandbagged strongpoints—just a line of foxholes with infantry sitting about in small groups. There were no artillery units, no motor vehicles, no wagons, and no horses.

There were no towns or villages anywhere nearby. What a desolate place for men to be fighting over. Most significantly, there were no signs of enemy soldiers anywhere, not even far in the distance. There did not appear to be any purposeful activity going on, like digging bunkers or filling sandbags. I am not sure what I had expected of the front, but it did not feel the same as what I remembered of front-line conditions at Orel last year.

"Where are the enemy?" I asked the captain.

He pointed toward the northeast. "They must be nearby," he said, "but I'm not sure where. They may be on the other side of that ridge you can see over there in the distance. We've seen no Russians at all for days. Headquarters reported some enemy movement farther east during the past week, but there's been no reliable information lately."

"I don't suppose the Russians broadcast news reports about where they are all the time?" I asked, and waited for his reaction.

He turned and looked at me. "No," he said with just a hint of a smile on his face. That subtle reaction to my feeble attempt at humour somehow bolstered my confidence in his leadership.

"Where are we?" I asked.

"In Russia," he answered without hesitation. Then in response to my blank reaction he added, "In the Ukraine, north of Charkov, if that means anything to you. As far as I know, the Donets River is somewhere over there," pointing toward the eastern horizon.

That night we took up our positions on the Eastern Front. The open ground would be our accommodations for the night. I instructed my men to dig foxholes large enough to provide cover in the event of a dawn attack. The three machine guns from my platoon were set up about fifty metres apart. The captain did not seem concerned about the possibility of a nighttime attack; but, as per our training, we posted two pairs of sentries to take turns keeping watch.

I had not slept in the open for over a year, not since the march to Orel. I lined my little excavated hole in the ground with grass, and bedded down for the night, my rifle and my automatic right beside me. Looking up at the stars, I felt small, exposed, and very much alone. I had disturbing visions of enemy soldiers crawling silently through the grass to slit our throats while we slept. Having spent most of the day marching, I was very tired and soon fell asleep. My last thoughts were of Gisela.

I awoke before dawn, stiff and sore. That hole was extremely unpleasant in spite of my efforts to make it comfortable, so I could not get back to sleep. The company awoke with the sunrise. A squad was sent back to the field kitchen for our food rations. We milled about for most of the morning.

Early in the afternoon I was summoned by the captain. "I want you to capture some Russian prisoners," he said, matter-of-factly.

The captain did not explain why they needed prisoners. Perhaps our commanders knew no more than I did about enemy activity. I guess they figured the simplest method of trying to find out what was going on was to capture some enemy soldiers and ask them. It seemed odd to me that one army could completely lose sight of the other. Was Russia so huge that entire armies could just get lost?

I had never done that before, so I asked how I was supposed to get those prisoners.

"Take two men with you and search until you find an undefended outpost, or a patrol, or whatever, and surprise them. You might find them over that way," he said, pointing northeast. "You'll think of something along the way.

"The Russians like to hide themselves in woods and holes, so be careful," he added. Once again I detected a subtle grin on his face.

"That's good to know," I said under my breath as I saluted to go.

As simple as that sounded, I guessed it was up to us to figure out how to keep from getting shot if we ran into enemy troops during our mission.

So I took two men with me and headed out across what should theoretically have been the no-man's land between the lines. After almost an hour we still had not seen any Russians. We occasionally stopped to listen for anything out of the ordinary. Every break in the ground might conceal enemy patrols that could shoot us before we knew they were there. The captain had mentioned that the Russians were probably on the other side of the ridge we had seen from our own positions, so I became very wary as we approached it. We were now at least two kilometres away from where we had started.

When we reached the ridge it turned out to be a long low hill with gently sloping sides. We turned southeastward, staying just below the crest. We walked through a field of grain that in some places came up to my waist. It would be difficult for us to avoid stumbling into an ambush. The sun was already in the west, and I remembered the lesson in Potsdam about being conspicuously silhouetted against the lighter background of field and sky, since the enemy would presumably be facing the setting sun from positions farther east. Hopefully there was no one out there to spot us. We had to rely on some good luck.

We heard nothing but the sighing of the wind and the continuous background racket of insects and birds. After cautiously coming over the crest of the hill we spied a large number of soldiers marching along a road in close formation about a kilometre away—hundreds and hundreds of Russians. They were infantry only, with a few on horseback, but without supply wagons, motor vehicles, or cannons. I oriented myself with my compass; they were heading north. We watched them for a few minutes from our vantage point near the top of the ridge, looked around carefully to make sure there were no other signs of the enemy nearby, and then started walking farther eastward. I assumed that all the enemy troops in this sector had left with that distant column; however, there might be a slim chance of finding some stragglers.

The soldier on my left suddenly ducked and motioned with his arm to get down. He silently pointed ahead. I listened carefully and heard voices, faint but distinctly Russian. I signalled to stay low, to spread out, and cautiously crawled ahead on my hands and knees toward the place where the voices came from. I got a whiff of the distinctive and unpleasant smell of Russian tobacco. Peering through the tall grass, I saw two Russian soldiers lying on the ground in a tiny clearing they had made by flattening the grain. The two were older men, probably in their forties, dirty and rough-looking, especially compared to good-looking boy scouts like us. Perhaps they were members of a rear guard, assigned to stay behind the main body of soldiers that we had seen withdrawing northward, or . . . perhaps not? My impression was that they were deserters. They made no attempt to follow the departing columns. Their heads were resting on their bedrolls and their rifles lay on the ground beside them.

We watched quietly for a few more minutes to make sure there were no other troops nearby. When I was sure that the two were alone I gave the signal. We leaped forward and yelled at them to raise their hands! They immediately jumped up, looking more surprised than scared. Their rifles stayed on the ground. We took them prisoner and marched them back to the battalion command post.

By the time we got back it was evening. A *Kübelwagen* (Volkswagen jeep) was parked at the side of the road. The captain was there, along with his adjutant and two other soldiers I did not recognize.

The captain actually seemed surprised to see us. He congratulated me on my ingenuity at capturing the two Russians, saying something about my being a "fine hunter." He asked where we found them and if there were other signs of the enemy. I reported the column of troops we had seen marching away northward. The adjutant retrieved a map from the *Kübelwagen* and spread it out on the hood. The captain asked me to show them where we had seen the column of Russians. It was a very poor map, looking more like a schoolboy's drawing than the military maps I had been trained to read at Officer School. I tried in vain to get my bearings.

"That depends on where we are on this map," I replied.

The adjutant pointed out landmarks and where he thought our location was. "This way is north, and that is about a kilometre," he said, forming a gap between his finger and thumb. I did my best to figure out where it was we had found the two prisoners, where I thought the Russian column was, and which direction they were heading. The major made some notes in a small handbook. He then offered each of the Russians a cigarette, which they accepted. One of the other soldiers present spoke Russian and translated the officers' questions to the two prisoners. The officers wanted to know where they were from, which unit they belonged to, if there were more Russian forces nearby, if they had seen any artillery or armoured units, which direction they had been heading, what their last orders had been, and so on. The interrogation appeared to be nothing more than a casual conversation about the day's events. The prisoners answered the questions without any attempt to be evasive, and the officers did not threaten or try to harm the prisoners. I thought it strange at the time that those two old Russian soldiers seemed completely at ease and showed no signs of fear or even discomfort with their situation as prisoners of war. Perhaps they were not completely content with life as soldiers in Stalin's army.

It probably would have made no difference anyway. From the look of those two I was convinced they did not know anything of importance. If I had been captured by the enemy I would not have known anything of importance either, and I was an officer. All I knew was that I was in command of the 1st Platoon, 3rd Company, Füselier Battalion 384. I had no idea which regiment, let alone division or army, we were part of. Soldiers were intentionally told as little as possible about the big picture so that they could not disclose anything of use to the enemy in the event they were captured and interrogated.

The officer asked if we could think of anything else. One of my men shook his head, the other just kept a blank expression on his face. The captain may have sensed my waning interest, as he waved his hand toward me in what passed for a salute and said, "That will be all, *Herr Leutnant*." I promptly saluted, and the three of us left. I do not know what happened to the two Russians after that. I assumed they would be no worse off as prisoners of the German army than they had been as members of the Russian army.

It was a revelation that my new status as an officer did not seem to count for much at the front. The task of capturing Russian stragglers could just as easily have been assigned to a corporal. It surely did not require any knowledge of military strategy or tactics such as I had learned during my two months of rigorous training and study in Potsdam. Apparently I was just another soldier out here in the wilds of Russia. My lieutenant's stripes carried no extra privileges whatsoever. All it meant was that I was now responsible for shepherding a platoon.

The next morning we were ordered to prepare to move out with the entire battalion. Presumably we were to try to catch up with the enemy. We picked up our gear, formed up, and moved out, heading generally northward. The other two companies were moving in the same direction. We were not occupying a stable line here at this sector of the Eastern Front, as there had been east of Orel last year. The situation was in a state of flux, as the captain put it.

We walked through monotonous countryside that appeared the same in all directions all the time—vast meadows and wheat fields, broken up by gullies or shallow valleys of rough pasture. We stopped in a village that was completely deserted to rest and eat some rations from our packs. After advancing slowly for hours we came upon a line of abandoned foxholes and short, shallow trenches. Perhaps they had been part of the Russian front line and the enemy had given ground as we approached? We continued for another hour or two. At evening we stopped and had our daily hot meal.

Once again we dug our little foxholes just in case of an attack. Other than the men of my company, I could not see any other troops nearby, not even other German troops. It made me feel uneasy not knowing where the enemy were. They could have been anywhere; a whole battalion could have been hiding in any of the fields we had passed that day. The new piece of ground we occupied looked exactly the same as the piece we had abandoned earlier.

The following morning we again headed north, and dug in again that evening. That series of movements repeated itself a few times for at least a week. It all seemed confusing and pointless. Some days we did not move at all. There was no concerted effort to advance with any sense of urgency, certainly nothing that compared to the pace of our advance in France.

"*Herr Leutnant*, are we going around in circles?" one of the soldiers asked.

"Damned if I know. Why? Do you have to be somewhere? You got a date?"

"I'm sure we slept here before. The ground squirrels look happy to see me again."

We encountered no enemy action during those seemingly pointless marches. Our headquarters staff, horse-drawn supply wagons, medical unit, and other support units always travelled a few kilometres behind us, and always spent the night that same distance behind any line we established. Columns of German supply wagons occasionally passed by on roads, sometimes far in the distance.

So far nothing about my stint at the Eastern Front had been particularly dangerous. We kept waiting for some kind of action, but nothing memorable happened during that first week in Russia. We often spent most of a day just sitting around. The big event of the day was when the field kitchen wagon pulled up and we were fed. Even though there was no shooting going on, I could not dispel the tension. I tried to convince myself that Russia may not be as bad as I had originally expected. Perhaps the front had finally settled down after two years of furious fighting and the situation would allow us to remain more or less inactive, guarding the frontiers of Hitler's Reich without any more serious battles? Perhaps it would be "all quiet on the Eastern Front," to parody Eric Maria Remarque's famous book.

An infantry battalion of the German army in Russia at that time was comprised of three infantry companies, each of which consisted of three platoons, together with communications, kitchen, and medical squads, as well as groups of personnel responsible for keeping the front-line troops supplied and in fighting trim. Sometimes a battalion would be assigned specialty units, such as heavy mortars or other small infantry howitzers, heavy machine guns, flamethrowers, anti-tank weapons, or engineers, to assist with particular situations.

Our company was led by an *Oberleutnant*, and under ideal circumstances a lieutenant would have led each of the three platoons. A platoon was called a *Zug* in German. Each platoon had three squads, which were led by corporals. The other platoon of our company was led by a *Feldwebel*. I was in charge of the first platoon, which had a complement of about thirty men. Regardless of rank, each platoon leader was called a *Zugführer*. The whole battalion was led by a captain. He usually communicated orders to the company commander by wireless two-way radio, who in turn gave orders verbally to me and the sergeant in charge of the other platoon. If we were too far apart to receive orders directly, the *Oberleutnant* would send his messenger, who always accompanied him. We were in close contact every day, to coordinate our movements and to provide mutual protection for each platoon.

I had no idea what was happening with our entire sector of the front, not even where "here" was. My only link to the rest of the army was my company commander, who told me what to do to carry out the orders he was given. We soldiers of 3rd Company, Füselier Battalion 384, had no choice but to trust our lives to our unseen commanders.

Late one afternoon, about a week after arriving in Russia, the entire company was advancing along a dirt road. As usual when we did not know the enemy's whereabouts, each squad advanced in single file, spread out with each man separated by at least five metres along both sides of the road. I was not particularly wary, as we had not seen any signs of the enemy that day and were not expecting to be involved in any fighting. As we approached a crossroad in the distance two shots rang out. Everyone instantly dove for cover in the fields beside the road. The metre-tall wheat hid us as long as we stayed down.

The shots were either a sign we had blundered onto hidden enemy positions, or it was sniper fire. We could not see any enemy and could not make out exactly where the shots had come from. If it was snipers, they could still be watching through the telescopic sights on their rifles for anyone foolish enough to expose any part of his body. A sniper armed with a telescope could easily hit a man from a distance of about a kilometre away, which was probably three times the range a rifle without a scope could achieve with any accuracy.

No more shots were fired, from anywhere. I ordered two teams to crawl forward in two wide arcs in the general direction from which the shots came to try to discover and hopefully eliminate the snipers. There was no point in risking anyone else's life by trying to attack snipers in concealed spots. For over an hour everyone stayed low. Then I spotted the two teams walking back toward us. The snipers must have left.

At first I thought we had all escaped intact, but then one of the men from the second platoon came running over to tell me the *Oberleutnant* had been hit.

I followed him to the depression near the side of the road where the company commander was being attended by our medic. He was lying face down, his trouser legs had been cut away, and there were blood-soaked bandages wrapped around his legs near the top of the thighs. There was a lot of blood on his uniform trousers and on the ground beneath him. He drifted in and out of consciousness as the medic finished dressing the bullet holes. I ordered two men to make a stretcher and carry him back to battalion headquarters. When they placed him onto the stretcher it was obvious that at least one of his thigh bones was broken.

The Russian snipers had picked out the company leader in their telescopic sights, as he was the only one hit. He had been near the lead at the time. It was not possible to have heard the shots and re-acted fast enough before getting hit, because rifle bullets travel faster than the speed of sound. It was a nasty surprise that the enemy were able to identify the company leader among the troops moving toward them. That did not bode well for infantry leadership at the Eastern Front.

As I watched the stretcher detail lift and carry the *Oberleutnant* back, the soldier beside me said, "You're now in command, *Herr Leutnant*."

"Yes," I replied. That was a fact.

So, by the middle of June 1943, our company was led by me, a lieu-tenant. I was also still responsible for commanding the 1st Platoon. Not much changed in a practical and meaningful way after I assumed com-mand of the entire company. The main difference was that I now had to direct and coordinate the movements of all three platoons, rather than just one. I was now responsible for the lives of some ninety men, rather than the thirty I had commanded until then. Those extra duties and responsibilities were not accompanied by any extra benefits or rewards. There were no crystal glasses or linen tablecloths here. I shared exactly the same conditions as the rest of the men in my company. Like every-thing else about army life, the circumstances of my command were not of my choosing.

As leader of an infantry platoon in the German army, you were expected to be in front when attacking and at the rear when retreating, making you the closest soldier to the enemy during actual battle situations. That may help explain why the casualty rate among officers was so high. It was considered essential to be closest to the enemy so that you would not order your men to do anything you would not do yourself. Your orders had to be competent and trustworthy.

Without really thinking about it, there was now a subtle difference between myself and the rest of the men of my company; an artificial gulf had been created between us. I could no longer think of myself as just one of the troops, as I had been in France, Narvik, and Orel. My men were no longer just my buddies. As their commanding officer, I was not only responsible for their safety, but was capable of exercising control over their existence. That distinction between enlisted men and officers is deliberately enforced by the army. As company commander I could be called upon to make tough decisions, which could cost any of them their life, so it was essential to maintain a measure of objectivity toward the men under my command. It would be much more difficult to order a close friend to risk his life than just another soldier from among the ranks. That necessary objectivity can come across as aloofness or arrogance on the part of an officer who does not have the personality to be a natural leader. In the army popularity can be irrelevant. What is important for an officer is to maintain the confidence and trust of his men.

I now received orders directly from the battalion commander and instructed my company in how to carry out those orders. Even receiving orders directly did nothing to increase my understanding of what was happening at the front. The entire series of movements by our company during that first week or so at the front seemed aimless.

A few days after taking command, my company was ordered to abandon our lines and move quickly to the nearby road, where we boarded some trucks. We were driven for at least an hour and got out near a complex of buildings at a crossroads—a collective farm. There were about a dozen very large buildings, partly surrounded by groves of trees and hedgerows along the edges of fields. We were to help another infantry company capture the buildings that they had already encircled. For some reason it was imperative we take the buildings before nightfall. Our orders were to shoot anything that moved in or around the buildings. Under no circumstances were any of the defenders to be allowed to escape. They must be partisans.

I ordered my machine-gunners to set up under cover in spots with a good view of the buildings. Communications were shouted back and forth, and across the wireless, trying to devise some way to overcome the defences. There was no cover between us and the central buildings. This had turned into a difficult and dangerous mission. I fervently hoped we would not be ordered to storm the buildings.

Machine guns suddenly fired from our perimeter and two men dashed toward the nearest building. They were not from my company. Automatic and rifle fire were immediately returned from the building. The two men beat a hasty retreat. After an hour of ineffective exchanges of small-arms fire a squad managed to reach the side of the nearest building. A grenade blew open the door. Several more were immediately thrown inside. The first soldier dove through the open doorway with his automatic firing, obscured by smoke and dust from the exploded grenades. Shots rang out from inside. He did not return, so he must have been shot dead. Damn stupid. Entering defended buildings through a doorway or window was suicidal.

Then a half-track carrier arrived, with a quadruple heavy machine-gun pod on the back. That weapon was capable of shooting down low-flying aircraft. It opened fire on the nearest building. The staccato roar sounded like an entire company shooting at once. A hole large enough for a man to pass through quickly appeared in the wall. Half a dozen grenades were thrown into the opening and the entire squad jumped inside. A few minutes later the sound of gunfire and grenade detonations ceased and the signal came that the building was clear. It was then used to provide covering fire for the attack on the next.

The half-track had run out of ammunition and withdrew, leaving us to attack the rest of the buildings without its firepower. Satchel charges were then used to blow a hole in the side of the next building, and the next. Some buildings turned out to be empty. If a building was doggedly defended the insides were set on fire. The outside of the buildings could not be set on fire, as the walls were made of some kind of masonry.

One building after another was captured until there was only one holdout, the largest, an imposing three-storey block with concrete walls and windows only on the third floor. It may have been a granary. I kept expecting the remaining defenders to surrender, as their situation was hopeless. They chose to fight to the death, even after the inside of the building was set on fire.

When we later searched what remained of the buildings I was astonished to find so few bodies among the shredded and charred remains. I did not count them, but it seemed like just a few dozen. During our assault I had assumed we were up against many hundreds of defenders.

Such a determined defence by so few was extraordinary, but understandable. Because of the savage terror campaign practised by the partisans, the fact that they always executed and often tortured prisoners, and especially because of their practice of trying to hide in civilian obscurity after committing brutal atrocities, we had standing orders not to take partisan prisoners. We had been briefed that any armed adversaries not in uniform were not legitimate soldiers and therefore not subject to the rules of conduct that governed the treatment of prisoners of war.

I never experienced partisan atrocities myself, but it was common knowledge that partisan gangs were savagely dangerous and completely ruthless. They were remnants of Russian troops that had been bypassed by advancing German forces. They operated behind the front by pillaging Ukrainian civilians and raiding poorly defended German storage depots, trains, supply caravans, and field hospitals. They often killed civilians, especially able-bodied men, during raids on Ukrainian villages, on the premise that anyone not with them was against them. Partisans were considered criminals and truly hated, as well as feared, by everyone in Ukrainian Russia at the time, soldiers and civilians alike. Their terror campaign made every part of this foreign land all the more hostile.

14 *In the Jaws of the Bear*

VERY EARLY ONE MORNING near the end of June 1943, we were awakened by the sound of approaching motor vehicles. We watched a German armoured unit drive by, heading northward. It included dozens of armoured cars and many hundreds of trucks and half-tracked armoured vehicles, some of them towing cannons and all of them full of troops. They threw up clouds of dust as they rolled by. The faces on the troops in those motorized units reflected grim resignation, not the indefatigable confidence I remembered of the triumphant panzer troops that had passed our artillery unit in France three years earlier. That experience had been exhilarating and exciting. Those panzer troops in France had responded to our cheers with broad smiles and waves as they rolled by. The men in this rolling column barely acknowledged our presence.

Watching that formidable armoured armada made me think that something big was up, something that required an assembly of heavy weapons.

Sure enough, a day or so after seeing the panzer unit pass by we received orders to advance to a specific objective, and with some urgency. We formed up after breakfast and advanced. My imagination frequently pictured Russian soldiers hiding in gullies or wheat fields, waiting to ambush us. The grim countenance on the faces of my men betrayed the tension we all felt.

The faint whistle of mortar projectiles caused everyone immediately to drop to the ground and try to take cover. That forced a halt to our advance. We regrouped and were ordered to dig in. Everyone quickly dug themselves a foxhole and faced toward what we assumed were enemy positions, and waited. Over the wireless I learned that a Russian infantry battalion occupied the top of the broad and shallow hill in front of my company. From my vantage point it was not possible to see them clearly, and we did not know if they were supported by any vehicles or artillery. We knew they had mortars. I spent the rest of the day looking for signs of enemy action through my binoculars. As night fell the tension level increased again, knowing that enemy troops were so near.

I was ordered to prepare my company to attack the enemy hill position the next morning. I passed my instructions on to the other platoon commanders to make sure the attack would be staged as ordered by the captain. Everyone prepared to go.

Long before dawn on July 4, 1943, we were awakened by the thudding reverberation of heavy weapons fire and explosions coming from an area to the north, very faint and almost continuous, but unmistakably the sounds of the monster of battle. It was too far away for the battle to affect us directly right away, but near enough to make me think that we would soon be involved. There was no sign of enemy movement from in front of our sector. We listened to that tumultuous symphony of hostilities for hours.

Groups of airplanes flew by overhead. Stuka dive-bombers came flying from the west toward that same battle zone to the north. The howling siren sounds made by diving Stukas were clearly audible, even though they were a long way away and the actual targets were not visible. The explosions could be heard and felt through the ground as the bombs hit—the ominous footfalls of the monster. Over the wireless the captain told me it was the beginning of a major German offensive and we were to be part of that assault.

Very slowly I lifted my head, stretching my neck just enough to peek out over the edge of my foxhole, careful not to become a target for a sniper and hoping to see some sign that the Russians had evacuated the top of the hill. There was no sign of enemy movement anywhere in front of our lines. Plumes of black smoke rose from the distant battlefield, flattening out into dark layers until they became a continuous smoky haze covering the entire northern sky, and gradually drifted toward us. The pungent smell of smoke soon permeated the air, faint at first, but becoming very strong by mid-morning.

I was feeling serious anxiety about the pending attack, my first attack against defended enemy positions. I knew what was expected of me, and I knew that all my men would also know what to do. We had undertaken many training exercises in Potsdam and Le Croisic that involved an infantry attack; but no matter how much faith I had that my training would preserve my life, it was impossible to dispel the apprehension of the impending fight. This time real enemy soldiers would be firing real bullets really trying to kill me. I dreaded the thought of having to get out of my foxhole and expose my body to enemy fire. The very stark reality that this could be the last day of my life stared me in the face.

The terrain between our lines and the top of the hill sloped gently upward and was covered with sparse clumps of grasses and weeds. It looked like a once cultivated field that had been left to return naturally to pasture. Because it may once have been ploughed, it was relatively smooth, with no holes, ditches, or even furrows in the ground deep enough to provide shielding from enemy fire. We would have to cross open ground with no opportunity to protect our bodies in the event the Russians stood their ground and fired at us from their concealed positions.

I had expected the signal to attack as soon as the sun came up, but we just waited and waited. Around mid-morning I realized that the knot I felt in the pit of my stomach might be my body telling me it was time to eat, rather than the terror of the impending action. Attack or no attack, I took out my pack and ate some bread and sausage spread. There were no signs of enemy movements in front of us, and no shelling or gunfire directed at us, but sporadic dull thudding sounds continued from the north. I spent much of the time swatting flies away from my face as the sun beat down. The insects in the field made a continuous scratching sound, as if the earth itself felt the itching. Life goes on for the bugs regardless of the foolish machinations of mankind. They would be here long after we were gone.

By noon we had still not received the signal to go. The waiting was nerve-wracking. I began to wonder if perhaps the attack had been called off. Perhaps Command had changed their mind? Perhaps the situation elsewhere at the front had altered and our attack would not be necessary?

"What the hell is wrong with you?" I chided myself. "Haven't you learned there's no use worrying about something you can't control?" There was nothing any of us could do but continue to wait. It was pointless to speculate as to what might be going on. The smell of burning from the distant battlefield was an insistent reminder of why we were there.

The captain came on the wireless. The attack would go at 1600 hours—in about half an hour. The tension level went up another notch. I passed the word to the other platoon leaders to get ready. I slung my rifle across my back and checked the ammunition clip in my automatic.

That short-barrelled, hand-held little submachine gun would be more useful than my rifle when attacking, because it could be fired in quick bursts while on the move. The clip held thirty-two rounds. It was not nearly as accurate as my rifle, but could concentrate a spray of bullets at a target, increasing the chances of hitting it. It was most effective at ranges of less than fifty metres, which is how far from the enemy I expected to be very shortly.

It was impossible to alleviate or just calm the tension and terror I felt over the impending action. The pounding in my ears was my beating heart, drowning out the bugs and the distant sounds of battle. I noticed my uniform was wet with sweat.

When the time came, the signal flare went up. This was it. The knot in the pit of my stomach worsened instantly, and a wave of intense heat flashed through my body. "Please let me survive this!" my mind screamed.

I yelled, "Go!" Everyone sprang out of their foxholes and headed for the enemy at a steady run. All thoughts of salvation or even survival disappeared from my mind. I ran in a frenzy. I could not turn back. I could not veer from my course. No clever tactics, no agile movements, no prayer, nothing could help me now. It was just a matter of luck.

At first all was quiet. Then the distinctive popping of mortar fire began behind us as our battalion's mortar company went into action. The projectiles whistled overhead and struck the brow of the hill ahead in rapid succession. I clutched at the hope that those little missiles would keep the enemy's heads down.

We were within about two hundred metres when the first shots of enemy fire came. Everyone immediately dropped to the ground, taking cover behind the nearest clumps of low-growing vegetation. Each of my three platoons had three machine guns, about fifty metres abreast, and the two outside machine-gunners from each platoon quickly set up their weapons and started shooting to provide covering fire, at which point the rest of us jumped up again and ran straight toward the enemy as fast as we could. The running men stayed in relatively narrow and straight rows between the fields of fire of our machine guns to avoid getting hit by our own gunners.

After running another hundred metres or so, the centre machine-gunners from each platoon and their ammunition carriers dropped to the ground and set up their weapons, and immediately began shooting.

As soon as they dropped all of the other men running forward also dropped to the ground and started shooting at the enemy. Then the two outside machine-gunners and their ammunition carriers jumped up and ran forward. The two machine-gun crews ran past us to a point some fifty metres ahead of the other line of advance. The two ammunition cases the machine-gunners' assistants were carrying prevented them from being able to shoot their weapons and defend themselves, so they were dependent upon the rest of us to provide covering fire. They then set up and took over the covering fire while everyone else again jumped up and ran forward. In that manner we were able to produce uninterrupted fire at the enemy positions. The leapfrogging procedure was repeated until we were close enough to make the final frantic charge, which we did yelling and screaming at the top of our lungs. At that point the supporting mortar fire stopped.

There was probably return fire from the Russians, but the ferocity with which we charged into the face of the enemy provided no opportunity to survey the situation, no time to adjust to whatever countermeasures the enemy would employ, not even time to think. We just ran straight forward, hoping the combined effect of the covering fire, the speed of the assault, and the screaming would create enough confusion and panic to rout the enemy. I had not gone more than a few dozen strides on my last dash forward when I saw Russian soldiers running away. A miracle!

A fence of barbed-wire coils loomed in front of me, staked to the ground. I took my rifle off my shoulder and laid it across the coils, stepped onto the rifle and over the wire, quickly picked it up again, and kept running. When we reached the line of foxholes the fleeing Russians had just abandoned I ordered everyone to stop and take cover. Russian soldiers were running in scattered paths down the far side of the hill toward a woodlot at the rear, into which they rapidly disappeared. When the shooting and screaming finally stopped, the quiet was almost startling.

I was absolutely thrilled to be breathing!

All the foxholes we found were empty. Everyone quickly found an abandoned hole and waited. My heart was beating furiously from the exertion, but the knot in my stomach was gone. The action that accompanied the opening shots had immediately caused all my senses to be completely absorbed in what was happening, overwhelming the fear

I had felt. The Russians must have recognized the determined intent of our assault and taken off before we were close enough to be within deadly range. I remained vigilant for signs of a counterattack. I radioed Command and was ordered to dig in and hold.

The other two companies from our battalion had also taken part in the attack. One group could be seen digging in farther south from us along the brow of the hill. They had charged the one flank of the enemy positions at the same time. That may explain why the Russians left as quickly as they did.

Perhaps the Russian commander had ordered the retreat because he was just not willing to risk the lives of any of his men for an inconsequential piece of ground that provided only a limited, short-term advantage? In retrospect their quick retreat may not have made them look very brave, but it certainly was smart. To underscore the point, they lost no one during that little skirmish. We lost the sergeant from the second platoon. As commanding officer of my company it was my unpleasant duty to report his death and send back his dog tag. That was heart-wrenching. He was the only son of a widow. What words could console her? What could the government possibly do to ease the agony of such an irrevocable loss?

We remained alert for any signs of enemy activity during the rest of the evening. Sporadic gunfire was heard from far away, but we did not move. I assumed the enemy soldiers had set up a defensive line at the edge of the woodlot into which they had escaped. That night was again nerve-wracking, knowing the enemy was only a short distance away. I assigned twice the regular number of sentries to keep watch all night. I slept hardly at all.

Before dawn I was told the woodlot had to be cleared of the enemy before we could advance again, as they would be behind us if they were not eliminated. The trees in the woodlot were all short deciduous trees, but the growth appeared so dense that it would be difficult to move through them. I was told that we would get assistance for our attack.

Suddenly, streamers of flames shot out along the edge of the woods. A flamethrower unit had crept up to the woodlot during the night. They repeatedly let fly with deadly streamers of flaming liquid. It had not rained since I had arrived at the front and everything was very dry. Within minutes the brush and trees were ablaze. The flamethrower squad moved along the edge of the trees, lighting more and more of the woods on fire as they went, until there was an immense wall of flames reaching high into the sky dozens of metres above the treetops. Eventually the heat became so intense that our men at the woodlot had to retreat.

We were then ordered to advance again, and moved in a circuitous route around the woodlot on the upwind side. The forested area was far too big for us to be able to surround it quickly, so I assumed that gave the Russian soldiers the opportunity to escape by retreating through the trees and out the far side before we got there. None of them came out the side we were facing. We kept going and the woodlot kept burning.

We had not gone more than a few kilometres when we encountered what were obviously well-defended enemy lines. So we quickly dug our own defensive line of foxholes facing the enemy. Then we waited. All night long the bright red glow from the burning woodlot could be seen behind us.

Radio messages went back and forth during the night. Before our next attack could be contemplated we had to determine the extent and strength of the enemy defences. Patrols were sent out to probe the areas between our lines. They reported that the Russians occupied well-constructed and extensive entrenchments, protected by rows of abatis, and completely covered with many coils of barbed wire. Their lines extended unbroken in both directions, through fields, meadows, woodlots, and a village. They had obviously had plenty of time to prepare for our attack.

It was a bit unsettling to realize the Russians had constructed this second line of defence in anticipation of our attack. Their commanders apparently knew the time and place of the German offensive, and long before I did. That did not boost my confidence in the competence of our military leadership at the highest level.

I figured we were outnumbered and outgunned; certainly not strong enough to attack such well-prepared defences. There was no artillery support available to us. The battalion's mortar company set up their little artillery pieces behind our positions. More patrols went out to try to find a weak spot in the enemy's lines, returning without discovering any easy way through. They did discover that the area in front of the Russian lines had been partially cleared of cover and sown with land mines. The following night squads of sappers were sent out to clear paths through the minefields. I did not envy them their task.

I was ordered to prepare my company to attack again. The plan was for us to sneak up close to the enemy along one small area that had been cleared of mines and then attempt a quick charge through the Russian defences at first light. I spent another restless night contemplating the chances of survival.

For some reason the order to advance did not come with the dawn. Instead, the mortar company began a barrage of the enemy positions as soon as it was daylight. That was soon followed by return fire from the other side. The mortar barrages went back and forth for most of the day, while we spent most of it crouched low in our foxholes.

The standoff continued for another two weeks or so, with only occasional and inconsequential barrages or brief skirmishes with reconnaissance patrols. We strengthened our defences by digging our foxholes deeper and connecting some with short trenches. We also covered sections with tarps and camouflage netting. Good thing, as it rained one day and the elaborate accommodations allowed us to stay relatively dry. Command must have deduced that any frontal assault on the enemy's well-defended lines by our meagre forces would have been futile. I wondered how the faraway German assault had fared, as we were unable to make any headway in our sector. Perhaps the front had stabilized again?

Then the distant sounds of battle began anew, again from far to the north. That was early in August. The next day those battle sounds came ominously closer. I tried to get information from Command about what was happening, suspecting we were in the path of a major enemy offensive, but was told nothing. The rumble of battle came inexorably closer and closer, until we could once again see and smell clouds of smoke. As before, airplanes flew overhead, some uncomfortably close. Then the inevitable was confirmed; Command expected an enemy attack the next morning. Reconnaissance had reported Russian artillery pieces moving toward our sector the day before. The monster had returned.

I kept hoping to receive orders to withdraw farther to the rear. It quickly became clear to me that Command was very confused as to what should be done. "Just get us out of here," I requested over the wireless, with sincere urgency. As far as we could determine the enemy remained dug in right in front of our positions. It crossed my mind that our commanders might be clinging to an old military maxim: "When in doubt, do nothing." I finally passed out in my foxhole in the middle of the night, exhausted from the tension.

The unmistakable tearing sound of incoming shells jolted me awake. It was still before dawn. I immediately ducked down into my foxhole. Boom! The ground erupted near our position. The order came over the wireless to retreat, immediately!

I yelled at the men on my left and right, "Retreat! Follow me! Stay together!" The order was shouted down the line in both directions. Everyone grabbed his weapons and scrambled out of his foxhole. It was just light enough in the predawn to see where we were going. At first the shells burst around us; then it appeared the barrage was heading away. That looked like a "creeping barrage" to me, the precursor of an infantry attack. During my training in the artillery, I had been involved in practising just such a tactic—fire at the forward positions, then keep raising the range to fire at retreating troops and to cover your own advancing infantry. Back then I had thought it clever, but on the receiving end I quickly lost my appreciation for its ingeniousness.

After we retreated about half a kilometre we slowed to a walk. Unbelievably, my wireless operator said he had just received orders to reoccupy our former positions. In disbelief I halted our retreat and called to confirm the order, screaming into the receiver and straining to hear the reply under the tumult of explosions. It was true! We had to get back right away. Counterattack?

The order was quickly passed along, and I waved the signal to charge. I headed in the direction we had come from, running as fast as my aching legs would carry me, assuming that we would run into enemy troops charging toward us. After a few hundred metres I dared to hope we would find our foxholes before the enemy found us. I prayed that Command knew what they were doing. At last our line of foxholes came into sight. I jumped into the nearest one. My messenger jumped into the next one. There was some confusion as to which foxhole should hold which man, but it sorted itself out quickly. I shouldered my rifle and prepared to shoot anyone running toward us.

I peered into the predawn light but could not see anything, which surprised me. Then I felt someone touch my arm. "I just got another message. We might have to pull out after all," my wireless operator said. The dawn lit the eastern horizon. He pointed toward the north. Through my field glasses I looked at a massive herd of Russians troops, coming closer. They looked absolutely endless. How the hell did they get here? I realized immediately that we had been outflanked. This was not good.

Then the sound of flying shells again accosted my ears, but instead of a loud explosion, each shell landed with a dull pop. A thick cloud of pale grey smoke quickly obscured my view toward the north. The enemy had dropped hundreds of smoke bombs into the area in front of us. That cloud would soon be right on top of us.

"Retreat! Follow me! Stay together!" I figured that within minutes thousands of screaming enemy soldiers would come charging through the smoke haze right on top of us. Off we went again, my lungs still trying to recover from the last rush. This time I led my men due south, which I figured was away from the charging throng. I repeatedly looked over my shoulder to check on my men and to see how far behind the Russians were. A dull roar could be heard emanating from the charging throng, like a soccer stadium full of madly cheering fans.

My rifle and automatic soon became very heavy. Knowing I was running for my life made me ignore the burning pain in my lungs and my muscles. It appeared to me that the entire battalion had abandoned their positions at the same time my company did. My body could not keep up the pace for long and eventually settled into a more sustainable lope. I checked repeatedly to make sure the rest of the company stayed together with me, and kept the position of the rising sun over my left shoulder to orient my direction. I had no idea where we were going, or if we would make it to some kind of safety.

Eventually I noticed some of the men lagging behind, falling onto the ground, unable to run any farther. I called a halt. The dawn had become bright enough to see the enemy were heading farther away, rather than following right behind.

Panting heavily and with my throat burning, I motioned for the wireless operator. We tried to radio the captain, but received no reply. There was enough distance between us and the masses of Russian infantry to be out of rifle range; however, we had to get out of this predicament, as I reckoned the Russians had breached our defences and gained so much ground that we would surely be trapped. We had to keep moving. After a few minutes I ordered everyone to move off again.

Just when I began to think we were heading away from danger, we came over the crest of a rise and there were about half a dozen small trucks and command cars, along with a large half-track, moving westward. Hundreds of soldiers were running along with them, German soldiers. As we got closer an officer in a *Kübelwagen* stood up and waved us on. "Fall in behind!" the major said. We quickly regrouped and followed the vehicles.

The *Kübelwagen* raced back and forth among our hastily assembled battle group. "Move, keep going!" the major screamed at us infantry, waving his arm, herding us along. Then I realized we were heading toward the enemy! We were going to counterattack. There was no time to think; otherwise, I might have considered attacking such a mass of enemy troops as completely crazy.

We ran after the Russians but did not appear to be able to get within rifle range of even the nearest group, as they were still moving. I was beginning to think our counterattack, and indeed the entire Russian assault, would just peter out and we would escape the day unscathed. Then the vehicles ahead turned abruptly and stopped. As we caught up near the crest of a rise masses of enemy troops came into view on the other side. Either they did not see us approach or they were so intent on continuing their headlong rush that they ignored our approach.

We stopped and immediately took cover on the ground. I shouldered my rifle and waited. Something else caught my eye in the distance. Trails of dust were being thrown up by the unmistakable silhouettes of Russian T–34 tanks among the charging infantry. The crew of our half-track vehicle took a tarpaulin off the back to reveal an anti-aircraft pod of four heavy machine guns. They had set up slightly behind us and started shooting.

My rifle felt like it weighed a hundred pounds, and I was breathing so hard I could not steady my aim. I aimed at the nearest target as best I could and squeezed the trigger. One of my machine-gun crews had set up nearby and the staccato burst from their weapon joined the chaos. The nearest Russians had spotted us, dropped to the ground to take cover, and fired back. The situation became so chaotic that it was impossible to figure out what was going on. My senses were so consumed with the demands of the moment that there was no time to look around or even think about the effects of the shooting, or any troop movements on either side. We may have attacked the exposed flank of the Russian torrent of charging men, but I really had no understanding of what was happening. It was absolute bedlam! The academic strategies about battles that I had learned in Officer School had completely lost any relevance.

Suddenly an explosion burst in front of me, quickly followed by more. Artillery shells or bombs exploded all over the place. Perhaps we had unexpectedly received heavy weapons support; either that, or the Russian gunners had misjudged the aim of their own artillery. The screaming of flying bombs was distinctive in the chaos. Airplanes flashed by overhead, very low in the air, adding their gunfire and roaring motors to the tumult of explosions, the heavy machine-gun fire from behind us, the machine guns from my flanks, and the rifle fire from everywhere. The enemy were quickly obscured by the smoke and dust clouds created by the exploding bombs. The shooting along my line and from nearby stopped, but the distinctive crackling of machine-gun fire continued from farther away.

"Dig in!" I heard someone scream. "Dig in!" I passed it on.

The slight depression in the ground was not deep enough to hide my whole body from view. I lay down my rifle and took my spade from my utility belt. Crouching low to expose as little as possible, I stabbed at the ground. The ground was very hard, and combined with the matted roots of the steppe grasses resulted in a thick, tough surface layer that was difficult to penetrate. I had previously dug through that barrier many times, but in this desperate situation it was a stubborn and frustrating foe. I could not raise my body to get better leverage for fear of being shot. Sounds of battle continued to accost my ears. This fight was far from over, so I frantically hacked at the black ground to excavate a tiny refuge in which to hide my body. I glanced up a few times as I dug to make sure there was nobody unfriendly rushing toward us. After a few minutes of desperate digging I had made a hole just deep enough to hide my body. By now it was broad daylight, but I could not see very far from my limited vantage point.

Then a signal flare went up. Before I had time to think it again sounded like a soccer stadium full of screaming fanatics. My entire field of view filled with charging enemy soldiers and I was momentarily transfixed by their sheer numbers. It looked like a thousand! They were not grouped in the relatively narrow lanes between covering fire like one of our attacks would have been. They were yelling what sounded like "Uraah! Uraah!" as they ran toward us.

I put my rifle against my shoulder, aimed at the nearest charging figure, and squeezed the trigger. He fell. Our machine guns then started shooting, at which the enemy immediately dropped to the ground to take cover. The sound of rifle fire now replaced the soccer stadium roar. I crouched lower into my hole, checked to make sure there was a full clip in my automatic, and put it beside me for when the enemy would be close enough. All my senses were focused on finding targets in front of me.

The attackers jumped up and another wave came charging toward us. I fired again, another man fell. Our machine guns to my left and right again spewed deadly bursts of bullets, cutting down many more. At such close range all the men in my company were now looking out for themselves, shooting at any target that presented itself, but trying to avoid exposing themselves to enemy fire. The mad chatter of the machine guns, the sharp pop of rifles, the scream and thump of exploding mortar shells, all added to the crescendo of the charging throng until the din of battle again became a symphony from hell.

Out of the corner of my eye I caught sight of movement. Two of my men had jumped out of their foxholes and were attempting to run away.

"No!" I screamed. Too late. They did not get more than a few paces before they fell. "Damned stupid!" I yelled in frustrated anger.

They must have been panicked by the noise and ferocity of the enemy attack as it came so near. "Stay in position!" I screamed at the top of my lungs, my voice surely lost among the din of battle. I turned and aimed with rage at the nearest attacker and fired. One less, then another, until my clip was spent.

The Russian commander must finally have realized they were not going to rout the rest of us from our foxholes. His soldiers were at a terrible disadvantage out in the open. When the Russians had retreated far enough to be out of deadly range, all shooting stopped, on both sides. With an inadvertent burst of emotion, I yelled, "Yaaah!" assuming the enemy attack had stalled. I reloaded my rifle and watched to see if they would regroup for another attack. I continued to wait, expecting another assault wave, but saw no sign of another massing of enemy soldiers. They had taken cover back at their starting line.

I sent our medic to check for casualties, figuring it was safe enough to risk having them moved back for medical attention. We were careful not to expose ourselves unnecessarily to sniper fire. When I got out of my foxhole I noticed the Russians made no attempt to shoot at us while we attended to our casualties, even though some must have still been close enough. Curiously, our vehicles, including the half-track, and the major, were nowhere to be seen.

We had half a dozen wounded in my platoon. One man had a ragged-looking wound in his cheek, just below his ear. One of my machine-gunners had been shot in the shoulder near his neck. Another man had been hit by two bullets, one in his left upper arm and another in the shoulder. A third had an ugly hole in his chest, and he looked bad. He was semiconscious and could hardly move. I knew he would soon be dead if we could not get him to a field hospital in time. He was one of the men that had tried to run away. The other man that had tried to run had been shot in the hip. He was unable to walk, but otherwise seemed in surprisingly good spirits. The badly wounded men were put onto canvas cape stretchers so they could be carried back with us. The machine-gunner and the man shot in the cheek were able to walk without assistance. I had no idea where the nearest field medical unit was, so we radioed for assistance.

"That was close," I said pointing to the prominent new dent in the top of one of the machine-gunner's helmet, made by a bullet.

He took it off and looked at it in amazement. "Many thanks to dear God," he said, with a grin that under different circumstances would have passed for joy on his face.

"He must have been looking after you today," I said. Clutching at small mercies just seemed appropriate.

We continued to watch out for another enemy attack. I also waited for new orders to tell me to retreat. Then I spotted dozens of Russians walking toward us in small groups. They appeared to be completely unarmed. I gave orders not to fire at them. They began to pick up their wounded comrades and carry them back to their own lines. Some of their casualties looked like they were dead. From what I could see in front of my platoon, they had lost many dozens of dead and wounded during that attack.

An hour earlier we had been trying to kill each other; now I felt sorry for these unfortunate victims of war, carrying out their sad duties.

Under the circumstances at the time the absurdity of that contradiction was not apparent to me. As soon as the casualties had been taken care of we returned to our foxholes and waited. The common humanity both sides had just shared during the execution of our sacred responsibilities to care for our wounded and fallen comrades in arms was quickly forgotten. Once again we were enemies.

There was no more action that day. From what I could tell, the masses of enemy troops accompanied by tanks had moved on until they were out of sight. Our little battle group had probably managed to delay only a portion of the enemy attackers. That evening the order came over the wireless to pull back. A flare would be sent up to give us a direction for our retreat. What a relief. I ordered my messenger to pass the word down the line and make sure the other two platoons knew to stay together.

I ordered the retreat as soon as it was dark. We carried our badly wounded with us on makeshift stretchers. As we trudged along I kept searching the sky for the flare, feeling nervous that we would encounter Russians in the darkness. Finally there it was, but incredibly far away! No matter; that beacon represented our only hope of salvation. I took a bearing on my compass and we headed off in the direction of the flare.

We walked for hours, slowed by the wounded. We had to ask for another signal flare to reorient our direction in the darkness. My chapped lips and parched throat were telltale signs of serious dehydration. We had not had a chance to refill our canteens for two days. Anyone can survive for weeks without food, but only a few days without water.

Finally we found our new command post. The first thing we did was look for the field kitchen to replenish our water. I was greeted by the captain. After asking about our condition the captain unceremoniously led us to our new position and told me to dig in and prepare to defend that new piece of ground. He made our desperate retreat and costly fight sound like we had just finished the shift in a day's work. There was no explanation for the choice of our new position.

The first chance after our retreat I lectured my troops on the stupidity of leaving your foxhole during an attack. "Stay put unless you get the order to leave. As long as our machine guns are operating, their attack will fail. Jumping out of your hole in range of the enemy is suicide." The two casualties that had attempted to run away underscored that lesson.

One of the machine-gunners casually mentioned that he ran out of bullets just before the enemy attack halted. He grinned as he said this, obviously pleased to have cheated death that day. The other two machine-gunners were also nearly out. We had been lucky. If another tide of enemy soldiers had attacked we would have been overrun. We had been greatly outnumbered at the start of the assault, and I guessed the enemy had plenty of men left to press their advantage if they had known we were so low on ammunition.

The following morning I scanned our new location and saw that we had dug in on a piece of ground that looked familiar. I recognized the hill positions that had cost our sergeant his life a few weeks earlier. Once again I felt the pain of his loss. The Russians eventually recaptured that same hill. The sergeant had lost his life for nothing.

The Russian assault on our small battle group had been blunted, but it did not matter much. German forces had given up many kilometres along a broad front that day. The Russian gains had probably been limited by their own exhaustion, not by any brilliant military strategy or fortitude on our part. With that many Russian soldiers taking part in the assault we could not have mustered enough firepower to stop them. A huge section of the front had shifted and we had been lucky to escape being encircled.

The men who were able to get medical attention rejoined us, including the man who had been hit in the cheek, which surprised me considering how nasty that wound had looked. He had a nice white patch on the side of his face, taped firmly to his head. "I'm going to look distinguished when this heals," he said, pointing to his cheek. "Like one of those generals with a fencing scar. That will make me irresistible to the ladies back home." He may have hoped they would send him home. Still, he was luckier than the man who had been shot in the chest. He would never be going home.

The next day the distant sounds of battle started again, but this time my company was on the receiving end of only sporadic mortar and small-arms fire. A company or so of Russian troops must have followed us during the night. They harassed us all day but did not approach close enough to be within deadly range. We were ordered to retreat again that night. Apparently the brunt of the enemy assault that day had been directed at a section farther out along one of our flanks. The distant sounds of battle were heard intermittently for the rest of that day, including the firing of heavy weapons, but nothing appeared to be happening in front of our lines.

Late that afternoon I was ordered to advance my company in the direction from which we could hear sporadic gunfire, which I assumed was the enemy lines. We were careful to stay low in the depressions that provided cover from bushes and trees.

We rounded the edge of the trees and approached a hayfield. On the far side, partly hidden by the backdrop of another woodlot, I spotted tanks. I immediately signalled a halt and ordered everyone to take cover, mentally preparing a plan to go around that deadly obstacle.

"Those are ours," said my wireless operator.

We quickly crossed the field toward the tanks. German armoured units were usually sent only to spots where the situation had become critical, and the presence of those tanks could mean a desperate and dangerous battle ahead for us.

There were about a dozen tanks in the group, along with some self-propelled guns, half-track vehicles, and motorcycles. The tanks looked like they had been at the front for a long time. Some of them were loaded with equipment and supplies on their backs and on top of the turrets. In the fading light it was difficult to tell what colour they had originally been painted. They appeared to be mostly a dull and dirty yellowish grey-brown, probably tinged by the colour of the dust in that part of the country. The smell of motor oil, gasoline, smoke, and freshly turned soil filled the air. The nearest had sooty marks on it, perhaps from driving over charred buildings. There were dents and holes in the steel plates that provided extra armour protection along its sides. Even though battered, dirty, and weather-beaten, those mobile armoured fighting vehicles looked somewhat handsome sitting there in the failing light, belying their manifestly deadly purpose. I was intrigued by their distinctly robust character, which exuded an almost comfortable quality, like huge mechanized toys.

Some of the tank crews were sitting on the ground beside their mounts, leaning against the wheels. A hatch at the back of one tank was open, and two men were apparently fixing or replacing something. There was activity around the other vehicles, but nothing that appeared urgent or even hurried. One man was sitting on an ammunition case beside the tank, drinking what smelled like tea. None of the tank men appeared the slightest bit wary.

The crewman drinking tea greeted us nonchalantly. He saluted when he noticed my officer's stripes. I politely returned the salute. "How's it going?" he asked, as if he were in a park and we were passing by on a picnic outing.

"Do you know where the Russians are?" I asked him.

"Oh, farther back," he said casually as he waved his hand over his shoulder toward the east. He appeared completely indifferent to what I perceived to be a potentially perilous situation. I knew that enemy forces were not farther back, but very near, and there were probably lots of them.

"What are you doing here?" I asked.

"Waiting for orders. Maybe we can stay here for the night. Enough sport for one day. Ivan can wait until tomorrow," he said, grinning.

I found that scene incredible. Here my men and I were being extremely careful to avoid getting caught by what I estimated to be very powerful enemy forces lurking nearby, and these fellows were sitting around as if they were at a summer camp. They must have heard the small-arms fire, yet appeared to be entirely unconcerned. I got the impression that unless the enemy were actually shooting at them from other tanks or anti-tank guns they were not the slightest bit worried. It was hard for a mere foot soldier to understand that peculiar mindset.

However, looking closely at their faces, I noticed that most of them looked more exhausted than relaxed. Their casual and strangely cheerful attitude could not mask the fatigue in their faces. They had obviously been kept very busy recently. Their armoured unit may have taken part in the noisy and furious engagements that we had heard earlier from afar. I did not know how many tanks were supposed to be in an armoured unit, but my guess was that it had to be considerably more than the number we saw here. We bid farewell to the tank men and reached our new position late that night.

Before dawn of that morning in late August we were again awakened by the sound of heavy-weapons fire. Shortly afterwards the sounds of motorized units moving could be heard, including the unmistakable clattering and squeaking noises of tanks. Those sounds were carried by the wind blowing from the west. The previous night we had dug in about a kilometre southwest of where we had last seen enemy soldiers, so battle noises coming from that direction were a very bad sign. In the pre-dawn light I scanned the horizon through field glasses and made out the outlines of dozens of tanks, accompanied by a great many troops, all moving southward. As the day went on I became increasingly uneasy that we would not get the order to retreat until it was too late to keep from being encircled.

That night I received orders from the captain that my company was to take part in an attack in the morning. Our objective was to cut off and encircle the enemy's advance units. Over the wireless the captain conveyed precise orders to instruct the three platoons of my company to coordinate our advance with the rest of the battalion. We had to be in position before 0500 hours, before it would begin to get light. Every piece of equipment in every man's kit had to be soundproofed, by covering everything that could make a clanking sound with soft cloth, especially canteens and gas mask canisters. I instructed my other two platoon leaders to advance together and to maintain contact all the way.

The most important thing to remember was to have a shit before dawn, because there might not be another chance for a while. Tension and stress caused by waiting for the order to attack stimulated a biological reaction in the digestive system, which may be nature's way of making the body as light as possible.

When we set off there was just enough moonlight to avoid stumbling over obstacles in our path, and we moved quickly. I repeatedly checked our direction with my pocket compass. After estimating we had moved at least two kilometres I called a halt to our advance. Suspecting we were very close to the enemy, I sent a two-man patrol ahead and waited. The thought crossed my mind that the Russians would probably also have sent out patrols to check their new perimeter. Hopefully nobody would stumble onto us. That would definitely spoil our surprise.

We waited, lying low and silent. I checked my watch. Ten minutes passed, then twenty, then half an hour. A shadowy figure suddenly loomed out of the darkness. My heart skipped a beat before I recognized my patrol. They had found the enemy digging in along a line of foxholes less than about 500 metres ahead—lots of them. I was worried about Russian tanks, but they had not seen any vehicles. I also asked about barbed wire and any signs that the ground had been disturbed, for land mines, but they had found none of that.

We moved silently ahead. It was impossible to see more than a few dozen metres into the night. We had to move forward undetected until we were close enough to dash across the last few metres onto the enemy positions. I passed the plan of attack to the other two platoon leaders down the line in both directions. I then gave the signal to move forward, and we set off toward an unseen and dug-in enemy, across unfamiliar ground, in the dark, with any one of hundreds of soldiers that could accidentally make a noise.

After a few hundred metres I became very apprehensive. When we approached the crest of a shallow swale we crossed an open field with no tall vegetation to hide in. We moved slowly, probing the ground ahead for anything that could make a noise that would give us away—snapping a dry twig, tripping over an exposed root, stumbling into a groundhog hole. I was especially alert for a tripwire. We were approaching the enemy positions virtually blind. After what seemed like an eternity, a silent signal from one of the men to my side caused everyone to freeze. Listening intently, I heard voices from ahead. We were now very near.

Everyone had better be ready to go. The waiting became excruciatingly tense. If any one of us made the slightest mistake we would be detected. I scarcely dared to breathe. My ears strained for the sound of footsteps. The dawn already coloured the eastern horizon with pale light. The chance of being spotted increased with the rising sun. I could make out the dark shapes of my men lying on the ground in either direction, A Russian patrol could easily have seen us if they happened to look our way. I rechecked my automatic to make sure the safety was off.

Finally, at exactly 0700 hours, the entire front erupted with a crescendo of artillery fire. I felt the familiar hot flash course through my body that accompanied action and gave the signal to go. All got on their feet and ran as fast as they could, straight toward the enemy. I had run about twenty metres when the first shot rang out. Our machine-gunners immediately started firing. A cacophony of gunfire and shrieking filled the air.

After a few more seconds of running as fast as my legs would carry me I was right in front of the nearest Russian foxhole. The soldier in the foxhole looked up and lifted his rifle toward me. I fired a quick burst from my automatic as I dove for the ground, landing hard only a few metres in front of him. I scrambled forward with my automatic in front of me, expecting the Russian to appear over the edge of the hole with his rifle. Within seconds I reached the edge. The Russian had not moved. I shoved him aside and tried to squeeze into the space beside him. My heart was pounding in my chest.

Looking up I saw many pairs of hands in the air. Obviously the element of surprise had created enough confusion and panic to force many of the Russians to surrender. The shooting around me quickly subsided. Hundreds of Russian soldiers were running away toward the north, rapidly moving out of effective rifle range. I searched for my radio operator and waited for orders.

Then I looked at the Russian in the foxhole with me, and really saw him for the first time. Until I stood up he had been pressed against my hip. He had an ugly hole above his cheek, where one of his eyes had been, and another in the top of his forehead. Blood was running down his face and soaking into the ground under his head. He was dead, and with the realization that I was responsible for his death a sickening, panicky feeling suddenly poured through me. It felt as if I was sinking beneath a pool of hot water. I slumped to the ground. That was the first time I had ever seen a man I had killed up close, close enough to touch him. He was a man like myself, or any of my fellows. How young he looked. I felt uncontrollably wretched at having taken his life. Knowing it had been him or me in the heat of battle made no difference.

"Prisoners, *Herr Leutnant*. What do we do with them?"

In a daze I looked up at the source of the voice without comprehending.

I could not move, or speak. My mind was consumed with the horror of that moment. The pain in my body would not let go. I am so sorry, I pleaded over and over, I am so sorry. I thought of his family, how his mother would cry. He reminded me of my own young brothers. What if someone killed one of them like this?

Sitting in that pool of sorrow, the activity swirling around me eventually diverted my attention. As I regained my composure it occurred to me that maybe I could not move because I had been shot. I checked myself for bullet holes and found none.

"Prisoners," he repeated, pointing.

As I stood up I could see dozens of Russians sitting in bunches, hands clasped on top of their heads. Others were unceremoniously being herded into small groups. I forced myself to focus on the task at hand. "Assemble them in a column and send two men back with them," I replied, pointing toward where I assumed we had come from.

I walked around to take stock of the situation, then told my radio operator to request new orders. Before I had a real chance to find out what to do next, I heard the distinctive whistling sound of incoming mortar shells. "Cover!" I jumped into the nearest hole. Everyone, German and Russian alike, dove for cover. Shells flew overhead and exploded in the midst of our newly won positions. Soldiers all around me were digging frantically to make or enlarge holes big enough to hide in. Thoughts of the man I had killed, whose death had affected me so profoundly only minutes earlier, had already slipped from my consciousness.

The battle continued unabated all around us for hours. Snipers kept everybody's heads down. The prisoners could not be taken back and we could not attend to the wounded. I was separated from my wireless operator. We had to stay put in our tiny holes in the ground for the rest of the day. Finally it became dark enough that we could attempt an orderly withdrawal. I was able to contact Command to confirm our retreat. We were forced to abandon our newly won positions in such a hurry that we could not stop to bury the dead. We gathered up as many wounded soldiers as we could and took as many of the Russian prisoners with us as we could find, including the walking wounded. Any wounded still hiding in holes within the battlefield would have to be left behind.

Gunfire repeatedly punctuated the darkness as we retreated through the night, sometimes uncomfortably close. That flight was incredibly tense. We could easily have blundered into enemy troops in the darkness. Although our retreat was orderly, I had no idea which direction led to safety, so I guessed as to which way to move. After hours of stumbling along I figured we had retreated far enough and ordered a halt. I told the radio operator to keep trying to contact Battalion Command for instructions.

Finally, around midnight, Command sent up a flare, which we could see far in the distance. Everyone headed in that direction. We eventually caught up with the battalion command post and, more important, the field kitchen. We were given bread rations. By the time I had eaten, dug another hole in the ground to sleep in, and curled up under my cape, I was at the limit of my endurance.

Russian infantry attack with T-34 tanks

As soon as I closed my eyes the face of the young man I had killed in the foxhole that morning leapt out of the darkness, pale and sad, accusing; the bloody holes in his face gross and distorted. That terrible vision joined a host of nightmarish images already haunting my subconscious.

The next morning I awoke stiff and sore. I had bruised myself when I landed hard on the ground in front of the Russian foxhole. The enemy were nowhere in sight. We had lost four men in that skirmish. The entire episode had been completely futile, in spite of the fact that our skilful and daring attack had itself been successful.

For my company that series of actions was part of the beginning of the tremendous Russian offensives in our sector of the Eastern Front. For the next few days we had to retreat every day, sometimes very quickly. The air was often heavy with the smell of smoke, day and night. We retreated through towns and villages that had been burned, as well as countless relics of battle, including derelict wrecks of armoured vehicles, trucks, motorcycles, wagons, and carts, and innumerable graves. My senses were often accosted by the stench of dead horses and bodies. We scrambled and scurried like mad to keep ahead of the enemy. Sheer good luck may again have helped us from being surrounded.

Eventually we were ordered to retreat far to the rear. We passed by the city of Charkov. Dozens of columns of dark, billowing smoke filled the evening sky. It looked like whole districts of the city were on fire. There must have been intense fighting in and around the city. We passed hundreds of wrecked military vehicles, including the broken and burnt-out hulks of tanks and self-propelled guns. At night the glow from fires still burning in the city could be seen for hours, gradually receding into the distance as we marched on.

That night was one of the nights we had to keep going, where we could not stop to rest at all. I lost much of my sense of time, as individual days became indistinct. Repeated forced retreats soon became exhausting, taxing my endurance and testing my perseverance. The fighting became a seemingly endless series of skirmishes for my company during the summer of 1943, trying to stay ahead of a relentless enemy.

I lost all sense of perspective, as my only concern was the section of front that my company was defending. The Russian offensive continued unabated, with the points of attack shifting repeatedly along different sectors over a very wide front. In spite of staunch and stubborn defensive actions by individual units, our forces were given no time to regroup and set up a coordinated and cohesive defence. It eventually became apparent that our commanders had been ordered to defend every metre of ground for as long as possible.

Our predicament was unrelentingly grim, much worse than anything I had experienced before or could ever have imagined. I was acutely aware that my life was in danger almost every day. I would have to learn battlefield skills and acquire self-preservation instincts quickly in order to have any hope of surviving. I would also need a great deal of good luck to return from Russia alive. We were caught in the jaws of the Russian bear.

15 *Hold Back the Tide*

AFTER THE START OF THE RUSSIAN OFFENSIVES in August, we were repeatedly forced to retreat. We quickly learned it was safer to move during the night and hide in our foxholes during the day. We had to dig foxholes in the pre-dawn hours almost every morning in order to be prepared to defend our position during the day.

Every man carried a short-handled spade. Sometimes the ground was compacted hard, requiring considerable effort to make a hole deep enough to be able to hide your whole body. Most meadows and pastures had a thick layer of matted roots through which we had to hack and cut before excavating the soil underneath. The dirt excavated from the foxhole was piled around the hole as extra shielding. The excavated dirt was usually much darker than the surface, so it was smart to spread the dirt out thinly to allow it to dry. As it dried it turned grey and blended into the surrounding ground. The last thing you wanted to do was to draw attention to yourself by making your hole conspicuous compared to the rest of the ground. All veterans at the front knew how to make a hole just large enough to provide protection from flying shrapnel or bullets, but small enough that the cape could make a tent over it to keep it reasonably dry in the event it rained. The intent was to fashion it so you could shoot with only your head and arms exposed. No matter how you fashioned it, it was impossible to make a hole in the ground comfortable.

Every infantry soldier carried a bayonet, but I had never used it to fight with. We would have done everything possible not to allow the enemy to get close enough for hand-to-hand combat. Repeated action had instilled in us strong self-preservation instincts, so I would have ordered a hasty retreat had I suspected we would be overrun, regardless of Command.

The prevailing tactics of advanced warfare, if "advanced" is the proper term, made the close-combat bayonet and pistol-type of fighting that had been commonplace in battles of earlier wars a rare event, at least judging by what I experienced. Our weapons made a difference, especially machine guns. Each German infantry company had nine machine guns, which by that time in the war were mostly the Model 42. It was similar to the older Model 34, but a relatively simpler design. It had a long, squared, black metal frame with a flared wooden stock at one end and a barrel in an elongated frame at the other. Like the Model 34, it had a folding bipod near the front to support its weight. Our machine guns had originally been equipped with a large folding tripod that supported the weapon in action, but they were cumbersome to set up and heavy to carry. The tripod also raised the gun too high to be practical under most battlefield conditions, so they tended to be lost soon after that series of retreats began. Most gunners relied on the small bipod near the front of the barrel to support the gun in action.

The Model 42 was a sound and reliable weapon, easy to operate, and quite accurate, even at relatively long ranges. It had an incredibly rapid rate of fire. It sounded like tearing linoleum when fired, not at all like the series of rapid pops made by Russian machine guns, or even the older Model 34. During battle the high rate of fire caused the barrel to heat up quickly, and each crew carried an extra barrel to replace the hot one before it warped from the heat. There was a quick-release lever on the barrel housing that was used to take out the hot barrel and slam in the new one. Very intense use could require that exchange more than once.

To be used most efficiently the machine gun required a two-man crew—one to aim and fire the weapon and the other to feed the bullet belts. The ammunition cases for our machine guns were heavy and cumbersome to carry when full. The ammunition feeder accompanied the gunner, sometimes occupying the same large foxhole. If necessary, the machine-gunner could feed the bullet belts into the breech himself, although it was then more awkward to operate, as he would need to stop shooting for longer intervals while reloading. In order to fire the weapon accurately the gunner had to expose his head and shoulders above the edge of his foxhole, which was of course dangerous; however, the stream of bullets that spewed from his machine gun discouraged enemy soldiers from exposing their bodies in order to reply accurately.

The soldiers assigned to machine guns understood the importance of their deadly weapons. The three machine guns were treated as our platoon's most precious possessions, the most valued protectors of our lives. As long as the supply of bullets held out, there was no chance for the enemy to overwhelm the machine-gun positions by charging it, no matter how fearless or determined they were. The machine-gun crews always tried to get their hands on as many ammunition cases as they could carry and store in their foxholes.

For an infantry attack to be successful the enemy would first have to dislodge or disable our machine guns. That could be accomplished with a direct hit from a mortar or artillery shell, or by crawling close enough to throw a grenade into the machine-gunner's foxhole, or by shooting the gunner. Attacking soldiers could get close enough to the machine guns only if there was sufficient cover to conceal them as they advanced. To prevent sneak attacks, we always tried to pick positions that provided an uninterrupted view across at least a few hundred metres of exposed ground in front of them.

Machine guns also made hand grenades practically useless in the predominantly flat and open countryside of the eastern Ukraine. It would have been extremely dangerous to get close enough to be able to lob a hand-held bomb with any effect, especially while prone. Standing up to throw it farther and more accurately at an enemy that was close enough to be hit would surely get you killed. After months at the front, we mainly carried the small egg-shaped hand grenades that could be hung on the utility belt.

During those series of rapid retreats, orders often came out of desperation, especially orders to counterattack a moving enemy unit. By that point in the war we all knew that our efforts would make no difference to the outcome of the war in the long run, and our endeavours would result only in delaying the Russian advance for a little while, each time at the cost of more lives. But the penalty for disobeying orders was court martial, after which you could be assigned to disciplinary units clearing minefields, or to some other hazardous activity. If the situation was critical, disobeying orders could mean being shot on the spot. I believe orders were given by our commanders to try to make the best of a deteriorating situation. The insanity of Hitler's order to hold any ground upon which the German soldier had set his foot was translated into much more pragmatic objectives at the front.

There was no room for idiots at the front. The pompous arrogance and political posturing of our leaders in Berlin portrayed in newsreel footage could not be emulated at the front. Military strategy and tactics at the company level had been reduced to accomplishing one very prag-matic objective — survival. Commanders who attempted feats that ob-viously flew in the face of reason would not survive for long. Company leaders who had lost the respect and confidence of their men could get themselves killed, as well as their men. I was always aware that if I expected my men to follow me and obey my orders faithfully, I would have to lead well. The men under my command were my responsibility and their fate could be in my hands, and that always weighed heavily on my mind. It was easily possible that, in spite of careful reasoning, a miscalculation, an oversight, a fear-induced hesitation, or a hasty deci-sion on my part could get someone killed. So far I had not made too many mistakes, as I was still alive and I had not given any orders that had directly cost a man his life.

Our commanders sometimes had sketchy information and poor maps to help coordinate movements with other units. We were often in countryside for which there were no maps available at all, compound-ing the confusion that rapid movements created. I never held a map in my hand during the entire time I was a company leader in Russia. I was given orders as to where to set up our defensive lines or which enemy position to attack by the battalion commander. He usually accompanied us after nightfall and told me where to dig in. I am sure he knew only what was happening within his own sector and had his own orders to follow.

The front was repeatedly in a state of flux. Command was probably in a repeated state of confusion. I sometimes had to make decisions without any assistance from Command, because the situation changed too rapidly and/or communications were not working. I then had to de-cide when to move, in which direction, where to set up a new defensive line, and which way to face it. It was probably as much by chance as by skill that we moved fast enough, or in the right direction, or picked sites that were defendable when the sun came up. There were also days at a time when it did not matter where we spent the day, or the night, because the enemy were temporarily too far away to be an immediate threat.

An infantry company in the German army was originally designed to have three officers, one to lead each platoon; however, given the brutal realities of the Russian front in 1943, a company would be

Front-line wireless

lucky if it still had two officers. If the company leader was killed or wounded the next in command took over right away, as I had in June. If I in turn were to be lost during combat, my place would immediately be taken by the sergeant from the other platoon until I could be replaced by another lieutenant. For the men at the fighting front, the high casualty rate for their officers was partly compensated by the fact that repeated combat had taught every soldier the essentials of tactics and survival, so that almost any front-line soldier could immediately take command of the situation if his immediate superior were lost.

Under ordinary circumstances my orders came quickly from the command centre behind the front lines, usually by wireless. For much of this desolate countryside there had never been any telephone wires installed, either Russian or German. If necessary, I sent my messenger back to the command post to receive orders directly from the battalion commander. The messenger could also relay my orders to the other platoon leaders in the event we were out of contact for a while. I made sure to keep him within speaking range whenever possible, and he was always in the next foxhole when we were dug in. One standing order that did not have to be repeated was for everyone in the company to always stay together.

The chain of command operated from the bottom up through the next larger unit, while orders always came from the higher level down to the bottom, and probably lost a great deal of strategic information along the way. I never saw the headquarters of our division, which was probably located many kilometres behind the front lines. I knew that division headquarters moved often, like our own battalion command post, in response to the moving battlefront. My captain would tell me as many particulars as he thought necessary to enable me to make decisions that were vital to the operation of my company, and no more.

As a lieutenant I was rarely told what part my company was to play in the overall strategy of defending a section of the front. Other than the approximate positions of the three companies of our battalion, I had no idea what was going on with the rest of the German forces in our small sector, let alone the entire Eastern Front. For me and my men the front was no larger than the ground we could see around us. Without having experienced such front-line conditions it would be difficult for anyone to understand how little the fighting men actually knew about what was happening.

One piece of information that I did learn was that Italian, Hungarian, Romanian, or other foreign troops from countries allied with Germany were sometimes holding a portion of the front near us. In September I knew that Romanian troops were in the line to our south. The use of foreign troops probably created its own set of problems, especially those associated with communications and coordination of actions.

News about other parts of the front rarely reached us. I was usually suspicious of any news that did reach us, because reality was often distorted to keep up morale. At the company level war was rarely the well-organized and efficiently executed campaigns that are portrayed on newsreels. Even if well-planned, actual combat could quickly deteriorate into a series of confused and even haphazard movements and engagements, the outcome of which could depend more on luck than strategy or skill. It was often essential to improvise and adapt quickly to any situation in order to stay alive, and the battlefield was a merciless teacher.

Some common-sense tactics helped us stay alive. For example, when moving in the open, day or night, we always moved in small groups with large spaces between them, and in single file. We made sure never to bunch up so as to not offer the enemy an easy target. If any shooting started only a few men would be within range at any time. In that part of the Ukraine the terrain was generally flat and characterized by almost endless, unremarkable features—meadows, crop fields, and wooded areas that were mainly within hollows or gullies where meandering streams ran in the spring or after a rain. Almost always we were ordered to dig in somewhere within a meadow, generally near the top or on the eastward-facing slope of a shallow rise in the ground, where it was possible to see across a good field of view. We avoided distinct features in the landscape, as they could be deliberately targeted by enemy artillery or mortar fire as soon as they were recognized as defended positions.

We usually avoided towns, villages, and collective farms. We encountered many villages, only because we traversed so much ground in our retreat. The eastern Ukraine was sparsely populated compared with western Europe, and there was only a fraction of the number of villages that the same amount of territory would contain in Germany. Fighting across open ground was bad enough, but house-to-house fighting would have been exceedingly dangerous, and trying to capture a town where the defenders could make a determined stand would be terrible. Luckily, my company was usually in the middle of nowhere.

Another consideration that may explain why inhabited places were usually avoided at the Eastern Front was that the army had issued a standing order against fraternizing with civilians. I am sure that order was sometimes interpreted and enforced rather loosely. Regardless, to us front-line soldiers, civilians were not considered combatants. No matter where we were, we mostly tried to avoid them. That attitude probably did not reach up from the ordinary foot soldier to the military high command, whom I doubt cared what happened to individuals. As I had learned in France, civilians often just got in the way of campaign strategies.

I had learned in Officer School that the reason German soldiers were forbidden to molest civilians or loot civilian property had more to do with maintaining discipline and morale than humanitarian motives. The army leadership had figured out that committing crimes against people or their property could diminish a soldier's self esteem, creating feelings of guilt or lack of self-respect. Human nature being what it is, a soldier could be less likely to make a selfless effort to save a comrade-in-arms if he considered him unworthy or had just lost respect for a fellow soldier who had committed a loathsome crime. The underlying value to the army of those standing orders was to produce effective soldiers.

MG34 machine-gun position in Russian village

MP40 automatic submachine gun

We had also been warned that Russian partisans sometimes booby-trapped deserted villages just before they abandoned them. Land mines could be buried in the main roads, or anti-personnel mines could be hidden on abandoned wagons, or in furniture, or under floorboards in houses, which would blow up when you moved their cover or accidentally touched them.

Most villages were deserted by the time we came upon them, although not all. We were sometimes ordered to burn a village when we left, ostensibly to prevent its being used by the enemy following us. That was literally a "scorched earth policy." Whenever the village was still occupied by civilians or it was evident they had recently left, that struck me as just mindless destruction. Regardless of how repugnant and pointless it seemed to me, orders had to be obeyed; but . . . I reckoned that since we were leaving anyway and would probably never be back, it would not matter that we were not very thorough in carrying out such orders. So I instructed my men to just pile some straw against the sides of some sheds along the westerly edge of the village and set those on fire. Hopefully that would make a grand enough display of flame and smoke to satisfy Command, especially when viewed from our headquarters, while leaving most of the buildings untouched. No one had any enthusiasm for burning people's homes.[10]

One of the more useful pieces of battlefield knowledge was to avoid forested areas. The Ukraine contained some extensive areas of forest or scrub, most of which were overgrown with relatively short and uniformly scruffy-looking trees which invariably resembled poplars to me. Even a small area of woods could hide a considerable force of enemy soldiers or partisans. They could be used as bases of operation or as conduits for troops to infiltrate through our defences. Remnants of enemy forces that had been bypassed by German spearheads advancing eastward two years before continued to operate in the conquered territory, as large parts of Russia could not be controlled or even investigated by German occupation troops. Digging in near any kind of forested area could be dangerous, as enemy soldiers could sneak up on us undetected during the night. If caught napping, a spade could cut your head off, silently and efficiently. In that case your life would not even cost the enemy a bullet.

Enemy forces in a woodlot were extremely dangerous. Defended positions in wooded areas were almost invulnerable to attack, as they could not be stormed, even with armoured and artillery support. Any

---

10   German rear echelon forces usually tried to clear civilians out of an area that was expected to be overrun by an enemy attack, not only to avoid civilian casualties, but also to keep the battle zone clear of refugees that could impede the rapid movement of troops and military vehicles. Many Ukrainians chose to leave with the retreating German armies, trying to avoid living under Stalin's regime after the war.

attempt to dislodge a hidden enemy could be very costly if they had time to dig in and construct defences. Those defences could include foxholes, slit trenches, underground bunkers and tunnels, barbed wire, abatis, concealed pointed stakes, pit traps, and land mines, all of which could be very difficult to spot from a safe distance. At night it was impossible to see anything in wooded areas. If possible, I always gave a wide berth to any wooded areas we passed.

We rarely knew where the enemy would be by the next dawn, not only because they deliberately tried to hide their strength and intentions from us, but also because the moving front created confusion and disorder that was difficult to monitor. The only certainty was that the enemy were never far away. We often saw enemy troops, but usually just out of rifle range. Sometimes we saw nothing of the enemy at all for days. We were aware that we were being forced to retreat over the same ground German armies had conquered two years earlier.

The Russians became very skilled at finding and exploiting weak points between strongly defended German positions, and at moving large numbers of troops and heavy weapons to parts of the front that were poorly defended. It happened to us more than once where enemy forces had breached a section of our lines with a determined offensive. As that breach was being expanded the remaining German units nearby retreated rapidly, including my company, trying desperately to avoid being encircled.

The Russians often sent out reconnaissance patrols, as did we, to verify enemy positions and strength, day and night. We posted sentries every night, as we always had to be wary of a night attack.

An enemy attack was almost always preceded by an artillery barrage, as a means of "softening up" our defences or to try to rout defenders from dug-in positions. We heard artillery fire coming from somewhere almost every day throughout August and September, and were on the receiving end of shelling more times than I care to remember. Incoming shells could be heard distinctly, and usually gave us time to take cover; although, one early morning artillery barrage late in August took us by surprise in the open as we trudged along a dirt road. Everyone immediately ducked into whatever holes, depressions, or other physical havens that presented themselves, and frantically dug into the earth like moles. Shells that burst directly overhead were the most dangerous, as they would send shrapnel flying down on top of

you. In a foxhole you made yourself as small a target as possible, relying on your helmet to keep from being hit in the head.

Our commanders had figured out it was more prudent to abandon
our line of foxholes in the middle of the night and dig a new line about
a kilometre farther back. When the next enemy barrage came at dawn,
it pounded the defensive line we had abandoned. Command then decided whether or not to try to reoccupy and defend the line. I guess that
depended upon how much the latest reconnaissance information could
be trusted. There were Russian infantry attacks that found nothing but
empty foxholes.

Our forces also used artillery barrages to try to destroy an enemy
attack or at least create enough casualties or enough terror to help
turn back the attackers. I had been trained how to call for pinpoint
artillery support. If the wireless failed for any reason, one man in each
platoon carried a flare gun to signal the artillery spotters regarding
the accuracy of support fire and to help make adjustments as needed.
The signal flare gun could fire different types of flares. There was one
colour to indicate that our barrage struck too far away to hit enemy
positions, and another to indicate that it landed too short to do any
damage. There was one type of flare that really came in handy when
my company was once fired upon by our own artillery. As soon as those
shells burst in our midst the signalman moved really fast and fired one
of those flares into the air to let the gunnery spotters know they were
shooting too close. We held our breath until the next rounds burst farther away.

All that knowledge notwithstanding, reality at the Eastern Front
meant that supporting artillery fire for any unit had to be sanctioned
by battalion command, or perhaps even higher up, and they must have
had their own difficulties, or priorities, as it was not always available
to us.

In the pre-dawn of another morning early in September we were
startled awake by a dreadful series of loud howling sounds. We saw a
spectacle of flame and fury as groups of rockets flew overhead—Katyusha rockets. They were one-and-a-half-metre-long rockets that were
carried to the battlefield and launched from specially designed racks
on the backs of trucks or modified tank chassis. We could see the salvos being launched from behind their lines. The repeated screeching
howl of hundreds of those rockets was extremely nerve-wracking. At

first I assumed they were aimed at our artillery batteries because some exploded well behind our lines, or they were just woefully inaccurate. But after a while of that barrage I noticed that the greatest number of salvos saturated an area to the south of where my company was. The poor bastards under that barrage would bear the brunt of another enemy attack. I passed the order to my men to prepare for another hasty retreat.

The Katyusha barrage was soon followed by the distinctive whistle of incoming mortar shells. For my company at the Eastern Front in 1943, mortars were the most common enemy artillery pieces used against us, and the most deadly. They were very difficult to defend against. They were simple to operate, even during strenuous battlefield conditions or inclement weather. The rate of fire could easily be dozens per minute from each mortar, depending upon how fast the operators could be kept supplied with projectiles.

Some of the Russian mortars, like some of their big machine guns, were equipped with little wheels, which made them look like a child's pull toy being towed across the battlefield by two soldiers. Once set up for action they quickly lost any semblance of a toy. The hollow pop of shells leaving the mortar tubes, as well as the whine of shells flying overhead toward us, were terrifying sounds that often formed part of an infantry skirmish.

The mortar bombs had a maximum range of less than three kilometres and produced less damage than the larger cannon shell; but dozens of them could be zeroed in on a machine gun until one would land close enough to a foxhole, or even right inside it, killing or wounding the soldier or soldiers manning the hole, or destroying the machine gun. If a soldier noticed his hole was being targeted, it was prudent to crawl out quickly and dig a new hole far enough away to avoid being hit. Such an escape attempt would of course be very dangerous if the enemy infantry were within rifle range.

Most Russian infantry companies had mortars, and I wondered why every infantry company in the German army was not also equipped with mortars. When I arrived at the Eastern Front in June 1943 our infantry battalion had a mortar platoon supporting us with the standard type of mortar we called *Granatwerfer* (literally, grenade thrower). I assumed that was common practice for all battalions. They were not assigned permanently to one company but were allocated to wherever they were considered most needed. Our mortars could be taken apart and carried in three pieces; the hollow barrel and bipod on the back of one man, and the large square base plate on the back of another. Other soldiers carried the projectile cases.

There were far too few mortars available to us to make much difference in beating back the recurring Russian attacks; however, by that stage of the war it may not have made much difference to us anyway, because mortars were probably a more effective weapon for attacking than for defending.

We also had to put up with attacks from sources other than the Russian army. Sometime late in August I had noticed an insistent itch on my abdomen near my belt line, along with an occasional irritation like a prolonged pinprick. That was accompanied by the subtle but unmistakable feeling of something tiny crawling up the front of my shirt against my skin. I slapped hard against my chest. When I got the chance I took off my shirt and saw a few reddish dots on my skin. "*Läuse?*" (lice) the man beside me said, verifying the obvious. His slight grin indicated what passed for amusement at the Eastern Front.

Damn! My clothes had been invaded by a company of the tiny vermin. I inspected my clothing but could not see any signs of them, nor could I feel anything in the uniform or the undershirt. Lice could hide in seams, where the cloth was folded over, and they are very tough. It was almost impossible to squash them even if you could hunt them down. If we had stayed in civilized accommodations for a while I might have had a chance to get rid of them by ironing the seams with a hot iron or a very hot bayonet, but in a foxhole in the middle of nowhere that was just wishful thinking. From then on I could feel them crawling up and down the inside of my shirt. My messenger once commented, "The little fiends are more persistent than the SS. I can just picture them goose-stepping all over my skin."

Since it was impossible to get rid of them, I had to endure their pinpricks as they sucked my blood, usually from my belly, small of my back, or armpits. Fortunately they did not feed all the time, and they really did no permanent harm, other than irritate me to the point of distraction. If I had not been so exhausted each night I probably would have been kept awake by those critters and they might have driven me crazy. I told myself I just had to learn to live on intimate terms with my tiny companions and that I would eventually get used to them. I hoped they would not reproduce too fast. They too were now part of the *Wehrmacht*, which was ironic, considering they were Russian lice. Anyway, I never got used to them. Nobody did. They remained a tenacious, relentless, infuriating scourge from hell for the remainder of my stint at the front.

We were occasionally supplied with new undershorts, an undershirt, and socks. My socks were usually very ripe by the time they were replaced, and the underclothes had often been repeatedly soaked with perspiration. It is incredible how delighted soldiers could be made to feel just by receiving something we had previously taken for granted. New underclothes also gave us a few hours' respite from the feeling of lice on our skin but, because they lived in our uniforms, they always came back. They may also have found delight in each fresh undergarment.

By mid-September the Russian pressure on our lines had been more or less constant for over a month. Overwhelming offensives repeatedly forced us to retreat, sometimes daily, to avoid being surrounded and cut off. There were few periods of relief from the necessity of spending the days hiding in a foxhole and at least part of the nights marching. Sometimes our line would be stable for a few days, but inevitably we would be forced to retreat again, scrambling to find relative safety farther back. I hoped our generals knew enough to take appropriate measures to keep us from being encircled, or overrun, or annihilated.

Our commanders had learned how to make formidable defensive stands and carry out quick and bold counterattacks that would often disorganize or cut off an enemy advance, causing their offensives to stall. That may help account for the fact that the Eastern Front was pushed westward as slowly as it was, in spite of the overwhelming numerical and logistical superiority of the Russian forces.

I never knew what part we played in the blunting of a major Russian offensive, the defence of a district, or just the strategic repositioning of the front. The objectives of the few counterattacks I led were always confined to enemy positions occupying a local feature within sight—a collection of houses, a road, a hedgerow, a section of railway tracks, or just a line of foxholes. Movements were mainly dictated by opportunity, such as spotting enemy troops moving past us in the adjoining fields. Sometimes we had to hold a road junction, a bridge, a deserted village, or an isolated railway station.

Any action at night was particularly dangerous. One such night skirmish happened when we blundered into a Russian position, and it deteriorated quickly into a confusing and perilous situation. The sounds of shooting were soon coming from everywhere. In the darkness we were just as likely to be shot by our own troops as by the enemy. It was impossible to coordinate my platoon's actions with the entire company, let alone the battalion. Not knowing which way to run, we just had to wait it out where we were. By morning the enemy had disappeared.

Considering the clamour of battle we frequently witnessed at a distance, my company had been relatively lucky up to then, as there were only a few occasions where enemy artillery or rocket fire hit us directly. Most skirmishes were fought at relatively long range, without having to engage the enemy in close and deadly fighting. Nevertheless, we suffered casualties that slowly but inexorably diminished our numbers. The Russian losses were always replaced with seemingly inexhaustible reserves of men and equipment. That was certainly not the case for us. My company never received any replacements. To make matters worse, I assumed that as time progressed the Russian soldiers facing us gained experience and fought with increasing confidence and ability, even though their tactics never appeared to change.

Late in September it rained. That was the first serious rain we had experienced since about the middle of July. It was not until then that it occurred to me that there had been a ten-week drought. I had no idea whether or not dry summer weather was normal for that part of the Russian Ukraine.

Every soldier carried a *Zeltplan*, a triangular-shaped cape made from oiled canvas with a motley camouflage pattern on it. As soon as it threatened rain I constructed my foxhole just big enough to hide in, but small enough to cover the entire hole with my little *Zeltplan*. The dirt was packed around the edge creating a little dyke that sloped away from the rim. The fringe of the cape was placed just over the rim and secured with sticks. If that tiny tent was set skilfully it should shed rain water down the slope, keeping the hole reasonably dry. I just hoped it would not rain for too long.

It rained all day. Everything became increasingly wet until there was no way to keep the water out, and no way to prevent the foxhole from becoming filled with mud. Rainwater eventually seeped through the soil, so that the sides of the foxhole could not be shored up to keep them from turning into oozing mud. I just had to bear it. The small excavation turned into a dismal, soggy wallow, necessitating frequent re-shoring and bailing to keep it from filling with mud. A muddy hole was a miniature hell. After it became dark enough I got out of the foxhole and sat under my cape in the rain, fighting a losing battle against the elements. Eventually the water soaked through my coat, my uniform, and my underclothes. It seeped down into my boots, which was absolutely vile. I felt like a wet dog.

Not only did every one of us get wet and muddy, but everything we touched became coated with mud. Just getting out for a shit was an arduous nuisance. Then everything became filthy, absolutely everything. If you could find some paper to wipe your ass, it would be wet and mud-stained. It is impossible to convey how miserable living in cold, wet mud really is, feeling as if trapped in the fetid guts of a malignant earth.

We packed up and marched off. I drew my *Zeltplan* over my head and tied it down in front, but my uniform stayed soaking wet, hanging very heavy on my body. It was quite cold at night late in September. Everyone hunkered down and endured it. I cursed the rain over and over. Finally the battalion commander ordered me to move my company and take shelter in the first village we could find away from the front. Good idea, as it looked like the rain would not let up. Command must have known it was important to try to keep us dry if at all possible. Getting soaked and chilled could lower resistance to disease and possibly lead to contracting pneumonia, or tuberculosis, or influenza, or some other damnable ailment, any of which could be as dangerous as being shot by a bullet.

With the rain came the inevitable return of the *Rasputiza*. The dirt road quickly turned to mud, which became worse as we marched, until we were slogging through the same energy-sapping morass that had beleaguered my march in the spring of 1942. Regardless of the strain, it was impossible to get any relief, since there was no dry place to sit, unless you took off your helmet and sat on it, which of course would become caked with mud.

Toward dawn we arrived at an abandoned village, only to find that the entire battalion had the same objective — to find some dry shelter. The houses were made of white, stucco-like material, not wood like the typical Russian *isbas*, and most had thatched roofs. They looked as if they had recently been abandoned. We opened the doors to several houses before we found one that was not already occupied by a ragtag crew of sodden soldiers. My whole platoon piled in.

There was no dry firewood in the house, so we smashed the furniture to make a fire in the tiled oven and stripped off our sodden and filthy uniforms, hanging them wherever possible to give them a chance to dry out. I stuck my bayonet in the wall and hung my uniform on it. We kept the fire going to stay warm. We washed mud off our bodies in the cold rainwater outside and dried our uniforms as best we could inside. It took hours of painstaking labour for us to clean our weapons. Some of the men were so tired they just collapsed in a heap on the floor, sleeping practically naked. Anyone that had to relieve himself was forced to go outside and get wet and muddy again, as there were no indoor facilities. We also had to get wet and muddy to retrieve our food from the field kitchen, as there was no room service.

The only advantage of heavy rain was that the enemy soldiers were probably just as wet and miserable as we were, and too preoccupied trying to avoid the rain themselves to carry out any sort of attack. We posted night sentries at the village outskirts anyway, just in case.

Finally it stopped raining. We waited for the roads to dry out. After huddling in our temporary home all day I was ordered to return to where we had abandoned our last defensive line, but that turned out to be futile, as the Russians had beat us to it. Again we retreated.

Inclement weather caused my *Zeltplan* to assume a disproportionate importance in my life from then on. It had a camouflage pattern on it, but for some reason our uniforms and greatcoats did not. Our grey-green uniforms must have been blatantly conspicuous against the background of vegetation in which we were usually trying to hide, especially when new and clean. The Russian uniforms were a drab, olive brown, which appeared to me to provide better concealment. I wondered why the German army continued to issue standard grey-green uniforms and never produced a camouflage pattern to help us blend into our surroundings. Anything that would make us less conspicuous to the enemy would have been useful. Perhaps the army decision-makers thought that after a week or two at the Eastern Front the uniform would become the same dull colour as the dirt in which the soldiers spent most of their time.

One night near the end of September we were taken back a long distance and loaded onto trucks in the middle of the night. That was so different it made me suspicious that something big was afoot. As the trucks rolled out most of us in the back of the truck immediately fell asleep. I certainly did. There was shelter and relative safety in the canvas-covered bed of that moving carrier, so I gave in to my exhaustion. Someone else—the driver—was temporarily responsible for my welfare, and I abandoned the wariness that had dominated my senses for the past three months.

It must have been a deep retreat, much farther and on a much larger scale than what we had been used to until then. The only thing I remember clearly was getting out of the truck to help push it through mud whenever it got stuck. During the night we must have crossed the Dnieper, because the next morning we dug in near the banks of a huge river. Although I did not attribute any special significance to it at the time, we were on the west side of the river. Interconnected earthworks had been constructed in our sector, including relatively large earth and timber bunkers, some bolstered with sandbag walls.

My company dug our own extensive fortifications, including interconnected trenches, large enough to enable us to stand upright without exposing our heads, as well as underground bunkers, with straw bales or wooden beds. It was exhausting labour, but resulted in relatively luxurious sleeping conditions. I expected that our heavily fortified lines on the west side of the river would help us make a strong stand.

No such luck. After a few weeks in our new position, we heard the sound of an artillery bombardment in the distance. Once again many airplanes flew overhead. Again we awaited the inevitable order to retreat. A few days after the artillery barrage we had to abandon our underground accommodations in a hurry. Apparently our flank had been breached and the front had moved again. Once more we were in danger of being encircled. If it had not been so dangerous, it could have been called routine.

Around mid-October we were issued greatcoats, mitts, and thick underwear. Good thing, as the weather turned very cold. I was not looking forward to another damn winter in Russia. At night the temperature quickly dropped below freezing. I then considered myself fortunate if the mud in my foxhole did not freeze before it was dark enough for me to get out without being shot by enemy snipers. Just washing became difficult. The nights became so cold I would not take my coat off, let alone my uniform, for fear of freezing.

If my boots and socks were to get wet, my feet could become frostbitten. On a cold night early in November the days of fighting had again left me exhausted. I awoke shivering with cold and became truly scared when I could not feel my feet. I carefully took off my boots and socks and massaged my feet and toes. I feared two of my toes could be frostbitten, the same toes that had barely escaped frostbite near Leningrad last year, but they recovered.

If a man loses some toes, especially the big toe, he cannot walk properly and has to be sent home, crippled but alive. In freezing weather wet socks may have caused as many casualties as bullets. I did not want to become one of those casualties, even though the thought crossed my mind that such an escape might be the lesser of two evils—the other being to stay at the front.

And "escape" expressed the appropriate sentiment. It was impossible to get out of our predicament without suffering a mishap. My world was confined to a very narrow strip of ground between the enemy lines and the German command posts at the rear of our own lines. We might as well have been in a cage, a cage that moved as we retreated westward.

Since escape was not an option, I kept telling myself that I could endure this torment, that it had to end sooner or later. There was another consideration that kept us here—no one could abandon his comrades, even if there had been an opportunity. I knew the men under my command depended on me to lead them through that hell.

I wondered why every man did not freeze to death sleeping in a foxhole during the cold of a Russian winter. There was nothing but your uniform, your greatcoat, and your *Zeltplan* cape to keep you warm. I was sometimes so cold I could not sleep at all. Some mornings it took a long time to revive to full function, numb from the cold. When combined with being drained of energy in body and spirit, my body moved like an automaton in the cold, seemingly without conscious direction from my mind. Amazing what the body can endure if it has to.

After months at the front it became impossible to keep my teeth clean. My toothpaste had run out by the end of September and, like most men in my platoon, I had worn out or lost my toothbrush. Cleaning my teeth then became a matter of scraping as much of the crud off as I could with a small piece of wood or a washcloth. But no matter what I did, there was no way to make my mouth feel clean. Like everything else about the front at that time, I just lived with it. Dental hygiene may not have been a high priority for the army.

The army did, however, place a high priority on maintaining discipline and the appearance of order. It was an unspoken policy that every soldier should try to be clean-shaven. Most of the men shaved as often as was feasible. The motivation was more than vanity, as it was easier to keep clean without a beard. If your beard became more than a centimetre long, the itching made you wonder what was living in there.

Each of us carried our own shaving kit, with a razor, a stick of shaving soap, and a little brush for lathering the soap. The soap looked like a small candle wrapped in paper, which was peeled back to expose more soap as it was needed. Other than that shaving soap, which the army issued, personal hygiene items were not supplied. Some of the men carried a small hand-held mirror. Those who did not have a mirror would usually borrow one. Everyone also had a facecloth for washing, and some men even managed to carry their own towel. Your tin cup could be used for lathering up the soap. Troops would requisition towels or other items in abandoned houses if they found them. Anything that could be used to make you feel cleaner was a precious find. Probably only caches of food were more valuable.

Every German soldier carried a round canister on his belt for storing his gas mask. Poison gas had been used as a weapon in the First World War, and the army commanders assumed it would be used again in this war. It was not, for which we should have been grateful. I guess highly mobile forces and a rapidly changing front had made poison gas an ineffectual weapon. Regardless, we were not allowed to lose our gas masks, and that canister was a constant clumsy part of our gear. Orders notwithstanding, I threw my gas mask away after the beginning of the forced retreats in August and used the space to carry my shaving kit, along with other toiletries. Some of the more pragmatic soldiers certainly did the same, and used those now handy canisters to also carry extra bullet clips, bread or found food items, and whatever other valuables they might acquire.

There were often opportunities to wash our faces and hands, or maybe rinse out our socks in a stream or water trough in a village. Detergent was unknown. In that part of the Ukraine there were very few streams, and rainfall was particularly scarce in that part of the country. Most of the watercourses we crossed had dried up completely by the end of July. Drinking water was always available from the field kitchen at night. Water quality was sometimes questionable, which was more than a matter of taste, as contaminated water could cause dysentery.

Shaving became truly grim by the beginning of November, when the nights turned very cold. Most of the men at the front sported short stubble by then. I must admit we were a rough-looking bunch.

The hair on my head also became a noticeable concern at the front. After weeks of not washing it became caked with dirt and sweat and my scalp felt grubby and itchy. At the beginning of my stint in Russia we had our hair cut regularly by the company barber, usually once a month. As the fighting intensified during the summer there were fewer and fewer opportunities to wash my hair or get it cut. So, if given the chance, most of us had our hair cut very short, with not much emphasis on style. By fall I was almost constantly preoccupied with self-preservation, so the condition of my hair was again relegated to a minor concern, something else I just had to get used to. A warm shower, with soap or detergent, along with clean clothes, were things dreams were made of.

Exhaustion also made everyone care less about the way they looked. I was in a stupor much of the time, and any opportunity for rest was used to sleep. The only opportunities we had to really rest or take care of personal appearance was when we retreated far enough that the enemy would not catch up to us for a few days and there was no imminent danger of an attack. But rest is not the right word for these short respites. It was the absence of being awake, but it was not restful. Sleep was fitful and uneasy, brief periods where consciousness just shut down.

War at the Eastern Front for me became a series of mind-numbing marches and long periods of anxious waiting, interspersed with short

The price paid by civilians—a burning Ukrainian village

bursts of furious activity that consumed all my energies. By then winning or losing the war had become completely meaningless. The sole objective of every man at the front was to live long enough to see the next sunrise.

When I stopped to think about it, everything we did appeared completely futile and ludicrous. After every desperate nighttime retreat we would again occupy hastily constructed foxholes, often in poor positions. I had assumed that if we had been permitted to organize and execute orderly retreats to more defensible positions that could have been prepared ahead of time, it would have saved a great many lives and perhaps allowed us to make a better stand against the Russians. But that desperate retreat across the Dnieper River demonstrated that such a strategy may not have made much difference anyway. The enemy had raced after us and managed more or less to keep up with our retreat.

We might as well have been ordered to hold back the tide. Trying to stop the Russian advance was impossible. No matter where we made a stand, no matter how courageously we fought, no matter what we did, that relentless red tide would overwhelm us eventually.

16 *An Army Marches on Its Stomach*

NAPOLEON HAD SAID THAT AN ARMY marches on its stomach. At the Eastern Front in 1943 I understood what he meant. It never ceased to amaze me that more than three million German soldiers could be fed at the front in Russia every day. That seemed like an organizational miracle.

Mobile field kitchens, which for our company were horse-drawn wagons, remained about two kilometres behind the lines during the day, preparing the night's meal. That separation would keep them out of sight and out of range of enemy rifle fire. The meal was invariably *Eintopf* (stew, or literally "one pot"), which was cooked in a huge kettle. It usually contained potatoes, vegetables such as cabbage, turnips, lentils, or carrots, and embellished with bits of meat or sausage. Sometimes it contained pieces of real meat, which probably happened when the kitchen unit had a chance to kill and cook a pig, cow, horse, or poultry. It was sometimes accompanied by fresh, or at least new, bread. I assumed the raw food sources came from local fields and farmers, since it was usually too fresh to have been transported all the way from Germany. Truthfully, I had no idea where it came from and really did not care.

Each night the horse-drawn field kitchen came up to the front and parked about fifty to a hundred metres behind the line of foxholes. By the late summer of 1943, the cover of darkness was usually the only opportunity to get a cooked meal, since there were many days we risked getting shot if we got out of our foxhole during daylight. In the summer daylight persisted until late into the evening.

Every soldier carried with him a *Feldgeschirr* (mess kit; literally, field dish), a rectangular tin, rounded at the corners, with a lid to keep the food from spilling and to keep it warm. As soon as it was dark enough a man from each squad would be sent back to the field kitchen with our tins to pick up our food rations. During nights when the enemy were nearby we could not make a campfire for fear of providing a conspicuous target to attract mortar fire. When we suspected the enemy were within rifle range we would not even have a lamp on anywhere. If there was no moon we would have to eat our food in complete darkness.

That may have been a mixed blessing, because the dark hid what we ate. Each soldier carried his own cutlery with him, so we just sat down wherever convenient, usually in our foxhole, and ate.

There was little concern for culinary etiquette at the front. In warm weather I just scraped out as much food from my dish as I could and then rinsed it out. There was never any detergent to wash it, but I always tried to make sure my food container was clean to keep the leftover bits from putrefying and causing food poisoning. After the weather turned really cold in November, I scraped out as much foodstuff as possible from the tin, then deliberately left it out in the open to freeze. That would retard the growth of bacteria. The icy residue was then chipped out of the corners the following morning with my bayonet to prevent it from contaminating the next meal.

We also received what had to do for coffee, what some of the Prussian soldiers referred to as *Mookefook*, which was made from roasted barley if we were lucky and some other roasted grain, or whatever, if we were less lucky. It never tasted as good as real coffee, which was of course impossible to obtain, but was probably no worse for us than the real thing. Sometimes there was tea instead of coffee, which tasted comparatively great. These warm liquids were somehow soothing, but had very little nutritional value. The fact that the water had to be boiled to make those drinks helped prevent dysentery.

The coffee or tea was brought in our *Feldflaschen* (canteen; literally, field bottle), a large steel flask covered with a layer of felt that helped keep the contents warm. The relatively soft felt covering also prevented the canteens from clanking loudly on our uniforms like a cow bell when trying to conceal our movements from the enemy. The canteen also carried water.

About once every three nights each soldier received a small loaf of heavy and hard rye bread, along with some cheese paste or sausage spread, which was either *Leberwurst* (liver sausage), or *Mettwurst* (a type of pale orange sausage paste). The cheese was mostly the soft type that squeezed out of a tube like toothpaste. Occasionally the bread would be accompanied by a little butter and a jar of jam, to be eaten for breakfast or whenever we had time.

Once in a while we even received special treats, such as apples or a piece of chocolate, which I appreciated dearly. Bottles of some kind of hard liquor, like schnapps or vodka, were usually available for a daily alcohol ration for those who wanted it. There was no prohibition against drinking alcohol in the German army. Each soldier also received three cigarettes as a daily ration. Not smoking or drinking probably kept me healthier than many of the other men.

Amazing how such a modest thing as a piece of chocolate or an apple could become the highlight of the week. Life for us front-line soldiers had been reduced to its most basic level. Our entire existence was preoccupied with just that—existence. Survival meant not getting shot or captured, getting enough food, trying to keep warm, and getting enough sleep to prevent total exhaustion. Concerning yourself with anything else was a waste of time.

Although the army food kept us alive, no one gained weight in Russia. If someone arrived at the front with some excess weight, he soon lost it. After a while everyone's body seemed to adjust to the food intake regimen and did not lose any more weight. There were no overweight soldiers among my troops. Strange how men of different sizes each survived on exactly the same amount of food rations.

There were a few days when we received no food at all, when the front had moved so quickly and so far that our position was not reported in time to battalion headquarters, or if a Russian assault had cut off the field kitchen unit, or caused it to flee beyond an accessible point. Then the bread and whatever other edible stuff we carried in our packs kept us from starving. As long as there was sufficient water to drink it was possible to survive for days without food, although the hunger pangs in my belly became downright bothersome at times.

Presumably the army tried to supply foods containing essential vitamins and minerals, and I believe there was a genuine attempt made to provide sufficient nutrition to at least keep us front-line troops healthy enough to fight. However, some of the men developed the distinctive yellow eyes of jaundice from the lack of vitamins. There were outbreaks of dysentery, if a batch of food was bad, or if the local water supply was contaminated. Needless to say, no matter what we received to eat, there were never any leftovers.

If a man became incapacitated from dysentery, he would be sent or carried back to the field medical station where he might have the opportunity to be nursed back to health. Usually anti-diarrhoea medication or proper nutrition would restore a man enough to be able to return to front-line duty within a week or so, unless he died of course.

If left untreated, dysentery could sap your strength to the point where your body would not recover. Many of the men lived with some form of digestive tract disorder much of the time; not enough to incapacitate them, but enough to make them feel wretched.

It was still forbidden by standing orders to plunder any farms or homes. Forbidden or not, we were sometimes in desperate circumstances where self-preservation forced the confiscation of food by our troops. I knew my men ransacked almost every house in deserted villages they came across, searching for food or articles that could make life at the front a little more bearable. It was scrounging, not looting, as the only "valuables" we took were food. If we came upon caches of stored foodstuffs we would eat as much as we could on the spot and then stuff as much as we could into our gear. For a short while in the fall we sometimes passed through orchards of plum or apple trees, where the men helped themselves to the fruits.

If troops became separated from their field kitchen for any length of time, I am sure they would kill chickens or other farm animals to supplement their rations if they could, but such opportunities were rare. Grazing cattle were rare at the front, even though the extensive meadows, hayfields, and cornfields produced cattle fodder. Farmers may have taken their animals with them when they abandoned a village, or more likely they were confiscated or moved by German rear echelon units.

So far my company was very lucky never to have been cut off from our supplies for more than a day or two at a time. Others were not so lucky. The fear of a terrible fate like that of the 6th Army was always lurking in a dark recess of my mind. It was easily possible that we could be surrounded and cut off from our supply lines, just like what had happened at Stalingrad. Those poor bastards must have eaten dogs, cats, rats—anything to survive. The spectre of Stalingrad haunted every German soldier at the Eastern Front.

The front was an alien world. It had its own rules of behaviour and its own motivations.

The feeling of fear was almost constant; however, after facing repeated dangers I learned to put fear into perspective. Not that we became fearless in the face of the enemy; it was more that fear somehow became relative to the situation at hand. When confronted with an attack there was rarely an opportunity to decide whether or not to expose your-self to mortal danger. You hid in your foxholes as much as possible, not just because you were afraid of getting hurt, but because exposing your body unnecessarily to enemy fire was stupid. You exposed only what was necessary in order to aim and fire. You stayed in position if ordered to do so. Your fears were irrelevant.

Fear of the enemy may not have been much of a motivator; fear of the consequences of disobeying orders surely was. Whether ordered to stay put or to get out of your hole and charge at the enemy, you did it, immediately and as efficiently as possible, in accordance with your training and knowledge. Military training had constantly reinforced obe-dience to orders, and that had instilled in every German soldier a con-ditioned response to obey commands that sometimes flew in the face of self-preservation instincts. Firmly planted in the back of my mind was the lesson that obedience to commands could help save my life.

Not only our training, but also the time we men spent together, helped each man disregard his own fears. There was a strong bond among the men. To help your comrades-in-arms in the face of danger was more than an obligation dictated by training or orders, more than team spirit, more even than the shame of appearing cowardly. It was a basic instinct, perhaps born of repeated conflicts shared by men with a common cause. I believe it would have been practically impossible for any of my men to abandon their comrades, even if they were in mortal danger. I could not have abandoned my men under any circumstances.

Terms such as courage, bravery, or valour were meaningless to front-line soldiers. At the Eastern Front in 1943, heart-stopping courage was not special or even extraordinary; it was commonplace. Soldiers did not consider their actions courageous, just necessary. Performing brave deeds in battle was more a matter of doing what had to be done to survive, rather than any noble ideas motivated by chivalry or cour-age. We were all aware that our lives often depended upon each other's selfless acts. In combat we soldiers rarely had time to contemplate the merits of our actions. We just reacted. There were countless acts of selfless courage at the front where men risked their lives to help their comrades that went unrecorded because the witnesses never got the opportunity to tell the tale.

Valour is a lovely concept when romanticized in movies or operas, but it means nothing to bullets, or shrapnel, or land mines, or anything else that could kill you in battle. Valour also means nothing to dysentery, typhoid, diphtheria, influenza, or the other common diseases at the front; or to freezing cold, mud, food poisoning, starvation, or any other evils that could kill you.

How farcical our leaders' political oratory about warfare was. Emotional rhetoric broadcast over the radio, or printed in newspapers, or shown in newsreels, about the war on the Eastern Front bore no resemblance to reality. I had heard politicians use phrases like "gallant soldiers covered in glory," or "noble actions," or other such bullshit. It might have been nice to just once experience anything that could have made me feel "gallant," or "noble," or "glorious" in Russia, but that was never the case. Glory is an abstract concept that exists only in the minds of those who have never even heard a shot fired at them, let alone fought at the front. It never entered my mind.

Hatred was also a meaningless emotion. Government propaganda had tried to instill in us a hatred for the Russians, but I felt no hatred for the enemy; it was not that personal. My men never expressed any hatred or even anger towards the enemy at the front. Russian soldiers were usually referred to as *Der Russe* (the Russian) or Ivan, an all-encompassing handy moniker that denoted no subjective judgements. Other than briefings about enemy activity, there was no reason to talk about the enemy at all. If the opportunity arose there may have been comments directed at Ivan laced with sardonic humour, perhaps as an attempt to make him appear less intimidating than he was, ridiculing his intelligence or fortitude or military prowess, but those were expressions of defiant contempt, not malice directed at real people.

Unless I actually spoke with one face to face, as with a prisoner, I never thought of the soldiers on the other side of the lines as individuals. I thought of them collectively as *Der Feind* (the enemy)—a vast, amorphous, and faceless war mechanism, completely impersonal and devoid of individual characteristics. Nobody in my company was stupid enough to take the Russians lightly, as we had no doubts about their ability to do us harm, but we recognized that they were just fellow soldiers caught in a situation not of their choosing.

Perhaps this detached attitude was essential to maintaining one's sanity in the midst of such insanity. When someone died or was terribly wounded, his comrades might say something like, "Poor guy, he got it." He was just in the wrong place at the wrong time. The death of a

comrade was perceived more as a matter of bad luck than as a deliberate act of murder. Even though death and injury were commonplace
parts of life at the front, the death of a comrade, a close friend, never
lost its impact.

Some of the men compared the Russian Front to hell. Not only my
fellow soldiers, but also innocent women and children, are victims of
war. Witnessing repeated horrible events made me question my faith in
the teachings of the Christian church. Shortly after arriving in Russia, we
had listened to a senior officer pontificating about God being on our side
and that defeat of the infidel Russians was a sacred duty for us defenders
of Christian values. What incredible bullshit, trying to convince grown
men that God was paying attention, let alone taking sides in such a sordid undertaking. It may have been that many of my fellow soldiers had
marched off to war convinced of the righteousness of our cause, at least
in the beginning. Once they arrived at the front and faced the reality of
warfare, such idealistic nonsense was soon set aside.

I had been brought up Lutheran, and there were other Protestants
and Catholics among the men. At the front any distinctions between
religious affiliations soon became irrelevant. Religious ceremonies, including mass or public prayer, which at first had seemed so important
in the lives of some of my men, especially the Catholics among them,
soon lost their meaning. My company had a chaplain, but the only time
he was distinguished from any other of the soldiers was when he administered last rites to a dying man. Some men may have attributed
an event that was nothing more than good fortune to assistance from
God. On the other hand, they may have attributed poor fortune to the
enemy, or to fate.

That is not to say that soldiers were not religious, or perhaps super-
stitious is a more appropriate term. Perhaps men clung tenaciously to
their faith as succour to help them abide the savagery and brutality they
confronted in that hell on earth. Some men prayed for divine interven-
tion when confronted with the possibility of imminent death. But my
common sense told me God would not help anyone in battle. Only your
wits, your weapons, your comrades, and especially good luck could
do that—and every soldier knew it. "Please let me survive this day"
was probably said more often than anything else in the face of danger,
imploring the God of Good Luck for assistance. Prayer may have eased
their minds, but it did not change their situation.

If it had not been for Gisela, I probably would have cared less about my own survival. My desire to see her again made me determined to live, to survive the nightmare of Russia. The desire to build a life together after the war drove me to try to outlast the atrocious conditions at the front. I kept telling myself over and over again that sooner or later the war had to come to an end and I could go home.

The most enduring feeling at the Eastern Front in the fall of 1943 was one of exhaustion; and "exhaustion" took on an entirely different meaning from anything I had experienced before. It was not simply the state of being overly tired; it was a debilitating condition that manifested itself as a numbing ache in every part of my body. The repeated and prolonged exertion insidiously sapped my body's strength, tearing down the ability to function effectively. I moved more by conditioned reflex than by deliberate will. Extraordinarily horrendous efforts to keep moving could cause my body to lose six or seven pounds in a day. Sometimes my consciousness just shut down, so that afterwards I had no memory of what I had just lived through. It felt as if I had become anaesthetized to everything except the sight and sound of immediate danger.

After weeks in the face of the enemy we soldiers at the front acquired much the same look, which has been termed "fatigued." It was not just the obvious and even expected exhaustion that results from days of exertion with little or no sleep; it was more subtle. It manifested itself as a sunken, hollow-eyed, slack-jawed look, where a man would not speak or even move for hours, often with his eyes open, staring vacantly toward the ground. A man would sometimes be so deadened to his surroundings that only a direct order shouted into his face could produce any response. Some soldiers became completely sullen, not moving or even reacting unless they were forced to do so.

Nevertheless, even without the slightest enthusiasm for anything or without a conscious desire to live, every soldier in my company became a very experienced veteran. Their survival instincts took over in the heat of battle, as if their bodies were functioning on autopilot. Hard-learned experience in innumerable skirmishes had taught them instinctive reactions that made them dangerous adversaries and trusted colleagues. Sometimes their quick and selfless responses saved not only their own lives, but the lives of their comrades, most of the time without realizing it and without thinking about it.

Even if on a rational level they considered life not worth living, many soldiers were motivated by a devotion to their comrades—their closest friends—and would defend them even if they had no wish to defend themselves. They thought of their platoon as their surrogate family. They probably also knew they were good soldiers, and were proud of that fact, if a feeling of "pride" had any relevance. That may have been all the motivation we had to cling to at the Eastern Front in 1943.

We cherished mail from home, and mail call was the most welcome event at the front. The mail came through irregularly, which is not surprising considering the circumstances of delivery. My company received mail about once a week, sometimes less often. A few of the packages in the mail contained treats, like chocolates or candies. Many of the men received mail from their families or girlfriends. I know it felt terrible to be away from wives, girlfriends, and families for so long, especially considering how little hope there was of returning home in the foreseeable future.

In my own case, I did not receive any mail from home the entire time I was in Russia. I also never wrote to my father. There was not much spare time, and most of it was at night when it was too dark to write. Writing paper and envelopes were scarce. Not only that, but I did not consider it useful to put my thoughts in writing to my father, or perhaps it just seemed too much of a chore. There was never any good news coming from Russia, and there was no point in complaining.

I received half a dozen letters from Gisela, which were absolutely precious. They were more than correspondence to convey information; they were a lifeline to a world that held out the promise of everything that I still cherished. Her letters contained mostly simple descriptions of ordinary events in her life, which then seemed like another world that I found difficult to relate to. The most important part of her letters was that she missed me and was waiting for my return. That would always rekindle the fervent hope of seeing her again.

Gisela's letters were addressed to "*Leutnant Albin Gagel im Felde*" (in the field), with my serial number on them. Each letter had a field posting number on it, a code for where I was stationed. She had no idea where on the Eastern Front I was serving, as the army would not have told her. Soldiers were forbidden to write any information about where they were stationed or what unit they were with. Gisela's letters had not been opened, so the mail did not appear to be censored. One letter mentioned something about her last letter, which I had not received. That meant the mail sometimes did not get through, which did not surprise me.

I missed Gisela very much, and wrote to her a few times. I could not bring myself to tell her how horrible life at the front really was, so my first letter just told her I was fine, sometimes even a little bored. As summer turned to fall my letters increasingly expressed the hope that I would come out of this predicament alive, although I took care not to mention how grim conditions were and especially not that my life was ever in danger. There was no need to cause her any unnecessary worry.

Mail did not always contain happy tidings. In one of her letters Gisela mentioned that the home front was becoming increasingly dangerous for civilians because of the ever-escalating Allied bombing raids upon Berlin and other big cities. A few of my men received letters with news that someone in their family had been killed or injured by bombs. One soldier, a tall quiet man, received a letter that his entire family—his wife and young daughter—had been killed in a bombing raid that had destroyed much of the city of Hamburg. When he read the letter he gripped his abdomen and just rocked back and forth for hours, moaning as if he had been shot in the stomach. I felt terribly sorry for him. We empathized with his pain, but there was nothing any of us could possibly say or do that could console him. Nothing worse could have happened to him. He had lost everything he lived for. His mood was agonizingly sombre after that. It became obvious that he did not want to keep living anymore. I now know it is possible to die of a broken heart.

Such was life at the Russian front in the fall of 1943.

17 *Night Moves*

BY EARLY NOVEMBER my company was defending a portion of the front that had recently moved to somewhere west of Kremenchug. The fighting had been haphazard and sporadic for a few weeks. We had been forced to retreat repeatedly because other sectors of the front had been attacked and thrown back. Those enemy advances were sometimes so far away that we may not even have heard any sounds of the fighting that had forced us to move. Even though a determined and overwhelming attack had not hit us directly, we could not avoid suffering casualties during repeated minor skirmishes.

My company had not received any reinforcements at all since we arrived at the Eastern Front in June 1943, over five months previously. I had made a request for replacements, but was told there were none available. The captain was aware that casualties were not being replaced, and troop strength was not anywhere near what it was supposed to be. He said that new units sometimes arrived at the front, just like we had in June, but those units were assigned to fill gaps where the need was considered greatest. Even though we did not receive replacements to make up for the men we lost, our ever-dwindling numbers were still considered to be a company, and we were expected to defend the same amount of ground as if we were at full strength.

An infantry company of the German army at that time was designed to consist of well over a hundred men. When I took command in July the company was still near full strength, having lost only the *Oberleutnant*. By the beginning of November we had been reduced to about sixty men. The lack of numerical strength was somewhat compensated by the fact that those sixty were seasoned veterans by then, whose experience was worth much more than the presence of many inexperienced recruits. My men were all tough and savvy, but no matter how skilful they were, we had probably just been lucky so far. Sooner or later we would find ourselves in front of a major enemy assault. Their reconnaissance was bound to discover how weak our defensive line was, and they would direct an attack right at our sector. I figured that by now I must have used up the majority of whatever good luck fate had allotted to me.

That night we were again ordered to dig in, once more in the middle of nowhere. Once again I spent a miserable night in a hole in the earth. I awoke to find a layer of wet snow covering the ground. No wonder I was so cold. As we marched off again I noticed that even at night our relatively dark uniforms must have stood out against the white of the fresh snow. I was happy to see the snow melt during the day, after which there was just a shallow layer of mud to contend with — nothing serious, but enough to stick to our boots and make walking exasperating. The mud also made it impossible to find a dry place to sit when we stopped to rest. Once again Mother Russia's General Mud let us know he was still on duty.

Probably a few days later, I was ordered to move my company to the top of a low hill a few kilometres from our present position. I was ordered to find a good vantage point overlooking the valley, dig in along the far side of the hill, and be prepared to defend that section of the front.

At the time I did not know where the main force of the enemy was; however, Command had told me that there had been considerable enemy movement, along with skirmishes to the north and south of our position, and that I should stay alert and report any signs of enemy activity. My company had certainly moved a lot recently. One thing I was sure of, the enemy were not far away. I assumed Command did not know where the bulk of the enemy forces were.

The situation made it necessary to move only at night. It was prudent to try to hide from the enemy the fact that my company, and indeed our entire battalion, was so under-strength that we were stretched dangerously thin. If that information reached the Russian commanders, it could invite the brunt of a full-scale enemy assault directed right at us. The thought of that very real possibility preyed on my mind more and more as the days passed.

After nightfall my company moved forward silently and carefully, with each platoon moving in single file and spread out. I was at the front of a squad as we walked across a meadow and approached a large field near the base of the hill on the other side of a road. There was just enough light from the moon to make out tepee-like stacks of harvested cornstalks interspersed throughout the field. I estimated that our destination at the top of the hill was still at least a kilometre away. I ordered a halt while my squad proceeded first into the cornfield.

Cautiously entering the field, I suddenly spotted a machine-gun barrel sticking out of a nearby cornstack. I motioned to the two men nearest me, pointed at the cornstack, and held up three fingers. At my signal the two men jumped onto the cornstack as I poked my automatic into the opening at the rear of the stack. We surprised two young Russian soldiers manning the machine gun, taking them prisoner.

I don't know why they did not fire at us, as they could have killed me and many of my men. Maybe they thought we were fellow soldiers? Maybe they had hoped to remain undetected if they just stayed still in the dark, allowing us to pass by? Maybe they were afraid that a firefight would also get them killed? Perhaps they had relaxed their vigil for a moment and did not notice us approach in the moonlight? Whatever, it was a very close call.

We quietly retreated from the cornfield with our prisoners. I had my machine-gunners set up their weapons in the swale at the side of the road.

We took the two prisoners to the rear of the company for interrogation. My messenger fetched a Russian interpreter. The German army in Russia contained many men from satellite states of the Third Reich, or from Eastern European countries such as Poland or Czechoslovakia, who spoke or at least understood Russian. Many Germans had been exposed to the Russian language before the war, either in school, or for business, or even political purposes. Army command tried to assign at least a few of those men to every company serving in Russia.

The two Russian soldiers at first appeared to be frightened at having been captured. When my interpreter asked them my questions they answered in a strange dialect he could hardly understand. Eventually he grasped the essence of their answers. They appeared almost eager to provide us with at least general information about their forces. We found out that the rest of their infantry company was in the cornfield that we had been about to go through. I asked how many men were in their company. "Many," they answered.

"How many?" I asked. "One hundred? Two hundred? Three hundred?"

One man nodded and said, "Da," to all three numbers. Both men looked perplexed. Perhaps their concept of a company was different from ours?

"How many soldiers altogether are in the cornfield?" I asked.

"Many," was again the reply.

It occurred to me that perhaps they could not count. When they were asked if they could count, both men emphatically said they could. But each time we asked how many troops were in their company the answer was the same: "Many." I eventually gave up, concluding that they really did not know. Maybe they could not count beyond the number of fingers on their hands.

"Any tanks with you?" I asked.

"No."

"Any cannons?"

"No."

"Any horses?"

"Yes."

I did not bother to ask how many. "What was your objective?"

"No idea."

I believed them. "Were you ordered to prepare to attack?"

"No."

I did not believe that. I checked for signs that either of them was drunk, knowing that Russian troops were sometimes given plenty of vodka prior to an attack.

Out of curiosity, my interpreter asked where they were from. Both gave the same name, which none of us had ever heard before. Obviously they were from a part of the Soviet empire very far away. One prisoner suggested that he would like to be taken to Germany, because life was very hard under Stalin's rule. He said that with a smile, making it sound like Germany was the land of opportunity. It had not occurred to me before that there were Soviet citizens who hated being in Russia as much as I did.

I figured we had learned as much useful information as those two Russians would give us, or could give us, so I returned to my men at the edge of the cornfield. I ordered two men to accompany me, crossed the road, and very cautiously proceeded into the field. Every few dozen metres we stopped and listened. It was now very dark and visibility was extremely limited. I was careful not to make any noise, knowing the enemy could not be far away. After about two or three hundred metres of slow and stealthy advance from one cornstack to another, I heard Russian voices coming from in front of us. That confirmed the two prisoners' stories. That also made the situation very scary. Holding my breath, I listened intently, but could not determine anything more about the enemy forces. Slowly and carefully we turned and headed back, feeling like someone was breathing down the back of my neck.

When we returned I ordered the entire company to dig in along the swale beside the dirt road that skirted the cornfield, and instructed them to be prepared for an early morning attack. I radioed Command to tell them what we had learned about the enemy.

Around midnight I was alerted to the sound of a horse-drawn wagon approaching along the road. My first thought was that this may be the head of a Russian column. We crouched in the dark beside the road and waited. A horse-drawn Russian field kitchen appeared out of the darkness. The driver and guard did not see us until we stood up and surrounded them, taking them prisoner and commandeering the field kitchen.

One of my men grinned as he patted the kettle. "Nice and warm," he said. Some cabbage soup was still in the kettle, and it tasted great. We also found wooden cases containing canned food. The labels on the tins read, "Chicago USA." That was disconcerting, as it confirmed that the United States was helping supply the Russian army. The tins contained corned beef, a real luxury, which we devoured like scavengers at a kill.

I sent two guards to take the two Russian soldiers from the cornfield and the two new prisoners, along with their now empty field kitchen, back to our battalion headquarters.

During the following hours I did not have to order anyone to be quiet or vigilant. I was sure that the Russians did not know we were so near; otherwise, they would not have lost their field kitchen. Perhaps the element of surprise would help us in the inevitable forthcoming fight.

An hour or so after midnight we heard the sound of horses walking back and forth in the cornfield. I knew that Russian scouts were often on horseback, as were officers. I heard Russian voices, sometimes with tones that implied commands. It sounded like they were advancing their troops in preparation for an attack. What to do? Do I order a retreat, and if so, which way and where to? There could easily be enemy troops moving toward our left or right flank. Retreating would mean leaving the relative safety of our concealed positions. If I did nothing the Russians would be upon us in a matter of minutes and we would be in a serious fight. The sliver of a moon was now gone, making it too dark to see anything at all in front of us.

When the sounds of voices and movement came close enough to risk our position being discovered I ordered a burst of machine-gun fire into the dark toward what I figured was the bulk of the Russian troops. That was followed by an immediate and eerie silence. We did not move and that silence lasted the rest of the night.

Russians or no Russians, I had been ordered to occupy and defend the far side of the hill ahead, so we prepared to advance at dawn. As soon as it was light enough to see I ordered the first platoon to move carefully into the cornfield. The Russians were gone; except for two, who were lying on the ground. One was dead. The other was still breathing, but only semi-conscious. I again felt that sickening, sinking feeling of pity and sorrow. He had lost so much blood there was nothing we could do to save him. The corporal drew his pistol, pressed the barrel against that poor guy's chest right above his heart, and mercifully shot him. We buried those two unfortunates as quickly as we could and moved on.

Perhaps our machine-gun burst in the middle of the night had tricked the enemy commander into thinking they were approaching an ambush from a much larger force than we actually were? Perhaps they knew something we did not? Perhaps I had erred ordering the machine-gun burst too soon? The two Russian casualties had fallen less than fifty metres from our position. If I had waited until they were upon us we might have killed or captured the entire group. On the other hand, we may have been lucky. The advancing force could have been large enough not to have retreated if they realized we were so near, and instead might have charged our position and possibly overrun my entire company. We may have been facing "many" more enemy troops than I had originally estimated, as they were accompanied by horses and a field kitchen and had posted advance scouts in the cornfield. Perhaps they were part of a large infantry force preparing for a major offensive?

I felt frustrated that we were not better informed about enemy movements or strength, so that I could make decisions more confidently. I hated placing my men in danger, even unwittingly. Regardless, none of my men had been injured that night, and I would now have to turn my attention to a new situation.

We continued on through the cornfield and reached the top of the hill with no further incidents. The Russians had withdrawn. My assigned objective was to defend the far crest of the hill, where there would be a clear view of the valley on the far side. I ordered my men to dig secure foxholes and be prepared for a possible enemy attack.

As the morning sun lit the eastern sky I could see that the hill we occupied provided a relatively good defensive site. The ground was sandy and firm, and not frozen, making it easy to dig into. Looking across the meadow we could see Russian soldiers also digging in about eight hundred metres away, on the side of the slope facing us. Between us there was mainly meadow covered with dead brown grasses and weeds, all less than a half-metre high. There was a small gully along the bottom of the valley, marked by a line of leafless bushes and shrubs. It was difficult to see anything clearly, as the early morning sun was still below the top of the eastern ridge and the entire side of the slope facing us was in shadow. I radioed the captain and asked for information. His reply was, "Keep your eyes open and be prepared. Report how many troops are facing you as soon as you know." He sounded like he knew less than I did.

As the sun rose higher individual features on the far slope became more distinct. My messenger handed me the field glasses. "Have a look," he said, pointing east. The light of the morning sun produced shadows of the men digging foxholes, making them show up as black marks against the otherwise grey-brown hillside. I counted hundreds of foxholes, many hundreds. There was far more than one Russian infantry company facing us.

I wondered why the enemy would choose to dig in over there, near the base of the slope along the far side of the valley. It seemed to me a much more vulnerable position than the one we occupied, as their hillside sloped toward us. Even though we could see them, and they could surely see some of us, no one opened fire. At that distance trying to hit someone would be a waste of ammunition. Even though our rifles could fire a kilometre, you had to be less than four hundred metres away to provide a good chance of hitting a target as small as a man. Snipers might have hit someone, but it was not worth the bother.

Then we spotted horse-drawn wagons moving along farther back. What was even more disturbing was a column of enemy soldiers crossing the crest of the slope toward the foxholes. We could soon be faced with thousands of enemy soldiers.

"This is it!" I said to myself. The massed attack I had dreaded for months was now in our face. This time we would have to bear the brunt of an assault. My imagination conjured up disturbing images of waves of soldiers flooding across the valley between our lines. The rest of the battalion may have been just as much under-strength as my company, so a massive attack could wear us down to the point where we would no longer be capable of holding the line.

The only way I could see out of our predicament was for speedy orders to beat a hasty and deep retreat. As the day wore on and the enemy forces swelled to truly intimidating numbers, I kept expecting the order to pull out, probably as soon as it was dark. By evening I still had not received any orders, so I got on the wireless and informed battalion headquarters of the enemy troops massing in front of us.

"Hold your position," was the reply.

"With what?" I asked. "I have less than sixty men in my entire company. We counted over a thousand Russians on the other side of the valley, and that was before it got dark. There could be many more by now."

"Just hold your position. We know the situation."

Small comfort that was. It was going to be another sleepless night. We could easily be outnumbered twenty-to-one by now.

Being outnumbered like that was uncomfortable, and even frightening, but not necessarily deadly. By itself, being outnumbered really did not mean much. I could not remember any time that we were not outnumbered in Russia. Experience had taught me that the most important element in determining the outcome of a battle was the position of the opposing forces in relation to each other. Even a large force attacking a well-defended line would have a nearly impossible task if they tried to break through. Sheer numbers meant very little to machine guns, which could mow down masses of attacking soldiers . . . as long as the ammunition held out. The enemy had to at least eliminate our machine guns, or attack with armoured vehicles or many other heavy weapons, to have any chance of producing a breakthrough.

I thought back to the attack last August, when massive waves of enemy troops almost succeeded in draining our supply of bullets before that battle ended. The spectre of another such assault, by even greater numbers, preyed on my mind.

I assigned extra men for sentry duty that night, and sent a squad to patrol our far-forward perimeter. They would fire a flare if they discovered a sneak attack. Even if the flare signals were to fail, I assumed they would shoot at anything that approached them in the night.

No matter how bad you think things are, they can always get worse. About an hour after nightfall we began to hear the unmistakable clattering and squeaking rumble of tanks approaching from behind the enemy lines. I looked over at my man in the next foxhole.

"This is not good," my messenger said, with deadpan understatement.

"You think?" I replied, commenting on the obvious.

We continued to hear tank movements for much of that terribly long night. It sounded like hundreds of enemy tanks were assembling behind the hill occupied by the Russian infantry, for quite a distance in both directions. We were in for it this time. Surely the order to retreat would come at any moment. Hopefully we would be ordered to move a long way back.

I radioed battalion command again and asked what was happening. The voice on the other end of the wireless said, "Hold your position."

"How am I supposed to do that?" I asked in as polite a voice as I could force from my lips. "They have tanks."

"Dig slit trenches," was the reply.

"That will help." My sarcastic retort came more out of exasperation than deliberate mockery.

"Hold your position. You have your orders." With that he hung up.

According to our training, slit trenches cut perpendicular to the line of advancing tanks would allow a man to move slightly sideways to avoid being run over and better position himself for attacking a passing tank with a magnetic charge or satchel bomb. That was something to look forward to. I passed the orders on, reminding the men to try not to make any new excavations conspicuous. Some of them might actually have constructed a few short and shallow trenches, although everyone was surely as tired as I was. I did not bother to check. I picked up my spade and scraped some dirt out of my hole, but was too fatigued to do any more.

I had of course seen tanks in action before, but only from afar. In France I had watched German armoured formations moving toward the front and charging across the battlefield. Watching those armoured units had been a fine sight. They had been part of the *Blitzkrieg* tactics used by the German military, where panzer divisions had used tanks and other armoured vehicles to drive deep wedges through enemy lines, then trap the hapless troops from all sides. I assumed those tactics had since been learned by the Russians and would now be used against us.

We had often heard enemy tank movements and seen tanks in the distance, and I had observed those tank movements with detached interest. The assembly on the other side of the Russian hill was an entirely new and different experience. It would be impossible for us to hold our own against a determined Russian assault supported by tanks. If we did not receive the order to retreat in time I was sure we would all be killed or captured.

Every infantry soldier had been trained how to try to survive a tank assault, and I replayed that training in my mind over and over again, searching my memory for some sublime bit of information that would help save us. I knew the theory. First you hide in the ground below the line of fire in your foxhole while the armoured machines rolled toward you. Then as soon as the tank approached your trench, you fired at the soldiers following the tanks. Infantry riding the tanks would also be crucial targets. The foot soldiers were more likely to get you than the tanks themselves. The tank drivers and machine-gunners were hampered by poor visibility. The tank driver's small viewing slit in the front of the tank was the only worthwhile target for rifle fire, forcing the driver to keep it closed and preventing him from seeing where he was going. Anyway, that was the theory.

During my training in Potsdam we were taught to use magnetic charges and satchel bombs to destroy tanks. Those anti-tank infantry weapons were effective only at very close range, close enough to get right up against the tank. My company was not equipped with any special anti-tank weapons, other than a few satchel bombs delivered to us during the night. The most vulnerable place on the Russian tanks was under the rear overhang of the turret. A bomb wedged under that overhang could blow the turret right off. A magnetic charge placed on the metal skin of the tank could also disable it. It could also disable you if you were too close when it exploded. If nothing else was available, a bottle or glass jar full of gasoline or kerosene could be made into a primitive weapon. A rag stuffed into the opening and lit on fire would ignite the gasoline as the bottle shattered against the tank. That bottle had to shatter over the grill covering the engine to be effective, to set the engine compartment ablaze, perhaps setting the fuel on fire, or at least making it too hot for the men to stay inside the tank. There were precious few glass bottles among the accoutrements of warfare here at the front.

Whatever the method, attacking a tank required nerves of steel, especially since you had to place the explosive on the tank right after setting the fuse. It could only be successful if you managed to avoid machine-gun fire from other tanks and their supporting infantry. In our current predicament all of that was just academic musing. I was so tired at the time that lengthy coherent thinking, let alone tactical planning, was probably beyond my capabilities.

In spite of the stay-in-your-foxhole lesson at the training field in Brandenburg, I had no delusions about the danger posed by attacking tanks. We had passed through former battlefields where the grisly evidence of a tank attack was all too obvious. Among the telltale marks left on the ground after a battle were scoured patches where the tank commanders had singled out a machine-gunners' foxhole. They had deliberately driven over top of them, then stopped one tread and turned the other, doing a pirouette with the entire tank on top of the men in the hole, crushing them into the ground. The men in the foxhole were not able to escape, because enemy machine-gun and small-arms fire would have cut them down the moment they leapt out of their hole.

Those disturbing thoughts and images just made me more stressed, further sapping my energy. The fact that we faced almost certain death if we stayed put produced pained, gut-gripping terror. Regardless, we could not retreat until ordered to do so. Fear, terror, anxiety, trepidation, frustration—all words to try to convey the feeling—could not even begin to describe the torment of that situation.

Suddenly I was startled to hear more tank movements, this time coming from our rear! I immediately supposed we had been encircled in the dark. My mind raced to formulate a plan of action to get out of this new predicament. We had to move, and fast! First I had to determine the strength and position of the enemy. Then I heard the wireless operator yell, "They are ours." What a relief. A panzer unit had been sent to help us.

Perhaps the massing of Russian armour had been spotted by one of our reconnaissance patrols or planes? Tanks were difficult to hide, especially when on the move. I now understood why Command had ordered me to hold our positions.

I had to investigate for myself. A few of us walked back from our fox-holes up the slope behind us toward the noise coming from a tank motor. In the moonlight I could make out a big gun being set up. From the high profile, the armoured frontal shield, and the four sets of road wheels, I recognized it as one of the formidable 88mm flak guns that were very capable of destroying tanks. It was set in a wide, shallow trench, camouflaged with small bushes and clumps of tall grasses, poised in ambush. A huge half-track carrier was parked nearby, and the crew were unloading wicker shell cartons and stacking them near the gun.

Following the crest of the hill, we next came upon a tank of the Panther type being moved into position in a large trench, so that only the turret was exposed above the surface of the ground, with its anti-tank gun pointed out over our line of foxholes toward the enemy. I was impressed with the efficiency with which that huge machine was set into place. A natural depression in the hill had been deepened to hide most of the body of the tank so that it would be difficult to be seen from the front, partly buried and camouflaged. It commanded a good view of the valley between us and the enemy. The crews had obviously done this sort of thing before. The sound of the motor from another of those mechanical monsters could be heard from farther away. Perhaps the darkness added to their aura, but those weapons of war were truly im-pressive to behold up close. Panthers were larger than the older tanks I had seen before, and carried a very powerful main gun that looked as long as a telephone pole.

I thought to myself that we must be holding a relatively important piece of ground if Command had decided to send such high-priced help to defend it. I felt some reassurance at their presence, thinking that we now stood at least a chance of surviving the coming morning.

I approached the tank crewmen in the excavated depression. They were uprooting clumps of grasses and tossing them onto the exposed turret to make it look like a natural part of the hilltop. One of the men greeted us, "Ah, infantry. How's it going?" he asked.

"Good to see you," I said with genuine enthusiasm. "How many panzers came with your unit?"

"Four," he answered matter-of-factly, "and three eight-eights."

"Four!" Only seven anti-tank weapons in total? Surely that was wrong? Surely there must be more? Perhaps they were already in place, hidden farther along the ridge? From the noises we had heard during the night, I was sure that hundreds of enemy tanks had gathered on the other side of the valley, hidden from view, poised to strike in the morning. What good would seven anti-tank weapons be against such a large force?

"Did Command tell you about the Russian forces facing us?" I asked him.

"Not much," he replied.

"Are they expecting an attack in the morning?"

"Probably," was all he said, with that customary manner when there was nothing else that could be done.

"We heard a great many Russian tanks. They assembled all night behind that hill on the other side of the valley over there," I said, pointing eastward.

"Really? Not to worry," he replied. "We'll get them."

That should have sounded more reassuring than it did at the time.

For us infantrymen tanks were formidable and intimidating weapons. Tank men had always struck me as somewhat dauntless, and perhaps even foolhardy. Maybe past successes made them assume they were invincible. The crewman seemed indifferent to what I perceived as a potentially perilous situation. It was hard for me to understand that mindset. Perhaps it was just a sham, designed to make their obviously dangerous job seem less dangerous in their own minds. Perhaps they had adopted the same fatalistic attitude as the rest of us here at the front—there was nothing you could do to change the situation, so just get on with the job at hand.

Walking back to my foxhole it occurred to me that the main purpose of armoured units was to spearhead attacks or counter major enemy offensives, so they were always sent to the most dangerous trouble spots and were often faced with the most powerful enemy weapons. Life in an armoured unit was perhaps not as glamorous as I had originally thought.

Assessing our own positions dug into the side of the hill, I was horrified to realize that we were caught right between two groups of steel juggernauts, with no place to get out of the way. There was nothing we could do but wait for the dawn.

18 *Sound and Fury*

THE DAY DAWNED CLEAR AND COLD, the temperature just above freezing. I shivered in my foxhole, in a daze from not having slept. I scanned the far slope of the valley but could not yet see anything clearly. I got out of my foxhole to pee, then quickly ate some of my bread rations. There was a suspenseful quiet that I knew could not last. Then the sound of a tank starting up behind the Russian lines broke the silence, then another, and another, then many more, until it became a continuous, ominous, rumbling overture to the attack. The monster had stirred.

The stress of the impending attack made my heart race, which helped to shake off the morning cold. Then a screaming howl made me duck—Katyusha rockets. The brilliant yellow flashes of exhaust trails could clearly be seen, as salvo after salvo of rockets were launched into the sky. A shrieking, terrorizing symphony from hell filled the air. Listening to that hellish shrieking I was certain that I would die that day.

When I realized that the rockets were not landing on top of us I gathered my wits and looked around. They must have been aimed at targets far behind our position, or perhaps the Russians were just gaining the range. Then another salvo struck much closer, with a series of multiple detonations reverberating from behind, perhaps on top of our hill, or at least close to it. A cloud of smoke rose up far behind the enemy-held ridge on the other side of the valley, silhouetted against the eastern sky and tinged with pink in the dawn's early light. The noise from those *Stalin Orgel* (Stalin's pipe organ), as we called them, was so intimidating I imagined that men with less rigorous training or battle experience than mine could have panicked and fled. I just huddled low in my foxhole and hunched my shoulders every time a salvo went overhead. Perhaps their purpose was more to frighten and panic than to destroy, because they did nothing to dislodge our troops or our armoured support weapons.

After what seemed like hours of Katyusha rockets, but was probably only ten minutes, the barrage ended. Before I had a chance to relax, the noise of tanks became noticeably louder. Looking over the edge of my foxhole I saw enemy tanks charging over the hill behind

Stalin Orgel, *Russian Katyusha rockets*

the dug-in Russian infantry positions. I recognized them immediately as T–34 tanks, the fast and powerful mainstay of the Russian armoured formations. As they rolled past their line of foxholes Russian infantrymen jumped up and ran along with them, using the tanks as moving shields. They would soon be within range.

I had counted about two dozen enemy tanks in front of my platoon when from behind me the loud crack of an 88 just about jolted me out of my skin. With that unmistakable first shot our anti-tank gunners began their deadly business. At the bottom of the valley between us, directly across from me, one enemy tank exploded with a tremendously violent boom, hurling pieces of burning debris that arced high in the air before crashing onto the ground. The infantrymen near it were flung about as if they were pieces of kindling. Some of them got up and staggered about aimlessly.

All hell broke loose. Shells screamed overhead. Ground-shaking explosions came from every direction. I instinctively ducked low into my foxhole every time I heard an incoming shell. For some reason tank shells sounded noisier than artillery shells, flying by with a higher-pitched scream. Considering there were only seven anti-tank weapons supporting us, they kept up an incredibly raucous fire. Return fire came from the Russian tanks that repeatedly stopped their forward rush to aim and fire. Stopping like that in front of our anti-tank guns made them relatively easy targets at that range. I saw three more tanks hit in rapid succession.

One looked like a steam locomotive as a jet of black smoke blew high into the air out of the top. Another suddenly shuddered to a stop, setting off a puff of dust around it. The turret was blown right off another, which crashed back down askew against the side of the tank.

One of our 88s was on the hill right behind my foxhole. Even though it startled me every time it fired, that distinctive crack was exhilarating and reassuring, as each shot meant the destruction of another enemy tank, one less antagonist for us to have to deal with. Every time one of the enemy tanks was hit I felt momentarily jubilant. The sound and fury of the battle was unbelievable, like nothing I had experienced before.

After a few minutes the air was so thick with black and grey smoke it was difficult to see what was happening. I could hear the rumbling of tank engines, the mechanical clanking and squeaking of their steel tracks, the bursts of cannon fire and explosions, all reverberating around me like a maniacal symphony. The acrid stench of smoke and cordite permeated the air, which stung my lungs. All that smoke, along with having to stay under cover, made it difficult to know how the battle was going. I felt very tiny and completely helpless. At any moment I expected to see one of those mechanical monsters loom out of the smoke in front of me and run me over. My rifle would have had no impact whatsoever on a tank. If the infantry following their iron shields could get close enough to overrun us we could all be killed.

The concussion of a shell burst was so close I felt a powerful slap on my ears, even though I had opened my mouth wide to prevent the pressure wave from bursting my eardrums. It was quickly followed by a shower of dirt raining down on my back. When I brushed the clods off my uniform, I checked to make sure there were no shrapnel holes in it. Still intact, I fervently implored the god of good luck to "Let me survive this day!"

In spite of the risk of exposing my head, I had to look out every so often to see if the Russian infantry were coming too close. Visibility was intermittently good enough to see that no enemy soldiers were within range. I listened for the distinctive soccer stadium roar that accompanies an infantry charge, but could not hear anything over the explosions and detonations from the big guns behind and in front of me. I again checked the clip in my automatic, made sure the safety was off, and set it right beside me. I glanced left and right. My men were still in

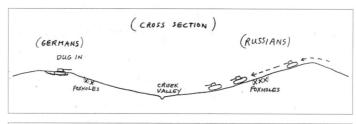

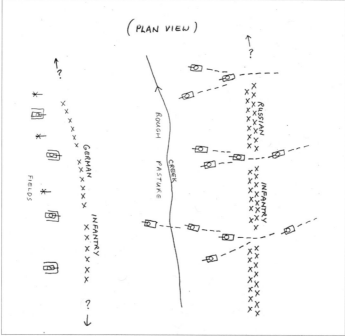

My sketch of the tank battle scene

position. As far I could tell, none of them had panicked and deserted their foxholes, in spite of the terror of the moment.

The retorts and explosions continued to ebb and flow across the battlefield. The anti-tank gun nearest me kept firing one shell after another in rapid succession. The next time I looked up, one enemy tank was heading straight at me less than two hundred metres away, closely followed by dozens of soldiers. I aimed and fired at the nearest one. Our machine-gun fire came from my left and right. Enemy soldiers began to drop.

Suddenly, the tank shielding them exploded with a blast so violent I felt it against my face. When I looked up again a thick cloud of smoke momentarily obscured the tank. I expected charging soldiers to emerge

German Panther tank

88mm flak anti-tank gun and crew

from that cloud. Another explosion made me duck again. I kept desperately looking for attackers, but could hardly see anything. The smoke not only clouded my view, but acrid fumes stung my eyes, causing them to water.

After a while the discharges from the guns behind me became intermittent, and the cacophony of shooting and explosions from all around became less concentrated, more sporadic. The battle seemed to be winding down, although it could just be a brief respite while the Russians regrouped. The muffled sounds of tank motors could still be heard from the valley.

Peeking out of my little sanctuary, the smoky haze drifting through the air began to clear, and tanks were moving back over the hill from where they had come. Black smoke continued to belch from destroyed tanks. There were no soldiers charging toward us now, only a few stragglers running back toward their lines. The incredible intensity of our defence had driven them back. Seeing their iron shields explode in front of them must have been very discouraging.

Finally the shooting stopped altogether. The absolutely marvellous realization that I was still alive swept through me. I had survived and was apparently unhurt. Hopefully it was over. That momentary feeling of exhilarating relief was followed almost immediately by a reflex reaction to remain wary, to scan the ground in front of my hole, and to be prepared to shoot at any attackers that might be crawling toward us through the grass. My heart was pounding in my chest, but I did not feel anything that could be called fear. That had disappeared with the first shots. There was a bitter taste in my mouth, my eyes were still smarting, and it was still painful to take a deep breath.

I had seen only the hits directly in front of me, so it was hard to tell how either side had fared in the larger battle. Scanning the valley I saw dozens of enemy tanks, most of which were burning wrecks, and whose fuel must be the source of all that black smoke. Others were not burning but obviously destroyed.

Although it seemed like forever at the time, the entire engagement had probably lasted less than half an hour. My foxhole momentarily felt almost comfortable, a snug little den in which to hide during the fury of the storm. I noticed my hands and uniform were covered with a fine layer of dirt and grey powder, but there were no new holes in me.

The rumble of tank motors could still be heard coming from behind the enemy-occupied hill. The intermittent sounds of detonations could also be heard from farther away, so apparently the battle was not over along our entire sector. There were bodies lying on the ground in the valley, but fewer than I had expected, given the fierceness of the battle. Soldiers were helping their injured comrades back to their lines.

My own survival made the situation look momentarily good for us. Reassured that more enemy were not coming, at least not right away, I raised my torso over the edge of my foxhole to see how the rest of my men had fared. "Everyone all right?" I yelled to my left and to my right.

"Ya," I heard from one man. "All good."

The tank battle had not caused a single casualty among my men.

"What a show that was," my wireless operator said.

And it had been. The clash of iron monsters had been terrifying but also fascinating; however, that was as much entertainment as I ever wanted to experience, ever again.

The wireless crackled again. Battalion command asked for a status report on the results of the engagement.

"There are dozens of wrecked enemy tanks in front of us. The other tanks have retreated back over the hill out of sight." I took another quick look toward the east, "The Russian infantry are still in position."

"How many?"

"It must be near a thousand," I replied, without exaggeration.

"Fine. Hold your position until further orders." With that he hung up.

"Fine?"

So we waited. The situation was still very tense. Unless the undamaged enemy tanks had managed to sneak away undetected, they must still be hiding on the far side of the hill. We waited the rest of that morning for another attack. Columns of smoke continued to belch from the wrecked tanks. Occasionally I took a hard look at the ground in front of us to make sure no enemy were approaching. By midday the situation had not changed. Perhaps the Russians would attack at night? That made sense to me, since the darkness might help hide their tanks and accompanying infantry.

By afternoon my curiosity got the better of me. My messenger and I, along with a few of the more inquisitive among us, went back to see how our armoured unit had fared. As we approached the top of the hill I was still feeling grateful that those formidable weapons were here to support us. To my dismay, the shallow pit that had sheltered the nearest Panther tank was empty. The 88s were also gone, along with all the armoured vehicles, except for one tank. Two crewmen were working on the engine under one of the large steel plates at the back of that tank. I also noticed that the steel plate on top of the body, just in front of the turret under the main gun, had been grooved and bent inward. It must have been hit by a shell. There was no indication on the outside as to what had been damaged inside the tank. A small *Kübelwagen* scout car was parked beside the tank.

A crewman looked up as we approached. "How'd it go for you chaps?"

"Looks like we all survived unharmed, thanks to you boys," I said sincerely. "How did you do?"

"Not too bad, I think," he said with a grin. "Better than Ivan," he added as he waved his hand at the still blazing wrecks at the bottom of the hill.

"That was one noisy show you put on."

"Ya, just like a travelling circus. This one is immobilized, though," he said as he patted the steel side of the huge Panther tank.

"Is he going to make it?" I said, pointing at the soldier lying on a stretcher at the rear of the tank. He had a bandage around his head and was barely conscious.

"Ya, Fritz forgot to duck. But he has a hard head."

"Where are the rest of your panzers?" I asked, genuinely concerned.

"They drove off an hour ago." He nodded toward the rear of the hill, toward the same dirt road where we had captured the Russian field kitchen the previous night.

"Are they coming back?" I asked hopefully.

"I think not," he answered. "They need us at another show."

"We could still use you here," I replied. "The Russian tanks can come back."

"Not likely," he said. "Reconnaissance told us they took off and headed south. Damn shame. Now we have to catch up with them again."

A few minutes later the sound of a motor could be heard approaching from the road. A tracked vehicle that looked like a tank without a turret on top came rolling up the far side of the hill. It pulled up behind the disabled tank. The crew got out and hooked two heavy cables onto its rear, and the *Bergepanzer* (recovery tank) slowly towed it out of the pit. The crew all climbed back onto their machines. So the last of the armoured unit that had fought so effectively that morning was towed away. The tank driver turned and looked back at us four lonesome figures and gave us a quick salute. It was actually more like a wave goodbye, as if he had just been here on a brief, friendly visit.

For me it was a much more emotional farewell. They would be dearly missed. I took a long look around; the Eastern Front had just become a much larger and scarier place. We had been abandoned by our saviours and were alone on that barren hilltop. I felt absolutely despondent. What would we do now? There was nothing for us infantry to do but return to our little holes in the ground and resume the defence of our sector by ourselves.

Before I had time to contemplate our fate, I heard one of my men yelling at the top of his lungs from the direction of our forward positions. "Ivan is coming!" Many hundreds of Russian soldiers were running toward us across the valley. We four sprinted across the last few dozen metres to reoccupy our foxholes. I picked up my rifle and prepared for the fight. Enemy machine-gun crews came with the charging throng, pulling their bulky wheeled weapons and carrying ammunition cases as they ran across the meadow. They would be our first targets. Men ran in small groups from one wrecked tank to another, momentarily hidden by the steel hulks or by columns of smoke. Soon there were too many of them to use the wrecks for cover and began running toward us in a throng. The soccer stadium roar assailed my ears. When the nearest attackers came to within about three hundred metres' range I aimed my rifle and squeezed the trigger. My machine-gunners immediately began firing.

The moment we started shooting the Russians promptly dropped to take cover on the ground. The screaming stopped, but that noise was replaced by the cacophony of gunfire, punctuated by the rattle of machine guns. Lying flat on the ground, the Russians returned fire. Even though they were at least partly hidden by clumps of dead vegetation, they were at a distinct disadvantage in the relatively flat ground at the bottom of the valley, as we were dug in and they were not. Some stayed near the relative cover of the wrecks of their own tanks.

Suddenly, a tremendous loud boom caused me to duck. One of the burning wrecks had exploded, sending showers of sparks and debris high into the air. That blast must have panicked the Russian infantry nearby, as they immediately began a hasty retreat, quickly followed by the rest. Perhaps the Russian commander did not know that we were now vulnerable, vastly outnumbered and completely without heavy weapons support. Perhaps the exploding wreck made them think our big guns were still hidden near the top of the hill? Sheer good luck may have intervened on our behalf that day.

By nightfall we were still in position. Some of the wrecked tanks were still burning and the fires provided an eerie glow, adding a surreal dimension to the battlefield.

I radioed the captain, hoping to convince him we should retreat. "Hold your position," was all I was told. Either the battalion commander was not fully apprised of our predicament, or he had been ordered to hold his sector of the line, perhaps because of action elsewhere. I asked for artillery support, or even mortars, but was told they were not available right away. I knew that meant not at all. We posted extra sentries in the event the Russians attempted a sneak attack during the night. I was not convinced the enemy tanks had gone for good.

We were issued more ammunition that night. I filled every satchel on my belt and every pocket in my uniform with rifle and automatic clips. Each of the machine-gunners carried black canisters of bullet belts back to their foxholes. I kept my automatic close beside me all night, fully loaded and with the safety off.

That night was just as scary as the previous one. After four months at the Russian front we soldiers were not prone to imaginary fears; however, that night I kept imagining enemy soldiers creeping up on us under the cover of darkness. Strange that the fear of impending action is stronger than any fear experienced during actual fighting. Perhaps it just seemed that way, as during a fight I was forced to concentrate all my faculties on the business at hand.

Sleep that night was a fitful series of quick naps whenever my wariness waned. On top of everything else it again turned very cold, well below freezing. I hoped it would not snow.

The dawn did not bring any relief. The Russian infantry had not left. I was sure they were preparing to attack again. What other reason would there be for so many men to remain facing us. At least there were no signs of tank movements. Some of the wrecks in the valley were still emitting wisps of smoke.

Through my binoculars I scanned for signs of machine-gun crews under the tanks, crews that could support an attack. Before I had a chance to make a clear assessment, the distinctive whine of incoming mortar shells pierced the air. Hundreds of enemy soldiers jumped out of their holes and charged toward us. This time the morning sun caused each man to stand out clearly against the ground behind him, creating very conspicuous targets. Once again we opened fire as soon as they came within deadly range, and once again they retreated almost immediately. Unbelievably, that pattern of attack and retreat was repeated a few more times during the day. They never got closer than about two hundred metres. The contest was becoming ridiculous. Each attack cost them more men, and each attack seemed futile.

I became concerned that our own casualties might be mounting. The most dangerous aspect of the fighting was the mortar bombardments that accompanied each attack. So far my little hole in the ground had not been spotted.

By evening the situation had not changed. For all the intensity of the tank battle and the repeated attacks by the Russian infantry, my company had survived those two nerve-wracking days without being routed or overrun. Their commander may have been ordered to keep us pinned down here to help other enemy forces gain some advantage elsewhere. All that speculation may be interesting in hindsight, but at the time I probably did not care why the Russians did what they did; I just worried about how long our ammunition would hold out.

I radioed the captain and was again instructed to hold our position until further notice.

After it was dark and we were able to get out of our foxholes I checked for casualties. The medic was attending a man who had been shot in the face. He was unconscious, but alive, with blood-soaked bandages wrapped around his head. He was carried back to the medical station on his *Zeltplan* cape. The medic said two other men had been wounded but were ambulatory. One man was dead. He had been hit in his foxhole by a projectile from a mortar. The force of the explosion had blown him into the air and turned him upside down, so that he collapsed back into his hole with his legs sticking out. That was an ignominious way for a brave young man to die. Once again I felt the sickening pain in my gut at the death of another comrade.

When he was pulled from his foxhole there was not much left intact. What was buried was hardly recognizable as a human being. His dog tag on the chain around his neck was snapped off and handed to me, to be given to the battalion commander. It, along with a letter advising of his death—a *Totenschein* (death notice)—that he had made the supreme sacrifice in the service of his country, would be all that his family would receive; cynically small tokens of a tragedy that would forever change their lives.

Regarding our immediate predicament, the tragic loss of two valuable men meant my company had been further reduced. We would have to defend the same piece of ground in the face of another attack the next day with even fewer men. If the Russian forces were being replenished during the night the situation could become even more desperate for us. The enemy might attack at night, so once again my life might depend upon my ability to stay alert. Fear competed with fatigue for control of my body. I was approaching exhaustion and knew it, but there was no chance for restful sleep.

We waited for orders to retreat, and waited, and waited. About an hour after dark the captain came on the wireless and ordered me to prepare my company to move

Totenschein *(death notice)*

out at a moment's notice, possibly to join a counterattack. Apparently Russian forces had broken through the German defences to the right of our position. I had learned earlier that our right flank was held by Romanian troops. Perhaps a determined Russian attack, possibly supported by tanks, maybe even the remaining tanks that had tested our defences earlier, had caused the Romanians to be overrun? Whatever the reason for that breach, it meant that our determined defence had been to no avail. That breach resulted in our right flank being exposed. There was now a real danger that we could be encircled and cut off from the rest of our troops and supplies. We would have to withdraw and regroup farther back, but I could not give the order until instructed to do so by the battalion commander, even if it meant staying exposed to obvious danger.

After what seemed like an eternity, I finally received the order to retreat westward and rendezvous at a new position much farther west. "How much farther west?" I asked.

"We'll set up about ten kilometres away," Command replied. That was unusually far, and indicated a desperate situation. Our entire battalion would also be withdrawing with us. The voice on the radio sounded very serious.

I ordered my company to move out and regroup on the far side of the ridge. We quietly abandoned the safety of our foxholes and moved westward. I had to make sure all my men were on their way before leaving myself. As we moved back between the cornstacks of the same cornfield we had passed through two nights before, I was convinced that masses of enemy troops must be moving in the same direction by now. The situation once again became very confusing. I kept listening for signs of enemy in the darkness, and hoped we would not blunder into them during the night. Still, any place farther west was bound to be safer for us than the hillside we had just abandoned.

Shortly after our last communication the wireless began to act up, then went dead altogether. My wireless operator did not know if it was a fault of his radio, or if our command post had gone silent. I was suspicious that battalion command had serious trouble of their own. Perhaps they had retreated so far as to be out of radio communication range.

That night I led my company through countryside that all looked the same, acutely aware that it was hostile ground. Shortly after midnight it started snowing, lightly at first, but more and more heavily, until it was impossible to see more than a few dozen metres. I used my compass to orient the direction of our withdrawal, and had a rough idea where we were heading in relation to where we had been; however, I could only estimate how far we had travelled by the time that passed. We stayed on the road as long as it went in the right direction, but veered off across fields when we had to stay on course.

Sometime after midnight the clouds dissipated. With a white layer of new snow covering everything the moonlight made for good visibility. That was good and bad. Good because we were able to see where we were going and keep a lookout for the enemy; bad because it also meant we might easily be seen by the enemy and blunder into an ambush. There was no sign of any troops anywhere, theirs or ours.

Even before the radio failed, reports about enemy movements had been very confusing. Now there was no communication with Command at all. I suspected the Russian assault had caused a major retreat, but had no idea how far the enemy advance had reached. We heard no sounds—nothing—from anywhere, for hours. Eventually I was sure we were nearing our destination and kept looking for signs of other units from our battalion. If we just kept travelling generally westward, sooner or later we should regain friendly territory.

As we rounded the crest of a shallow hill a sudden machine-gun burst made everyone dive for cover. In the moonlight I could make out the silhouette of a lone Russian T–34 tank, partly veiled against the shadowy backdrop of a woodlot. It was not moving, there was no engine noise, and there were no crewmen in sight. We took cover behind the crest of the hill. Even with the moonlight, the lay of the land prevented us from seeing very far. I ordered two men to scout the area ahead to make sure there were no other armoured vehicles or soldiers about. They came back and reported that they had not found any signs of other enemy in the area. The tank appeared to be completely alone. It must have been part of the previous day's assault and had been disabled at that spot, or had just broken down, or run out of gas.

That was enough excitement for me. Better leave that armoured strongpoint alone. Other than a few satchel bombs, we had no anti-tank weapons with us. No use risking anyone's life to try to knock out the tank, especially since it was not mobile. I just hoped the tank commander did not have a radio to notify the rest of the Russian army of our position.

I reckoned that we had travelled about as far as I had been ordered. We had probably put a considerable distance between us and the Russian units that could have been following us. The moon would soon be below the horizon, making it too dark to see anything. I was near the end of my endurance, as were the rest of my men. I ordered the company to dig in and wait for dawn. I ordered a man at a time to stand watch, one hour at a time.

The next morning dawned cold and cloudy. It was snowing again. I scanned our perimeter for signs of enemy soldiers, but saw none. The lone T–34 was still there. One of my men got up and approached the tank. He yelled at it, calling for the Russians to surrender, which was somewhat comical. He looked like a mouse walking up to a sleeping cat and telling it to give up. There was no reply from inside the tank. The tank men had slipped away in the night.

We were still in a serious predicament. Finding that single enemy tank so far back meant that at least part of the massive Russian offensive had reached well beyond our present position. We were now behind the enemy lines.

Everyone ate whatever rations they had left in their kit and then prepared to move off. I had no way of knowing what lay ahead of us. My only sensible option was to stay on a westward heading. Worried that some of my men could get lost in the snow, I instructed them to stay together. Other than the guidance provided by the little needle on my compass, we were proceeding virtually blind.

We plodded along in single file, slow but steady. I was in a daze, trusting more to fate than to any rational strategy, when I felt a hand on my shoulder. The man behind me put his hand to his ear. I immediately signalled a halt. Very faint muffled popping sounds came through the snow—battle sounds. The falling snow made it difficult to distinguish the direction those explosions came from, or from what distance. The consensus was from the west. That confirmed my suspicion that the fighting front had shifted far past us. We had no choice but to keep walking toward those sounds, even though it meant heading toward danger.

It stopped snowing. Columns of smoke could be seen in the west. The familiar smell of burning permeated the air. I knew we had to move quickly if we were to have any chance of rejoining our forces. We would also need some good luck. The snow-covered ground would make us very conspicuous. I looked for some feature in the landscape that would allow me to pass through the Russian lines without being detected, and without being caught in the middle of a battle. The countryside looked much the same in every direction. Only the fires provided some kind of landmark that could help orient our direction. We passed through stubble fields and fields where the corn was still piled up in tepee-like stacks. We walked along shallow depressions and followed lines of shrubs and tall weeds that marked fencerows and the edges of dry watercourses along the bottoms of swales, anything that would help conceal us or provide some backdrop other than snow.

By late afternoon we were moving cautiously along a dirt road when we approached a relatively large village. Streamers of smoke streaked the sky, rising from the remnants of burned buildings. This presented a predicament, as the area around the village was flat and barren, with absolutely no cover, so I reckoned the safest route for us to take would be the road through the village. I called a halt and ordered a scouting party ahead to investigate.

When the scouts returned they reported that there had been serious action recently, but it now appeared clear and deserted. I signalled the advance and we moved forward along the road. We had stumbled onto part of a vast former battlefield. We passed the wrecks of dozens of armoured vehicles, some of them still smouldering. Passing one mangled wreck, the unmistakable stench of burnt flesh assailed my nostrils. There had been an intense fight, perhaps to capture the village itself. Tank treads had left long parallel gouges in the ground, making ugly scars upon the landscape. Fresh graves dotted the battlefield near the sides of the road, pockmarks on the landscape.

I was very wary as we entered the village. Snipers, or other living remnants of the battle, might still be around. Many of the buildings had been destroyed. The acrid odour of charred wood was very strong. I felt sad for the poor people who had lost their homes and perhaps everything they owned.

Suddenly I spotted movement. Everyone immediately took cover. I signalled a squad to circle around and approach from the far side, and another to approach from the opposite side. When we flushed out our quarry it turned out to be a few dozen older women and an old man. They looked terrified. One woman started wailing, rocking back and forth, waving her arms toward the burnt-out remains of a house, toward the sky, and toward the graves. The other women joined in, and it became a chorus of sorrow. Other apparitions began to emerge from the ashes, more pitiable civilians. I felt terrible. There was nothing we could have done to help those poor people. We did not even have any food to give them. Their wailing lamentation was one of the most pitiful sounds I had ever heard. Hopefully for them the war was over.

It was not over for us, and we had to move on. That scene of destruction, combined with the battle noises we had heard earlier, made me even more apprehensive that the front was still moving, and was so far beyond us by now that it might be very difficult for my company to catch up to our army. I kept expecting to see Russian troops moving headlong toward the front. I reminded everyone to be on the lookout for any kind of movement, particularly coming upon us from behind.

What to do next? I could wait for radio communication to be restored. I did not have any hope that our own units would somehow find us. The situation was proving to be a thornier problem than I had originally anticipated. I had not been trained how to cross the confusing no-man's land between the lines and approach our own troops without being mistaken for enemy soldiers. There was no alternative but to continue heading westward. The Russians may not have set up connected positions along the entire length of the leading edge of their newly recaptured territory. With a little luck we would find one of those unconsolidated gaps between their forces.

I had no idea where the remainder of our division might be. We walked on and eventually spotted activity a kilometre or so ahead. The first objects that could be clearly discerned were the black silhouettes of tanks and vehicles, outlined by the late afternoon setting sun. Scanning the landscape through field glasses, I could make out the distinctive shapes of Russian T–34 tanks clustered in small groups and scattered across a wide arc from north to southwest. That was disappointing but not unexpected. The terrain may have hidden many more than I could see, as well as infantry and perhaps field guns. I assumed that we had stumbled upon an entire Russian division that had halted for the night. I also assumed we had reached the rear of the enemy side of the fighting front.

There were no obvious large gaps visible where I felt we could safely pass through, although there was what looked like a woodlot in a shallow valley toward the southwest. We would stay hidden until dark. Those armoured units might be the vanguard of more Russian forces, and I became increasingly apprehensive that we could be discovered by Russian infantry, trapped, and captured. To underscore that reality, one of my men from the rear of the company came running forward to report he had seen moving vehicles. I accompanied him to a rise in the ground. Through field glasses I was able to see what looked like farm tractors with caterpillar tracks, towing huge cannons along a section of roadway a kilometre or two away, accompanied by horse-drawn wagons and infantry. It appeared to be a Russian artillery unit moving forward. They were not heading directly at us, but could pass close enough that we risked being detected if we stayed where we were. No more waiting. We had to make our move now.

It was dusk as we set off again, following the low point of the valley as much as possible, taking advantage of every hedgerow and bush to stay out of sight. With luck we might pass through the area where the lowest concentration of enemy troops appeared to be. By the time we came near enough to the closest enemy group to risk being detected it was totally dark. We moved slowly, in single file, roughly parallel to the enemy, searching for a gap. Running into a Russian patrol now would be disastrous.

There were clusters of lights in the distance, campfires, and I often heard the sounds of voices. One of the lit areas turned out to be a Russian field kitchen, feeding the soldiers. They were making no attempt to hide their presence, which probably meant there were no German troops nearby. The field kitchen reminded me that we had not been fed for two days and the rations each soldier carried had all been eaten.

In the darkness I had no illusions that finding a route through the enemy positions would be more a matter of luck than skilful scouting on our part. I counted on the enemy tank men being as nonchalant as our own panzer troops, so they would not be on the lookout for German infiltrators or stragglers. After about an hour of heart-pounding tension we came upon a roadway. As we dropped to the ground I realized we were suddenly very vulnerable, as the meadow we had just crossed had no tall vegetation for cover, and the road would probably be guarded. Although I saw none, there had to be sentries, as well as sleeping enemy soldiers, nearby.

On the far side of the road there was a dense stand of small, thin trees, all bare of leaves and no more than about four or five metres tall. I guessed it was the edge of the woodlot I had spotted with the field glasses earlier. It looked tempting as a possible escape route. I judged that the relatively small trees made it unsuited for hiding large numbers of troops. The dead leaves and twigs that littered any forest floor would make it impossible for us to move silently. Regardless, I figured our best chance to reach safety would be to go through it.

There were about sixty men in my company, which meant sixty opportunities for a mistake. I gave orders to the nearest squad leader that he was to take his squad over the road and into the trees. Once in the woods they were to head due west, maintaining absolute silence. Hopefully they had only a few hundred metres to go before they were clear of the nearest enemy group. If we did not hear any shooting within about a quarter of an hour, the rest of us would follow, one squad at a time. That way, if one squad happened to be detected, the others might still have a chance to escape. If everything worked according to plan the whole operation should take less than an hour, and we would be well past the Russians long before dawn.

The squad leader started to crawl toward the road. "No," I said. "Stand up and walk, as silently as possible, but slow and steady. And shoulder your rifle, that way you might be mistaken for Russian guards if you are spotted. Make sure your men are not wearing their helmets."

The first squad set off. Fifteen minutes passed with no sounds of gunfire; in fact, no sounds at all. I motioned for the next squad to cross the road, then the next. The more that left, the less I worried about detection and hurried the next group along. I went with the last squad. I took a quick glance left and right, then walked across the road, holding my breath.

Once inside the woods my initial appraisal of the bush was confirmed. It was overgrown with small, skinny trees, making rapid and especially quiet movement impossible, although the trees were not dense enough to obstruct movement. The ground was spongy and wet in spots, with occasional sections of shallow standing water, covered with a thin crust of ice. My boots and socks soon became soaking wet. We relied on the first squad's point man to keep us on course and just followed the path the previous groups had made. I used my compass to verify our heading. We made excruciatingly slow progress.

After what seemed like hours of slogging through that dense wet bush we eventually emerged into a stubble field. I was sure we were far past the Russian lines. I had no idea where our own lines were, but assumed they were not far away. Not wanting to risk being shot by mistake, I sent two men ahead to try to contact friendly troops. They set off across the field and disappeared into the night. After about five minutes I ordered everyone to move forward, again due west, carefully and in single file. After another half hour of this edging forward I was sure we were near or even inside German-held territory, or at least territory not controlled by Russian troops.

Finally we saw a light blink on and off in the distance, the signal that it was safe to approach. We walked across the intervening space and returned to our side. I momentarily felt relieved and safe again, if such a concept could have any relevance under those circumstances.

The troops we had found were not part of our battalion, but they were German. A sergeant escorted me to the battalion command post. I reported the concentration of Russian armour that we had seen that night, as well as the artillery unit. He radioed his headquarters to find out where the remainder of our battalion was. It took a few tries, but eventually word came back as to where my company was supposed to be, which was a few kilometres away.

My men had already found holes in the ground to bed down for the rest of the night; however, we were ordered to rejoin my battalion immediately. By morning it may have become too dangerous to move in the light. Everyone was expecting another enemy attack. It took another hour of marching in the dark before we rejoined our battalion, by which time I was close to total exhaustion; however, I had to report in to the battalion command post.

The captain greeted me, heartily shook my hand and said, "Congratulations, *Herr Leutnant*. We heard about your magnificent action and escape. You have earned the Iron Cross Second Class. Good job."

I stood there dumbfounded for a moment. Iron Cross? Second Class? My mind was in a daze, my body immersed in that dull ache that comes from prolonged exertion. My initial reaction was almost annoyance at being detained. "Thank you," I heard myself utter, more out of conditioned courtesy than genuine gratitude. I was far too fatigued to care about some trinket. All I wanted to do was dry my socks, get something to eat, and sleep. I could not remember why I had been so impressed by soldiers who had worn the Iron Cross at Officer School.

That tank skirmish was just one of a series of horrendous battles fought along the southern part of the Eastern Front in the summer and fall of 1943. At the time I knew nothing of the larger picture.

19 *The Longest Day*

FOR THE NEXT FEW DAYS we were forced to move almost every night, sometimes under very confusing and uncertain circumstances. Somehow my company managed to stay ahead of the Russians with rapid but orderly retreats. We were repeatedly harassed by mortar and small-arms fire, and fought repeated minor skirmishes, but at relatively long ranges. The sounds of battle were often heard during the day, sometimes uncomfortably near. The "routine" of marching a kilometre or so during the night and then digging a defensive line of foxholes to prepare for a dawn attack allowed for very little sleep. Those harrowing front-line dances were played out until November 21, 1943.

During November my company had lost twenty-one men—seven dead, eleven wounded, and three missing in action—bringing our complement down to less than fifty from the original of more than ninety front-line troops that had arrived at the Eastern Front back in June.

Strangely, the deaths of so many young men were regarded like everything else at the front at that time: it was part of the routine, an almost ordinary event. I had gradually become callous to death, at least outwardly. The first death I had witnessed in combat, that of my comrade at the artillery barrage in France, had been a terrible, traumatic, heart-rending experience that had left a deep and lasting impression. Now, after years of warfare, I had developed a kind of immunity to the constant reality of death. "Body counts," the army termed it. But regardless of how commonplace it was, it was impossible to forget that they were human beings who had families, homes, and social lives before dying in Russia. Now they had each become part of the ground in an obscure part of a foreign country far from home.

To an outsider that typical soldier's attitude toward death would appear to be incredibly heartless. But it was not heartless, just necessary. If a soldier allowed his feelings to preoccupy his consciousness it may not have been possible to function at the front. After the carnage of a fight was buried or carted off, I forced myself to put the whole episode out of my mind as quickly as possible, as if it had been a bad dream.

While my company had received no replacements to replenish our ranks, I was still responsible for defending a section of the front that was sometimes as much as a kilometre wide. That meant only one man for about every twenty metres. I assumed similar conditions prevailed at other sectors of the front. That was not enough to stop the relentless Russian juggernaut. The loss of more and more of my men could no longer be compensated by the fact that those that survived were experienced and battle-hardened. By then we did not need additional battlefield experience to teach us to stay alive. There was a limit to how long we could keep going under those conditions. In the face of constant onslaughts by an enemy with a numerical superiority, no amount of soldiering skills would help us in the long run.

By then we were all more than tired. The strain had left me more fatigued than I had ever been before. It felt as if I was mentally anaesthetised as well as physically exhausted. I was convinced it would only be a matter of time before all of us were killed or captured.

During the night of November 21, 1943, we had retreated from Russian troops who were occupying a line I estimated to be about two kilometres away. I had no reason to believe they would not still be at that position in the morning. There was no indication from Command that they expected an enemy attack. During the night we again dug our little holes in a line of defence. I was with my platoon, which by then had been reduced to eighteen men. One of my machine-gunners was positioned about thirty metres to my right, the other at least that far away to my left, and the third about a hundred metres or so beyond that. The second platoon, led by a sergeant, was positioned farther along the front line to our right, and the third platoon, led by a corporal, was beyond the second a few hundred metres farther away.

I awoke with the dawn, and immediately sensed danger. The sounds of voices, very faint, but distinct, were coming from the direction of the rising sun. I raised my head very carefully, just enough to peer through the dead vegetation in front of the rim of my foxhole and looked eastward, but saw nothing. Realizing that the sounds I heard could only be enemy troops, I knew we were in big trouble. Here we were, dug in, confronted with an enemy who was also dug in within extremely close range. The enemy had followed us during the night and had dug in less than a hundred metres away. We were trapped, and so were the enemy. Even if we were ordered to retreat it would have been impossible under those conditions. As it turned out, the second and third platoons had dug in along a curved line that angled away from where the enemy had dug in.

A few moments after noticing the enemy's proximity I saw the machine-gunner to my right unexpectedly partly stand up in his foxhole, probably to stretch. He must not have noticed anything amiss in front of our lines. I immediately yelled, "Jäekle, get down!" Too late. A shot rang out from the enemy lines. His head tilted down as his hands clasped the front of his chest, and he collapsed into his hole.

Damn! I felt momentarily sick. That was a painful reminder of just how quickly a moment's carelessness could cost a life at the front. But there was no time to ponder his fate. I was expecting the enemy to attack at any moment. For the rest of us, Jäekle's machine gun was essential for our survival. I yelled over to the man next to him, about twenty metres distant, and ordered him to take over the machine-gunner's position.

Without hesitation he got out of the relative safety of his own foxhole and crawled on his belly like a lizard over to the machine gun. The area between the opposing lines was almost completely flat, but it was covered with clumps of short, dead, brown grass, the tallest being knee-high at best, which provided just enough cover in the dawn's light for him to make it without being seen. At that range he would have been shot dead if any of the Russians had spotted him. Still prone, he managed to pull Jäekle out of the hole and got in himself.

"He's dead," he yelled toward me as he manned the machine gun. He was a very young man, probably twenty years old. Our survival may have depended on that soldier's courage that day.

One of the little tricks I had learned to help me survive an enemy attack was to stick a piece of wood, or short branch, or my bayonet if no wood was available, into the ground at an arm's-length distance from the side of my foxhole, and drape my *Zeltplan* over it. Hopefully it would be more noticeable to enemy marksmen than my head and shoulders. I had also learned that it was better not to wear my helmet during a firefight, mainly because it was bigger than my cap and stuck up too high, making a more conspicuous target. Besides, the helmet only protected my head from bullets that struck a glancing hit, or from flying shrapnel or dirt. I had already learned back in France that a direct hit would pass right through the steel anyway. It was better to wear the smaller and less noticeable cap than the larger and more visible helmet. The cap also helped keep my head warm in the November cold.

The Russian attack came within minutes of Jäekle's death. It started with incoming mortar shells, quickly followed by enemy machine-gun fire. I shrank down into my foxhole as low as I could get. I noticed a slight movement out of the corner of my eye. Peeking over the edge of my foxhole at my canvas draped across the little stick, it twitched twice more within a few seconds as bullets flew through it.

I knew that as long as the Russian machine guns kept firing, their soldiers were not going to get in front of them. As soon as the enemy barrage ended I shouldered my rifle and prepared for the infantry charge. Enemy soldiers jumped out of their foxholes and came running toward us, some crouching low, firing from the hip as they ran. The only opportunities for cover between our lines were the clumps of dead grass. The light from the rising sun made each charging figure clearly visible, a dark moving form silhouetted against the sky.

The moment our machine guns sprang to life the enemy dropped onto the ground to take cover. None of the attacking soldiers made it more than twenty metres toward us. Eventually all gunfire ceased. The mortar barrage had also ceased. They did not charge again, so I assumed that they had crawled back to their holes.

As soon as all the targets disappeared from view I quickly reloaded my rifle. After a few minutes of silence I figured the attack had failed. Not so. An hour later they came again. The Russians made repeated, furious attempts to overrun us. The pattern was always the same: a short barrage of mortar and machine-gun fire followed by men jumping out of their holes and running at us. Our machine-gunners held them off each time. They would retreat as soon as they realized it was suicidal to approach too close to our positions. Most of them never got more than a few dozen metres before they turned and ran back to their holes. They suffered casualties every time. After each attack I kept a wary eye out just in case anyone might be crawling toward us through the dead grass.

I wondered where they were all coming from, and how many men they had. The idiocy of their attacks was baffling. It was incomprehensible to me why the Russian commander kept ordering his men to risk their lives in obviously futile efforts.

My men were all veterans who kept a cool head under fire. The machine-gunners waited until they had clear targets and then fired a short, well aimed burst. Those killing machines had demonstrated their effectiveness countless times in battle. As far as I could tell, there were not enough enemy soldiers facing us to mount an overwhelming massive charge, so as long as our machine guns were operable and the supply of bullets held out it was impossible to overrun our position, no matter how many times they came at us.

The enemy could not overwhelm us by sheer weight of numbers, so the Russian commanders may have deliberately changed their tactics. Now the enemy charged with a few men at a time, perhaps testing our defences, probing for weak spots in our lines. If they met deadly and determined resistance during those probing attacks they would quickly fall back and regroup. If they found a weak spot they would surely pour troops into that area to overwhelm any remaining resistance and break open the line.

On that day, either the Russians in front of us thought we were the weakest point in that sector of the front, or they were coordinating their attack against our positions with another attack somewhere else. I am sure their commander was just following orders, whether it was smart or not. At that stage in the war it was doubtful that he could not figure out that our machine guns would defeat his frontal assault tactics. Whatever the reasons for their repeated attacks, it seemed an appalling waste of young men's lives.

Waiting for the next assault it occurred to me that, since about the beginning of August until late in November 1943, my life had been in danger almost every day. I knew that sooner or later my luck would run out. What could I expect? Once again the stark reality that there were only three ways out of the Russian front tormented me. The first, to be killed, still did not appeal to me in spite of my miserable lot. The second, to be taken prisoner, was as good as being dead, because I suspected no prisoner would ever come back from Siberia, or wherever they were sent. The best thing that could happen to me was to be wounded seriously enough to be taken out of the front and sent back to Germany, but not seriously enough to be permanently crippled.

After repeated, intense exchanges of gunfire I looked over at my little cape canvas and noticed that it had several bullet holes in it. There were still none in me, although I had noticed a distinctly hot rush through my hair earlier. A lull in the shooting gave me the opportunity to look at my cap. There was a neat round hole in the front and another in the rear. One centimetre lower and the bullet would have hit the top of my skull. Two centimetres lower and I would have been dead. Very close is still a miss. There was no time to reflect upon my luck; the enemy were upon us again. I put the cap back on my head and put my rifle against my shoulder.

A sudden movement in the grass in front of me caught my eye and I instinctively aimed and fired. The shot went right through the middle of a helmet, and the man behind it did not move again. A Russian soldier had crawled through the knee-high grass toward the front of my position and had momentarily raised his head to look ahead. He was a very brave man, but now he was dead. I admonished myself for allowing my vigilance to falter, even for a brief moment. I had not slept more than a few hours for days and knew I was on the verge of exhaustion, but that would not matter to any Russian who got the opportunity to take a shot at me.

The fighting was so close I am sure that any time I aimed and shot at one of the enemy I killed him. At a distance of less than a hundred metres I could hit any target bigger than an apple with every shot, let alone anything the size of a man. My rifle could hold five bullets at a time, and few were wasted. Much the same was surely true for the other men of my platoon. I reckoned the enemy must have lost at least thirty men in less than an hour, plus many more wounded, just within the section of no-man's land in front of my platoon's foxholes. Who knows how many they lost in front of our entire company?

There were rifle fire, machine-gun bursts, return bursts, smoke, the stench of gunpowder — the familiar trappings of battle — but no charging enemy. Perhaps they were crawling forward under covering fire! I started to really worry when I was down to two rifle clips, although I still had my automatic. It was very dangerous to expose my head and upper body enough to get a good look or to fire my rifle accurately. Because I could not see any soldiers running toward us, I assumed there must be plenty of them hiding in the grass. I raised myself up a little to get a better look at the ground in front of my foxhole, my rifle against my shoulder, desperately searching for approaching attackers. There were others still manning their foxholes — there! I quickly took aim at a soldier who momentarily looked like he was also aiming at me. I saw him clearly. He was so near.

Suddenly it felt as though someone hit my right arm with the blunt end of an axe. I slumped back into my foxhole. Everything went strangely silent, and I saw myself as if detached, moving in slow motion. Then came the traumatic realization that I had been hit by a bullet. Strange feeling, almost serene. The sounds of battle seemed to have disappeared.

A steady, ringing buzz filled my head. It was like being under water. My mind groped for some explanation. Perhaps it meant I was in shock, perhaps I would be paralyzed, perhaps it was a prelude to my own death? As if in a dream, I saw my father's face. What would he think now? Still in the dream, I imagined Gisela being alone in a hostile world.

Slowly I again became conscious of the sounds of battle. Surprisingly, after that initial shock, there was no more pain. Very carefully, I took off my coat and the right part of my jacket, curled back the right sleeve of my shirt, and saw a messy pink hole about the size of a large coin on the inside of my right arm, just below the elbow. There was another smaller and neater hole on the inside of my arm a few centimetres above the elbow. There was surprisingly little bleeding from both those holes. The lower half of my forearm drooped noticeably toward the ground as I tried to lift the arm, which meant both bones were broken. I could not move my right hand. Then the holes began to ooze blood, so I bandaged the arm as well as I could with my shirt sleeve and the strap from my rifle, being careful to keep the forearm as straight as possible. I assumed I was in shock, because there was so little pain and I had started shivering. I wrapped my jacket and coat around me and huddled in a small ball as low into my foxhole as I could get.

What a miserable state to be in, unable to help my men defend us, and practically defenceless myself. Feeling so dejected, it was too great an effort even to move. I almost despaired. Every vestige of control over my own destiny was gone. "Get a grip," I admonished myself. "You're not dead yet!"

There may still be a chance, as the remainder of my platoon could still defend us. My little hole in the ground now took on increased significance as my only safe haven; for I would have to remain there until it was dark again, provided we were not overrun. I figured my rifle would no longer be of use to me now, so I took my pistol out of its holster with my left hand. Awkwardly, I forced myself to turn and peer over the edge of my foxhole. Apparently that latest attack had also been beaten back. I did not want my men to find out that I had been wounded, so periodically I yelled toward those in the adjacent foxholes, asking if they were still all right, just to let them know that I was still there. I tried my best to stay alert, watchful for any movement in front of my foxhole. My pistol was more a psychological prop than an effective weapon in the event the Russians came close.

The enemy tried two or three more times to overrun us during that interminably long day. I kept expecting to see a Russian soldier loom over my foxhole and shoot me, but my men beat them back each time they attacked. As long as the machine-gunners remained in position there was a good chance I would come away from this day alive. All our lives were once again in their hands, and the supply of bullets for their guns.

Every once in a while I would notice a twitch in my little tent— another hit. That canvas must have had a dozen bullet holes in it by then. The number of hits meant some enemy soldiers must have singled out individual targets. I imagined they were getting closer and closer, perhaps digging their way toward us in shallow grooves across no-man's land until they would be right in front of us. I expected a grenade to roll into my hole at any moment, and imagined being able to toss it out with my left hand before it exploded. I felt terribly helpless hiding in my hole like a trapped animal. Please, let me survive this day!

After several hours I was on the verge of unconsciousness, possibly due to shock, compounded by exhaustion from days of sleep deprivation. I shook my head and gritted my teeth, trying to stay conscious. Over and over I kept telling myself to stay alert. But no matter how hard I tried to stay awake, I repeatedly passed out, each time waking with a momentary panic. Each time I was grateful to still be alive. Sometimes not even the sound of gunfire could keep me from nodding off.

When I lifted my jacket to examine my arm it made me feel momentarily flushed, and I had to overcome a reflex to throw up. The ragged bandage around my forearm was a bloody mess. I shivered uncontrollably at times, probably more from the trauma of the bullet wound than the cold, because the sunshine helped warm me.

By late afternoon the situation had not changed. There had been a lull in the shooting for a while, so I thought about eating my bread ration, but did not feel hungry. I drank some water from my canteen, but it felt as if I had to force the water down my throat. The hours ground by ever so slowly. A grim determination to survive kept me fighting unconsciousness all day. I had never longed for nightfall as much as I did on that day. Let me survive this day!

Nightfall brought a lull to the fighting, but we still had to be careful. When it was finally dark enough that neither we nor they could see each other anymore, I ordered my messenger, who was in his hole next to mine, to tell everyone to the left of him to retreat. I made sure all the men to my right did the same. I did that without waiting to receive the order to pull back. I would have ordered my men to retreat even contrary to any order to hold our positions, because our predicament was absolutely hopeless. It would only have been a short time before the Russians would have destroyed us. I was not going to force my men to spend the night within such deadly range. Even if my company could have avoided being overrun, I was positive the Russians would break through one of our flanks and encircle us, probably during the night.

There were no obvious emotional reactions on the part of my men when they saw I had been wounded, at least none that I saw. I was probably too dazed and exhausted to be concerned about their responses.

The medic quickly attended to our casualties, including me. He looked at the blood-soaked rifle strap around my arm and nodded his head. "Good enough," he said, and told me to go to the medical aid station.

I saw another man walk back to the first-aid station, with assistance from another soldier. Jäekle's body was placed in his tent canvas, to be carried back with us so that he could be buried. Considering the fury of the past day's fighting, it was incredible that no more men had been lost. There may have been other casualties, but by then I was beginning to feel strangely detached. I knew that my responsibilities to my men were ending. Someone else would now have to lead them.

I ordered my messenger to radio battalion headquarters that I had been wounded and that our company was now without an officer. I also told him to inform the captain of our retreat. Over the wireless he received acknowledgement from Command, and a terse concurrence to pull back.

"Yes, sir!" he said into the radio, with as much mock enthusiasm as he could, then looked at me, half exhausted, and in a completely deadpan voice said, "Good idea."

"You think?" My reply may have been just as deadpan.

We made it back to battalion headquarters, which was a dug-out bunker near a road. The captain saluted me, then looked at my arm and smiled, which I thought was a strange reaction. "Good job," he said. "You will probably be going home now." He made it sound like I had just won a prize.

Before we parted I asked him to recommend that my three machine-gunners receive the Iron Cross First Class, and that the rest of my men receive the Iron Cross Second Class. They had all gone through a terrible ordeal and had done what had to be done with distinction, regardless of their own safety. He agreed. I was sure he knew very well what we had endured.

A new lieutenant was assigned to replace me as company commander. He arrived within the hour. He was tall and thin, with pale features and a pleasant demeanour. How young he seemed. He was probably in his mid-twenties, about the same age as myself, but it did not occur to me that I, too, was still a young man. After years of military service, and especially the last five months of intense combat, I thought of myself as being much older than my twenty-five years. I felt sorry for that young man, and for all the men I was leaving behind.

Eventually I became vaguely aware of an unusual feeling beginning to take hold of me. The prospect of leaving that awful place was possibly starting to make me feel optimistic, if not downright ecstatic! Walking back to the medical aid station out of earshot of the others, I started singing for joy—exhausted, traumatized, partly delirious, but singing! I knew my wound might allow me to escape the horror of the Russian front. It had been the longest day of my life, and it turned out to be one of the luckiest. Of the three ways to leave the Russian front, being wounded was the best.

The medical aid station, or field hospital, was another kilometre away. Considering my condition, I was probably lucky to have found it by myself. Calling it a medical aid station or any kind of hospital may have been kind, as it turned out to be just a few tents, one quite large, set up beside a covered wagon, next to a large dug-out bunker. There were soldiers and medical personnel about, with many soldiers lying on stretchers outside the tents.

One of the aides guided me inside the large tent. It was lit by kerosene lanterns hanging from the ceiling. The first thing that struck me was the smell; it reeked of urine, blood, and alcohol. There were cots along the inside walls, every one occupied by a casualty. Although I did not investigate their wounds, some of them appeared much worse off than I was. There were also narrow tables, stands, dividers, pails, and other tools of the body repair trade, as well as cases of what must have been medical supplies. I did not care what it looked like, I was so happy to be there. The way I felt, I would walk all the way back to Germany if I had to.

The man that had been shot in the shoulder that day was also there. He lifted his greatcoat and showed me his new white bandage, which had been wrapped right around his shoulder, arm, and chest. "A lucky shot," he said with a gesture of his free hand toward his bandaged shoulder. I noticed he was smiling. I too had to smile, and understood the reason for all the smiling.

The station had two medics and about a dozen assistants. They were busy looking after other casualties. One of the medics finally had time to attend to me. He took off my blood-soaked field dressing and examined my arm. There was still no pain, even though the medic confirmed that both forearm bones were broken and I could not move my right hand. Examining the holes, he asked if I had been given a tetanus shot recently.

I had, just before coming to Russia, along with diphtheria and cholera shots. I remembered that inoculation distinctly because it had made me feel slightly ill for days. He cleaned the arm and poured antiseptic over the holes. The antiseptic came out of a large glass bottle and it stung sharply on my skin. It was probably vodka, which may have been the only antiseptic available. He straightened the forearm and bandaged it tightly between two slats of wood, as a makeshift splint. He told me he could not repair the damaged arm properly here in the field. My arm was put in a sling and I was dismissed. All in a night's work.

For the rest of the night I moved like an automaton, going where they pointed me and doing what I was told. A truck pulled up to the first-aid station, and the wounded were put into the back and driven away. Sitting in the dark in the back of the truck, I felt incredibly grateful to be heading away from the front, damaged, but alive. I was grateful to the Russian soldier that shot me. If I were ever to meet him later, I would recognize his face and would have to find some way to show my gratitude. His bullet in my arm was my ticket out of hell.

20 *The Lifesaver*

AFTER THE FIRST-AID STATION, the other walking wounded and I were driven westward to some place away from the front. It was probably cold and uncomfortable on the bench in the back of the truck, but to me it felt better than a chauffeur-driven limousine. Not much of that ride registered in my mind, probably because I was only semi-conscious.

Our first stop was on the outskirts of Kirovograd. We were helped out of the truck by a crew led by an old man, none of whom spoke German. Another old man wearing a mask over his nose and mouth, the kind painters wear, lined us up in the yard. He used a large metal pump to inject a smelly grey powder inside my clothes, down my collar, up my sleeves, under my shirt, into my pants, up my pant legs, inside my boots and socks, and into my hair. At that delousing station it barely registered in my exhausted state that those damnable body lice were being asphyxiated by that powder of retribution.

After we had all been thoroughly powdered we got back on the truck and were carried on to our next stop. I had not eaten since the evening of the previous day, but it hardly mattered. I was so tired I immediately fell asleep.

We finally arrived at the train station. As we climbed from the truck the scene that unfolded in front of me was nightmarish beyond anything I could possibly have imagined before. There were many hundreds, maybe even thousands, of wounded soldiers at the station, waiting for the train. There were men sitting or lying on the platform and in the approach street, many on stretchers, a few being attended by medics, others just sitting on the platform, or standing on crutches, or leaning on each other for support. The lights from the station highlighted the white bandages covering arms, legs, and heads. There were men with their entire head covered in bandages, including their eyes, so that other soldiers had to guide them when they walked. I could hear baleful and strangely hushed moaning from everywhere, as if emanating from the ground itself. I was gazing upon a scene from hell, filled with a wretched collection of unfortunates. Apparently I was one of them.

At last the train arrived, very late at night. All the casualties were ushered on board. Many had to be carried onto the train on stretchers, some were helped by others to climb aboard and find space. I found an empty spot on a wooden bench seat, laid my head back, and promptly fell asleep. The last thing I was conscious of was the vile smell in the train, a fetid mixture of oil, sweat, blood, antiseptic, and delousing powder.

The entire train must have been designated just for the wounded. That was an aspect of the war I had never seen or even imagined before. Here was an entire trainload of maimed bodies, carrying what was left of once strong and healthy young men back from the front. I was astounded to learn that it was one of many regularly scheduled trains, picking up casualties from the front every night in the summer and fall of 1943. So many wounded would have been unimaginable to me before that day. I had never before thought about the cost of the war in terms of suffering on such a stupendous scale.[11]

Every one of those men had a mother and father, and may have had a wife, brothers and sisters, maybe even young children. My thoughts went back to the teachings of the Lutheran Church during my upbringing, to the number of times I heard the phrase, "Give thanks to a loving and caring God." It was now difficult to imagine there could be a caring God that would permit the type of atrocities that war begets, unless God does not have the power to interfere, or does not exist. I could not think of a point to the suffering that had been inflicted on all those lives. My attitude was more than a disdain of the institutional authority of the Church; it was a personal mistrust of the higher authority. Thinking back, I had completely lost my faith in God.

That first night on the train, nerves and nightmares kept interrupting my sleep. I was troubled by feelings of terror and urgency. I dreamt that I was back in my foxhole, under attack, desperately searching for my rifle, trying to avoid being shot. I heard a distant voice shouting. Something touched my arm! Terror gripped me! They found me!

---

11   From July 4, 1943 when Hitler launched *Fall Zitadel* (Operation Citadel) until the Russian capture of Kiev in November 1943, the German army suffered more than 900,000 casualties. The Russians lost at least that many. Civilian deaths were never counted.

As consciousness returned the soldier in the next berth was shaking me to wake up. "You were yelling something about attack," he said. He had to assure me repeatedly that I was safely on a train, heading back to Germany. I must have been almost delirious at times, suffering from physical exhaustion and mental fatigue. I certainly felt half dead. I had seen other men at the front crack from the stress and psychological trauma caused by prolonged front-line combat, but it had not occurred to me that the strain had also affected me so profoundly. Like most young men, I had naively been sure that kind of thing only happened to others.

Not that I was unhappy. Knowing the train was carrying me farther and farther away from the front made me very happy indeed, but it was a restless, emotional, roller-coaster ride in a dream-like world. Eventually the monotonous clattering and gentle rocking of the moving train helped me relax enough to sleep for most of the trip. We stopped frequently to service the train. Those that could stretched their legs and used the facilities. We were fed from mobile field kitchens at the stations. Those that could not get off were watered, fed, and tended by medics and nurses on the train.

I have no idea how many days I spent on the train, but it could have been at least three. Eventually we arrived in Warsaw. Most of us were ordered off the train, loaded onto trucks, and driven to a hospital in the city. The truck passed through districts that were crowded with civilians. The hospital looked like a relatively new building, with clean and modern facilities.

Those that remained on the train probably required special treatment or long convalescence for very serious injuries and were sent on to Germany. Those of us that got off in Warsaw may have been ones the military doctors judged could be patched up easily and sent back to the front. Because only my right arm had been damaged, I might have been considered a candidate for speedy recovery and subsequent speedy return to the front.

Most of my first day in the Warsaw hospital was spent sitting on a chair in a hallway with other casualties, waiting. We casualties looked like misplaced derelicts. The hospital was a confusing place, busy and crowded. In Warsaw I had expected to meet people that spoke Polish, but all the medical personnel and patients I met spoke German.

Hours after arriving a group of us soldiers were ushered into a large washroom for a shower. The water was barely lukewarm and the soap smelled of lye, but it felt wonderful to wash months of grime from my body, not to mention that smelly delousing powder. I was absolutely ecstatic to get out of my uniform. Some of the soldiers had wounds that were serious enough that they had to be helped to wash. At first I was careful not to get my bandages wet, but after a few moments of revelling in the sheer pleasure of feeling the water on my body, I let everything get wet. I assumed the bandages would soon be changed anyway, as they smelled terrible. That shower washed more than dirt and stench from my body. With the draining water went much of the fear, tension, and horror, as well as the physical exhaustion, that had permeated my existence for months. Amazing how such a simple thing as being clean again can make a person feel miraculously rejuvenated.

After we washed we were escorted to a large storage room near the showers containing piles of uniforms and undergarments. An orderly helped us find new underclothes, as well as new uniforms. I found a pair of trousers that fit reasonably well and put them on. Good riddance to my old filthy and worn-out ones. It felt especially great to be alone again, not having to share my uniform with my former tiny companions, the Russian lice. If there was any energy left in me to experience such a thing as a feeling of victory, that was it—the lice had finally been defeated.

Each of us was then assigned a bed in a ward. Mine was a lovely clean room with only three other soldiers. A nurse came in and took the bandages off my arm. They were still damp, and discoloured with purple and brown stains. The nurse applied antiseptic to the two holes on the inside of the arm and also to another hole on the outside of the forearm, just above the wrist, a hole I had not noticed before. My forearm was a mess, not just from the holes in it, but also because it had swollen up in a hard swelling. The thick bandages wrapped around the wooden splints had kept the forearm together. It perplexed me that I still felt very little pain, other than a dull ache throughout my entire right arm. Whatever, I was now in a hospital and trusted the medical staff to know what to do.

A doctor examined me and explained that the bullet had entered the outside of my right arm just above the wrist, where the small hole was, came out where I had bandaged the silver dollar-sized wound on the inside of the forearm, and re-entered the inside of my upper arm, where it lodged near the bone. He explained that both bones inside my right forearm had probably been shattered into many small splinters. The bullet may have severed the main nerve in the upper arm, which would explain why I felt so little pain. He said the injury was too serious to be treated in Warsaw and that I would have to go back to Germany to have the arm repaired. As traumatic as the diagnosis of my arm could have been, it did not bother me. I was just glad to be alive, and the prospect of going back to Germany for a while made me feel even better. That bullet wound was not only a very lucky gift of fate, it was a lifesaver.

That evening I ate in the hospital. It was my first meal in six months not eaten out of a mess kit. It may have been standard hospital fare, but to me it tasted absolutely marvellous. The setting helped — a clean building that was lit and heated, at a real table with real dishes, and amidst civilians, including women. Just about anything would have been better than another feeding at the front, but that initial meal impressed me as uncommonly luxurious at the time.

I had not had a chance to shave since long before being wounded, so I was sporting a full beard. I was proud of that luxuriant growth, that symbol of manhood, and perceived myself to be rather sophisticated-looking. After spending a whole day in the ward, however, I noticed that the nurses were ignoring me. They were all young women, the first attractive women I had seen in half a year, and I felt slighted by their lack of attention. Had my usual charming personality also been impaired by the front?

When I asked one of the nurses how she liked my beard, she curtly said, "You look forty years old."

I shaved the first chance I got. Damaged or not, it was important to look good.

Shaving was awkward and clumsy, as everything had to be done with my left hand. In the bright light of the washroom I looked in a mirror objectively for the first time in months. I hardly recognized myself. I was gaunt and much older than I remembered myself to be. Mother Russia had exacted a heavy toll.

Regardless of my appearance, I felt better after shaving. It was good to be part of civilization again, dressed in clean clothes, feeling clean, clean-shaven, and warm, with pretty nurses to tend to me. During my waking hours I was deliriously grateful that fate had delivered me out of the nightmare of the Eastern Front. That night was not so agreeable. My sleep was pervaded with vivid images of dangerous situations and feelings that I had to be wary. My subconscious would be screaming at me not to let myself fall asleep. I awoke to see the soldier from the next bed leaning over me. "You were dreaming. Calm down." My heart was pounding in my chest. It was a relief when I became aware of where I was.

The next day at the Warsaw hospital I found myself feeling strangely out of place, awkward, and uncharacteristically unsure of myself. It was more than just being uncomfortable with my now use-less right arm. I had never before experienced a crippling injury, but now I was a casualty and would have to rely upon others to make me whole again. It was even more than that; it was almost as if I some-how recognized that I may have been emotionally scarred as well as physically damaged by my experiences at the front. I wondered if my injuries would affect me permanently, so that I would no longer be able to function properly in civilian surroundings. Whatever scars warfare had left me with, my most fervent hope was that my soldiering days were over.

I now had time to think of things other than fighting for my life. I scrounged a pen and some paper and wrote a letter to Gisela. I ardently wanted to see her again and wondered how she would react to my in-jury. Left-handed, my handwriting looked almost illegible. I felt like a child, having to learn to write all over again. I also wrote to my father in Michelau, telling him that I had left the Eastern Front because of a shot in the arm, but that I was safe in a Warsaw hospital. I was careful not to sound too pleased about being wounded. No need to portray the front as so horrible that it would give him and the women living at home more cause to worry about my brothers still away at some fighting front.

The following day I was transferred to a *Lazarett* (hospital for sol-diers) in Heiligenstadt, which means City of the Holy, in western Ger-many. It was a lovely hospital in the heart of the city. It had been a convent before the war. Like the hospital in Warsaw, it too was crowded and busy. I was assigned a bed in a small room with another soldier.

The nurses in the Heiligenstadt hospital were all nuns, who wore their traditional black dresses and white-rimmed hats. The habits made them look very formal and intimidating, and indeed they conducted themselves in their duties as if they had been empowered with divine authority to run the place and the soldiers. The nurses were splendid people, caring, kind, and considerate. I was impressed with their efficiency and marvelled how they never let the plight of their patients get them down. They treated everyone as if they would soon be completely healed, and refused to let anyone feel sorry for himself, no matter how badly he was injured. Their staunchly optimistic attitude was vital to the recuperation process for wounded soldiers. They were absolutely indispensable, doing their best to repair the damage caused by the Nazi oafs back home who were responsible for our plight.

My arm was finally put in a real cast so that the shattered bones could heal properly. The doctor explained that it was not possible to realign the bones as two separate bones, since the bullet had created too much of a mess. The bones had already begun to fuse together and would eventually form one solid mass. Luckily they had fused straight. The doctor also told me that the nerve must have been severed, which would explain why I could not move my right hand and why I felt so little pain. He warned me that a severed nerve would not heal by itself. If the nerve was only damaged it might recover, but that could take a long time.

I was pleased to hear that the healing could take a long time, despite the realization that the long-term prognosis might mean permanent disability. If the arm healed enough to enable me to fire a rifle again the army would send me back to the front. As long as I was unfit for combat I had a good chance to stay away from the fighting and possibly survive the war.

In the Heiligenstadt hospital I was given the *Verwundetenabzeichen* in Black (the German equivalent of the American Purple Heart) for being wounded in battle in the service of my country. I was also given the Iron Cross Second Class and the Iron Cross First Class. The medals and certificates were handed to me in the hospital by the senior medical doctor, who read a brief note with the mandatory praises and accolades, followed by a handshake and congratulations. That was it. The only witnesses besides the doctor were a nurse and the other soldiers in the ward.

The Second Class certificate was dated November 21, 1943. I vaguely remember being told by the captain in charge of our battalion that I had earned the Second Class shortly after the tank battle in the

Citation for being wounded in battle   *Iron Cross, First Class*

valley. That had not been important enough to me to hold a prominent place in my memory. The First Class was dated December 12, 1943. It must have been for the battle during which I was wounded. The order to award this medal came from the battalion commander at the front, who must have observed the action through his binoculars. Apparently he had been impressed enough to award that acknowledgement of "meritorious conduct in the face of the enemy," as the doctor had put it.

How strange that two incidents were singled out for special recognition. There had been so many situations where I had no choice but to risk my life in the fury and confusion of combat. I thought of the men I had fought with. There were countless acts of courage that merited the Iron Cross, performed by soldiers under extreme adversity, that would never be rewarded or even acknowledged because the witnesses were mere fellow soldiers. Bizarrely, a German soldier would likely only be awarded the First Class after he had already received the Second Class. Only the First Class was actually a metal cross; the Second Class was just a ribbon.

At the time I allowed myself to feel pleased with such a symbolic decoration. As if those little trinkets somehow compensated for the hardships and deprivation the army had forced me to endure. I understood how silly being decorated was, but still could not suppress the satisfaction I felt at being recognized for "bravery." No wonder the practice of awarding medals endures.

Actually, during combat I had no choice but to do what had to be done at the time. It had been circumstances, more than deliberate courage, that had forced all of us to act "heroic." My own feelings were irrelevant, as it did not matter what deeds the medals were for. What was significantly important was that wearing the Iron Cross and the *Verwundetenabzeichen* provided tangible proof that I had served at the front in active combat, and with distinction. It bestowed a certain assurance, in my own mind as well as that of others, that I deserved to be here among civilians in the relative safety of Germany, instead of back at the front.

There were a lot of men much worse off than me. My roommate, a sergeant, had lost his right leg just below the knee. He had been in the hospital a long time, as the stump had healed over. He was waiting for an artificial leg. When the prosthesis finally arrived, he acted as if he had just been assigned a new and complicated job he had to master. Fitted with his new mechanical leg, he put a crutch under his arm and doggedly tried his best to walk. It was obviously awkward and painful for him, but after truly tenacious effort, he managed to walk down the hall and back without a crutch. When he returned he sat on the bed and looked up at me. He almost smiled as he quietly said, "Now I can begin to feel like a human being again."

I had written to Gisela from the hospital in Warsaw, and as soon as I arrived in Heiligenstadt I wrote to her again. Being back in civilization greatly increased my longing for her, as there was now a possibility of actually seeing her again. I hoped she would visit me.

On Saturday afternoon of the weekend before Christmas, Gisela arrived at the hospital. When she entered the room my heart leaped for joy. It felt so good to put my arms around her, I wanted to hold her endlessly. She was even more beautiful than I remembered. She was so happy to see me and relieved that I had returned from the front with no more than a cast on my arm. Before receiving my letter from Warsaw she had not heard from me for almost two months and had feared that I might never return.

"I owe some Russian near Kirovograd for being here," I said. She shared my view of my arm injury as a lifesaver, the only reason we were able to be reunited. I also showed her my Iron Cross, which I considered a serviceable memento of my time in Russia. "This is what you get from the army for risking your life long enough," I said matter-of-factly.

"It must have been dreadful for you at the front," she said. She knew very well that the army did not award the Iron Cross easily. I did not want to tell her how horrible the Russian front really had been. When I showed her the bullet hole in my cap, she looked like she was going to cry. I put my good arm around her and quietly said, "Don't worry, I'm very lucky." Then added, "I might have to get a new cap."

We spent the rest of the day together, which was wonderful. She talked about her job, her friends, her mother, all topics that until recently had no relevance in my life. I was somewhat surprised to hear that her mother spoke of me often, which obviously meant she missed me. Not much of what was being said during our conversations registered, as my mind was consumed with the joy of being reunited. After the hell of Russia spending time with Gisela was like spending time in a magical, fairy-tale world.

One of the nurses found Gisela a place to sleep for the night, a tiny cubicle with a bed and a nightstand. It was very kind of the nurse; otherwise Gisela would have had to leave that night. We spent most of Sunday together, which was very precious.

After Gisela left I felt terribly lonely. She meant more to me than anything else in my life. This would never do; I had to think of something to let us be together. The next day I applied for a transfer from the hospital in Heiligenstadt to one in Brandenburg.

My request was granted and, just after Christmas 1943, I was transferred to a large hospital in Brandenburg. It was a much newer building than the *Lazarett* in Heiligenstadt. I was initially assigned a room that I shared with three other convalescing soldiers, but since there was not much that could be done with me as long as my arm was in the cast, I became an outpatient and stayed with Gisela and her mother.

Naturally I spent as much time as I could with Gisela. We celebrated New Year's Eve together. It truly was a new year for me. I felt a renewed optimism that we would survive the war. For the time being, we felt safe in Brandenburg.

Gisela belonged to a Hitler Youth girls' choir that visited the local hospitals and sang for the convalescing soldiers. That volunteer service had been requested by local government officials to help boost the soldiers' morale. She asked if I wanted to accompany the choir on one of her singing tours, but I politely declined. I recognized my limitations. Not only did I not think I could manage such an escapade gracefully, but I did not want to subject her, or any recuperating veteran, to the sound of my singing voice.

Sometimes we went to the Café Graf for a social evening with friends. Gisela usually wore a hat when we went out. She said it made her look more mature, so that the social police would not bother to check her papers regarding the curfew. She made it obvious that she was with me whenever one of the curfew enforcement types came into the café. Initially my cast was an interesting conversation piece, as Gisela's friends wanted to know how I had been wounded, but the novelty wore off quickly and it became just an inconvenience. I traded stories with other convalescing veterans as to how our respective tickets out of the front were obtained. I often thought about my comrades left in Russia and felt truly sorry for them.

After six weeks the cast on my arm was removed. The holes where the bullet had penetrated the skin were closed, covered in bright pink scars. The scar on the inside of my forearm was particularly large and colourful, and slightly raised above the level of the rest of my skin, which was surprising since it had been a hole.

"There it is," the doctor said as he felt the back of my right upper arm, "the bullet."

I reached around with my left hand and felt a hard lump deep under the skin, about halfway between the armpit and the elbow.

"That may have to come out," he added, "No hurry, though. Your body will form a cyst around it." The doctors were so busy treating so many mutilated cases that something as trivial as a bullet lodged in the arm was not a priority. I could live with it for as long as necessary.

The doctor asked me to try to move my arm and my hand. The hand drooped noticeably, and I could not lift it. The range of movement of my wrist joint was greatly restricted, to only a few degrees inward. Concentrating, I could cause my thumb to press against my index finger a little tighter, but was completely unable to open my hand even the least bit. It felt as if I no longer had any muscles to open the hand. The fused bones in my forearm prevented me from rotating my forearm more than a tiny bit, so that my hand was held permanently palm inward.

Because my arm had been constantly bent at the elbow in an "L" shape for so long, I could not straighten my arm. The muscles on the insides of my arm felt shorter than they had been before the injury. It surprised me how much my arm had atrophied in less than two months. The doctor explained that I would have to undergo extensive physiotherapy to regain functional use of my arm; however, the fused bones in my forearm meant that I would never be able to rotate my wrist more than a few degrees and my right palm would face inward for the rest of my life. I cared less about the hand problem than the mention of the physiotherapy.

"How extensive?" I asked.

"Perhaps months," he answered.

To my way of thinking, the longer the better.

The next day I started physiotherapy at the hospital. At first it involved repetitive exercises designed to straighten the arm. I had weights pressing my arm onto a table to try to straighten it, and spent hours carrying a pail of water to pull the forearm down and strengthen my grip. There were also exercises designed to strengthen the muscles, such as lifting weights for hours at a time. I had to learn how to place objects into my right hand by deliberately separating the fingers from the thumb with my left hand. No amount of trying would hold the hand open at all, so the index finger always rested against the tip of the thumb. The hand felt alien and awkward, as if it were disengaged from the rest of my arm.

The therapy also involved treatment designed to stimulate the damaged nerve in the hope it would heal by itself, including electrical shock and deep pressure stimulation of my forearm and upper arm. It took weeks of therapy before my elbow resumed anywhere close to a normal range of movement. Although the physiotherapy gradually increased the strength of my grip and increased the mobility of my elbow and wrist joint, it did not improve at all my ability to open my hand. I began to wonder if my right hand would remain permanently useless.

War or no war, Gisela and I enjoyed being together. I longed to be with her forever, so I thought seriously about the prospect of getting married. On her eighteenth birthday I formally asked her to marry me. I was ecstatic when she said yes.

When we told Margarete we wanted to get married, she let us know that she thought Gisela was still too young. Regardless, I was undaunted. Gisela had let me know that her mother adored me and expected me to make a good husband. It must be obvious to her that I loved her daughter and would do everything in my power to make her happy for the rest of my life.

There was also a very practical reason to get married sooner rather than later. By 1943, women were being drafted by the government to serve in train yards, factories, hospitals, and farms, or as support personnel for military posts in places who knows where. Married women had a better chance of being assigned work in their hometown than single women. Only women with children under three were allowed to stay at home without working. Also, because she had apprenticed for a trade, Gisela had not served in the *Arbeitsdienst* and might still be conscripted for that unpleasant duty. If she were married she could have a good chance of not being transferred to some work station far away. I doubted my status as an officer would influence the authorities, especially if conditions in wartime Germany became worse.

There was another reason in the back of my mind. If fate were to decide that I should not survive the war, I very much wanted that she be my wife, not just a girlfriend. As my widow she would receive my veteran's pension from the government, whereas as my girlfriend she would receive nothing.

A few days after announcing our engagement, Gisela's mother handed me a gold chain bracelet, obviously of excellent quality. She told me to take it to a jeweller to try to exchange it for two wedding bands. I was astonished at her generosity. Unlike money, gold had lasting value. The jeweller had a few rings for sale in his store, but there were no ration cards issued for such frivolities. Without the stamps the jeweller would not have sold me two rings for all the money in Brandenburg, but we could trade one gold item for another. So we bartered the deal. The jeweller may have got the better of the gold, but we got the two precious rings. As per German custom, I put the smaller one on Gisela's left hand, to signify she was now engaged. When we were married it would go on her right hand.

I asked Gisela if she wanted to meet my family. She enthusiastically said, "Of course." The army granted me a few days off from physiotherapy to visit my home. I wrote to Turko that we would arrive in two weeks' time for a weekend visit. Gisela arranged for time off work to accompany me. I found out after the trip that the little truant had told her employer she was ill.

As we approached the Michelau train station Gisela commented on how scenic the countryside was in Oberfranken, with its tree-covered hills, manicured little farm fields, and numerous quaint villages. That comment made me look at the landscape with a renewed perspective, as I had always taken the picturesque aspects of my home for granted.

I eagerly anticipated the reunion with my family as we walked from the train station to my father's house. I opened the door and announced our arrival. Aunt Gustel came rushing out of the kitchen to greet us, followed by Turko and Karl. Big hugs and kisses all around. As we entered the kitchen, it was full of wicker, cane, raffia and bast, as the area was being used as a workshop for the family basket-making business. That was a total mess to my way of thinking. I was trying to make a good impression on my fiancée and my family did not even clean the place up and make it presentable. How embarrassing. I let Aunt Gustel know I thought she and Turko were making my family look like country bumpkins. She just laughed at my silly complaint.

We sat at the kitchen table and out came the beer and a bottle of wine, along with some preserved fruit and sweet cakes. Excellent. At least my family's hospitality had not diminished. My little brother Karl, my older brother Hermann's wife, Anna, and her two young boys, Richard and Adolf, also joined us. My other three brothers were away in the military. Turko knew only that Hermann was in Russia, and that Oskar had joined the *Kriegsmarine*, the German navy. He had no idea where Edwin was, but assumed he too was in Russia.

We talked for hours, catching up on the latest news about family, friends, and acquaintances. I received appropriate sympathy for my damaged arm. Aunt Gustel especially seemed genuinely sad about my useless hand. Gisela listened politely to all the stories from Michelau and the latest gossip, but said very little. Turko said we were going to the Zum Schärfner pub for dinner. Turko was a regular at Zum Schärfner, and we were greeted like celebrities by the owners, Nickolaus and Lotte Spitzenpfeil. They had been close friends since childhood. I gathered that Turko had made a deal with Nickolaus, so that our meal would not cost him the fortune in ration stamps that it otherwise would have.

Dinner was filling and delicious. There were boiled potatoes, potato dumplings, some preserved vegetables, and a small piece of fatty pork for each, all smothered with marvellous onion gravy, as well as lots of good rye bread. There was *krapfen* for dessert, donut-like pastries that were absolutely delightful. I felt somewhat smug that my family could treat us to such a delicious meal at that time. Gisela made a point of mentioning that she was delighted with the restaurant's almost miraculous ability to prepare such a wonderful meal. That was exactly the right thing to say to win Lotte's heart.

After dinner we had some more beer and hours of jovial discussion. Anna eventually brought politics into the conversation, bragging to Gisela about her big-shot *Gauleiter* brother in München. Anna may have been a staunch supporter of Hitler's regime because of her brother's position. I knew Gisela disliked politics and hated Hitler's government, so I was astounded when she listened attentively to Anna's prattling and even nodded acknowledgements at what was said. Everyone else had already heard Anna's stories and ignored her as much as possible without being impolite, but in Gisela she had found someone new to listen to her. None of us argued with Anna's opinions, because we really did not care what she had to say.

When we returned home that night I looked at Turko, searching his face for an indication of what he thought of my fiancée. "Well?" I asked.

"*Ah schöns Weib*," ("A lovely 'woman'") Turko said emphatically.

That was a compliment, but qualified and perhaps begrudgingly given. The term *Weib* is slightly condescending, relegating a woman to lesser status than a man. It can denote a possessor context, as if she is prescribed by necessity, but not necessarily wanted. I recognized that this was more than just a male chauvinist comment. He could obviously see that she was beautiful, and smart, but I knew that Turko had wanted me to marry Helga, the only daughter of Turko's good friend Mini. Helga was nice, but I had no interest in her. Turko may also have harboured some latent or subconscious suspicion about Prussians, whom most Michelauers still considered foreigners. Notwithstanding any underlying motivation that may have tinged his comment, I was satisfied with my father's acknowledgement of her appeal.

There were tenants living in my former bedroom on the second floor of my father's house, so we were assigned the tiny but cozy bedroom on the third floor, under the roof. Gisela was impressed with the fact that my family owned their own house, and such a large house at that. In Brandenburg only the very rich could afford to own a house. Gisela's observation greatly enhanced the value of property in my mind, and owning our own home became an abiding ambition for me from that day on.

I hoped Gisela would not think Michelau too parochial. "What do you think of my family?" I asked her, taking it for granted that she would now consider herself part of "us." I just assumed she liked them, because of course I loved my family and considered everyone in it to be excellent, kind, caring, and steadfastly supportive.

"I didn't understand a word they said," she replied.

"What?" It had not occurred to me that our local dialect was that much different from her *Hoch Deutsch* (High German) manner of speaking. I now understood why she had been so silent at the dinner table, and especially why she had listened so politely to Anna's political sermons. I should have noticed something was amiss when she had remained quietly attentive for so long; after all, Prussians have been known to express their own opinions on occasion. I promised to be more helpful in overcoming the language barrier in future.

The next morning I could tell that my sweetheart was less than impressed with the plumbing in the house, or rather the lack thereof. There was a toilet on the main floor, but it was nothing more than an outhouse inside the house, set over a large concrete septic tank. I explained that a local farmer came and emptied the tank every so often and used the manure to fertilize his fields. That was an environmentally responsible recycling method, used in Michelau long before recycling became fashionable in the rest of the western world. There was no running water in the house, so pails of water had to be brought up from the hand pump in the basement for cooking, cleaning, and washing. Laundry was particularly hard work that was traditionally left to the women of the household, which also left Gisela unimpressed.

I took Gisela on a tour of my village. She was surprised at how large Michelau was, and how industrialized. She had expected a tiny farm village from the way I had described it, and was amazed at the scale of the local wicker industry. Besides Zum Schärfner, we also visited another of the neighbourhood pubs, Die Krone, where I introduced her to many friends and acquaintances. Conscious of Gisela's difficulty with the local dialect, I tried to make sure she understood at least the gist of conversations. The only men my age in Michelau at the time were soldiers on leave or convalescing casualties. It was disappointing to have missed seeing most of my close friends from my youth. I was pleased to have Gisela by my side, and wished more of my friends could have met her.

My lame hand came up in conversations. I subtly made sure it was noticeable enough that there would be no need for me to explain why I was not at the front. Everyone, especially the women, sympathized with my disability. The veterans, including those of the First World War, probably understood that it had been my ticket out of Russia. I had not brought my Iron Cross with me from Brandenburg and I did not bring it up.

A few of the older people in the pub asked about the course of the war as they suckled on their beers. Perhaps because I was an officer stationed in Brandenburg, they may have assumed I had some kind of inside knowledge about future happenings. "What will happen out of this war?" I was asked. "Is there any hope we can still win?"

What a question. Any reasoning person could figure out that Germany could not win the war. I had been convinced the war would be lost from the time America entered the fray. Every scrap of information from the Eastern Front indicated that the Russian army was unstoppable. It was only a matter of time before we would be fighting inside the borders of Germany itself. Unless someone got rid of Hitler very soon and somehow negotiated a peace, there was no way to escape Russian occupation.

"Perhaps," I replied, with as much optimism as I could feign, "Hitler may have a secret weapon which could change the course of the war." It was common knowledge that German scientists had recently developed rockets that could reach all the way to London, England. Picking up on rumours about the development of super weapons, I added, "Hitler may soon have an atom bomb which could do so much damage that the Allies would be forced to give up."

That may have mollified the older men and women in the pub, but I knew it was just a dream. The defeat of Germany was inevitable. Gisela even made a sardonic joke about the situation. "Enjoy the war," she said. "The peace is going to be worse."

"There may be some truth to that," I added, remembering the aftermath of the First World War in Germany. The thought of living under Stalin's thumb made me wince.

Those social gatherings were sometimes bittersweet, as I was confronted all too often with the painfully sad news that someone I knew well would not be returning from the front. I was particularly despondent after meeting the mother of three boys I had gone to school with. All three of her sons had been serving on the Eastern Front. When she received news that her two older sons had been killed she immediately requested that her only surviving son be returned from the front. It was government policy that the last remaining son of any family could be returned home if all his brothers were killed in action. Before the army had a chance to pull him out of the fighting front, he too was killed. I could not imagine anything more grievous than losing a child. To lose all your children was a staggering tragedy.

We spent two full days with my family in Michelau. Anna had essentially taken over running the entire household when she married Hermann. We gave her our ration stamps so she could buy more food, and she did a marvellous job of preparing wonderful meals. As a soldier I did not get regular ration stamps, as the army supplied everything, including meals, but I had received food ration stamps for this little holiday. Generous hospitality was not only a Bavarian tradition, it was a sacred obligation.

After our short holiday in Michelau we returned to Brandenburg. Gisela and her mother continued to go to work every day, and I spent four hours in physiotherapy at the hospital every day. I also spent a lot of time just walking around the city. It was not very exciting, but it was infinitely better than spending time at some military outpost. The Allied bombers that repeatedly flew over Brandenburg on their way to Berlin kept reminding us that it was still wartime.

I learned to write with my left hand, which at first was very awkward and slow. Everything felt backward, and the pen would catch on the paper, causing blobs and scratches. But after weeks of practice I became quite proficient at writing with my left hand, developing a serviceable if not elegant style.

One evening near the end of April 1944, there was a knock on the front door of Gisela's mother's building. We heard an exchange of words at the front porch. Our seventy-year-old landlord sounded quite distressed, "I can't let a stranger into the house." Suddenly a wave of joy flashed through me, as the other voice was very familiar. I rushed downstairs to see my brother Oskar standing in the doorway. What a wonderful surprise! We greeted each other with big, back-slapping hugs. I felt great joy at his being alive and well.

I introduced him to Gisela and her mother. O was on a two-week holiday from the *Kriegsmarine* and had decided to visit his older brother. When he reached Brandenburg he had no idea where Margarete Winkelsdorf lived, so he had gone to the city hall and asked the officials for her address. Everyone in Germany had to have their address registered with the municipality in which they lived, so the clerk was able to tell him.

O had plenty of stories to tell about his adventures with the navy. He had served on an armed landing craft, escorting freighters and tankers to German outposts on the coast of the Black Sea. He described running the gauntlet of Russian warships and attack airplanes. His storytelling talents made his exploits in those foreign outposts sound exciting; however, he too found his military service mostly tedious, boring, and lonely, even though it was sometimes dangerous. I understood his sentiments very well. Neither of us had any news of Hermann or Edwin to tell the other.

I showed him the Iron Cross, which he acknowledged with curiosity and pretended to be very impressed. He sympathized with what he knew it took to be decorated with that little metal token. I showed him the cap I had brought back from Russia. When he saw the hole made by the bullet he said, "You got some dumb luck." He admitted that during all his escapades in Sebastopol and on ships in the Black Sea, where he had been bombed, shelled, and strafed, no instrument of death came as close to him as that bullet came to me. I also delighted in showing him where the bullet was lodged in the back of my arm. That internal lump and the holed cap were now mere curiosities, souvenirs of an ancient adventure in a distant land.

O spent two days with us, after which he had to return to active duty. It was such a pleasure to see him again. It reinforced the family bond that was still the foundation of my world and affirmed how precious a family really is.

Early in May 1944, I was sent to a hospital in Potsdam to be operated on by a nerve specialist. Because so many men had been injured during the war, out of necessity German medical experts experimented with innovative techniques to rebuild or rehabilitate damaged bodies. They were going to try out an experimental procedure for grafting nerves on me. They had nothing to lose by trying something new, since I was useless to the army with my hand the way it was. I had ambivalent feelings about that procedure. A successful operation could mean that my arm would be returned to useful function, which would be a good thing in the long run, but it could also mean I would be repaired enough to be sent back to the front.

The Potsdam hospital was very old, with thick stone walls and medieval-looking arched windows and doorways. Some of the rooms had high, vaulted ceilings, all made of stone. It may have been a monastery at one time. The entire inside had been renovated with the fixtures and equipment necessary to operate a hospital. Electrical conduits, water pipes, and ducts ran along the walls, and there were hot-water radiators in every room. Light bulbs hung on electrical cords from the ceilings, with steel lampshades painted white. Those modern utilitarian fixtures looked starkly out of place in the medieval stone setting. The effect was to produce an institutional environment that was utilitarian, but decidedly bleak.

I met Dr. Bunne, the surgeon who would perform the operation. He told me there was no guarantee with the procedure and that it could be risky, but there was a reasonable chance it would result in at least a partial recovery of the use of my right hand. He also said that there was probably nothing that he could do about the permanently restricted rotation of my right forearm. He was very matter-of-fact about the whole thing, calm and unpretentious. His demeanour gave me the impression that he was competent as a surgeon, which alleviated some of my apprehensions about going under the knife. It mattered little what I thought anyway. The army had decided that the nerve operation was needed, so Dr. Bunne was just carrying out orders. The operation would take place the next morning.

I felt no pain when I awoke, only a slight dizziness and dryness in my throat, along with a dull feeling of pressure in my right arm. The bullet had also been taken out, and was presented to me after the operation. It was flattened in front and slightly deformed along one side, which must have happened when it hit my bones. I cherished that lump of lead as the symbol of my deliverance from the Eastern Front.

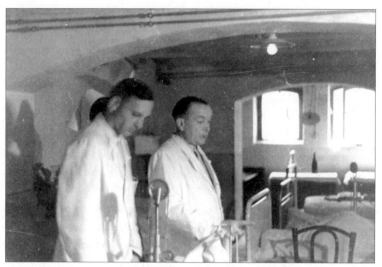

Dr. Bunne, Potsdam hospital, May 1944

Schwester Bertha and The Boys, Potsdam hospital, May 1944.
The soldier on the left had one leg amputated just above the knee,
and the soldier to the left of the nurse has no left arm.

About a week after the operation the bandages came off. There was a bright, fifteen-centimetre-long scar along the inside of the elbow on my right arm, partly covering the hole made by the bullet. There was also a new scar on the back of my upper arm where the bullet had been removed. The stitches looked like alien hairs across the scars. The doctor asked if I could open my hand. Well, I tried, but could not; however, it felt like there was more sensation in my hand, as it was painful to move the arm and close my grip. The whole arm ached.

Dr. Bunne had cut open such a long section of my arm to find the cause of the problem. The radialis nerve had been crushed against the bone by the bullet but had not been completely severed. It had taken very delicate and careful surgery to free the nerve from the damaged bones and repair it. "Nerves are very tough. It will probably take a lot of physiotherapy to regain the use of your hand, but I am sure it will recover."

"Thank you, doctor," I said.

"Ya, that's my job," he replied. "You are very lucky. I operated on three men that day for damaged nerves, and yours was the only one I think successful. You'll soon be fit for duty again." He said that with a grin.

"Ya, thanks a lot," I said, with a grin.

Gisela came to see me a few days after the operation. When she asked about the results of the operation, I said, "I still can't open the hand, but I can feel tingling and painful sensations in my arm that were not there before the operation."

She smiled and seemed pleased, then took a deep breath as a concerned look came over her face. "Hopefully you won't recuperate fast enough that they send you back to the front."

"The war will be over soon," I said, trying to sound reassuring.

Potsdam is about twenty kilometres west of the heart of Berlin, close enough that I heard the sounds of bombers in the sky every day. A few of us recuperating patients were on the grounds outside the hospital one afternoon when I counted what must have been a thousand bombers passing overhead from west to east. I recognized them as huge four-engined American B–17s, flying in formations, in groups of about one hundred each. It took almost an hour for all of them to pass overhead. The deep droning sound of that many motors was very ominous, and made all the worse because I knew their purpose.

Our fighter planes were nowhere to be seen. The anti-aircraft batteries were concentrated in and around the city of Berlin itself, but there was no way those flak guns would be able to stop that incredible airborne onslaught. We could not tell if any of the bombers were shot down. The dreadful dull thudding reverberation of distant exploding bombs could be heard for over an hour.

I could only imagine the devastation that rained down on the city that day. Berlin was a big city with about three million inhabitants at the time, the great majority of which were civilians. That may have been an unusually large raid, but there were bombing raids on one German city or another every day and every night in 1944. Living conditions must have been appalling for citizens in the big cities.

I was sent back to the hospital in Brandenburg. A few days later the stitches were taken out. I immediately went back to physiotherapy. The staff had set a rigorous schedule of daily sessions for me, which included painful exercises to work the muscles in my arm and hand. This time the electric treatments, which they called "galvanizing," produced acute sensations in my forearm and hand and caused the muscles in the hand to contract repeatedly without my control. The hospital staff were making a determined effort to get my arm back in shape.

At first I could not open my hand or do anything noticeably better than before the operation, but after a week of trying I was able to open my hand just a bit. After that there was slow but steady improvement in my hand's mobility, dexterity, and strength. That meant my right hand and arm would eventually be restored to reasonably competent function. I could soon be serviceable enough to be capable of firing a rifle. It was now only a matter of time before I would be sent back to the front.

21   *Someone to Live For*

GISELA CONTINUED TO WORK at the Kaufhaus Riedel department store as a decorator, specializing in the design and installation of window displays. She had quite an artistic flair, which impressed me very much, probably because I have no artistic ability at all. I met her every day at closing time and walked her home. Most evenings we went out to a café, usually the Café Graf. Sometimes Gisela's mother came with us. Margarete continued to work at the Arado airplane factory.

We discussed wedding plans for hours at a time, at least Gisela and her mother did. Eventually, I suggested we get married in Michelau. I figured we could have a better wedding party there, as it would be nearly impossible to provide a decent wedding dinner in Brandenburg. My family would be able to organize a traditional party in Michelau with the help of friends and neighbours. Michelauers always rallied for a good cause like a wedding, an attribute probably typical of most rural communities in Germany. Any excuse for a party was a good one. Weddings were important social events. It would also be easier for Gisela's small family to travel to Michelau and find accommodations than for my relatively large family to come to Brandenburg. Michelau was also not being bombed at the time, so we would not have to flee to the basement in the event of an air raid.

I wrote to my father to tell him of our plans to marry in Michelau. The army granted me a week's leave to get married.

We had to get permission to marry from the state. To be able to get a marriage licence we had to show the local Nazi officials at the Brandenburg city hall our family genealogy, to make sure there were no "undesirables" in our heritage. We were specifically asked if we had any Jewish blood in our ancestry. Although that question was obviously ludicrous to any rational thinking person, it was the law at the time, and we knew the government employees were only doing their job. Nevertheless, it was disgraceful to be required to show some stranger our family history, not because we were ashamed of it, but because our government forced its citizens to undertake such base behaviour in the name of nationalism. That was surely a source of national embarrassment felt by most Germans.

Gisela's family tree had been assembled before the war. Her Aunt Helene had hired a professional to research their family's history, which could be traced back to Franciscus Josephus Fredericus Müller, born in 1768 to Johann Georg Müller, birth date unknown, in Dürr Kunzendorf, Silesia. My family history was obtained from the church in Michelau, which was the only source that I knew about for any citizens of Michelau. It could be traced back only four generations, as the ink had disappeared on the old documents in the damp church basement.

Because Gisela was only eighteen years old we had to get her father's written permission to get married, so we went to visit him at his restaurant. Gisela had told me that her father was a German navy boxing champion during the First World War, and that many of his friends called him "Boxer Willie" for years. I also knew that Gisela harboured some resentment towards her father, blaming him for her parents' separation. My impression was that she had not had a very happy childhood and that he had rarely been there for her while growing up. With that in my mind, I prepared myself to meet a very rough character who would be stern and aloof.

He was a tall man, powerfully built, with dark hair slightly balding on top, and carried himself with a confident, erect posture. He greeted me with a broad smile and a firm handshake with his huge hands. In spite of that somewhat intimidating first impression, he struck me as an agreeable enough man, cordial and hospitable. He appeared genuinely pleased to meet me. He set a beer in front of each of us and we had a surprisingly congenial visit.

He asked about my hometown, my family, how we met, about my arm, and about all manner of things in our lives. He asked about our plans for the future, and especially about my continued service in the army. He hoped for a speedy end to the war, so that it would not interfere with our prospects for a happy life together. Coincidentally, he had just received his conscription notice to rejoin the *Kriegsmarine*. At fifty-four he was not considered too old for military service. That indicated the desperate need for bodies to fill the ranks of the armed services in Germany by that stage of the war. His four-year service in the German Navy in World War I should have been enough.

He signed his consent to our marriage and wished us the best. I was left with the impression he cared very much about his daughter's welfare. As we shook hands goodbye, he said he hoped to see us again often. I hoped we would too.

I had given Gisela money to try to buy a wedding dress. Money was not a problem because of my earnings from the army, but money alone would not buy any clothes without the requisite clothing allocation stamps, and we did not have anywhere near enough stamps to buy one from a store. After a few weeks, however, she astounded me by coming home with a length of beautiful white material, along with a long white veil. She explained how Eva Chine, one of the salesclerks at Kaufhaus Riedel, abetted by the supervisor of the clothing department, had scrounged together loose and single ration stamps until they eventually accumulated enough to make up the total needed. Eva and her co-workers had surreptitiously misplaced stamps that had been turned in with purchases and that were supposed to be pasted into the stamp book, to be returned to the authorities for more goods when full. Those wayward stamps ended up in Gisela's hands. The supervisor was an elderly lady who had married late and then sadly lost her husband to the war. She told Gisela, "I will help you. No one should have to wait as long as I did to get married." That was quite a display of loyalty and affection toward Gisela. Eva also sold Gisela the lovely long veil to go along with the dress.

A close friend of Margarete's, whom Gisela had always called Tante Alice, made the wedding dress. She was a dressmaker, and a good dressmaker was hard to find. All the younger ones had been conscripted to work in factories for the war effort, and any older, retired ones would not have had any incentive to make dresses because of the uselessness of the money.

On Saturday June 3, 1944, we boarded the train for Michelau. Gisela's mother and Aunt Helene, Margarete's sister, went with us. I asked why Helene's husband, Franz Schütte, did not come with us. Helene replied that he had recently been arrested by the Gestapo and taken to a camp, to Dachau. Her use of the word "camp" might have been her way of trying to soften the reality that he was in a prison camp, one that would come to be known as a concentration camp. Helene did not explain why he had been arrested. Her inquiries as to his status had not been answered by the authorities. I could see that her husband's plight was very stressful for her, but did not appreciate the seriousness of that incarceration at the time. I knew nothing about the true nature of a concentration camp and most people in Germany did not either. Considering the grim nature of such prisons, the government deliberately kept them a guarded secret.

Gisela bought the train tickets for all the women in our group. As a soldier in uniform, I had received my tickets from the army. The conductor checked all our tickets with a serious and intractable manner. Perhaps his attitude was a sign that the authorities were becoming increasingly paranoid about German citizens moving about within their own country.

When we arrived at my father's house my family was excited about the upcoming wedding, not the least of whom was me. I was surprised and happy to see Edwin at home. He was on holiday from his posting in Russia. He enthusiastically agreed to be best man for the wedding. According to Turko, Hermann was still with the army in Russia. No one had heard from Oskar since his visit to Brandenburg six weeks ago.

Unpacking Gisela's wedding dress was a huge social event. The ladies of my family were astounded by the lovely material and the long veil. Michelauers would probably have been willing to lavish money on a dress, but it was virtually impossible to buy a wedding dress anywhere in our little village or in the entire district.

A few days later the family were gathered at the kitchen table when the news came over the radio that Allied troops had landed in Normandy. That event was not broadcast in nearly the manner due such a major news story; just a curt, matter-of-fact announcement. The next day's newspaper carried a surprisingly low-key coverage of the landings, a few paragraphs on the front page. In spite of the deliberate attempt to downplay the seriousness of the invasion, I knew what it meant. If the Allies were not defeated on the beaches and prevented from getting a foothold on the continent, it would spell disaster for the German armed forces. There was no way Germany could win a two-front war. I remembered news reports of the Allied raid on Dieppe back in August 1942, when German propaganda had a field day with that fiasco, touting it as a failed invasion. This time the news coverage again proclaimed that our forces were pushing the Allied troops back into the sea, but their bravado was not as convincing. Normandy was apparently a full-scale invasion. Even though I was a German soldier, I secretly hoped the Allies would advance quickly into Germany, to bring the war to a speedier conclusion. Since Germany could not win the war, it would be better if the British and Americans conquered Germany than the Russians.[12]

12   The Allied invasion of Normandy—D-Day, June 6, 1944—was a momentous event in World War II and a huge Allied success, opening the Western Front. The German news media steadfastly refused to acknowledge the overwhelming realities of repeated disasters suffered by Germany, always assuring the German people that they were just temporary setbacks.

When I casually mentioned that the Normandy invasion might signal the beginning of the end for Germany, Anna became incensed. She said it was the duty of every German citizen to support our troops and our country's leaders, no matter what. I immediately dropped the subject, but was incredulous that anyone could be so naïve at such a late stage in the war.

Turko added that we should not give up so soon. He had heard rumours that German scientists were developing a secret weapon that Hitler would soon unleash on the Allies and yet win the war. After all, Germany had already developed the "V" weapons that were capable of bombing England all the way from Germany. Those rocket bombs were being publicized in German newspapers and radio reports as just the beginning of a whole new generation of scientifically advanced weapons that would reverse the current tide of the war.

It was even harder for me to believe that Turko could be so naïve. Perhaps he mentioned Hitler's super weapons just to calm Anna down. Perhaps he had been impressed with other technological advances that had been developed since the beginning of the war, like mechanized armies, dive-bombers, radar, artificial gasoline, as well as rockets, so that he may actually have believed another technological miracle could yet change the course of the war. Regardless, the Allied invasion was a news event far removed from my family's current preoccupation. We were busy with preparations for the wedding.

I tried to find a car to rent for the wedding, but it was impossible. Even before the war there had been few automobiles in Michelau. By then all automobiles, except those belonging to doctors and political leaders, had been confiscated by the military. Once again friends came to the rescue. A good friend of the family's, Olga Aumüller, had an expediting business, which involved transporting merchandise from local manufacturers to and from the railway station for shipment. She didn't have a car, but she did have a buggy and a team of horses. For our wedding, she agreed to drive us from the church to have our picture taken and then to the reception.

To make the marriage legal, the Friday before the wedding we went to the *Rathaus*. The *Burgermeister* (mayor) witnessed the legal contract of marriage, and the certificate was registered in the registry office. That was the only record of our marriage recognized by the government, which did not recognize a minister's pronouncement in a church, no matter how many people witnessed it. Since around 1870, when

Otto Von Bismarck had made civil wedding certificates mandatory, the church ceremony served only to satisfy religious and social customs.

A church wedding had its advantages. It provided a social ritual whereby all our friends and relatives could witness our vows and share in the celebration. Many people in Michelau were devoutly Lutheran, and the sacred aspects of the wedding were important to them. In fact, my father's sister had gone out of her way to ask me, "Are you two getting married in the church?"

"Of course, Tante Gustel," I answered.

"Good," she said with a satisfied grin. That was obviously important.

June 10, 1944, dawned bright and sunny. A beautiful summer day to match the elation I felt in my heart. It was our wedding day.

I did not have any civilian clothes with me, as all soldiers had to wear their uniform at all times in public. I did not even own any civilian clothes at the time, so I dressed for the wedding in my formal dress uniform. The church gardener brought a bouquet for Gisela to carry at the church, ingeniously fashioned out of white lupines which had been growing on the church grounds, embellished with lacy green asparagus leaves.

As many of our close relatives and friends as possible celebrated our wedding with us. Also in attendance were Turko, my brother Edwin, Anna and her two young sons, my *Paate* (godfather) Albin Werner and his wife, Albine, my father's sister Auguste, Gisela's mother, Margarete, Gisela's Aunt Helene, and my youngest brother Karl, who was fifteen at the time. Besides our family members, everyone in Michelau that knew the family and could fit into the small Lutheran church attended the ceremony. Some of the older ladies may have been curious to see the "foreigner" I had brought home. Many of them would have considered it quite an event for their little community—an international wedding. I of course knew everybody in the church. I hoped Gisela's mother and aunt felt at ease, since they were the only ones present from her side of the family, and the only other Prussians.

As I stood at the front of the church with my brother Edwin, I looked about the pews. Everyone was dressed in their finest, many fidgeting in their seats waiting for the bride. Then the church went quiet, the organist struck up the wedding march, and everyone turned to look toward the back of the aisle.

I was awestruck when I saw Gisela. She was absolutely stunning, a radiant bride in her resplendent white dress. I thought my heart would burst with joy. Watching her walk down the aisle that day left an indelible image in my mind, one that will accompany me for the rest of my life. She will forever be the beautiful bride I married that day.

She took my hand as we stood in front of the minister. The entire ceremony lasted about half an hour. As we looked into each other's eyes I knew our marriage would last a lifetime. I remember hardly anything of what the minister said. It was probably a standard, simple Lutheran wedding ceremony, with text dictated by church traditions. What I do remember is the promise I made when I said "I do," a promise I have kept to this day.

As soon as we stepped out of the church we were showered with the traditional confetti and greeted with big cheers. I received congratulations from everyone, and big hugs and kisses from the women. My hand was still more or less useless, so shaking hands with the men was a bit awkward for me. It was truly a joyful occasion.

Olga was waiting outside in the horse-drawn carriage, with the top down. She had put on a formal black tuxedo outfit, complete with a black top hat, and even managed to put flowers in small holders behind each of the horses' ears. It looked absolutely splendid. Riding down the street with my new bride felt like we were in a royal wedding carriage. Olga drove us the five kilometres to Lichtenfels to get our wedding picture taken.

We owned a small box camera at the time, but there was no film to be had in all of Michelau. However, a school friend was a professional photographer in Lichtenfels, and I talked him into taking our wedding picture. He had been discharged from the army after losing a foot. I paid for the film with money, but realized the picture was more or less a gift. The picture turned out beautifully, even though Gisela was concerned about her dress draping onto the floor, which I had not even noticed.

The reception dinner was held in my father's house, in the kitchen of Hermann and Anna's floor. Their section of the house consisted of two small bedrooms, one for the two of them and one for their two boys, as well as the large kitchen. The immediate family members were there, as well as Albin and Albine Werner, and Gisela's mother and aunt.

Newlyweds, June 10, 1944

As I thought about how fate had been kind to me, my thoughts flashed back to the serious events I had survived. I turned to Gisela and said, "If I could have found the Russian soldier who shot me, I would have invited him to the wedding."

The guests and other friends of the family had earlier brought over some food to make sure the wedding dinner was an excellent meal. There were boiled potatoes, potato dumplings, carrots and other vegetables, some eggs, bread, and, best of all, two rabbits. A rabbit was quite generous, since meat was strictly rationed. One of the rabbits had been given to us by another Gagel, a distant relative who raised rabbits and chickens in his backyard. The rabbits were a wonderful treat. The two ladies Turko had hired did an excellent job preparing the meal.

We even received some wedding presents: a small cooking pot, a few porcelain bowls, a tablecloth, and a six-place set of cutlery from my *Paate* (godfather). Gisela was astounded that during such hard times, when material goods were so scarce, people could be so helpful and generous. She was profoundly touched by the food, the presents, and the wedding celebration itself, and thanked each of the guests for their generosity.

At the end of the meal Gisela leaned over to me and said, "I still can't understand what everyone is talking about." The language barrier notwithstanding, we enjoyed ourselves immensely. After the dinner, we listened to some music on the radio and sang songs, told stories, and drank a few beers and some wine, until well into the night. A joyous time was had by all.

Then it was time for bed, our first time as husband and wife.

I was now a married man, which was suddenly a very intimidating realization. This was a brand new adventure, which "we," not just "I," would travel together. Whatever lay ahead, I loved her with all my being. I was convinced that love would triumph over any adversity. After all, if a world war could not hold us back, what possibly could?

The next morning I told Gisela we had received a wedding gift from the army. Because I was an officer, the *Wehrmacht* had given us a card permitting us to purchase enough pieces of furniture to set up our new household. That was nice; however, having the means to buy furniture was one thing, finding furniture was another. My officer's pay was sufficient to provide us with the money, but the problem was finding some decent furniture to buy. Any clandestine trading would have been extremely risky, as the authorities would arrest and jail anyone caught trading without using the *Reichsmark* and the appropriate ration stamps.

With the army's gift card in hand we set out to find furniture. We almost despaired when there was absolutely no furniture to be had in any of the stores in Michelau or Lichtenfels. Then Tante Gustel told us she knew the proprietor of the sales outlet at a factory in Nürnberg, where we might find pieces to buy. Nürnberg was the furniture manufacturing capital for the entire region, so optimistically we set off on the train. When we walked into the furniture factory we were pleased to see that there actually were pieces displayed in the front room. By 1944, many store window displays were still quite attractive looking, but the store interiors were always practically empty.

In the reception area we were met by the proprietor, an older man. "Can I be of assistance?" he asked very politely.

"We came to buy some furniture," I explained.

"This is a factory," he said. "We have nothing for sale."

"We have the stamps." I said and showed them to him.

"Sad to say, but I cannot help you," he said. "Here we only make furniture for the army."

"The army gave us this voucher," I replied, and showed him the card.

"We have nothing for sale at this time. Perhaps you can come back later."

"I am Albin Gagel. My aunt, Gustel Gagel, Görge's Gustel, suggested we come here to see you personally," I said.

That seemed to change his attitude considerably. "How is Gustel?" he asked with a grin. "Is she getting any taller?"

"No," I answered, with a smile, "she's getting shorter and shorter all the time, just wearing herself down."

We exchanged stories about Gustel, which only someone who knew her well could have told, until he eventually became more comfortable with me. "Everything we make here is supposed to go directly to the army. I can't just let you buy anything or else one of the workers in the factory might think I made an illegal deal. You never know who to trust," he said, gravely. "I have an idea," he said, pointing his finger at his temple. "You are an officer, so just pretend to be on duty, as if you are on a military commission assigned to pick up furniture for your garrison quarters. I'll take you back into the shop and you can pick the furniture you want. That way, any of our overly patriotic employees won't need to get suspicious."

Thank you, good old Tante Gustel.

Gisela could have exposed our little ruse if she had come with me into the factory, so she remained behind in the reception area. I had to decide by myself which furniture pieces to buy. That could be a more dangerous thing to do than fight in Russia. If Gisela disliked my choice I might have to live with the consequences for years.

He led me into the factory and pointed out the pieces of furniture that I could choose from. There were about half a dozen matching sets in a few different styles. I knew something about furniture, having helped make wicker furniture in my father's workshop before joining the military, so I looked for pieces that were well constructed. I settled on matching sets in a nice light stain, with two beds, two night tables, a chest of drawers and a clothes cabinet for the bedroom, as well as a kitchen table with four matching chairs and a kitchen cabinet for the kitchen. The furniture was made from birch, and was sturdy and handsome. I hoped Gisela would like it. We could not send it back after it was delivered.

We decided to have our furniture shipped to Michelau, as we planned to move there as soon as possible due to the danger to Brandenburg from Allied bombings. We figured that Michelau would never become a target because it was too far south and too small to be of any military significance to Bomber Command.

On our way back to Michelau I asked Gisela if she wanted to stay behind in Michelau with my family when I returned to Brandenburg. I could request a transfer to whatever military garrison was nearest Michelau as soon as my physiotherapy was completed. That was provided I was not sent back to the front. She said she would rather stay with me. Not only that, but she doubted she could get permission from the authorities to leave her work.

We slept two more nights in my father's house uninterrupted by sirens and bombs, which was heavenly. That was our honeymoon.

Gisela gave her wedding dress and veil to Hanna Gruber, who wanted to get married soon. Hanna was thrilled to get such a beautiful and magnificent gown for her wedding. We never found out what happened to it after that. It may have adorned a few more brides in Michelau, perhaps for years afterwards. It may still be in Michelau, having been passed down to another generation of brides.

22 *Christmas Trees in the Sky*

LIFE IN BRANDENBURG SETTLED into a routine for me, my wife, and her mother, if "routine" is the appropriate word. Our sleep was interrupted almost every night by the wail of air-raid sirens, announcing Allied bombers flying overhead on their way to bomb Berlin. Occasionally bombs were dropped on Brandenburg, perhaps leftovers from a Berlin raid, or bombardiers getting rid of their bomb load because Berlin may have become shrouded by clouds. Every time the bombers came we would go to the basement of the apartment building, just in case.

The ever-escalating threat of bombing attacks made me increasingly concerned about Gisela's and Margarete's safety. Brandenburg had military targets that Allied Bomber Command might consider worth bombing, including the Arado Flugzeug Werke. There was also the Opel factory, which made trucks, and the Brennabor plant, which made bicycles, all of which could become targets. Our apartment was only a few blocks away from the Arado factory where Gisela's mother worked. Brandenburg was also a major garrison town. Even if Brandenburg's targets did not attract bombers directly, I suspected the incidents of random bombing would increase.

In July I again asked Gisela if she wanted to live in Michelau with my family until the end of the war. To my surprise, she did not react enthusiastically. She pointed out that all her friends were here, and she had her job to think of. Besides, she did not want to leave her mother all alone. When I suggested her mother go with her, Margarete insisted she would not be allowed to leave her job. Gisela was my wife, and we could claim that Michelau was our home, but it would probably have been impossible to convince the authorities to let Margarete leave her job.

We decided it would be best to make our home in Brandenburg after the war. I had to agree with Gisela's assessment that Michelau afforded rather limited career opportunities for both of us. The prospect of working in my father's basket-making business did not appeal to me at all. Still, the dangerous situation in Brandenburg made Michelau seem very attractive in the short term. It was possible to sleep through the night in Michelau. Eventually Gisela agreed to let me take her to Michelau, so she could at least try living with my family. We would figure out some way to have her mother join her later.

Gisela first had to go to the city hall to report that she was leaving Brandenburg to live in Michelau. That *Abmeldung* (deregistration) was mandatory for every German resident. That was not just to comply with government regulations; it was the only way to be sure of getting her allotment of ration cards. There was another very pragmatic reason everyone had to report any changes in their residence at that time. The war had created an extreme housing shortage, so it was essential that the authorities keep track of every single living space within the country, to ensure that everyone could be housed. Many people had been evacuated from the big northern cities after their homes had been destroyed by Allied bombing and relocated in smaller communities in southern and eastern Germany.

While at the *Rathaus* Gisela asked for sufficient ration stamps to last her until she could be issued new stamps in Michelau. She also had to get permission to quit her job at Kaufhaus Riedel. After receiving the necessary clearance, we packed most of Gisela's personal belongings, almost filling two small suitcases. Early Saturday morning we said goodbye to Margarete, went to the train station, and set off for Michelau.

This time we were not in Michelau for a happy occasion, and I sensed that my family now greeted us with some reservations. Whatever their reactions, she was now my wife and a member of the family, and I expected her to be treated as such. Turko said everything would be fine; Gisela would stay in the attic bedroom. That seemed acceptable to everyone.

The evening after our arrival in Michelau Anna burst into the house absolutely incensed. She had just heard on the radio that there had been an assassination attempt on Hitler. That was July 22, 1944. "How could anybody do such a thing?" she raved. "What treason!"

Gisela and I sat stunned at hearing such news. "Have you got nothing to say?" Anna demanded of Gisela, as if that event should invoke passionate outrage in my wife.

"Is he still alive?" was all Gisela managed to utter. I was pleased to hear no hopeful tone in her voice.

"Of course," Anna replied.

We listened intently to the radio that night and the next day. Apparently a few high-ranking army officers had planted a bomb in Hitler's bunker and tried to blow him up. Unfortunately, to my way of thinking, Hitler was only slightly injured. The Nazis immediately capitalized on his narrow escape, determined to convince the people of Hitler's personal invincibility. Official news broadcasts during the days following the coup attempt made it sound like Hitler was protected from harm by a divine shield. We know now that there were many other such attempts on his life from within the ranks of the *Wehrmacht*.

When Gisela and I talked about the assassination attempt in private, she confided that she found it incredible that Anna could act indignant that someone had tried to kill that maniac. Hitler was the reason for our national calamity. He was responsible for so many lives having been lost or destroyed. She said she wished that Hitler had been killed, as it would have given us hope that the war could soon be over.

I thought about what would happen if Hitler were killed. Who would take over? I doubted the Nazi government would capitulate, as that could result in a civil war between those factions that wished to continue the Nazi struggle and those that wanted to end the war at any cost. Even if the top military commanders could get rid of the Nazis and take over the government, how could four million of our fighting men at the front be withdrawn without a wholesale retreat and complete abandonment of Germany's defences? I doubted the Russians would accept any kind of peace terms short of unconditional surrender. After all, it was only a matter of time before they would be invading Germany itself. And what would the Western Allies do? The death of Hitler would have created a very complicated situation.

Regardless, I expected life in Germany to become even worse as a consequence of that assassination attempt.

I had to be back at the hospital in Brandenburg the next day to continue physiotherapy. I asked my family to help Gisela adjust to life in Michelau. It felt good to know she would be relatively safe in Michelau. Back in my mother-in-law's apartment in Brandenburg I discovered I missed my wife very much. Our tiny apartment then seemed very large indeed. The momentous repercussions associated with the Nazi reprisals against the conspirators of the failed coup made little impact on my personal daily routine. Those events in Berlin mostly affected high-ranking public figures. I just felt lonely. I tried my best to keep busy, but each day's activities were somewhat aimless, as if I were lost in my own neighbourhood. Gisela had truly become part of my life. More than that, she was part of my identity, my sense of self, and it felt as if that part of me was now missing.

About a week after leaving Michelau, the front door opened and there was Gisela. I was ecstatic, but also surprised to see her. She told me she had left Michelau because she could not stand staying there any longer. There was nothing for her to do and she quickly became bored. She said she missed her mother, her friends, her job, and especially me. Listening to her describe living in Michelau, I sensed there may be other reasons for her leaving. My wife was an emancipated and assertive young woman. The small-town mentality and parochial attitude of most people in Michelau, including members of my own family, may have become unbearable for her. Turko was usually working, and when he was not he would probably have been at the local pub, where he usually ate his main meal of the day. Anna and Gustel had their own meals separately and did not include my wife in their dinners. So Gisela had no access to a hot meal and had to live on bread and whatever else she could get with her ration cards.

Also, Gisela still had difficulty understanding the Michelauer dialect. She told me that Gustel had made a deliberate attempt to speak to her in *Hoch Deutsch*, at least in what Gustel must have thought was the proper German language, but that only made the language barrier worse. Even after she began to understand the dialect she could not speak it well, sometimes misinterpreting the connotation of words or misusing particular expressions. I also knew she was proud and somewhat shy, so she could have felt very isolated.

She summed up the whole episode by saying she preferred the daily threat of bombs in Brandenburg to the interminable boredom in Michelau. City girl. Anyway, I was glad she was back, even though I again worried about her safety.

When Gisela returned to Brandenburg her old job at Kaufhaus Riedel was no longer available. Window displays had become a non-essential service. She had to report to the *Arbeitsamt* (state employment bureau) to get another job. The clerk at the *Arbeitsamt* told her she would be assigned to work in a factory. That really did not appeal to

Gisela. She knew from her mother how tough factory work was. Factories were also likely targets for Allied bombers. So she kept talking with the clerk, trying to be as pleasant and charming as possible. Eventually he said, "Just a minute." After reviewing her file he asked her, "Can you type and do shorthand? We have a secretarial position available."

Without hesitation she replied, "Yes, I can type, write shorthand, and take dictation." Actually, she had not typed a word since she took typing in the *Handels Schule* (trade school), and knew she was woefully slow at it. She also could not remember much of her shorthand. Anyway, she made herself sound convincing enough that the clerk believed her credentials, or charming enough for him to give her a break.

"They need a secretary and library clerk at the office of the *Granatwerfer Kompanie*."

The *Granatwerfer Kompanie* (Mortar Company) occupied what used to be the Pestalotzi School for mentally handicapped children, a three-storey building near the heart of Brandenburg that had been turned into a barracks. The former classrooms and treatment rooms were now dormitory rooms for soldiers. There were clean washrooms, offices, an exercise room, and meeting rooms. Gisela's job was to keep track of the reference library books, type official letters, and generally do filing and assorted paperwork for the soldiers in the company. Although Gisela learned very little of what the soldiers did at the garrison, and cared less, they were probably there training in the use of mortars before being sent to the front.

Margarete continued to work at the Arado Flugzeug Werke as a welder, a job that before the war was usually reserved for men. She told me that at first she had great difficulty learning to make proper and secure welds, especially since most of the airplane parts were made from aluminum, but she eventually became quite proficient at it, although the arduous nature of the job never diminished.

I went to the hospital every day for physiotherapy and to eat lunch. When not at the hospital my time was my own, so I did chores around the apartment, including bringing coal up from the basement for the stove and getting potatoes for the evening meal. I went shopping for necessities, sometimes standing in line to get our allotment of food. I also cleaned the floors and fixed things around the apartment.

Perhaps because of doing those domestic chores, Gisela's mother began calling me "Julius." She may have whimsically associated my chores with the customary duties of a butler, and the stereotypical name for a German butler was Julius. So I reciprocated by calling her "Julchen," which has the connotation of "Julius's little one." That moniker somehow seemed appropriate. Like many nicknames, it had no obvious explanation unless you knew the story behind it. Anyway, the name stuck and soon everyone we knew was calling her Julchen. She accepted her new name with good humour, as I accepted being called Julius.

Now that Gisela and I were husband and wife, we realized that Julchen's little apartment would eventually become uncomfortably small for all of us. As we planned to live in Brandenburg after the war, we decided to try to find a place of our own. Both of us assumed that the Americans would occupy most of Germany, probably as far as the Oder River, well to the east of Berlin. Neither of us expected the Russians to advance as far west as Brandenburg. We imagined life under American occupation would not be intolerable and therefore gambled that it was better to get a place as soon as possible, since the housing shortage could become even more acute as the war approached its inevitable end. In September 1944, Gisela and I went to the *Wohnungsamt* (state housing bureau) at city hall to ask for an apartment.

The clerk was a typical bureaucrat, formal and rigid, who obviously took his job very seriously. At the time, all civil servants had to be members of the Nazi party, unlike soldiers, who were not allowed to join the Nazi party. At first he gave us the usual line about how space was very limited and there was just nothing available. We were not refugees and probably did not look like we were living in the street, so he felt no compulsion to help find us a place. My officer's uniform did not seem to impress him in the slightest. I was beginning to think we would have to walk away unsuccessful.

Then Gisela said, "I'm pregnant, and we have to have room for a baby."

Surprised as I was by that revelation, I played along and tried to look as much the part of a concerned and responsible father-to-be as my acting ability would allow.

He looked gravely at my wife, then at me, and finally said, "Let me look again." He left the room. I looked at Gisela. She just shrugged her shoulders. A few minutes later he came back with a file folder, "There's a small one-bedroom apartment for rent."

Gisela immediately said, "We'll take it," without even checking to see how big it was.

The apartment was in a two-storey building in a recently built housing project near the edge of the city, about four kilometres from Julchen's home. It had a large combined kitchen/living area, a single small bedroom, and a tiny bathroom. We met the young woman who was vacating the apartment. She had recently become a widow and the authorities had deemed her apartment too large for one person, so she had to go live with her parents. Her husband had fallen in Russia and she was obviously distraught over her loss. I felt terrible for her, but at the same time felt fortunate that we were now able to live together in a place of our own.

The apartment was not furnished, so we wrote to the store in Nürnberg where we had purchased our furniture and asked that it be sent to our new address in Brandenburg. In the meantime, Gisela's mother scrounged through her belongings to provide us with at least rudimentary comforts. She gave us a few dishes, a coffee table, a night table, two chairs, a chest of drawers and, most important, two featherbed comforters and pillows. Those items were enough to live relatively comfortably. The pillows helped us to sleep on the floor. Later we also managed to obtain a bureau for the kitchen/living room in which to store our few belongings, especially clothes.

It was a good thing we did not depend upon the furniture from Nürnberg, because it never arrived. We eventually suspected that it may have been lost. The store may have been bombed, or Allied planes may have attacked and wrecked the train it was sent on; after all, it was wartime.

Gisela and I continued to spend many evenings at Julchen's place, partly because she appreciated the company and partly because it was furnished much better than our place.

The repeated bombings made it necessary for the authorities to enforce a total blackout every night. Every evening we hung heavy blankets over all the windows to prevent any light from shining into the street that could have been used by enemy bombardiers for targeting. Those blankets also had another purpose—to help keep shattered glass fragments from flying through the front rooms and cutting us to shreds in the event a bomb blast blew the windows into the apartment.

One mid-October night we were again roused by the familiar sound of air-raid sirens, followed by the sound of airplanes approaching from the west. As I went to adjust the blanket on the window I noticed a cluster of very bright lights high in the night sky. It must have been a bundle of flares that was somehow held aloft, perhaps by a parachute or a balloon, producing a light show that reminded me of our Christmas tree illuminated by candles when I was a boy. I went outside to have a better look. As I gazed in fascination at that aerial spectacle another cluster of lights lit the sky about a kilometre away, and then another, and another, even farther away. The four clusters of lights formed roughly a square of Christmas trees in the sky. Suddenly it dawned on me what they were.

I ran into the house and yelled, "Gisela, we have to get out of the house right away." I took a deep breath and calmly said, "The bombers are coming. Those flares are marking a target, and this time we are in the middle. The basement may not be good enough protection this time."

We quickly threw on our coats and ran out of the house and down the street to an open space area near the Görden See hospital grounds. Dozens of small trenches had been dug into the ground around the edge of the grassed area, between rows of mature fir trees. As at the front, those small holes were the best protection against exploding bombs. I explained what I had learned from my military training to my terrified wife. "As long as you duck down below the level of the ground, you'll be safe."

As we crouched inside one of the little trenches we were joined by many other people seeking shelter. The drone of heavy bombers approaching high in the sky became louder and louder, until the sound was almost directly overhead. Then we heard the unmistakable and dreaded sound of falling bombs. Bombs make a distinctive whistling sound, and hearing it made you hold their breath while trying to discern how far away they were. Then there was a heart-stopping moment of silence just before the bomb hit. The sound of the explosion, along with the tremors, indicated how close it had struck. Hearing the explosions also momentarily produced a huge feeling of relief, knowing you had survived.

The raid on the city lasted only about half an hour. I wondered if the Arado Werke had been targeted. When the all-clear siren sounded we quickly headed back to our home. A red glow in the distance, along with the unmistakable smell of smoke, meant that parts of the city had been set on fire. We were relieved to see nothing had been destroyed in our neighbourhood.

Very early the next morning I went to Julchen's home to check on her. As I approached her neighbourhood on the trolley there were many residential buildings that had been damaged, including one apartment house right across the street. The roof and upper floors had collapsed, sealing in the lower floor. A work gang of women and a few old men were frantically clearing rubble, directed by a man in uniform wearing a fireman's helmet. The owner of the house had been taken to hospital, and one of her daughters was still trapped in the basement. I immediately pitched in, lifting bricks, parts of walls, roof, rafters, furniture, and other pieces of what had been homes. After about an hour of frantic work we had cleared an opening into the basement and found the little girl, under the stairwell, unhurt. The fireman was satisfied that there was no one left in the rubble. The work crew continued to clear the street of bricks and glass. I wished them well and continued on to Julchen's home.

She was unhurt but visibly shaken. "Do you mind if I spend the night at your place?" she asked. "I'm scared to death that the next bomb will hit my building."

"Of course," I replied. "Was the Arado factory hit last night?"

"No," she replied, "but the fiends will surely try again!"

It was probably the first time Brandenburg itself was the deliberate target of a bombing raid, and perhaps it was just naïve of us to assume that the bombers had been after military targets. The bombers surely would come again. So Julchen slept in the kitchen/living room for a few nights, until the fear of another air raid in her neighbourhood subsided.

In spite of the rationing, the austere living conditions, the arduous physiotherapy, and the periodic bombing of the city, Gisela and I spent almost four months together in matrimonial bliss. The therapy slowly but steadily improved the utility of my arm and hand until there was noticeable recovery.

On a cold day in November the inevitable happened. The doctors assessed the condition of my arm as being sufficiently restored to be able to fight again, even though I could hardly hold a rifle or a pistol with my right hand. I was sent to Dresden to join a group of other of-ficers, some of whom had also recently recuperated from combat in-juries and were being prepared to return to active duty. Each of us was billeted in a private residence but met every morning in a former conference room in an old building that may have been a hotel or even a resort before the war.

Dresden was incredibly crowded. There were probably hundreds of thousands of refugees in the city, mainly Germans who had been driven out of East Prussia and Silesia, areas that later became part of Poland. There were also Ukrainians, Romanians, and Hungarians, who were also fleeing Stalin's advancing armies.

Dresden is a very old city. Historically, it had been the seat of the Saxon kings and had been an important medieval trade centre. The city contained hundreds of ancient cathedrals, castles, estates, monasteries, and other heritage buildings, as well as one of the oldest universities in Europe. The predominant architectural style of the old buildings could be characterized as baroque. Many of the churches, former royal resi-dences, museums, and other institutional buildings contained priceless works of art, as well as historical books and artefacts. It was by far the most significant and historically valuable heritage site in Germany. The Saxon kings had lavished great efforts into making it a beauti-ful showpiece. The extensive parks and gardens associated with the castles, manor houses, and estates of former royalty were especially picturesque. Even within Germany, Dresden had acquired a reputation as a cultural masterpiece—"The Pearl on the Elbe."

In late 1944, Dresden was the only big city left in Germany that had not been bombed into rubble by the Allies. That may have been because it was situated far from any industrial areas and the Allied leaders had no other strategic reason to bomb Dresden. There were no military bases there, and no factories producing military equipment or supplies. They may also have recognized and appreciated the value of the city's architectural and cultural heritage. The Allies must also have been aware that it was crammed with refugees fleeing the Russian armies.

My duties included more than therapy. All of us officers had to take part in serious callisthenics for hours every day to get into shape, as well as rifle and pistol practice. It was reasonably easy for me to hold and fire a rifle again, but using a pistol with my still convalescing right

322   FÜHRER, FOLK AND FATHERLAND

hand was practically impossible. It was actually easier to use a pistol with my left hand than my right. I knew it would not take long before I would be sent to the front, so I worked strenuously to return strength to my right arm, conscious of the fact that skilful use of my weapons would be essential to my future survival. The retraining routine also included refreshing my knowledge of procedures and practices for leading an infantry company, including some new procedural requirements that had recently been introduced by the Regime.

The failed assassination attempt in July 1944 had caused Hitler to initiate radical measures designed to increase his absolute control over every aspect of life in Germany, including the military. One obvious indication of the shift of control from the army to the Regime was that we were now required to use the extended-arm Nazi salute and say, "*Heil Hitler*" (Hail Hitler), when saluting another soldier or greeting any government official, rather than the regular military salute. Every time I had to make that insipid and pompous gesture it made me feel like I was inside an insane asylum.

The atmosphere among the officers with me in Dresden was noticeably different from what it had been in Le Croisic almost two years earlier, when I had felt like part of a powerful and proficient army. Back then, I still trusted the competence of army organization and leadership. There had also been a strong *esprit de corps* among the men who went with me to Russia in 1943. Here in Dresden I considered everything we did to be a sordid waste. I was now inside a different world, one that was pervaded and dominated by a sense of futility, desperation, and fear. A sense of inevitability dominated our conversations, as there was nothing any of us could do to change the calamity that was descending upon our homeland. I and my fellow veterans were resigned to the fact that the occupation of Germany by foreign forces was unavoidable. We were careful not to openly express any negative opinions regarding the government's conduct of the war, which might undermine morale and could be overheard by someone deluding himself into doing his "patriotic duty." Even though mostly unseen, the presence of the Gestapo could not be dismissed from my mind; they could be anywhere. Since the assassination attempt on Hitler's life and its aftermath, a type of paranoia about possibly offending the wrong government official controlled everyone's public behaviour, and that paranoia influenced every aspect of life, even in the army. I certainly did not want to be hauled in front of some Gestapo fanatic, facing charges of treason.

Soldiers then had to live with the perception that our senior officers would be making decisions and giving orders based upon conformity to Nazi directives, and not upon sound military strategy or even traditional procedures. In light of the monumental military blunders Hitler and his cronies had already perpetrated, we could not help but be pessimistic about our future. I was being forced to serve the personal interests of the Nazis, which had nothing to do with the best interests of my nation.

In mid-December we heard the astonishing news that Germany had mounted an offensive on the Western Front. The radio broadcast touted it as an "irresistible onslaught," which had broken through the American lines in the Ardennes and surrounded an entire American army around Bastogne. I was surprised that the German army was still capable of any kind of large-scale offensive. The attack must have been carried out by the very last well-equipped panzer divisions on the Western Front. That attack had some initial success, probably because the inclement weather and overcast conditions over the battlefield grounded the Allied air forces. I suspected that as soon as the weather cleared the overwhelming numerical superiority of the Allied armies, and especially the Allied air power, would destroy our armoured units and defeat that desperate attack.

Why would Hitler mount such a hopeless offensive? The only reason I could think of was as a political ploy to shore up the flagging morale of the German people by showing them their armies were still capable of pushing back the enemies of the Reich. I felt no enthusiasm for that battle on the Western Front, as I did not want the Western Allies to be held up any longer on their push into Germany.

As the days passed news reports of the battle became less and less enthusiastic. After the weather cleared it became apparent that the offensive had stalled and had turned into an appalling battle of attrition. Eventually the media could not hide the fact that Hitler's "breakout into France" had failed completely. In the end the Battle of the Bulge, as it was later called, would prove to have been completely futile, serving only to cost the German army on the Western Front most of its heavy equipment and invaluable supplies, as well as a great many lives. It did nothing to change the course of the war, which could not end soon enough for me.

News reports from the Eastern Front could not hide the fact that Russian armies were relentlessly advancing westward. There were no morale-boosting news reports of German offensives in the east. The Russians were encroaching all along Germany's eastern borders and were already in East Prussia. The terrible number of casualties coming out of the east was compelling testimony as to the dismal nature of the fighting. On a personal level, knowing that I was in Dresden on the first leg of my return journey to that front was not morale-boosting either.

Gisela visited me in Dresden at Christmas. I introduced her to my fellow officers at our hotel. We went out and had a nice dinner in a local restaurant. She thought that was wonderful, like being on a romantic date. After dinner we went for a long walk through the neighbourhood. Gisela had never been to Dresden before, and I had not seen Dresden before I had been sent there by the army. I was used to old buildings, but Dresden was truly a city straight out of the Middle Ages. The artistry and craftsmanship of the builders of these architectural masterpieces were evident everywhere, from the smallest homes to the most majestic cathedrals. In spite of the circumstances and the overcrowding, the city was meticulously clean. Even during these times of adversity, the people tried their best to make their surroundings beautiful.

Dresden was not a garrison city, so we met few soldiers in the streets. Except for the scarcity of military-aged men in the city and the obvious crowding caused by the influx of refugees, it was easy to imagine life here during a happier time.

That evening we were sitting at the kitchen table with the lady of the house where I was billeted, when the sound of an air-raid siren started. Gisela immediately stood up and asked the way to the basement. The lady of the house looked up and smiled at Gisela. "Don't worry," she said with a reassuring tone in her voice, "Dresden will never be bombed."

"Why not?" asked Gisela.

"There's nothing in this old city that would interest Bomber Harris," she said, referring to Sir Arthur Harris, Commander-in-Chief of RAF Bomber Command. "There are no factories making things for the military. Dresden is like a great big art museum." She continued to talk about life in Dresden, concerned about the increasing number of refugees that were streaming into the city from the east, as there was already an acute housing shortage. She considered that more of a temporary inconvenience than a serious hardship, and had faith in the government's ability to resolve the problem. Apparently she also had faith in the good will of Bomber Command.

Gisela could only stay with me for two days before she had to return to work in Brandenburg. As it turned out, she only had that one opportunity to visit me in Dresden.

23 *Marsch Kompanie*

ON JANUARY 30, 1945, I was ordered to report to Naumburg an der Saale, a city in central Germany. In Naumburg I became company leader of a so-called *Marsch Kompanie* (March Company) that was part of the Grenadier Ersatz Bataillon No. 53, a new infantry battalion that was being assembled. I had never heard of a *Marsch Kompanie* before, the name given to each of the three companies in our contrived battalion. I had also never heard of an *Ersatz Battalion. Ersatz* means simulated or replacement, as opposed to the genuine original. It may have been something the state had recently dreamed up.

The whole battalion was being put together from soldiers who had come from different branches of the armed forces. Some came from anti-aircraft units whose equipment had been destroyed. A few were former *Luftwaffe* support personnel who were no longer needed by our formerly formidable air force, as there were few planes left to fly. Some had been sailors from our formerly mighty navy. There were also men that I would have considered too old to be able to survive the rigours of the front. Others were mere boys. *Volkssturm* came to mind (People's Storm), as they looked like members of the collection of civilians the Nazis had organized into a civil defence force. The *Volkssturm* were mostly young boys and old men aged sixteen to sixty, armed with whatever weapons were available, and told to defend the Fatherland when the enemy arrived on their doorsteps. We saw a newsreel of Hitler inspecting a row of such kids, shaking their hands, and obviously exhorting them to die for their country. What a sickening spectacle. Surely even the people closest to Hitler must have been disgusted with him by now.

Many of the men in my new *Marsch Kompanie*, like myself, were casualties who had been repaired enough to be plunged back into the front. Some were not fully recuperated, as they limped noticeably or exhibited some other handicap. I was well aware that our disabilities could impair our ability to function effectively in battle.

That ragtag collection of soldiers in my *Marsch Kompanie* demonstrated the wretched condition of the *Wehrmacht* at that late stage of the war. They were definitely not what the army would have considered

Marsch Kompanie, *March 1945*

suitable for the infantry. They must have been hastily assembled on orders from the Regime. At least all the officers I met were experienced soldiers. The battalion commander was probably in his early thirties. He was a congenial sort, with a quiet manner and a good sense of humour. He had a wife and two children at home. He was probably not a professional soldier, as he displayed none of that haughty or detached demeanour that characterized some career officers.

It had taken weeks to collect enough men to form a battalion, to organize and assign all the men into units, and to train them to function cohesively together. The training they received consisted mainly of some target practice to make sure they could all shoot a rifle and an automatic, a few lessons in how to handle a machine gun, how to throw a grenade, and how to handle other basic infantry weapons. They were also taught to dig foxholes while under fire. There were few instructions concerning tactics, unless being told to duck into a foxhole when hearing enemy gunfire or incoming shells could be called tactics. The main emphasis was on how to obey orders according to infantry rules and how to stick with your unit.

One aspect of their training made me wince. They spent hours marching in formation, remaining in straight rank and file as they paraded to and fro, wheeling in unison on command. They even sang songs as they marched, the same songs I had sung on marches with soldiers of a bygone era. They were taught the art of manipulating arms, presenting arms, shouldering arms, and standing at attention with their rifles during inspection. The exercise ended with a rousing charge across the field, still in formation. It was hard to believe that any army instructors still practised such parade-ground manoeuvres. Those dressed-up skills looked splendid on the parade ground, but I knew they were totally useless in combat.

It troubled me to see that their training was certainly not enough to turn these men into competent soldiers. I had no idea what conditions were like at the Eastern Front by then, but imagined they would be at least as grim as when I had left in November 1943. The feeble-looking assembly of displaced remnants, recuperating relics, and raw recruits that I now commanded bore little resemblance to the efficient fighting force that had been assembled in Le Croisic in 1943. There was no grim determination in their faces, no self-confidence in their gaze, no manifestation that any one of them would be a dangerous adversary in battle. I tried to imagine what it would be like to lead such lambs into the jaws of the bear. I doubted those men could be relied upon as I had repeatedly relied upon the courage, skill, and steel nerves of those at my side in Russia in 1943. Most of the men in my *Marsch Kompanie* were not infantry soldiers; they were just bodies in uniforms.

Soon after arriving at the military base in Naumburg I was promoted to the rank of *Oberleutnant*. The entire company was assembled in formation and the battalion commander asked me to step forward and pinned a diamond onto my shoulder strap. He then announced in front of all the men that I was now a first lieutenant. I dutifully pretended to be honoured and pleased, but there was no pride in receiving that promotion. My duties would not change. My rank would make no difference to the stark reality of conditions at the front. An army clerk recorded the promotion in my *Soldbuch*.

The fighting we would soon be part of would not only be completely futile, it would be a sad waste of lives. Our *Ersatz Battalion* could not possibly make the slightest difference to the progress of the advancing Russian hordes. I suspected that part of the reason it was taking so long to get our group ready for front-line duty was that the officers in charge tried every tactic, short of insubordination, to stay away from the fighting front as long as possible.

While in Naumburg the entire company had to participate in a sharpshooting contest. That was either part of the rifle training for the new soldiers in the company, or it was supposed to be entertainment. We spent the day on the rifle range at the garrison, where army judges assessed our marksmanship. After the very serious use I had made of my rifle at the front I considered that contest a farce, like we were a bunch of adolescents playing with toy guns. The country was on the brink of collapse, with no resources left to stem the tide of enemy armies closing in on Berlin, and our commanders had time to put on a sharpshooting contest. Perhaps those responsible for holding the contest were pretending everything would be just fine, if only we practised our military skills diligently and obeyed orders faithfully.

Regardless of my opinions, we all had to participate. In spite of the damage to my right arm I was still a very good shot, so I received a slip of paper commending my abilities. As if I needed some hackneyed recognition of my marksmanship. The contest failed as a ploy to pretend we were having fun; however, it was a favourable waste of time that provided another day's delay in returning to the front.

I sincerely hoped we would not be sent to help defend our nation's capital. I kept anticipating some sign that the government was ready to sue for peace; after all, British and American armies were rapidly advancing from the west, and Russian armies had already reached East Prussia. The best news possible would have been that the Nazis had capitulated.

Ironically, I remember wishing that I could have stayed in Dresden, and that my new assignment was the worst thing that could have happened to me. But it was not.

On February 13, 1945, just two weeks after I left, Dresden was bombed. The entire bomber might of the American and British air forces combined to obliterate what was once a beautiful city that had stood majestically and peacefully for centuries. The attack lasted two nights and a day. German news media denounced the senseless brutality of the raid, announcing that many thousands had been killed, including many refugees fleeing the Russians. If I had not been sent to Naumburg in preparation for my eventual return to the front, I could have been among the uncounted souls killed in that air raid. Once again fate played a hand in my survival.

I thought about what had happened to the Pearl on the Elbe. Why had the Allies bombed that beautiful city, when it was blatantly obvious that the war would soon be over? Surely the Allied commanders would not think that Hitler would sue for peace after the last large city in Germany was in ruins, or that any citizens or even military generals could organize any resistance to topple the regime? It was common knowledge that Churchill disliked and distrusted the Russians, and may have feared that Stalin had ambitions to take over all of Europe at the end of the war. Was it that the American or British leaders just wanted to show off the might of Allied air power to Stalin? If that was indeed the reason for the Dresden raid, it would forever be a testament to the bombastic arrogance and moral corruptness that is inherent in such political power. Whatever the contrived reason for the attack on Dresden, there was no excuse. The destruction of Dresden and the killing of those uncounted civilians and refugees was as evil a crime as any perpetrated under the pretext of "this is war."[13]

In March my company was sent to Wittenberg, on the Elbe River about ninety kilometres southwest of Berlin. In Wittenberg I was billeted in the house of a nice lady in a pleasant neighbourhood. I began to hear rumours that my company was going to be sent to the Western Front. If those rumours were to prove true it would make me very happy. Every German soldier considered being captured by British or American forces on the Western Front as their best possible fate. The other officers with me in Wittenberg also thought they were preparing to go to the Western Front. My company was ready, or about as ready as that group of misfits could be, to return to front-line duty, so when I did not receive orders to move out to the Western Front it made me suspicious that something unusual was going on at a higher level of command.

I wrote to Gisela as soon as I arrived in Wittenberg, asking her to visit me, as it may be my last opportunity to see her again before returning to the front. Mailing the letter, I had considerable reservations about the mail service, as the repeated bombing of rail lines and aerial attacks on trains were making it difficult for the mail to get through.

To my delight, I received a reply from Gisela that she could come for a brief visit on the following weekend.

Early Saturday afternoon on March 31, I met her at the Wittenberg

---

13   News reports at the time, which usually downplayed the extent of deaths and destruction to the German people, described civilian deaths as more than 250,000. The incendiary bombs created a firestorm that sucked the air out of the burning city, suffocating those that had fled to their basements in a vain attempt to escape death.

train station. We spent a wonderful, happy two days together. Gisela mentioned that in Brandenburg decent food was becoming scarce. Even non-rationed foodstuffs like vegetables were difficult to obtain now that it was wintertime. I imagined that similar conditions prevailed in all the larger German cities. I just took it for granted that the army could find enough food to feed its soldiers.

Gisela told me about her new job at the *Granatwerfer Kompanie*. She worked with two other secretaries. One was named Erika, who had been working there for a while. Although only a few years older than Gisela, she was already a war widow. Working in an adjoining office was another secretary who worked for the sergeant of the company, and she more or less ran the office. By coincidence, she had been a classmate of Gisela's in the *Handelsschule*. Gisela and Erika knew practically nothing about secretarial work and their typing skills were rudimentary. The sergeant's secretary was a proficient typist, so she ended up doing most of the office typing. Consequently there was not much for Gisela and Erika to do; however, they still had to be on duty during business hours. Mostly they filed and retrieved reference books for the soldiers. They actually spent much of their time knitting or reading. Gisela and Erika conversed a lot and soon became close friends.

Ignoring Germany's national paranoia, where everyone had to be careful about what they said to avoid being accused of undermining the morale of the people, Gisela had casually told a young soldier in the *Kompanie* that she thought the war was surely lost and that it would soon be over. During the conversation that baby-faced young man had expressed no opinions at all about the state of the war, which should have been a signal to Gisela that he could not be trusted. That idiot soldier denounced her to his superior officer, the *Kompanie* captain, saying that Gisela was spreading defamatory remarks about the government's conduct.

The captain happened to be Erika's boyfriend. He told Erika to tell Gisela to keep her mouth shut about her political opinions. Luckily that incident turned out to be nothing more than a lesson in political correctness, rather than a potentially serious infraction of the state's authoritarian rules. Gisela could have ended up in a prison camp, as had happened to too many of the Reich's citizens by then.

During our Sunday afternoon walk Gisela and I happened to pass by a work gang digging small trenches along the side of the street in a park, supervised by two armed German soldiers. From the sound of their voices they were English prisoners of war. It was a cold day and digging those trenches was unpleasant, but not gruelling, work. One of the English prisoners was complaining to the guard in stilted German mixed with occasional English that it was contrary to the Geneva Convention regarding treatment of prisoners of war for his men to be forced to dig trenches. The guard patiently explained in a thick Tyrolean accent, mixing German with the occasional English, that the trenches were designed for their own safety, to protect them in case Churchill's bombers attacked the city.

That argument was accompanied by gestures and body language that are universally comprehensible regardless of nationality. A few of the prisoners gave their spokesman suggestions to try to convince the guard to stop or at least stall the work. The Englishmen were not shy to express some conspicuous expletives directed at Hitler himself. Gisela had taken English in school and caught the gist of the conversation. The whole episode looked like a comedy routine in a movie. There had not been the slightest sign of animosity or recrimination on the part of the Englishmen, or any intimidation or threat of force on the part of the German guard for what could have been viewed as a challenge to his authority. Both parties seemed to understand the limits of the situation perfectly. That episode could have happened only with Englishmen, which most of my countrymen considered not just equals, but distant relatives. I doubted Russian prisoners would have been given such respect. Anyway, they constructed neat and straight little trenches, which I hoped no one would ever need.

We spent that evening socializing with my landlady, Frau Irmgard. She invited Gisela to spend the night, which she gratefully accepted. She made Gisela and me feel like welcome guests. "We all have to do our share during this terrible war," she said. We talked about all kinds of things late into the night, accompanied by the radio and cups of the ubiquitous *Malzkaffee*. She treated us very graciously, making a big fuss about our newlywed status. Her husband was serving in the military and she had not heard from him in almost two months. She was obviously worried about him.

Thinking back on the men we had buried in Russia in 1943, I felt sorry for her and struggled for something to say that might console her. "Don't worry," I said. "He may be a prisoner of the Russians and will be returning home to you as soon as the war is over."

City life, Germany, 1945

"Those beasts will send him to Siberia," she replied.

"Maybe not. All the Russians I met were reasonable people." I said that sincerely, but without conviction. Prisoner would be better than dead.

She was heartbroken about the destruction of Dresden. Her sister lived in Dresden with her two children, and she was worried about their safety. "Did they have to do that? The war is almost over."

"A shame," I replied, "a terrible shame. A crime." What could anyone say? None of us grasped the true scale of the tragedy of Dresden's destruction at the time.

The day after Gisela arrived I received my orders to report early Monday morning with my gear.

The following morning Gisela and I arrived at the Wittenberg station to find the entire battalion preparing to board the train. We were told by Command that we would not be heading directly into action, but that the train would be going north toward Berlin, as the first leg of our journey to the Western Front. That news made me suspicious that we were being sent to take part in the defence of Berlin, which I feared would be a terrible and catastrophic battle.

I was preparing to say goodbye to Gisela when she told me she was coming with me. She figured that because we were told the train would be travelling northward to Berlin, she might be able to travel all the way back to Brandenburg on the same train. I said it may not be safe for any civilians to ride our troop train. She insisted. Admittedly, the idea of spending a few more hours with her was very appealing, so I let her aboard. The battalion commander knew what was going on, but said nothing, even though Gisela may have been the only civilian on the train, and the only woman.

Every available space on the train was filled with soldiers and their gear—every bunk, all the compartments, the aisles, and almost every spot on the floor of every wagon. It was practically impossible to walk along the aisle. Many of the soldiers gave us questioning looks.

The train left the station in broad daylight. After a few minutes I noticed we were heading east! That was a surprise, and surprises are usually unpleasant in the military. Obviously the army had lied to us about going to the Western Front, perhaps to prevent anyone from being tempted to desert. Gisela's enthusiasm for that train ride vanished. For her own safety, we had to get her off the train as soon as possible.

After about an hour the train pulled into a large marshalling yard, with at least a dozen parallel tracks, and stopped. Outside the windows I could see that the yard was crowded with soldiers, thousands of soldiers. It looked like a grey-green sea of bodies in every direction. Although our train was stopped, the doors of the coaches remained closed. Everyone was ordered to stay on board. There were other trains in the station beside ours, probably all filled with troops destined for the front. Just then Gisela spotted a passenger train approaching the far side of the yard from the east.

It was impossible to get out the door, so I opened a window as wide as possible and looked down. There was no platform beside the train but, no matter, this had to be it. I put my arm around her, moved her closer to the window, and said, "You have to hurry."

She looked down at the ground and at the size of the window. "Help me out."

"It's a long way down. Do you think you can make it?"

"Of course," she said without hesitation.

I asked the nearest soldier to help us. Gisela took off her coat and climbed onto the bench. We lifted her up and out through the window. I gripped her wrists and slowly lowered her to the ground. Other soldiers came and helped her down, to the accompaniment of enthusiastic whistling and cheering from the crowd of troops. I dropped her coat and suitcase down to her. She only had time for a brief glance back and a quick wave of her hand, before she turned and disappeared into the sea of soldiers, heading back toward where hopefully she could catch that train heading west, back to Brandenburg.

Once again we were parted. There had been no time for any tearful goodbye. This time leaving her felt worse than ever before. The terrible realization that I might never see her again tormented my mind and gripped my heart. For the first time in my life I felt what it was like to truly love someone in a way I had never known before. My longing was made all the worse by the knowledge that I was being forced to risk my life on a lost cause, the hopeless cause of one fanatically stubborn lunatic.

I slumped into my seat and prepared for the inevitable. Instead of leaving right away, the train sat on the siding until late into the evening. At first I assumed we were going to travel at night to hide the train's movement from enemy airplanes, but when we still had not moved well after dark I began to wonder what was going on. Around midnight I fell asleep on the bench.

The next morning we were still there. Looking out the window I could see that the rest of the troops in the station had left during the night. There was activity in the marshalling yard, with a locomotive coming and going, moving wagons, but we continued to sit at our siding. The entire battalion stayed on the train all that day. We slept in our seats and got off occasionally to be fed and to use the facilities. I had no desire to rush my return to the front, but even so, the situation became increasingly tense. The train was abuzz with rumours. When my men asked me what the wait was all about, I had to tell them honestly that I had no idea.

When the train finally started moving out on the afternoon of the second day, it headed westward! That raised my hopes that our commanders considered the end of the war to be so close as to obviate the need to return to the Eastern Front. But our withdrawal did not last for long. After about half an hour of moving slowly west the train stopped again, and we sat for another night. Finally I searched out the battalion commander. He looked me in the eye and said, "*Leutnant*, stay with your men. The less you know, the better."

I began to get an idea of what was going on. It must have been that the officer in charge, probably of a higher rank than our captain, perhaps with the co operation or at least agreement of other senior officers, was trying to keep us from ending up on the Eastern Front for as long as possible. That ploy was an astonishing and very courageous gamble on his part. There were still plenty of Gestapo around, as well as the *Feldgendarmerie* military police, who were assigned to arrest or even shoot any soldiers that tried to desert.

That display of individualism was another sign that I was not alone in my conviction regarding the desperate state of the German armed forces at the time. It also reinforced my suspicion that conditions awaiting us at the front would be precarious indeed. By then every German soldier knew that his probable fate was either death or to become a prisoner of war, so facing the Russian army would make it impossible to surrender to Western troops.

The next morning we watched the engine being taken from the front of the train and coupled to the other end. The train moved out and we were on our way—east. During that slow and serious trip we passed through Görlitz, a city on the Neisse River.

The train finally stopped at the edge of a village in the middle of partly wooded countryside, typical for that part of Germany. The entire battalion disembarked, and we marched into a large walled farm complex, consisting of houses, stables and sheds, all surrounding a wide courtyard. I did not see any civilians. It was obviously a staging area, which I assumed was near the front. The troops spent the night in whatever accommodations were available, sleeping in farm buildings, mostly on hay or straw bales in the barns and sheds. I was lucky enough to have a bed in one of the farmhouses.

Very early the following morning the battalion was assembled in companies and platoons, and we were fed from the mobile field kitchen. I thought I could hear the faint and ominous sounds of heavy weapons fire coming from the east, but it was probably my imagination because no one else indicated they noticed anything. I just hoped we would not be thrown into the middle of a deadly battle. I did not miss having some buffoon make another idiotic speech about our sacred obligation to defend the Fatherland.

Around noon the entire battalion set off. Groups of civilians passed us going the opposite direction—refugees. Once again I was confronted with the heart-wrenching reality of innocent people caught up in the maelstrom of war. After marching eastward for hours we stopped at the side of the road. There were barren fields nearby where the stubble from the previous year's grain crop was still on the ground. The three companies were each assigned to dig in along a line at the edge of a woodlot. I could not see any particular strategic importance to the piece of ground we were to defend. As in Russia two years earlier, our horse-drawn supply wagons, field kitchen, and the headquarters unit were stationed a kilometre or so behind our line of foxholes. There was no sign of the enemy.

So I was back at the Eastern Front near the beginning of April 1945, somewhere near Görlitz, about one hundred kilometres east of Dresden. The most notable difference between now and my past visits to the Eastern Front was that this time we were not in faraway Russia; we were digging in on German soil. When I took stock of the situation it was not what I had expected, even though our defensive line was set up in the customary and familiar manner dictated by infantry training, similar to what it had been in Russia in 1943. There was no evidence of any recent fighting anywhere. The villages we had passed did not appear to have been damaged. We were not in immediate danger. By sheer luck my company had been assigned to defend a portion of front far to the south of Berlin.

All things considered, circumstances could have been worse for me. We heard rumours that there had been heavy fighting in the defence of some cities. It was common knowledge by then that Russian armies had reached the Oder River, which is less than a hundred kilometres east of Berlin, along a broad front. I was told by the captain that our sector of the front had been quiet for some time before we arrived. There were no heavy weapons accompanying our company; in fact, there were no armoured vehicles or artillery pieces to be seen anywhere. Hopefully that meant Command did not anticipate a major enemy attack.

It was cold and uncomfortable sleeping in the open that first night back at the front. I had not slept outside for fifteen months, so the ground felt unyieldingly hard. It was also wet. I laid my cape over some boughs lining my foxhole at the edge of the trees and curled up in my greatcoat under my blanket. It became so cold after dark that I woke up shivering and was kept awake for most of the night. But at least it was quiet; no one was shooting at us. I just had to get used to outdoor life again.

At dawn I scanned the terrain to the north and east, expecting to see enemy forces, but saw nothing. Scouting patrols were sent out to reconnoitre the areas toward the east and north. Without the help of reconnaissance planes to spot enemy activity our commanders were practically blind. Surprisingly, nothing at all happened that entire day. Supposedly the enemy were not far away, but our scouting patrols returned after seeing and hearing nothing threatening. My company remained in position, with our nine machine guns set up in strategic locations, providing a good field of fire toward the east.

It was not until the third day back at the front that the wireless brought news of enemy activity. They had been spotted advancing from the north a few kilometres away. Though not visible from where we were, the captain said there were "huge" numbers of enemy infantry, accompanied by motorized units. I received orders to retreat a few kilometres due south. Luckily we did not get a chance to test the effectiveness of our defending capabilities against "huge" enemy forces. We waited until dusk to retreat and then set up a new defensive line. That short march was repeated the next night, not with any desperation, but as an orderly withdrawal. Obviously the Russians were not in any hurry. Supposedly they were moving, but thankfully they were not attacking. Supposedly, because we saw nothing of the enemy. The front in front of us remained more or less quiet.

Late the next evening we were moving along the side of the main road leading into a village, facing the setting sun. As the company approached the closest house two fighter planes suddenly burst from over the rooftops and flew right over us. I immediately dove for the shallow ditch at the side of the road. I assumed the rest of the men would do the same, but when I looked up only a few men had run for the ditch. Most of them just stood in the middle of the road watching the planes roar by. The planes banked steeply and made a tight circle higher in the air until they flew straight back toward us.

"Take cover! Everybody off the road!" I screamed at the top of my lungs. This time every man scrambled toward the line of trees at the side of the road. As the fighter planes roared nearer, rounds from their machine guns raced along the ground ahead of them, coming uncomfortably close to us huddling among the trees. A minute later everything was quiet again. I reassembled my company and hustled them into the village. Miraculously, nobody had been hit, although some of them had obviously been shaken up.

From then on we were much more cautious, and kept a sharp eye out for aerial attackers, which the men referred to as *Jabos*, short for *Jagdbomber* (hunter bombers). We mostly stayed put, especially during daylight hours. Airplanes frequently passed overhead. Sometimes Russian fighter planes flew right over our lines, appearing suddenly from behind tree cover at very low altitude, each time startling the daylights out of me. Luckily, or perhaps because we took great care to be invisible from the air, my company was not attacked again. I learned that the cloudy and wet early spring weather was our friend, because it grounded the airplanes, even though it was accompanied by cold rain, which made conditions miserably uncomfortable.

I assumed that our short, leisurely movements were ordered to avoid direct confrontation with enemy forces. Whatever the strategy dictated by Command actually was, we avoided a fight. Eventually enemy troops came into view in the distance, probably part of the massing forces that the captain had told me about. Even hours later, they did not show any signs of moving to attack.

The next morning we actually did have to engage in a firefight. We were surprised by an approaching Russian unit that was unaware we were so close by, dug in at the side of a road and screened by a line of trees along the fenceline. It was broad daylight, so we would have had no chance to get away without being seen. Command ordered me to hold my ground and prepare to attack the enemy flank as they passed by. The Russian infantry were advancing in a column that looked like at least a company in strength, possibly more, and I assumed it was the advance unit of a much larger force. I ordered a short machine-gun burst long before they were within deadly range, as a warning rather than as an attempt to destroy them. They immediately took cover and returned fire. That halted their advance long enough for us to escape as soon as it became dark. We suffered no losses during that haphazard skirmish. When Command asked why we had fired so early, I explained that it was difficult to keep inexperienced troops from panicking at the sight of the enemy. I assured the captain that there would be disciplinary action to make sure it never happened again, and then promptly put the incident out of my mind.

In addition to the standard infantry weapons, we had been issued weapons that were designed to be used against tanks, called *Panzerfaust* (armour fist). They were ten-pound armour-piercing shells attached to the front of a disposable metre-long tube filled with a propellant charge. The theory was to aim the tube at a target, release the safety pin, and press the firing lever. Although the projectile could fly considerably farther than a hundred metres, it had to be fired within a range of much less than a hundred metres to have a reasonable chance of disabling a tank, making it extremely dangerous to use. You not only had to avoid being shot by the tank's machine-gunners or supporting infantry as you approached your target, or it approached you, you also had to avoid the flying shell fragments as the projectile exploded on the tank. It could just as easily explode against the ground, or a tree, or a wall if you were in a built-up area, or some other obstruction, especially if your aim were less than perfect. If it struck a glancing blow it might not even penetrate the armour. If the tank exploded when hit the tremendous blast and flying fragments could also injure or kill you.

Another anti-tank weapon was the *Panzerschreck* (tank terror), which was similar to the American bazooka. It was a two-metre-long tube that fired a small rocket capable of destroying any tank it hit within an effective range of up to about two hundred metres. The troops commonly referred to them as *Ofenrohr* (stovepipe), because of the way they looked. Unlike the *Panzerfaust*, the firing tube could be used over and over again, as long as there were available rocket projectiles. It was a much better weapon than the *Panzerfaust*, with better armour-piercing capability and greater accuracy at longer range. It was also much more sophisticated and therefore more costly to produce than the *Panzerfaust*, so consequently it was scarce. My company had many dozens of *Panzerfaust* but only two *Panzerschreck*.

Both of those anti-tank weapons were noisy to use, and produced a conspicuous puff of white smoke that would reveal the holder's position the instant they were fired. Enemy machine-gunners or sharpshooters could immediately concentrate fire at anyone within or near that obvious cloud. Because of the dangerously close range that was required to make them effective, I surmised that *Panzerfaust* were more or less suicide weapons.

I fervently hoped we could avoid encountering any forces supported by armour. The few veterans in our company may have known enough to stay out of harm's way in a firefight, but the men from the other branches of the armed services, and especially the young recruits, could not be expected to cope well under fire. Their woeful lack of infantry training and inexperience could cost them their lives. They rarely chose good spots to dig foxholes, where the field of view would permit them to see the enemy without being seen. I feared they would react irrationally in the heat of battle.

Considering the futility of the situation, it was amazing that few of the men expressed their fears and none cracked. There was still a camaraderie that would have made it impossibly impolite for anyone to abandon his fellow soldiers, or even to complain about their predicament. Although mostly unseen, the enemy presence caused a sense of foreboding that was inescapable, constantly felt by everyone, which we had to deal with. Sometimes there were opportunities to express what could be called humour, perhaps as a way to relieve the stress, as if refusing to acknowledge the reality of the ever-present danger. The disparity in age between the older men who had been gleaned from other services and the much younger raw recruits was often a cause for some verbal sparring. To make light of the situation, I heard a veteran say, "Ah, no worries, you can get used to the taste of vodka and the smell of *makhorka* (Russian tobacco)."

"I'm sure you'll even like borscht. I hear Siberia can be lovely in the summertime."

Discussions about female companionship, or dating, or a normal family life in future were often tinged with mockery. One of the younger men asked one of the older fellows if he had a daughter for him when the war was over. "So you want a wife?" the older man replied. "Maybe you can have your pick of a big Russian *babushka*."

None of us was eager to fight and perish so very near to what we all knew was the end of the war. Resistance was not only stupid, it could be suicidal. Notwithstanding reality, I was well aware that we could be ordered to hold a position, regardless of the danger. But the days of lightning counterattacks or determined resistance in the face of overwhelming odds were over for me. My main objective was to stay out of harm's way. As long as I was able to command my company I would do my best to avoid a firefight with the Russians. Our little band of infantry could not have put up any sort of meaningful resistance, let alone have any hope of turning back a determined enemy assault.

Russian soldiers were not our only enemies. While trying to avoid the Russians we also had to remain far enough forward not to be considered deserters by the *Feldgendarmerie*. That was easier said than done, as they could be encountered almost anywhere. I never went back to our command post. I trusted our battalion commander to do his best to keep from placing us in jeopardy. Hopefully we would not receive completely foolhardy orders.

Even though there appeared to be no way to escape the eventual Russian occupation, surrender to the Russians was out of the question. I knew that, if necessary, my men would fight fiercely to keep from being captured. Everyone feared being sent to a prison camp in Siberia. Also, we were now on German soil, and misplaced patriotic zeal could make the men fight fervently. I noted sadly that the most noticeably fearless and reckless-acting of the defenders of the Fatherland under my command were also the youngest. They had not been given time to learn how callous and uncaring bullets and bombs are. Their obvious efforts to appear brave were pathetically out of place. I suppose they suffered from youthful enthusiasm and a desire not to appear boyish in front of the older men, but this was not the time to be a hero. I told them, "Obey orders. Avoid taking foolish risks. Keep your heads down. Stay alert. Do not draw attention to yourself. You're not allowed to risk your life without my orders to do so!"

Other than that one skirmish, we endured more than a week at the front without engaging the enemy in any kind of serious battle, and without losing anyone from my company.

We eventually crossed the Neisse River, a tributary of the Oder. After the last of the battalion had crossed the bridge there was a huge "boom" from behind. The bridge had been blasted. On orders from Hitler, German army sappers destroyed all bridges as they retreated, in a vain attempt to slow the Russian advance. Such a shame. That old bridge was a marvellous example of almost artistic engineering, constructed with care and attention to detail, an architectural jewel of stone and steel. How could rational people so casually destroy the heritage of future generations for the sake of holding up the inevitable for a few days? Acts of deliberate destruction, which would be punishable crimes in times of peace, were now considered not only acceptable, but necessary because "it was war."

On probably April 13, 1945, we were somewhere north of Görlitz, dug in on the west side of the Neisse, which we could see winding through the valley from south to north about a kilometre away. Once again there was no evidence of any fighting in our sector; however, enemy aircraft flew overhead repeatedly. That night I received a report that enemy vehicles had been spotted moving toward us from the east, which brought back frightening memories of the Russian tank attack I had survived in the fall of 1943. ·

The next morning I assumed that enemy forces were gathering nearby, but had no idea where they actually were. Battalion command obviously had no idea either, as I was ordered to try and find out. I ordered another soldier to accompany me on a quick reconnoitre ahead and made sure that he was a veteran, just in case we ran into trouble.

We were walking along a cow trail through a gently sloping pasture, parallel to the river, when suddenly I heard the distinctive whine of an incoming mortar shell. I immediately dropped and flattened myself onto the cow trail, which formed a small depression on the ground. I assumed my companion did the same. From the concussion of the blast and the dirt that rattled down onto my back, the shell had exploded very close by. It had come out of nowhere. I listened for more. Nothing. I looked over my shoulder and asked, "Are you all right?"

"No," was the strained reply.

I scrambled over to where he was, staying low to the ground. He was lying on his back with his head and shoulders propped up against the uphill edge of the cow trail, holding his right arm with his left hand. The right sleeve of his uniform was shredded and there was blood pouring down the arm and onto the ground.

I took out my bayonet and cut open the sleeve. I saw a bloody mess that made my heart race. Just above the elbow, the bone was shattered and there were bloody strips of sinew, muscle, and skin joining the forearm to the rest of his arm. A piece of shrapnel had severed the main artery in his arm, and the grip of his left hand was not enough to stem the flow of blood. There may not be enough time to get him back to a first-aid station before he bled to death, especially if we were under fire. The bleeding had to be stopped in a hurry.

I was just about to take off his coat and rip his shirt sleeve to strips to create bandages when he said, "Just a moment. Inside the right pocket of my coat is a cord."

I reached into his coat pocket and to my surprise withdrew a metre-long piece of sturdy thick cord. Just the thing we needed to make a tourniquet!

"Please, can you tie off my arm above the wound to stop the bleeding?" he asked, surprisingly calm considering the circumstances.

My dexterity was hampered by the impairment of my own right hand, but apparently the tourniquet worked, because the blood stopped spurting and slowed to just a slow drip.

I scanned the terrain but could not see any signs of enemy troops anywhere. The woodlots in the area prevented seeing far in any direction, particularly toward the east. Could the mortar shell have been fired by our own troops? Considering the large number of inexperienced soldiers among our ranks, it may have been a mistake by a mortar squad of our own battalion. I took a chance that we were not targeted by enemy mortar men and decided to get back to our lines as quickly as possible, otherwise my wounded soldier might die.

As we set off I noticed the hole left in the ground by the exploding mortar shell, which had landed about ten metres in front of me, yet it was my companion who had been hit, about two metres behind me! The piece of shrapnel that destroyed his arm must have flown right by me.

He kept holding what was left of his right arm against his body with his left hand as we hurried along. By the time we got back there was a lot of blood on his uniform. I assigned another soldier to take him back to the first-aid station right away. When the escort returned he said the old soldier's arm could not be saved and would have to be amputated, but he would live.

After that experience I reassessed our situation here at the so-called front, and took stock of the circumstances of my command. My responsibility for the lives of my men weighed heavily on my mind. I resolved from then on to do whatever I considered necessary to preserve our lives, even if it meant disobeying orders. I began to analyze possible options for getting away from the fighting altogether. After very careful deliberation I made up my mind that as soon as the opportunity presented itself I would take my whole company back from the front, across the reserve lines, if any existed, and desert. But I could not trust every man in the company. There may be a misguided patriot among us who still believed the Nazi propaganda and would consider it his patriotic duty to turn me in.

I reckoned that units of the *Feldgendarmerie* would be stationed about one kilometre behind our front-line positions, usually with the command posts of individual battalions, and spaced at intervals that would allow them to monitor the entire front line. Military police usually worked in pairs and were universally despised by every front-line veteran, and feared. I took their potential interference very seriously. It was their job to catch deserters and bring them to a military court. All they had to do was check a soldier's *Soldbuch* to know which unit he was serving with to find out if he was not where he was supposed to be. Such a "court," nicknamed *Fliegende Kommando* (flying commando) squads, would be convened immediately, expediently composed of whoever was available, perhaps two commandos and a *Geheim* SS officer. It could take only a few minutes to decide your fate. They had the authority to shoot anyone they suspected of being deserters. They may have liked their jobs, as they were always stationed behind the fighting front, hiding behind their shield of authority.

I was not too worried about those policemen, suspecting there were not enough to stop us. Yet it was rumoured that reserve troops, probably SS, were stationed behind the front assigned to prevent any regular troops from deserting. I doubted those rumours, because it seemed improbable there were enough able-bodied men to maintain a second line of troops, especially considering there were not even enough men to maintain a continuous first line. Enough of my men were veterans who could easily rout a few military police; however, if any fanatical patriot got away to inform army commanders responsible for our part of the front, we might end up facing a large force determined to stop our little mutiny. Another company from our own battalion could possibly be made to follow orders to attack ours.

I walked from our dug-in positions to check for myself what might be in store for us if we moved back from the front. Sure enough, after scouting the roads about a kilometre behind our lines for over an hour, I spotted two *Feld Gendarmé* types under a tree beside a house at the outskirts of a village. I recognized them by the crescent-shaped metal breastplates they wore suspended across their chests. Although it was difficult to see clearly, they appeared to have a wireless set with them. I moved laterally for another half a kilometre or so, keeping a careful lookout for more of them along the roads, but saw none. I returned to my men convinced that the rumours about rear guard reserves were greatly exaggerated.

My most worrying problem was a complete lack of knowledge about the larger situation. The pervasive uncertainty about what was happening all around us meant we would be taking a big gamble. It was impossible to make an informed decision. The usual army protocol of providing only need-to-know information was still very much in effect. It was difficult to know if the other company commanders shared my sentiments, or if they would oppose our attempt to leave the front. I suspected the other commanders to our immediate left and right may have been practising a strategy for survival similar to my own.

I wrestled with the alternatives — stay and be killed or captured by the enemy forces massing on the other side of the valley, or leave and take my chances that we could pass undetected through the voids between German troops and military police. It was possible that Russian forces could already have passed our lines and we would be captured anyway. My company had been lucky up until now and our good fortune could not possibly last much longer. I decided to opt for a strategy committed to survival. We would move back far enough that all of us could have a chance to strike out for our homes. If we were confronted with troops opposing our retreat, I would decide then whether to fight or turn around.

I was ready to seize the first opportunity that presented itself to put my plan to the test.

24 *To Flee or Not To Flee*

GISELA MOVED BACK IN WITH her mother after I left for Dresden. By then bombers flew over Brandenburg almost every night, sometimes even during the day, on their way to and from Berlin, and bombs occasionally fell on Brandenburg. Gisela and her mother had to shelter in the basement almost every night. If they happened to be away from home when the air-raid sirens started they would flee to a bomb shelter near their workplace, or knock on the nearest door to seek refuge in their basement. A few huge concrete bunkers had been built to serve as air-raid shelters for civilians in the downtown area. The bombers usually came shortly after dark, so the two women did not undress completely for bed every night, as there may not have been enough time between the air-raid siren going off and the first bombs falling to change clothes and make it to the basement. In case the house were hit, you would also be properly dressed to be seen in public, provided of course that you survived the air-raid. You also wanted to be dressed in case you were injured in the attack and had to be taken to hospital.

Each apartment of Julchen's building had its own storage stall in the basement, four along each end wall, which was used to store some of the eight tenants' possessions, including coal, wood, potatoes, and preserved foodstuffs. The only space remaining within which to huddle while awaiting the all-clear signal was very small—about four square metres—beside and under the stairwell. There you sat or stood, terrified, until the raid was over. After months of repeated bombings Gisela began to think that maybe Michelau was not such a bad place after all.

By the beginning of April rumours abounded that the Russians were preparing for their final assault on Berlin. Many people listened clandestinely to the BBC radio broadcasts from England. The government had outlawed listening to the BBC, so anyone overhearing the sound of English-language announcers coming from your apartment could report you to the authorities. The German government also broadcast an interference sound over the same wavelengths used by the BBC that was sometimes so strong, all you could hear was a constant wailing, rising and lowering in pitch like a police siren. Despite the law and the irritating interference, those radio broadcasts from England were one of the few methods for German citizens to get news about what was really happening with the war.

Gisela and her mother would sometimes turn the radio on very late at night, just loud enough to be heard close up, to listen to the BBC news. Gisela had learned English in school, so she could understand the gist of the news and translate for her mother. One night they heard that American troops had crossed the Elbe River near Magdeburg. Hopefully that meant they would reach Berlin before the Russians. They had not heard of any fighting in Berlin, so assumed that the Russians were not yet close enough to capture Brandenburg.

She also heard rumours that the Russian soldiers had been given permission, perhaps even encouraged by their government, to rape the German women. The purpose of that deliberate Stalinist policy may have been to terrorize German civilians and demoralize the German soldiers still in the field. As far as Gisela was concerned, the terrorizing part worked very well. She was determined not to allow herself to be captured by the Russians.[14]

After visiting me in Wittenberg she decided to leave Brandenburg and tried to convince her mother to leave with her. Julchen was very reluctant, knowing she was not allowed to be absent from her job without permission and was afraid of the consequences of being caught. When rumours that the Russians were preparing to attack Berlin became pervasive, Gisela and Julchen finally decided to make a run for Michelau on their bicycles. They packed as much in their knapsacks as they could carry, which amounted to a few of their most precious belongings and some food. Gisela had serious misgivings about whether or not Julchen had the stamina or the stomach for such a perilous undertaking.

Julchen was afraid for good reason. The Nazi regime had forbidden citizens to travel more than sixty kilometres from home without formal written authorization, mainly for their own safety, because vehicles could be attacked by Allied airplanes. Also, the roads were needed for troop transport and must not be clogged with civilians. There were police checkpoints on the roads, where everyone had to show their

---

14   That policy was officially admitted and denounced by the Russian government long after the war as one of the greatest mistakes perpetrated by Stalin's regime.

papers. Julchen's job at the Arado factory was part of the German arma- ments industry, which was of course considered strategically important by the regime, so if she did not show up at work, the *Bonzen* types would come looking for her.

Regardless of the risks, on Saturday, April 14, 1945, they both re- ported sick to their respective employers. Immediately afterwards they left home and rode their bicycles along the secondary roads. After about twenty kilometres of riding Julchen started lagging behind and then stopped. When Gisela turned back for her mother, she said, "I can't do it. You go on without me."

"We can slow down and you can make it," Gisela implored.

"I'm so sorry. I have to go back before they catch me."

Gisela was torn, but understood her mother's distress. She felt bad for her, but also loved and cared about her. She resigned herself to the fact that they would not make it together and accompanied her mother home again.

Julchen's fear was legitimate; however, Gisela was still in a pre- dicament. She could escape on her own, but would have to leave her mother in Brandenburg to fend for herself, knowing that the Russians might eventually occupy the city. Or she could stay with her mother and risk being caught by the Russians herself. After much discussion, Julchen suggested it would be best if Gisela left to join her husband in Michelau and leave her behind.

Gisela's dilemma would not let her sleep. The struggle between leaving her mother and saving herself weighed heavily on her mind.

25 *Between the Lines*

ON APRIL 15, 1945, MY COMPANY was still in position somewhere north of Görlitz. We were dug-in near a road at the edge of a woodlot on a small hill, overlooking the west side of the Neisse River valley. Word came over the wireless that the Russians were preparing to cross the river. There were still no signs of the enemy, but Command confirmed the reconnaissance reports about Russian troops massing on the other side of the river. During the day we heard what sounded like sporadic skirmishes, mainly small-arms fire. We had occasionally also heard large explosions. From the destruction evident along our recent retreat, *Wehrmacht* sappers must have been busy destroying everything they thought would be of use to the enemy. If we were to be faced with a large offensive I hoped we would be able to flee fast enough to avoid disaster. I wanted the chance to at least try to implement my escape plan.

Before daybreak on April 16, my world erupted in a pandemonium of almost continuous heavy-weapons fire. A truly gigantic artillery barrage thundered throughout the early morning, close enough to scare the wits out of me but far enough away that our particular position was not hit. It was difficult to identify where it was coming from. It seemed to surround us, muffled by trees and distance. After what seemed like hours of roaring from the throat of the battle monster it became strangely quiet for a while.

As the sun rose higher above the horizon I expected to be accosted by a massive assault, as that barrage had to be the start of another Russian offensive. Then swarms of airplanes flew by overhead, heading west, in waves. The muffled thudding sounds of battle, distant but distinct, kept us alert all day. That could only mean serious trouble. We spent some very anxious hours hoping Command knew what was going on. I ordered my men to be prepared to move out at a moment's notice and gave them a rendezvous point on the other side of the woodlot at our backs. I would have pulled my men out on my own discretion if I had been reasonably sure as to which direction to go. We still had not seen any enemy troops.

About mid-afternoon, I could wait no longer. I was just about to lead my men out of there when I received the order to move my company north along the edge of the river valley. Our action was to be coordinated with other units of the battalion. Northward was perpendicular to westward, which I presumed was the general direction of the enemy thrust, so I was suspicious that our manoeuvre was part of an attack into the enemy flank.

Over the wireless I asked the captain if this was preparation for a counterattack. He said to stand by. I suspected he had a superior officer standing over him at the other end of the line, so dropped the subject. Still, north may be as good as any other direction. Perhaps he knew something I did not know.

Before heading out, I wanted to have one quick look around. I got out of my foxhole and turned to look up the road that ran along the base of the hill beside the edge of our woodlot. With my first glance eastward I was astonished to see Russian infantry approaching along that same road! Enemy troops were crossing a pontoon bridge over the Neisse. It looked like thousands! I quickly sprang back into my foxhole. I knew we could not get out of there in time, so ordered everyone to stay hidden.

For hours the Russians marched along the road in orderly columns less than fifty metres away from our positions as we crouched in the woods by the edge of the road. There were even motorized units, including trucks, jeeps, and armoured half-tracked vehicles, as well as officers on horseback, among the seemingly endless columns of infantry. That intimidating sight must have been part of the offensive we had heard begin earlier. As dusk approached still more troops came from the east. They looked absolutely endless.

I was amazed that they were marching out in the open, seemingly unconcerned about possible German counterattacks. Their commanders must have known that effective resistance was no longer feasible for German troops in that sector of the front. Now the enemy were just marching into Germany, virtually unopposed.

The Russians had no idea our soldiers were so close to them; but it really did not make any difference, as we would have been hopelessly outnumbered and outgunned in a fight. If I had received the order to attack I would not have obeyed it. Having assessed the fighting capabilities of my company of misfits, I knew they would have been next to useless in any kind of battle with experienced Russian soldiers.

The front swept past us, leaving us stranded deep inside Russian-held territory. I passed the word along. Everyone was to leave on my order once it was dark enough and reassemble at a rendezvous position on the other side of the woods to the south. "Beware of scout patrols," was one of my last commands.

When the shadows of the setting sun were deep enough to hide our movements, I signalled the retreat. We quietly crept out of our holes and snuck away to our rendezvous location. Checking the numbers upon arrival, I discovered that the third platoon was missing. I began to worry that they had not received my orders to withdraw. Slow reactions to orders could be expected of the men in my *Marsch Kompanie*.

I decided to go back and find them. I waved at my messenger to accompany me. We knew where the missing platoon was supposed to be. Re-entering the forest, I could see only a few metres in front of me. What feeble light was left in the late evening was mostly obscured by trees. In the twilight I was eventually able to distinguish the faint outlines of a few men walking toward us—our lost platoon. I waited until they were close enough that I could be heard without yelling too loud. "Over here. Hurry up and follow us," I said, waving my arm.

"Rooki wehr!" ("Hands up!") They were not our men! In seconds we were surrounded by Russian soldiers.

I felt the hot flush of fear, or more like intense anger with myself for such an imprudent lapse in vigilance. There was no way out, and as soon as that realization hit me I made no attempt to fight or flee. Any sudden movement by either of us would certainly have been the end of us both. As much as I feared becoming a prisoner, it was certainly better than being shot dead on the spot.

Deliberately and obviously I raised my hands over my head. One Russian motioned for us to remove our weapons. I very carefully took the rifle from my shoulder and lowered it to the ground, then my automatic. I undid the ammunition belt with the pistol holster, bayonet, canteen, canister, and helmet on it, and handed it to the nearest Russian.

They frisked our uniforms to make sure we were not carrying any concealed weapons. They were also looking for loot, as they took our wristwatches and my compass. One of the Russians tried to take my wedding ring, but my second knuckle was swollen and it would not come off. For a moment I feared he would cut my finger off just for that small piece of gold, but he eventually gave up.

They escorted us to a nearby village. We stopped in front of a farm-house that was being used as a command post. I assumed we were going to be interrogated before being sent off to a prison camp. My messenger was taken into the farmhouse while I was held outside. Five minutes later he came out with his Russian escort, apparently un-harmed. I was looking for some indication as to what was in store for me, but he only glanced quickly toward me and shrugged his shoulders. Then it was my turn.

Inside the farmhouse there were six Russian soldiers in the main room. Four were sitting at the big kitchen table with some papers or a map in front of them. Two guards stood at the sides of the door, armed with rifles. The light from the lamp over the kitchen table revealed that two of the men at the table were officers. Both appeared quite young, probably younger than I was. I suddenly felt very conspicuous in my officer's uniform, fearing that the Russians might think I knew more than I actually did.

One man spoke and understood German quite well and he acted as interpreter for the Russian commander. He asked which battalion and regiment we belonged to, where we had positioned our defensive line, how many troops were left in our sector, and if we had artillery units with us.

"Grenadier Ersatz Battalion No. 53," I answered. "The last I saw of my company, they were heading west as fast as they could go. Our battalion was put together from a collection of misfits and old men, none of whom wanted to fight anymore." That probably meant nothing to him anyway. I hoped my messenger had said much the same thing.

After that "interrogation" the commander said something to one of the guards, who grabbed my arm and brusquely moved me out the door.

I was struck by how casual the interrogators had acted. Even though it was a tense situation I was left with the impression that those Rus-sians were regular people. After all the propaganda I had heard about what beastly subhumans they were supposed to be, their congenial de-meanour was surprisingly disarming. The commander's unshaven but youthful appearance indicated he was probably not a career soldier.

My messenger and I were taken to an old barn at the edge of the village, a few dozen metres from the road, the same road along which the advancing Russian columns were still marching. The two guards stayed outside the door. My eyes gradually became accustomed to the darkness inside the barn. Pale streaks of moonlight came in through narrow slits between the boards at the back. It was a large, shed-style barn, used for storing hay. There were about two dozen other German prisoners inside, sitting or lying on hay bales on the dirt floor. I did not recognize any of them.

I was convinced we would be held in there only temporarily and would eventually be sent to a prison camp, where we would be handed over to the same type of thugs that peopled our own military police. I immediately started looking for a way out.

I approached the German soldier nearest me and asked if he had discovered a way out of the barn or if he or any of the other prisoners had tried to escape.

"What's the use?" he said. "They'll shoot you if you break out of the barn. And where are you going to go, anyway? Outside is now Russian territory. You'll just be captured again."

"Maybe not," I replied. "They cannot be everywhere."

"Even if you make it, what then? You want to rejoin the army so they can put a gun in your hands again? You just risk getting killed."

"I want to go home," I said with sincere determination.

"There's no escape out there," he said despondently.

Unbelievably, he had resigned himself to his fate. None of the others showed any interest in escaping. I had a different assessment of the situation. There must be empty spaces between the advancing Russian and the retreating German troops, a constantly moving no-man's land between the armies. Also, the troops we had seen were moving forward in long, orderly columns along the roads, so they were encountering little, if any, resistance. There had to be voids that we could hide in, moving but unoccupied pieces of ground. If we could get out of here quickly enough the Russians would not be too far ahead for us to get in front of them. It was certainly worth the try, but only if we moved right away.

Whatever their physical condition or emotional state, I did not think the rest of the captured German soldiers in the barn would be helpful in our attempt to escape. I told my messenger to concentrate on trying to find a way out. If we could escape, the others could follow if they wanted.

At the bottom of the rear wall some of the boards were half-rotten. Very carefully and quietly the two of us broke away pieces of wood and scooped out enough dirt from the floor under the wall to make a space large enough to crawl through. I hoped that the men at the front door were the only ones assigned to guard us. When the opening was large enough I turned onto my back and inched my way headfirst under the barn boards. As soon as my head and shoulders were outside I looked left and right. The moonlight illuminated the outline of the forest a few hundred metres away. Between the barn and the forest was a pasture that did not provide any cover high enough to hide a man. I squeezed the rest of my body out through the opening and then crouched beside the wall to assist my messenger's exit. He slipped out easily.

We walked silently toward the forest. The dark backdrop of the woods might help to conceal our outlines even if the guards were to look our way. After a heart-pounding few hundred strides across the field we reached the woods. As soon as we were behind cover we looked around to assess which way to go. We were north of the road where the Russian columns were still marching westward. It must have been close to ten o'clock at night. I wondered if they would stop for the night. Whatever their plans, we had to try to get ahead of them.

We headed westward, walking quickly and generally parallel to the Russian troops moving along the road, far enough away to remain unseen. Since they were still not meeting any resistance they had no reason to leave the road. We were extremely wary, especially when we were forced to traverse open ground or roadways, and made wide detours around any built-up areas. Even when we went through woods we were alert. It was common procedure for an advancing army to send scout patrols along their flanks to protect themselves from a surprise ambush. It was probably just such a patrol that had apprehended us in the first place. We moved all night. As it was too dangerous to walk during daylight, we searched out a secure hiding place in a woodlot as soon as it became light. We covered ourselves with branches and leaves and tried to catch some sleep.

I awoke with a start to the sound of motors. I froze and held my breath, then slowly lifted my head to look around. It was fully light. I reassured myself that we had not been detected. Again, Russian soldiers were marching along the road, accompanied by motorized units, similar to the massive troop movements we had seen the previous day. Again, the sounds of battle reached my ears, not nearby but distinct enough for me to recognize heavy artillery fire. The Russians must have run into German resistance after all. I feared that we were caught right in the middle of a main force. There was no way to get an accurate picture of the situation, so I decided to wait until darkness to resume our flight. Units of Russian troops moved past us on the road for hours that day. There must have been a huge offensive with a major breakthrough to necessitate almost continuous forced marches.

By the second night my stomach let me know it had not been fed for almost two days. We had to find some food. The hunger pangs in my stomach were so strong they forced me to risk being caught again. In the middle of the night we carefully approached a farmhouse at the edge of a village, which turned out to be abandoned. We searched the cellar and found some jars of preserves, mainly pickles and sauerkraut, which we devoured like scavengers. We were just about to leave when I discovered two large smoked sausages hidden in the oven, a veritable treasure which could keep us going for days. I scrounged a small kitchen knife with which to cut up the sausages and two bottles for carrying water, and we were off again.

We had originally remained on the north side of the moving columns, but soon became aware that there were Russian forces on both sides. The strategy of moving only at night worked well for us. During daylight hours we found secluded hiding places in woodlots or thickets where we slept or just rested. At night there was usually just enough moonlight to be able to see where we were walking, but not enough to be spotted. We avoided villages or any inhabited places that looked like they might be occupied. Surprisingly, we saw no signs of the aftermath of battle, such as graves or derelict equipment, or even burned buildings. We probably walked about fifty kilometres, always heading generally westward.

About four days after escaping the barn we awoke to an eerie silence. There were no sounds of fighting to be heard from anywhere. Looking around, we were completely alone. We had found our void between the lines. Perhaps the Russians had turned southward or northward while we slept. I suggested to my travelling companion that now may be our chance to make it to friendly territory, if "friendly" was the right term under the circumstances.

We were then faced with a different dilemma. We had to be careful to avoid running into German troops, or worse, military police. I assumed there were still German forces, however isolated and perhaps retreating, ahead of us. Under no circumstances did either of us want to end up back in the front line facing the enemy with a rifle in our hands. Still, we had to move on and risk being apprehended if we were going to make it home.

I decided it was worth the risk of travelling during the day as well as at night in order to cover more ground. By the end of the day, all signs indicated that we were well within German-controlled territory, far away from any kind of fighting units. From then on we kept a watchful eye out for the *Feldgendarmerie*, or anybody that looked like he might be police.

At the time I assumed we had been lucky to have slipped through a gap in the German defences, because we never encountered any soldiers at all. Actually, it may have been that any semblance of a military defence had completely disappeared within the area through which we travelled. Regardless, having been captured and briefly detained turned out to be quite fortuitous, because it got us away from our company, who may have become stranded deep inside Russian-occupied territory with little hope of returning home.

During our sojourn as fugitives my messenger and I had a chance to get to know each other a little. Before, there had never been any opportunity for us to talk on a personal level, and our relationship would have been dictated by our duties within the military chain of command. Now we could talk to each other like two normal human beings. His name was Armin. He was probably about twenty years old, and spoke with a hint of a southern accent which at first made me think he was Austrian. He said he had spent much of his youth in Vienna, which is where he picked up the accent. He had an easygoing and affable disposition. He had recently been drafted and perhaps still considered this an adventure. He had a girlfriend in Wittenberg whom he had not seen or heard from in months, so naturally he was keen to get back to her. He was a good fugitive who kept a cool head, followed orders appropriately, and did not do anything stupid.

Another day on the road and we reached a crossroads with a sign pointing southward that read "Wittenberg — 12 km." That was where Armin wanted to go. I wanted to continue toward Brandenburg, as I was worried about Gisela. We assessed the situation and discussed our options. I knew roughly which route to follow to get me to my destination and estimated that Brandenburg was now only about seventy kilometres away, in a generally northward direction. I figured I could outdistance the advancing Russians enough to allow me sufficient time to reach Brandenburg, rescue Gisela and her mother, and escape to Michelau. One of the last news reports I had received from battalion command, before my brief detention, said that the Americans had crossed the Elbe, which meant I had a good chance of ending up in American-occupied territory. I also assumed that if the Russians reached Berlin before the Americans, they would be held up for days in a bloody battle for the city. There was no need for us to continue our flight together any longer, so we decided to go our separate ways. We wished each other heartfelt good luck and parted company.

26 *Refugees*

GISELA SPENT THE WEEK after her initial attempt to leave Brandenburg on April 14 agonizing over her options. She knew that the Americans had captured Bavaria about the middle of April. She also heard rumours that the Russian assault on Berlin had begun and that there was intense fighting in Prussia east of Berlin. The BBC provided no details about Russian army movements and German radio gave no reliable information at all. She was worried the Russians would show up at her doorstep at any time. She had hoped it would be the Americans, but those hopes were dashed when she heard that they had abandoned their drive on Berlin. She was convinced that the Americans still occupied the territory on the other side of the Elbe River.

She made up her mind to leave without Julchen.

At work on Tuesday she told Erika that she still did not feel well and that she might be off sick the rest of the week. Being too sick to work was the only acceptable excuse for not showing up. However, the authorities were rapidly losing their grip on daily activities in the city. Perhaps no one would care if Gisela left her job, or at least would not do anything about it? Perhaps Erika could cover for her? She trusted Erika.

On Thursday evening Erika called on Gisela and told her it was becoming increasingly difficult to make excuses for her absence. Gisela decided to leave early Friday morning, April 20. She packed as many personal belongings as could fit into a small knapsack, including a change of underwear, some family pictures, some sandwiches, and, most important, her Hitler Youth card, the only identification papers she had.

April 20 happened to be Hitler's birthday. To mark the occasion Allied Bomber Command targeted Brandenburg with an early-morning air raid. Gisela had fastened her knapsack to her bicycle and was just preparing to say goodbye to her mother when the sirens sounded. As usual, she and her mother immediately ran into the basement. It was a full-scale raid. When they emerged, clouds of smoke could be seen billowing skyward from all over the central part of the city.

That air raid made Gisela more determined than ever to leave. She looked at her mother, who tried her best not to show her anxiety. They hugged each other for a long time. Julchen pulled herself away and said, "You better get going," wiping tears from her cheeks. Gisela left not knowing if she would ever see her again.

To get out of the city she had to cross the Havel River via the bridge, which meant going right through the bomb-damaged city centre. There were more piles of rubble and shattered window glass in the streets as she rode along. The glass shards particularly concerned her as they could puncture the tires of her bicycle, which would mean the end of her flight. She chided herself for having waited so long. She also resented Bomber Command for callously destroying her beautiful city, especially as they knew the war was practically over and the city was defenceless.

She dismounted and gingerly walked her bicycle among the rubble, passing firefighters attempting to put out roaring house fires. Policemen were directing civilian work crews clearing debris and trying to dig out survivors and bodies. Other crews were working to fix broken water pipes, gas lines, and cables, some inside huge bomb craters. There were women, children, and old men trying to salvage whatever they could from their shattered homes. Nurses were attending the injured. Horse-drawn ambulances were carting away the injured and dead. Through the fires, the smoke, the noise, and the frenzy of activity, nobody paid attention to one young woman walking by with her bicycle. She thought to herself, if I get through this with no flat tire, then fate wants me to make it.

When she reached the Havel River bridge she was relieved that it had not been destroyed. She quickly crossed over into the Neustadt district of the city and continued to pick her way through more bomb-damaged streets until she eventually reached the outskirts of the city. She never rode so far so fast in her life. She headed for Wittenberg and figured she could reach it by the end of the day. She hoped to spend the night at the house of the lady where I had been billeted just before being sent back to the front a few weeks earlier.

The farther she rode her bicycle the more apprehensive she became about being stopped by the military police. The roads were crowded with all sorts of travellers, and some of them looked quite rough, including foreign workers and soldiers, some of whom may have been deserters.

She got off the road every time she saw a vehicle or a group of men approaching and acted as if she was just a local teenage girl out on a short errand. Sometimes she could not avoid strangers, so when they came close by, she would smile and make a flippant remark if anyone asked where she was going. That strategy apparently worked well, as no one asked to see her identification papers and no one accosted her.

The farther from Brandenburg she travelled, the more her concerns about being apprehended became irrelevant. There were more and more refugees on the roads heading toward the Elbe River. Although she could not be certain, surely even the contemptible *Bonzen* types could figure out that the war was over, so that the insipid rules of the regime were no longer enforceable. That was good and bad: good in that there was less to fear from the German authorities; bad because there was now no rule of law to control any potential violence that may befall travellers.

Eventually Gisela reached an unmarked intersection in the middle of nowhere. She stopped and looked left, right, and straight ahead. Which way now? It was starting to get dark. Suddenly, she heard male voices approaching from behind. Her heart raced. What to do? She turned and stared at three men approaching on bicycles. They looked like a work gang. "Which way to Wittenberg?" she asked with as much bravado as she could muster.

They continued riding past her. "Kid, hitch yourself to the back of the line and follow us. The Americans bombed the railway tracks in Wittenberg, and we're going there to fix them," one of the men said as he rode by.

What a lucky break. She tagged along behind them and reached the outskirts of Wittenberg just after nightfall. She bid farewell to her three travelling companions and headed for the house where I had been billeted.

The lady of the house answered the door and, recognizing Gisela immediately, invited her inside. She gave her a warm meal and offered to let her stay in a small bedroom. That night Gisela fell asleep exhausted, thinking about her mother's safety, the whereabouts of her husband, and her own future. She had left her entire life behind and wondered whether she would ever be able to return to Brandenburg. She too was now a refugee.

27 *To the Rescue*

IN THE MEANTIME . . . after parting company with Armin at the cross-roads near Wittenberg, I took a calculated risk that it was safe enough to travel along the main paved roads in order to make better time. I became increasingly worried about Gisela's safety as I headed for Brandenburg. The Russians could not be far behind.

The first village I encountered along the road was completely deserted. I searched some abandoned houses for food. It was obvious that the owners of one house had left recently and in a hurry; dishes were still on the table and warm ashes smouldered in the stove. In a bedroom some clothing had been strewn on the bed. That gave me an idea. If I were to be caught by the German military police I might be arrested or shot as a deserter. If spotted by Russian snipers, they might be less likely to shoot a civilian than a man in uniform. If apprehended by the Russians, I feared that my officer's uniform would single me out for mistreatment once I reached a prison camp. Given the circumstances, I was convinced that the odds of avoiding trouble were better in civilian clothes than in a lieutenant's uniform. It was time to disguise myself as a civilian.

I put some wood in the stove and made a fire to burn my *Soldbuch*. I did not want to carry anything on my person that would identify me as a soldier, and that book was an irrefutable indictment that I was a German officer. With my *Soldbuch* in ashes, the proof of my years of service in the *Wehrmacht* disappeared. I also burned my uniform. My self-preservation instincts were stronger than any sentimental attachment to the trappings of my rank. It felt strange to be in civilian clothes again after so many years in uniform.

The deserted villages and lack of civilians in the area were beginning to worry me. Perhaps the Russians were closer than I had reckoned? I might have to move much faster in order to stay ahead of them. I needed a bicycle. I searched storage sheds, barns, entranceways, hallways, and yards, and finally found an old bicycle among some farm implements. The tires were still firm enough to ride. Off I rode in my continuing quest to reach Brandenburg, and at a much faster pace.

I travelled along what I figured was the most direct route to my destination, passing through half a dozen villages and one small town. I frequently passed what I assumed were refugees on the roads, mostly groups of women and old men riding bicycles, all heading generally westward. I rode all day, gambling that the widespread chaos would have caused the disintegration of any semblance of order or authority in the country, making it unlikely that any military police would be on the roads. It made sense that everyone would be more concerned with escaping the Russians than enforcing any of the dying regime's brutish laws. However, I could not be sure what was really happening in the remaining vestiges of the Third Reich, partly because I had been detached from any reliable source of information for so long. There may yet be fanatical Gestapo types around who might try to exercise whatever of their former authority they believed remained to them. There may also be former prisoners of war or deserters who would not be overly concerned about the well-being of a lone traveller, especially one who had a bicycle. There was no way of knowing who was friendly and who was not among the many groups of refugees on the roads.

As I pedalled along I often concentrated on listening for any distant sounds of battle, but heard nothing. I assumed the Russian offensive had stalled or been diverted. Still, I wondered how far ahead of the Russians I really was.

Riding always northward, I eventually reached the outskirts of Brandenburg in the evening of that spring day. I became very wary and slowed down to assess the situation in the city. I had expected to encounter German troops, but surprisingly there was no identifiable military presence to be seen anywhere. It occurred to me that any remnants of the German army still functioning would probably have been sent to defend Berlin.

Proceeding into the city I looked for some indication that the Americans or the British had captured Brandenburg. It made sense to me that they should have reached Brandenburg long before the Russians, because they surely would not have met any determined resistance from German troops. However, there were no signs of military occupation troops. There were few people in the streets at all, and those I saw were women, children, or old men.

Where were the Russians? That was the question that continually preyed most on my mind.

I decided to go straight to my mother-in-law's house. I walked my bicycle cautiously along the sidewalks, staying close to the buildings, trying to be as inconspicuous as possible. I was on the lookout for anyone in a uniform, or any man of military age for that matter, since I had no idea what someone from the Gestapo would look like. I was especially watchful for anyone wearing the distinctive steel breastplate of the *Feldgendarmerie*. Blundering into one of the military police types now would have been the worst thing that could happen to me. If I were to be caught and charged as a deserter, those fellow countrymen would be more dangerous than even the Russians.

Approaching the central part of the city it became increasingly evident that Brandenburg had been bombed repeatedly. Parts of the old city were in ruins. Many of the buildings in the heart of the city were just empty shells, with walls still standing, but without roofs and nothing but rubble inside and onto the street. In some areas every window in the buildings facing the street had been shattered. I picked my way carefully among the broken glass. All window openings of undamaged buildings were covered with curtains or blankets. I skirted around huge bomb craters, some half full of smelly brown water. There were work crews in the streets trying to clear debris.

The closer I came to Julchen's neighbourhood, the more I worried about her and Gisela's safety. On Grossgörschen Strasse, where she lived, there were quite a few bombed-out buildings, including the one right across the street from her apartment.

I arrived shortly after dusk. When Julchen opened the door she looked very surprised, then hastily pulled me inside, took a quick glance outside, and closed the door behind us. We hugged each other reassuringly. She was truly pleased to see me alive and well. Her expression quickly turned to one of dismay, as she told me that Gisela had left just the day before.

The day before! How incredible that we had missed each other by such a narrow margin. As disappointed as I was that Gisela was not with her mother, I was pleased that she had left early enough to have had a good chance to escape the Russians. Gisela and I had discussed how to deal with that possibility before I had left for the front. We had agreed that if she thought capture of Brandenburg by the Russians was imminent, she would flee to Michelau. Both of us had concluded there would not be much to worry about if the Americans or British were to capture Brandenburg, in which case she would stay at home.

Julchen and I talked while she scrounged around for something for me to eat—bread, some leftover potatoes, and cold cuts—and made two cups of *Malzkaffee*, which was all greatly appreciated. I was happy to see that the electricity still worked in her apartment and was somewhat surprised that it was still possible to get running water from the tap.

I asked her if she had heard any news of where the Russians were. All she knew was that the authorities were expecting a monumental battle for Berlin. That news made me less apprehensive about the proximity of Russian forces, as I assumed they would be held up for days, if not weeks, trying to take the capital before they could move westward on to Brandenburg. The German forces defending Berlin would surely fight ferociously, and in every quarter of the city.

I felt sorry for the defenders of Berlin. If the Russians eventually surrounded the city the remaining German troops and civilians caught in the trap would be doomed. Hitler would not permit anyone to leave the city. Before the war Berlin had about three million civilian residents. Those remaining were mostly women, old men, and children, as well as hundreds of thousands of labourers who were prisoners of war, and of course the soldiers assigned to defend the city. I could only imagine the calamity that would befall the victims of that inevitable bloodbath.

Julchen told me that she had not seen any German soldiers or military personnel of any kind for at least a week. The regular uniformed police, as well as the military police types, seemed to have disappeared. Perhaps they had been commandeered to serve in the defence of Berlin, or made themselves scarce because they were worried about the reprisals they would inevitably face from German civilians after the end of the war? There was now no representation of law and order in the city at all, and she told me she had feared for the future and her own prospects. Everyone she had recently spoken with felt the same way.

I was curious as to why she had not left with Gisela. Julchen explained that she had tried, but the long bicycle ride had proved too arduous for her. Also, she was afraid to leave because she knew that any Germans caught by the police more than sixty kilometres from their home could be arrested. Her fear of the authorities was understandable, as that fear had been instilled in the mind of every German for over a decade. She was still hopeful that the Americans would reach Brandenburg any time now.

I suspected the situation was precarious, and decided we had to make a hasty departure. I suggested she pack her most valuable possessions in whatever we could transport with us on our bicycles and be ready to leave before dawn the next morning. The expression on her face communicated just how genuinely reluctant she was to leave her home. That was understandable, as almost everything she owned, everything she had worked for all her life, would have to be abandoned. Leaving would be heartbreaking.

We would try to reach the Elbe River and cross it to what I guessed, and certainly hoped, would be British- or American-occupied territory near the city of Magdeburg. From there we would head south to Michelau. She did not commit to going with me, and I do not know if she packed for the journey. I decided that if I could not convince Julchen to accompany me, I would have to leave without her. I had to reach Michelau to be reunited with my wife. But right now I felt absolutely exhausted, so excused myself, climbed into bed, and passed out.

I awoke to the sound of my mother-in-law in a state of panic. She stammered something about Russian soldiers outside in the street, which immediately jolted me awake. I pulled aside the blanket covering the window and peered out into the pre-dawn light. A motley group of prisoners was being herded down the street by armed Russian soldiers, while other soldiers were going from house to house. Two soldiers were rapidly striding toward our apartment building. The knock at the door told me it was too late to avoid being captured again.

Julchen said, "Hurry! Let's go down to the basement to hide." So I grabbed my shoes and jacket and both of us scurried downstairs. The landlord and his wife, two other women, and a boy probably less than twelve years old did the same.

As we huddled in the semi-darkness, I thought that our attempt to hide was stupid; there was no way out. I was acutely angry with myself for allowing this to happen to me, especially after being so careful for so long. The front door upstairs burst open and we could hear heavy footsteps tramping through the building. They were searching every room. It was only a matter of time before they found us. Sure enough, the door to the cellar opened and a Russian soldier cautiously came down the stairs holding a rifle in front of him. He looked us over, pointed at me, and motioned for me to go upstairs. The others stayed behind.

The two Russian soldiers then brusquely escorted me out òf the building at gunpoint. I did not even have time to say goodbye to Julchen. I was very worried for her safety, but was powerless to do anything to protect her.

I was also quite concerned for my own safety, because I expected the Russians to shoot me as soon as they discovered I did not have any papers on me. Perhaps burning my *Soldbuch* had not been such a good idea after all. What if the Russians thought I was a Nazi?

It did not matter to the Russians whether anyone was in uniform or not. All males, from teenagers to old men, were taken prisoner and marched out of the city toward what I suspected was going to be a dreadful labour camp—and I was one of them.

28 *The Last Ones Across the Elbe*

GISELA HAD INTENDED TO LEAVE first thing in the morning after arriving in Wittenberg, but Frau Irmgard was happy to have some company and asked her to stay a while. They both believed that the area would soon be in American hands, so Gisela did not feel compelled to leave immediately.

Late in the evening of that second day there was a knock at the door. Who would be out so late at night? It might be the authorities, which could only be bad news. Irmgard went to the door and after a brief exchange came back into the room. "Gisela, there is someone here to see you," she said.

Surprised but cautious, Gisela went to the door. Who even knew she was there?

A young woman introduced herself, then asked, "Are you Gisela Gagel?" Never having seen her before, Gisela hesitated to say anything until the woman added, "Albin's wife?"

Her curiosity aroused, Gisela said, "Yes I am."

"Please come with me. There is someone who wants to meet you."

Gisela looked at her host, who gently nodded approval. She obviously knew the young woman, so Gisela decided to trust her.

"I'm Armin's girlfriend," she said quietly, which meant nothing to Gisela. "I did not want to say so in front of anyone else, but Armin was Leutnant Gagel's messenger in the army. He is at my house right now and wants to talk to you."

"Albin's messenger?" She hoped that meant good news.

Around the corner and another block farther they turned into a house. Once inside Gisela was introduced to a young soldier. She suspected he was a deserter on the run, judging by his dishevelled state as well as the fact that he did not want to venture outside.

Armin introduced himself and then briefly told her the story of his escape and flight from the Russians with me.

She paid close attention. "Where is he now?" she asked, hoping for a moment that I was hiding nearby.

"When we split up he was on his way to Brandenburg to meet you.

That was this morning."

"Why didn't he stay with you?" She asked.

"He thought you were still in Brandenburg." He added, "I'm grateful to him for making me escape with him. I would not have had the nerve to try it by myself, but I trusted him and had faith in his instincts. I owe it to him that I'm here."

Gisela almost cried. She was glad to hear that I was still alive, but feared I would be captured in Brandenburg. She remembered that our plan had been to go straight to Michelau if Brandenburg would be in danger of capture by the Russians. Out of frustration she said, "That hero. I hope he changes his mind about looking for me and goes straight to Michelau."

Gisela thanked Armin for the information, said goodbye and wished him good luck. She was grateful, and astounded that he had found her in Wittenberg. Apparently news travels very quickly in small towns.

Gisela fretted over her options. Should she wait for me in Wittenberg, being so close? Armin had found her, perhaps so would I? After much deliberation she decided to follow her original plan and continue her trip to Michelau sooner rather than later. She also suspected that rumours about the impending American occupation of that part of Prussia might turn out to be false. Her fear of falling into Russian hands was greater than any apprehension concerning the uncertainty surrounding Michelau's fate. Her most immediate priority was to get across the Elbe River. So, early in the morning, she told her hostess she was leaving. Gisela gave her as many of her ration stamps as she could spare in appreciation for the food and shelter. Frau Irmgard gave her a loaf of rye bread to take along.

She got back on her bicycle and headed out of town toward the Elbe. There were now hundreds and hundreds of civilians on the roads, all fleeing toward the river. The ever-increasing groups of refugees provided a certain safety in numbers, possibly protecting them from "guest workers" (former prisoners of war) who could try to rob or harm individual civilians. Many walked beside their bicycles, some of which were laden with bags and possessions. Others pushed handcarts, small wagons, or baby carriages, also packed with belongings.

Gisela soon found herself in the midst of one of those groups of refugees, walking her bicycle. Beside her walked a small man wearing civilian clothes that did not fit well. He was carrying a large leather briefcase, which was obviously very heavy. She took pity on him for having to carry that burden and offered to let him put his pack on her bicycle carrier. He gratefully accepted. So she pushed her bicycle with her knapsack and his briefcase on the back while he walked behind steadying the load, which worked fine. They did not talk much, other than exchange pleasantries and names. His name was Herbert. Gisela mentioned that she had hoped the Americans would be on this side of the river by then. Herbert also hoped so, but thought not; however, and most important, he believed they occupied the other side.

They were heading for the bridge over the Elbe that led to the western side. After a while they reached a crossroads where they could see that the bridge over the Elbe had been blasted. The centre span had completely collapsed and was below the surface of the water, making it impassable. They continued along the road parallel to the Elbe until they came to a restaurant. It had probably been a tourist spot for tour boats before the war. They agreed to take a break and went inside. The place was packed with people, most of them probably also refugees, but eventually they found an empty table. The only items on the menu still available were beer, camomile tea, and *Malzkaffee*. They ordered two coffees.

"I'm hungry," said Gisela's new-found travelling companion.

"Me, too," replied Gisela. She then leaned forward and quietly added, "I have a small rye bread in my knapsack. We can share it."

"Wonderful," replied Herbert, also quietly. "I have more than papers in my briefcase; I have sausages."

He reached into his jacket pocket and took out a pocket knife. It turned out that Herbert had three large smoked salami sausages in his briefcase, which explained its weight. Even though they were sure no one would have cared that they brought their own meal into a restaurant, they tried to hide the fact they had as much food as they did. Notwithstanding any guilty feelings, they proceeded to have themselves a shamelessly decadent feast.

After their clandestine dinner, the conversation turned to finding an opportunity that might get them across the Elbe. The restaurant was near the edge of the river, and both assumed there were no bridges still intact anywhere along the Elbe.

Herbert said, "Wait here, I'll be right back," and went into the kitchen. He left Gisela sitting at the table wondering what was happening. She was not prepared to swim across the cold wide river and leave her precious bicycle behind. Not only that, but what would she do if she did make it, with no food and nothing but the wet clothes on her back? It was only April and the weather was still quite cold.

After an uncomfortably long wait, Herbert returned. He sat down and whispered to her, "I have arranged for a boat across the river for both of us. Get ready to leave when I get the signal. We can sit here and wait until then."

So they waited and waited, making small talk to pass the time. She figured Herbert was about thirty-five years old or so. He had a wife and two small children waiting for him in a small town in Westfallen, and he had been in the army since the beginning of the war. All the while he kept an eye on the kitchen door. Noticing Gisela's increasing apprehension, he quietly said, "Just try to relax. There's nothing else we can do."

Finally, toward evening, the proprietor came out of the kitchen and motioned to Herbert to follow him. Time to go. They got up, casually walked out the door, and followed him around to the back of the building. The proprietor led them down to the water's edge, where they and two other women and another man in civilian clothes climbed into a rowboat.

Gisela noticed Herbert was without his briefcase. He had bribed the boat owner with his precious sausages. Perhaps he took Gisela along as repayment for her kindness in letting him transport his heavy pack on her bicycle. The proprietor told Gisela to leave the bicycle behind, but she refused, so he rowed the five refugees, along with Gisela's precious bicycle, across the Elbe. Gisela was as nervous as she had ever been. Helping refugees cross the Elbe was risky, as the men could have been deserting soldiers, which Gisela's companion surely was. The risk was worth it, as the far side of the river held out the promise of freedom.

On reaching the far shore they climbed out of the boat, thanked their benefactor, and congratulated each other on their escape. The rowboat owner left to return to his restaurant. Walking across the flood plain they met dozens of other refugees who had recently crossed the river. "Where to now?" Gisela wondered as she stood among the milling crowd. Nobody seemed to know what to do next. Before they had a chance to devise a plan they heard the sound of a motor and saw a jeep approaching. Gisela almost panicked when she saw a five-pointed star painted on the hood of the jeep. Herbert noticed her agitation and said, "The *Amis* (German slang for Americans) have the white star; the Russian star is red."

The jeep stopped in front of the group and two young American soldiers jumped out. One of them spoke German. "Wait here!" he shouted at the crowd.

Then another jeep pulled up, with two more soldiers. One of them looked like an officer. Pointing and gesticulating, he spoke to the German-speaking interpreter who turned to the refugees and announced, "He said you will all have to go back. This is a war zone and there is still fighting going on in this area."

Gisela listened for any sounds of shooting in the distance, but heard nothing. It seemed inconceivable that there was fighting anywhere in the area. They did not seem to be in any danger from anything. Being suddenly faced with the alarming possibility of ending up in the hands of the Russians was particularly exasperating after the effort they had gone through to reach what they thought would be freedom on the west side of the river. One of the other women started crying and said that she would kill herself before going back. The men in the group protested that everyone had surrendered, so there was no need to go back. Gisela had not seen any armed soldiers during the entire time she had been on the road. There was therefore no justification for the Americans to send them back.

Gisela made up her mind to run for it if they tried to ship her back. The flood plain was covered with clumps of bushes and tall weeds which could provide possible hiding places. Thinking about the situation she realized there was no boat to take the refugees back anyway, so the entire confrontation was confusing and pointless. She decided to be patient, reckoning that eventually the Americans would have to take them.

And they eventually did, for whatever reason. The interpreter and another soldier escorted them up the embankment out of the flood plain to the road where some army trucks were parked. About a hundred civilians were already assembled alongside. The interpreter then ordered them to form two lines. "Soldiers to one side, women and civilians to the other."

Herbert hesitated for a moment, then walked over to the soldier's side. No one would have believed he was a civilian anyway. Gisela said goodbye and a heartfelt thank you to her brief travelling companion and benefactor. She knew she might not have made it across the Elbe without his help. After the refugees split into two groups the former soldiers were loaded onto transport trucks. Herbert's last words to her were, "I hope they won't turn us over to the Russians." Gisela hoped so, too. She will never know, as she never saw him again.

The women and other civilians were ordered to get into another truck. Gisela clung tenaciously to her precious bicycle, but one of the soldiers firmly said no and forcefully took it out of her hands. She had no choice but to leave it behind. She clutched her bag with the priceless half rye bread in it, thinking they might want it also, but was allowed to keep it. The other refugees were also permitted to hang onto their meagre personal possessions.

They were driven to a village a few kilometres away, which turned out to be Pratau, reaching it just before dusk. There they were assembled in the front courtyard of a large, two-storey house, and waited. The interpreter went into the house, which was the American military command station for the area. When he returned he explained that they would be taken one at a time into the house for questioning.

When it came to Gisela's turn she went into a waiting room and sat down on one of the chairs that had been set up along the wall. There were soldiers and civilians working at desks or moving about very purposefully, all seemingly busy with administrative duties. Some were German. A young American officer came out and motioned for her to follow him into another room. He was tall and handsome, with blue eyes and blond hair. Once inside, he turned to her, looked her in the eye, and said in perfect German, "I am a Jew."

Gisela was very surprised by his statement. She had expected to be interrogated about her activities and to be asked for identification, but his unexpected approach took her completely by surprise. As she gazed at his blond hair and blue-eyed face she searched for some indication as to what he wanted.

"Did you not hear me?" he continued. "I said I'm a Jew."

"Yeah, so?" Gisela replied, still perplexed.

"Don't you want to jump at my throat?" he continued. "What do you think now, you who are one of the 'master race'?"

Gisela was so astounded by his comments that she was speechless for a moment. That was the first time she had ever heard the term "master race."

"I don't know what you've been reading," she replied, having no idea where he had learned such strange notions. She had no intention of being anything but polite.

He told her to sit down and asked, "Were you in the Hitler Youth?"

"Of course, everybody was."

"Well at least you are not lying about it," he replied.

He then said, "You Germans are really going to have to work hard now."

Gisela was not sure what he meant. The first response she could come up with was, "Naturally, but unemployment would be worse," a sarcastic remark that might have got her into trouble.

"What?" he asked.

"Yes," was all that then came out of her mouth. She had no idea what was in store for Germany after the war, or what to expect from the American occupiers.

"I'm surprised you are married," he said, pointing to her wedding band. "You look too young to be a married woman."

"Yes, I'm married," she replied. "I'm on my way to rejoin my husband."

He then picked up some forms and took out a pen. "Where are you going?"

"Bavaria," she replied.

"That's a long way away," he said. "Do you have family there?"

"Yes. My husband's family."

"How do you plan to get there?" he continued.

"I was going to ride my bicycle, but your soldiers took it away from me," she protested.

"It's late. You will need a place to stay," he said, and left the room. She sat there waiting, not knowing what to expect next. After a few minutes he returned, handed her a piece of paper with an address on it, and told her to go there. Apparently a family in the village had a room available. "At least that will keep you out of the refugee camp," he added. As she got up to leave he politely showed her out of the room and into the entrance hall. He called another soldier over to escort Gisela to the house. "Goodbye and good luck," he said.

"Thank you," Gisela said, then added, "What about my bicycle?"

He said something to the other soldier in English. "This man will get you another one," he replied.

So the officer turned out to be a nice guy after all.

Gisela accompanied the soldier to a row of dozens of bicycles stored at the side. The soldier said something in English and pointed at the bicycles. Gisela hesitated, not sure if he expected her to find her own bicycle in that row. She walked back and forth, but could not find her own bicycle, and finally turned to him and shrugged her shoulders. He walked up to the row of bicycles, picked one out, and pushed it toward her. "Good?" he asked, with a smile.

"Yes, thank you," she replied, in English.

She took her new bicycle a few blocks down the main street of the village to her new lodgings, escorted by her "guard." At the house she introduced herself to the landlady and handed her the form she had received from the American officer. She was to stay in a tiny room, which was just big enough to hold a bed and a chest of drawers.

Gisela paid the lady of the house for her room with money and her board with her precious ration stamps. The landlady had two daughters almost as old as Gisela.

Gisela realized she would have to be patient before resuming her journey to Michelau. The war was not officially over, and the Americans had announced that civilians were not allowed to travel on the roads because they were needed to move troops. After twelve years of living in a totalitarian regime she was used to obeying the authorities. However, she planned to leave as soon as things settled down. As it turned out, there was a lot of military activity in the area, day and night, especially long truck convoys passing through the village. There would surely be checkpoints on the main roads. She would have to wait for the right opportunity. She wanted to be reunited with her husband in one piece; however, the area was occupied by the Amis, so she felt relatively safe.

The room where she stayed faced the main street, and the girls of the house would sometimes hang out the window and flirt with the Yanks, even after the 9 p.m. curfew. The American soldiers were forbidden to fraternize with "the enemy," and that included German women; however, human nature being what it is, soldiers would often stop to chat with civilian girls. That was until an officer or military policeman came along, when they would quickly pretend they were just passing by. Gisela's understanding of English, however limited, made her very valuable to the two girls of the house. That was the first time Gisela regretted not having paid more attention to her teacher during English classes.

On the second day of her stay in the village, Gisela was walking along the main street when she heard a friendly "Hello." A young American soldier approached her. "Remember me?" he asked. "We met on the flood plain the day you crossed the Elbe."

"Ah, yes," she said, "the interpreter." She had not recognized him at first without his helmet. They struck up a conversation and she learned a few things.

He said that her group was among the last ones to cross the river. "You should be glad you made it," he told her. "I heard rumours the Russians raped women they caught."

"I know I was lucky," she said.

"Where is your destination?" he asked Gisela.

"Northern Bavaria," she replied, sure he would have no idea where Michelau was.

"Bavaria?" He sounded surprised. "The Main River might become the border between Russian- and American-occupied Germany. General Patton is already in Bavaria, but our boys might have to leave and give much of it to the Russians."

Gisela was dismayed to hear such news. She knew the Main River flowed right through Michelau. Her mind raced. Was Turko's house on the north or south side of the river? Which side would be Russian?

He continued, "It looks like the province of Thüringen might also be given to the Russians, as well as all of Saxony."

That sounded completely implausible to Gisela, because Thüringen was entirely on the west side of the Elbe. Plus, the American army had captured all of Thüringen and she could not imagine they would hand it over to the Russians after all that effort. Anyway, she thanked him for his concern.

She weighed her options. She would try to find out more about the situation in occupied Germany. The prohibition against civilians using the roads was still in effect, so she decided it was better to wait for a more opportune time before striking out for Michelau.

29 **POW**

IN BRANDENBURG, THE RUSSIAN SOLDIERS rounded up every man and boy in the city, regardless if they were in uniform or civilian clothes. There were boys among the prisoners that could not have been older than thirteen, and old men who must have been in their sixties. We were gathered into small groups, which gradually became larger and larger until we filled the centre of the street in a long column, three or four men wide. We were herded like farm animals down the main streets of Brandenburg.

As we marched I kept looking for an open doorway through which I could quickly duck out of sight. At the same time I kept a watchful eye on our guards, trying to see where every one of them was all the time. But none of the doorways we passed appeared to be open. I could not risk bolting across the ten metres or so of pavement to a doorway unless I was sure the door would not be locked, otherwise the guards would probably shoot me on the spot, as there were at least two guards within rifle range at all times.

The column grew until there must have been thousands of prisoners. We marched northward out of the city, escorted by what was not more than a platoon of Russian soldiers.

Some of our guards were mounted on horseback. They appeared very alien to me, like no other soldiers I had encountered before. Many of them had distinctly Asiatic features, with very straight black hair, flat noses, and small eyes. Even their speech sounded unlike any Russian dialect I had ever heard.

After about two hours on the road two of the mounted guards became embroiled in an animated discussion. One, a corporal, was waving his arms and gesticulating with his riding crop toward the front of the column. His voice became louder and more agitated. Then, incredibly, he struck the other rider with his riding crop! To my astonishment, the other man struck back! They continued their jousting match for almost a minute, circling each other, pushing their mounts into each other, and repeatedly striking out with their crops. I was astounded by that behaviour, as it would have been unthinkable in the German army.

The second rider then wheeled his horse around and galloped off to the front of the column. The corporal seemed completely nonplussed and calmly went back to his position at the side of the column. Such violent behaviour was apparently an acceptable method of resolving differences of opinion among these Cossacks.

We were not allowed to talk during the march. If a guard suspected anyone of whispering to another prisoner, he was slapped across the back of the head with a riding crop or jabbed with the butt end of a rifle, accompanied by a spiteful admonition. I did not talk to the men next to me. There was nothing to talk about anyway.

I tried to keep track of the direction we were moving in, which I judged to be generally northward. We passed through a few villages, but saw very few civilians.

I do not think there was any deliberate abuse of any of the prisoners, but the forced march eventually became very tiring, for the guards as well as the prisoners. Even the soldiers on horseback began to appear fatigued as the morning wore on. We stopped around noon for a brief rest at the side of the road. I was hoping to be fed; however, there was no field kitchen to be seen and we had just passed through a village.

After about half an hour's rest we were ordered back onto the road and the march resumed. As the relentless plodding continued, my enthusiasm for trying to escape gradually waned, and I resigned myself to the fact that unless something completely unexpected happened, there would be no opportunity to escape. By late afternoon my stomach began to compel my attention, as I had not eaten since the little snack Julchen had given me last night. During that entire first day on the road we received nothing at all to eat.

Late that evening we approached a village and were led into a *Bauernhof*, a large farmyard at the centre of a rural farm complex enclosed by two-metre-high stone walls that were connected to the farm buildings. We were allowed to drink from the well, like cattle at a trough. We spent the night in the farmyard. The guards occupied the residences and as many prisoners as possible were crammed into the storage sheds. Most of us just slept on the dirt inside the crowded open courtyard. As far as I could tell, only two Russian soldiers were assigned to guard us, and they stood outside the gate. Other guards may have been posted at strategic spots, but I could not see them. The only possible escape routes would have been through the gate or over the wall, both of which were probably covered by armed guards. Regardless, I was too fatigued from exertion and hunger to care much about escape. We prisoners in the farmyard huddled together for warmth in the cold night air. I doubt anyone slept much.

The morning of the second day we were fed. We lined up at a table beside a field kitchen in the yard. The first group were given bowls and as many spoons as were available and ate. The bowls and spoons were then handed to the next shift, and so on. The Russians had slaughtered a cow, so the food was cabbage soup with some beef in it. Calling it soup might be a misnomer. The cook had boiled water in large kettles, thrown in a pile of cut cabbage, and added chunks of dead cow meat. There were no spices and no salt, so it tasted horrible. However, if hungry enough, you will eat almost anything and be grateful for what you got. That bowlful of odious soup would help keep me alive. Surprisingly, the Russian guards were given exactly the same meal.

After being fed we were permitted to use the closest outhouses and lavatories in the village, which took hours. We were then ordered to line up and were once again herded along on the road leading north.

As we trudged along I could not help but be fascinated with the mounted guards. One of the horsemen was particularly memorable. He was a small man, with a short, almost flat nose, half-closed black eyes that drooped at the outside corners, and jet black hair which seemed to stick straight out of his head. He moved as one with his horse, which I never saw him dismount during our two-day trek. I never saw him wash himself, or stop to urinate, but did see him eat what looked like hard dark meat and drink from his canteen while sitting in the saddle. I was sure he even slept in the saddle. He seemed physically attached to his horse. His horse was also relatively small, especially compared to the large farm horses I was used to—short-legged, with a dark brown, long-haired coat, and a peculiar deep and rounded lower jaw.

That horseman had an amazing ability to make his horse do any manoeuvre he wanted, without the slightest hint of a gesture or verbal command. I saw him reach down and pick something off the ground at the side of the road, without the horse deviating from its path or even changing stride, and immediately right himself, without any visible effort.

Despite his alien appearance he was not disagreeable. I never saw him take his rifle from its position slung across his back. He hardly ever spoke and seemed totally indifferent to everything around him. I am sure he could not speak or understand any German. As far as I could tell, he may not have spoken any Russian either. Most of the time it appeared as if he paid not the slightest attention to us. Sometimes he was napping as he rode along beside the column, his chin on his chest, his horse with its head down, matching the pace of our strides. At least he was entertaining to watch, that half-man, half-horse being.

By late afternoon of that second exhausting day we arrived at our destination, the Döberitz prison camp. It looked almost identical to the *Arbeitsdienst* camp near Irlbach where I had started my compulsory service to the state some six long years ago.

Entering the camp I surveyed the surroundings before we crammed into an open area beside a row of barracks. There seemed to be no order or even organization in the camp, as if there were no one in charge. Groups of prisoners were milling about everywhere. Other than a few Russian horsemen, who just ignored us, I could not see any Russian guards.

We stood or shuffled about in the open, not knowing what would happen next, until late in the evening. Then about sixty to eighty of us were ordered into a barrack. It was completely empty inside; no beds, no stove, no wash facilities, not even straw bales—nothing, just a wooden floor. It may have once been an exercise hall. After we were crammed inside, the guards left us and closed the door, after which the interior was pitch-black.

Surely this was not to be our quarters, I thought to myself. Perhaps it was a temporary holding pen until we were assigned to more permanent accommodations? Most of the prisoners just sat down and waited, as did I. An hour must have passed without anyone coming to fetch us. Some of the prisoners lay down on the floor and fell asleep. Eventually, it dawned on me that we were to spend the night in there, so I tried to make myself comfortable on the bare floor. After the past two gruelling days' march I was very tired. At least there was a roof over our heads. Might as well make the best of it, I thought, as this may be home for a while. There were no facilities inside, so every time someone had to urinate, they knocked on the door and the Russian guard escorted them to the toilet.

Suddenly, the distinctive sound of gunshots made me instinctively flatten myself onto my stomach. The shots did not come from nearby, but not from far off either. Perhaps the guards had shot at someone trying to escape? I felt uneasy lying in the dark, listening for more shots, but heard none. I again fell asleep on the floor.

"Out! Out!" Two Russian guards shook me awake and yanked me off the floor. What now? It was the middle of the night. I was taken to an administration building. Two Russian guards stood in the entrance hallway. No one was talking, and no one looked happy. Then a door opened and a German prisoner was brought out by a Russian guard. Interrogation!

My mind raced to prepare a credible story as to why I was not in uniform and why I had no identification papers on me. Before I felt at all prepared for the interrogators, it was my turn. The room looked as if it had been an office, brightly lit, containing a large desk in front of the far wall behind which sat three Russian officers. There was a big table to one side, behind which sat two more Russians. They were all wearing uniforms with identification tags I had not seen before. I guessed they were military police types. One of the men sitting at the desk was writing. The two armed guards stayed in the room by the door. I was not asked to sit down.

The first thing they did was make me take off my shirt and lift my arms. They were checking to see if I was a member of the *Waffen SS*, as every SS soldier had his serial number and blood type tattooed on the underside of his upper arm. After satisfying themselves I was not SS, they let me put my shirt back on. Perhaps they would have killed me if I had been with the SS? Come to think of it, if I had grown a few centimetres taller I might have been a candidate for the *Waffen SS*. Right then I considered myself fortunate to have been just an ordinary soldier.

I knew I had to remain calm. There was no way I wanted them to know I was an officer, as they might be inclined to give officers special mistreatment. I figured the more harmless I appeared the better.

"What is your name?" the interpreter asked in almost flawless German.

"Albin Gagel," I told him.

"What is your father's name?" he asked.

"Hartmann Gagel," I told him.

"Where is your home?"

"Brandenburg," I replied.

The officer clerk was writing down my answers in a large binder.

One of the officers got out of his chair and walked around the desk until he stood in front of my face. He then stared me right in the eye.

I was unsure how to react. Should I avoid his gaze and look straight ahead as if he was not there, as I had learned to do as a soldier, or look back as if we were social or business acquaintances? Avoiding his stare could be construed as guilt or be recognized as military training, while returning his gaze could be misinterpreted as arrogance or aggression. I did not want to appear arrogant, like a career officer might appear, and I was certainly in no position to be aggressive. I looked him in the eye momentarily and then looked around at each of the other men in the room. The silence became excruciating.

"Why are you not in uniform?" the interpreter asked, almost casually.

I had expected that question as soon as I knew I was in for interrogation. "I was discharged from the army because my arm is lame." It was the best story I could concoct on such short notice, and rolled up the sleeve on my right arm to show him the scars. I mimicked the former uselessness of my right hand, the way it had been before the nerve operation, and exaggerated the seriousness of the injuries. "The bones in my arm were shattered and the main nerve was severed, so I was no use to the army."

The other officer then came up and very deliberately and meticulously examined the arm. He even tried to rotate the forearm, which of course was not possible. Neither officer showed any indication as to whether or not he believed me. One spoke to the interpreter in Russian.

"Where did you receive the wound?" the interpreter asked.

"At the Eastern Front," I said.

"Ah!" the officer in front of my face said emphatically. Obviously his suspicions had been vindicated. Obviously he also understood some German, or at least that I had been in "*Russland.*" He again said something to the interpreter.

"How many Russians have you killed?" the interpreter asked accusingly. There was a deadly serious look on the officer's face now.

"I don't know," I answered. "I was a corporal with an artillery battery."

"Where were you stationed in Russia?" the interpreter asked.

"In the Ukraine," I replied. "South of Kiev, until November 1943."

"Did you see any partisans in the Ukraine?"

"What do partisans look like?" I suspected a trap in his question.

"Civilians. Did you ever fight civilians?"

"No, we were not permitted to go near civilians."

"Did you not see civilians?" he asked.

An image of the *babushkas* in the potato fields near Orel flashed through my mind. "Yes, on my way to the front, I saw women working in fields."

"You are obviously a soldier," he continued. "You look like you were an officer. Were you an officer in Russia?"

"No," I lied. With over a week's growth of beard on my chin, I figured there was nothing about my appearance that would suggest I was an officer.

"Where is your uniform?"

I repeated the story about being discharged because of my lame arm. "I spent a year in hospital trying to regain the use of my arm. I even had an operation, but nothing helped. I was not fit for the army with one useless arm." I avoided looking at the faces of the officers, not wanting to look like I was checking to see if they believed me. I felt very tense, but kept telling myself to stay calm, stick to my story, and think before answering any question.

There was another discussion in Russian between the interpreter and the officers. "Where are your papers?" the interpreter asked. "Why have you no *Soldbuch*?"

"My house was bombed in the middle of the night last week. I got out in time, but everything inside burned up. All my identification papers are gone, even my ration cards."

"Why did you not get new papers?" he retorted.

"The authorities had abandoned the city. There was no way to get new papers."

That answer generated a comment from the officer clerk.

"What were your duties with the German army in Russia?"

"Clean up the spent casings. Tend to the horses. Dig holes and trenches in the ground." Under the circumstances, my experiences near Orel in 1942 would surely provide a better image for my interrogators as examples of my duties at the Eastern Front than my actions on the retreat to Kirovograd in 1943.

"Did you destroy buildings in Russia?" the interpreter asked.

"I never knew where the shells landed. I just followed orders."

"Did you burn any houses in Russia?"

"No," I said.

"You saw houses burn, did you not?"

"Yes."

"Did you order your men to burn houses?"

"No." That may have been too hasty an answer to a dangerous question, so I added, "I was just a corporal in the artillery."

"What city did you stay in while in Russia?"

"I never stayed in a city. I was always in a hole in the ground at the front, or in underground bunkers."

"You must have been in Russian villages, even at the front."

"Yes. My unit passed through villages during our retreat in the Ukraine."

"Did you meet civilians in those villages?"

"No, they were deserted."

"Did you take anything from a Russian house?"

"No," I replied, surprised at that kind of question.

"Did you confiscate any food?"

"No."

"Did you steal any horses?"

"No."

"Did your men steal any horses?"

"I never saw anyone steal horses."

"What division were you with?"

I hesitated for a moment, as if trying to recall. "At first it was the 88th Infantry Division, but I am not sure which division I was assigned to later," I replied, hoping that little piece of information would mean nothing to them.

"Who was your commanding officer?"

"I can't remember," I replied. "It was 1943." I thought for a moment and then gave him the name of who I thought it might have been.

The interpreter leafed through his binder on the desk. He said something to the other officers. I understood the word "*nyet,*" meaning "no" in Russian, which raised my tension level a few degrees. What would they do to me if they found out I was lying? My interrogators had not been belligerent or even threatening; still, I wondered why they wanted to know so much about my service history in Russia. I feared they would send me to a labour camp or coal mine in Siberia if they could prove I had committed some act they considered criminal while in Russia.

They deliberated back and forth in Russian, and then repeated some of the same questions again and again. I kept telling myself to stay calm, be patient, think, breathe. Finally, with a wave of the officer's hand, I was dismissed. The whole interrogation had probably lasted less than ten minutes, but had seemed like hours. The two guards escorted me out of the building. Where were they taking me now? The shots I had heard a few hours earlier suddenly loomed ominously in my mind. Did they execute prisoners whose answers they did not like? I was relieved when they took me back to my barrack. I assumed that was the end of that. That empty black enclosure felt almost comforting.

In the morning we were led out to use the toilets in the adjoining building. We were allowed to move around outside our building, but were not permitted to walk freely about the camp. Thankfully we were not marched off to work, so at least it was not a labour camp. Shortly before noon we were fed from a field kitchen, with a bowlful of the same repugnant cabbage and dead cow soup we had on the road the day before. By then I was ravenous and would have eaten almost anything. It was the only meal of the day.

Döberitz was a big camp, covering dozens of acres. There were rows and rows of barracks and extensive open areas. Administrative, maintenance, and other specialized buildings were situated within and near the main compound. The whole complex was set in the middle of very flat countryside, with areas of marshland visible in the distance. It was not part of any town and there were no large urban settlements nearby, although two small villages could be seen in the surrounding countryside. It was a typical utilitarian facility, but not really designed to be a prison. The group of barracks and associated grounds were enclosed by a chain-link fence about three metres high, topped with three strings of barbed wire. There were guards posted along the outside of the fence every hundred metres or so, armed with automatics, but there were no observation towers manned by armed guards.

There must have been some ten thousand prisoners in Döberitz, guessing from what I could see. Most were German soldiers, but there were also many civilians, some of whom were old men or teenaged boys.

The following night I again heard shots, similar to the previous night. Hopefully that was not going to become a routine occurrence. Later that same night I was again roused out of my sleep and taken to the same interrogation room as on the previous night. Evidently my trials were not over yet. The same officers asked me the same questions. Obviously they had not believed my story about being discharged because of my lame arm. Once again they behaved without any threat of violence, and once again I was very careful to hide my identity as an officer. I made sure my story was exactly the same as on the previous night, and continued to feign the uselessness of my right arm.

This time they tried a slightly different tactic to convince me that it was all right to tell them everything that happened in Russia. "The war is almost over," the one officer said in an almost amiable manner. "We have been brothers-in-arms, sharing the same dangers. Germany will be governed by Russian authority. We all will have to live together, sharing the same fortune. You have nothing to fear."

While I appreciated the logic of what he said, I did not trust his motives.

"How do you think you will like Russians living in Germany?"

"I look forward to peace and understand things will be different after the war."

"How did you get along with Russian people in Russia?"

Back to reality. "I never met any Russian civilians in Russia. I was stationed at the front in the Ukraine."

More questions. I stuck to my story telling myself over and over again to stay calm and to think before answering any question, and to avoid saying anything that could be construed as a confession to any kind of crime, however obscure. At the end of that second interrogation I was again taken back to my bare-floor building.

Unbelievably, the same thing happened on the third night. I began to surmise that my interrogators were Soviet secret police, who were looking for any pretext to send Germans to a prison in Russia. This time they asked more about my recent activities in Germany. Perhaps they suspected I was a member of the Gestapo, or was some other Nazi official because I was not in uniform. I was worried they would not give up until they found a reason to send me to Siberia. I hoped the conspicuous lameness of my arm would make my captors judge me as being unfit for hard labour in a Siberian gulag or an underground mine. I understood that this could turn into a very long game, to try to wear down my resistance.

Once again there were no threats or violence as I stuck to my story.

Once again they returned me to my building after the interrogation.

I continued to fake the lameness of my right arm wherever I went about in the camp, just in case one of my interrogators saw me. Most of the men in the barrack with me were also taken out and interrogated, one after another.

We received very little food—only one meal per day, near noon, consisting of potato and/or cabbage soup, with one small piece of rye bread as hard as wood. The soup usually had some kind of greasy meat in it that tasted terrible. Some of the men supplemented that meal with raw potatoes that had just been dumped into a large storage bin. Others had discovered raw rhubarb growing in patches near the fence at the back of the complex, which they gathered and ate. Many of the prisoners became sick with dysentery. Fortunately my system seemed to be capable of digesting just about anything, but I had a difficult time swallowing raw potatoes, as they seemed to constrict the passageway in my throat. It surprised me that my body would reject any kind of food, as I expected to be able to eat almost anything edible if hungry enough.

We may not have been deliberately mistreated, for it seemed the Russian soldiers did not fare much better for food and amenities than we did. In fact, they sometimes shared cigarettes with their prisoners. Most of the time the guards just ignored us completely.

After about a week in Döberitz I wished we could have had a shower or a bath, or at least been given the chance to wash. There had been no opportunity to clean myself since I left Wittenberg almost a month ago. The interior of our barrack smelled terrible. I also wished the food allocation would improve. The very meagre rations were beginning to tell on my waistline, which was already thinner than it had ever been. I tightened my belt another notch. Only sleep relieved the hunger pangs in my gut.

Whenever outside my barrack I surveyed the compound in an effort to discover a potential method of escape. Even if I did not end up in a Russian labour camp, I still might starve to death, or die of dysentery or something worse. The memory of the countless prisoners I had seen wasting away in that makeshift prison camp in Russia in 1942 now haunted me. My fear of ending up like them verged on paranoia. I was convinced that the longer I stayed in Döberitz the worse things would become.

From brief conversations with other prisoners, I concluded they had very little interest in trying to escape. Most of them were of the opinion that it was only a matter of time before the war ended and we would all be released and allowed to return to our homes. I considered that opinion a bit optimistic and perhaps just wishful thinking. Who knew what would happen, even after the war's end? In my opinion it would be foolish to trust the Russians to let us go. The soldiers who had captured us seemed like decent human beings, but who knew what kind of thugs the occupation governors might turn out to be?

My barrack was near the outside edge of the camp, about thirty metres from the chain-link perimeter fence. Even with three strings of barbwire on top, I presumed it could be scaled, provided you could do it while out of sight of the guards. There were large lamps about fifty metres apart all along the fence. The guards were stationed about one hundred metres apart, just outside the fence. Each guard usually stood at his post or paced slowly back and forth, probably bored to distraction. None of them looked particularly alert. Still, I took them very seriously, as each one carried a rifle and an automatic, and surely had orders to shoot anyone they did not recognize.

A few days later I was lying on the floor close to the door of my bare barrack late in the evening, almost asleep, when the door opened and a young Russian officer leaned into the doorway. He briefly looked around, and perhaps because I was the first to catch his eye, motioned for me to follow him, which I did. I had no idea what would happen, but was not afraid. He had smiled politely and there was nothing intimidating or suspicious about his behaviour. We walked along the fence until we came to a large gate that was guarded by a lone sentry. He led me through the gate and, just outside the compound, we entered a small building that had probably been a commandant's residence when Döberitz was an *Arbeitsdienst* camp.

Inside there were two other Russian army officers, sitting at a table eating a meal. They looked up at us when we entered and greeted us in Russian, with a smile. To my immediate relief, they were not the ones who had interrogated me the previous nights. The building contained two more rooms at the back, probably bedrooms.

The officer who brought me pointed to three pairs of leather boots by the wall, with shoe polish and brushes beside them. They obviously wanted me to clean and polish their boots. My instincts told me that they were reasonable people and I did not need to feel afraid. I did not bother to exaggerate the lameness of my right arm; however, the wound had left my hand with only limited function, and that was probably obvious. I cleaned and polished the boots to the best of my ability, all the while the smell of the stew they had been eating tormented my empty stomach.

After I finished the last boot, one of the officers motioned to have me sit at the table and then gave me a bowl of stew with beans, potatoes, and meat. I was dumbfounded, but did not waste a moment accepting it. I tried my best to appear composed but was so hungry I probably wolfed down that meal in seconds. I was ecstatic. It tasted absolutely wonderful. In that prison food was the most precious of rewards. I had lived with almost constant gnawing hunger pangs since being captured. After finishing my meal the officer who had brought me took me back to my barrack. He was quite polite during the entire time and even said what I assumed was "good night" in Russian when he left.

The next evening the same thing happened. Judging by their manners and mannerisms, as well as the tone of their conversations, I deduced that these young Russian officers were well-educated, cultured, and quite obviously decent human beings. Because they had fed me, they were saints in my eyes.

In spite of the reassurance that Russians can be nice guys, I kept looking for some means to escape. The longer we stayed the more I was sure we would not be released. Even if the soldiers running the Döberitz camp were well-intentioned souls, there was no reason to trust the Russian government. Regardless of the other prisoners' opinions, or what the guards told us, I did not believe we would be allowed to return home. I was convinced the Soviet leaders wanted all captured German men to work in Russia, like slaves, as part of the reparations that were sure to follow the war. Stern reparation payments had been required of Germany after the First World War and there was no reason to believe it would not happen again. So I kept alert for an opportunity to escape.

30 "The Russkies Are Coming"

IN THE MEANTIME . . . Gisela was not in any hurry to leave her temporary quarters in Pratau. The American occupation troops were a reassuring presence that would keep her and the inhabitants out of danger, as she assumed things would now settle down to a protracted occupation by American forces. She felt comfortable in obeying the prohibition against civilians using the roads that had been issued by the American Command. Her host was gracious and friendly, and she socialized with her and her two daughters. There was no reason to feel compelled to continue her journey to Michelau right away. So, on May 3, 1945, Gisela was still in her temporary quarters on the west side of the Elbe.

On that morning she was awakened by the sound of truck motors. Looking out the window with one of the other girls of the household, they saw a truck convoy leaving the village, full of American soldiers. Some of the GIs whistled and waved at the girls in the window.

"Where are you going?" she yelled.

Through the din she eventually distinguished two statements. "We're leaving. The Russkies are coming."

"What?" she yelled in disbelief. Maybe her interpreter friend had been right after all? She quickly got dressed, packed her knapsack, and prepared to leave immediately, destination Michelau.

The Americans had set up checkpoints every few kilometres, at almost every settlement, but she felt confident that any remaining troops would not show any interest in one woman on a bicycle. She believed the authorities were only looking for soldiers. Still, it was better to avoid the guards, so she continued along country roads, always heading in a southerly direction.

In spite of the prohibition against travel by civilians, the roads were full of refugees and she always travelled in a group to keep her precious bicycle from being stolen. Gisela usually walked her bicycle on the road to Michelau, rather than rode, because most of her fellow travellers did not have bicycles.

Each evening a designated spokesman would ask a farmer if the group could spend the night in the barn. One night an elderly farmer came into the barn and gave the group of hungry travellers some hot boiled potatoes. She marvelled at how kind and generous people could be during times of adversity.

On one of the mornings on the road the band of travellers awakened to the news that the war was over. It was May 9, 1945. There was no celebration, no emotional expressions—no dismay, no joy, not even relief, among the band of refugees. They just looked at each other. "What now?" Gisela said, more as a statement expressing the futility of all the nation's efforts during Hitler's reign than a question about Germany's future.

She arrived in Michelau a few days after the end of the war. Turko, Gustel, and Anna and her two boys were at home. Everyone sympathized with her having to flee her home, leaving all her possessions, and especially her mother, behind. By then everyone believed the rumours that most of Prussia east of the Elbe River, including Brandenburg, would remain in Russian hands as part of the armistice agreement between the victors of the war.

Gisela hoped that I had not been captured by the Russians. She too believed the common rumour that all German prisoners of war captured by Russian troops would end up in Siberia. She told the family about meeting Albin's military messenger in Wittenberg and how ironic it was that they had missed each other by so close a margin. Gisela feared for her mother and for me, as she did not know what was happening in Brandenburg.

A few days after arriving in Michelau, Gisela went to the housing bureau in the *Rathaus* to register for living quarters, as it was too crowded at Turko's house. She made no headway with the old attendant, until, in exasperation, she said, "Don't you want to know my name?"

"Of course," he replied, with routine politeness.

"Gisela Gagel," she replied.

"Gagel?" He perked up right away.

"Hartmann's Albin's one," a co-worker said. "Turko's daughter-in-law."

Suddenly things changed, and she was treated like family. "Don't worry, Frau Gagel, we will find you something nice."

By coincidence, an old farmer friend of the Gagel family, whom everyone in Michelau called *Der Alte Heiner* (The Old Heiner), happened to be in the office at the time. When he heard the name Gagel mentioned he immediately took Gisela aside by the arm. He told her he had a spare room in his house and would rather have Albin's wife get it than some stranger.

Gisela moved into that spare room the next day, in the same farm-house where I had worked as a boy.

During those days by herself in Michelau she waited for news about me, praying that I would return. She had not received any letter from her mother, so she hoped that Julchen was unharmed. She hoped that I had not been captured by the Russians. She did not know whether or not I was even still alive.

31 *"Voiena Kaput"*

A ROUSING CHEER SUDDENLY REVERBERATED through the Döberitz camp. My curiosity aroused, I took a chance and opened the door to our barrack. Looking out I noticed that the guard who usually stood near our barrack door was nowhere to be seen. The guards outside the fence were also not at their posts. Then I heard music. Music? Two Russian soldiers came into our building and shouted *"Voiena kaput!"* obviously jubilant. The Russians were celebrating, complete with boisterous singing and lots of drinking. Germany had surrendered, and the war in Europe was officially over. It was May 8, 1945.

The Russian guards were now acting like they were our long-lost buddies — friendly, sociable, jovial, handing out cigarettes to the prisoners, offering them swigs out of their vodka bottles. It was an incredible sight to see my fellow prisoners, most of whom were terribly thin, unshaven, dirty, smelly, and ragged-looking, acting as if they were attending a neighbourhood soiree. A few men in our barrack could understand and speak Russian well enough to carry on conversations with the guards. The Russian soldiers were saying that we would soon all be released and allowed to return to our homes. I think the guards and most of the prisoners actually believed that.

I certainly did not believe it. What I did believe was that the occasion might provide an opportunity to escape, and tonight would be my best chance to do so. If they partied hard enough, and especially if they all became drunk enough, the guards might just relax their vigilance long enough for me to slip out unseen. I asked around among the other prisoners if any of them would be willing to join me in an escape attempt. Most showed no interest, seemingly convinced they would soon be released. Maybe they were just too afraid of being shot if they were spotted trying to escape or if they were caught in Russian-occupied territory. Many were too emaciated or debilitated from previous wounds or dysentery to make capable fugitives.

Finally two older guys agreed to try to escape with me. Both were soldiers but, like me, were in civilian clothes. One had an old wound in his right leg just above the knee, which had not yet healed completely. He said it was just a flesh wound and really did not bother him, even though he limped noticeably when he walked.

After nightfall the singing and drinking were still going strong. The door of our barrack remained open, and there were still no guards to be seen at their posts. When it was completely dark, probably around 11 p.m., the three of us agreed it was time to leave. I told them to wait at the front door for my signal. I stepped out the door, edged toward the corner of the building closest to the fence, looked around and, seeing no guards, waved to my two cohorts to follow me. We walked quickly away from the barracks over to the fence. I resisted the temptation to run and told the other two to walk with a steady pace. If the guards spotted three men running it would have appeared much more suspicious than three men walking.

With repeated furtive glances over our shoulders, we followed the fence toward the gate I had seen during my brief career as a boot polisher. We were careful to avoid the boot owners' quarters. We encountered no one during the walk to the gate, which to my amazement was unlocked, and we simply walked out of the camp. There were no more fences and no sentries outside the compound. I was still wary, as there might be guards posted outside the camp perimeter.

When we reached the cover of a hedgerow beside a road we took our bearings. Judging by the road signs we had passed during our march to the camp, I knew roughly where we were. I believed that Döberitz was just north of the railway tracks that led to Magdeburg, a city on the banks of the Elbe River toward the west. My plan was to find the railway line, which I figured was nearby to the south, and follow it westward until we reached the Elbe. The last information any of us had was that the other side of the river was occupied by the British or perhaps by the Americans, at least by occupation forces from the free world. Both my companions agreed that the other side of the Elbe River held out the best promise of freedom.

We set off, moving quickly and deliberately. We tried to avoid open ground, which was difficult, as the countryside was generally flat, with extensive pastures, meadows, and even some marshy areas, but with enough patches of trees and hedgerows and other cover to help avoid being detected. We looked back repeatedly for the first hour or so, but did not see anyone following us.

Within an hour we found the railway tracks. What a relief. It meant my reckoning was correct. The tracks were on top of an embankment, elevated about two metres above the surrounding terrain.

After a few minutes' walking westward along the tracks we noticed light from a window up ahead, close to the tracks. We cautiously approached what turned out to be a signalman's shack at a road crossing. Under normal circumstances it would have been occupied by a signalman whose job it was to lower and raise the traffic barriers when a train came by. Judging from the rust on the tracks, there probably had not been a train along here for quite a while, possibly weeks, so the light in the window made me assume there were Russian soldiers inside. We made a wide detour around that potential pitfall and returned to the tracks when we considered ourselves safely back in the darkness out of sight of the shack.

We walked for hours, until just before dawn. We talked very little, and only in whispers, fearful of attracting any attention. We were in the middle of fields of standing wheat beside the track. It was not tall enough to hide in, so we headed for a line of weeds and bushes that marked a drainage ditch. We hid in the box culvert where the drainage channel ran under the railway tracks, where we had a good chance of not being seen during daylight.

There was just enough space in our hiding place for us to rest most of that day. Once in a while one of us would look around just to make sure no one was approaching. Toward evening we surveyed the area to get our bearings and to help plan our next move.

There was a village a few kilometres away, and as soon as it was dark enough to risk leaving our hiding place we headed toward it. We could tell there were people there, as many windows showed lights on, but could not tell if there were any soldiers among the civilians. I told the other two to stay put as I went to the door of the nearest house, took a wary look around, and knocked. An elderly man opened the door a crack and peered outside. He looked at me very apprehensively until I spoke to him in German, telling him that we were three fugitives trying to get home. He was relieved to discover we were German and not Russian, and invited us in. I signalled my two companions to come out of their hiding place.

Inside the house the man introduced us to his wife, who offered us coffee and bread with jam, which tasted absolutely magical. They were very friendly and genuinely happy to see us, but advised that we had better not stay too long because the Russians had already searched their house and property twice before. They told us that during the searches the soldiers had not been violent or abusive, but they had taken their watches and their jewellery. They had also confiscated most of their food. He had not been arrested because he was far too old to be in the army.

The old couple had hidden some smoked sausages, as well as a large bag of flour, under some junk in their barn, to prevent it from falling into the hands of the Russians. When we left that night the old woman handed me a pouch into which she had put one of their precious smoked sausages and a loaf of bread. We thanked them wholeheartedly for sharing their precious food with us. "Never you mind," he said. "I hope someone else will be kind to our son, wherever he is." They wished us good luck, and we were on our way again.

We returned to the tracks and continued westward. After hours of walking, we had made good progress and I became increasingly optimistic about our chances of reaching the Elbe in a few days. The Russians could not be everywhere, and there were still German civilians who were prepared to help us. As we continued along the tracks we approached other railway crossing shacks on the way, always making wide detours around them. As dawn began to light the eastern sky we hid in a clump of willow trees that grew along the edge of a watercourse beside the tracks. We ate our sausage and bread and then slept for most of the day. We resumed our westward flight at night, still following the tracks. We made detours around all villages and very deliberately avoided a town large enough that we were sure must be occupied by a garrison of Russians.

The dawn of our third day as fugitives found us on the tracks, out of sight of any houses or people, in the middle of extensive meadows. I felt nervous about being so conspicuous, but as it became light I began to relax somewhat as there was no evidence of people anywhere. There were no large villages in sight and no signs of any military presence at all. We were about half a kilometre away from a woodlot. As the meadows on either side of the tracks offered no safe hiding places, we agreed to head there as quickly as possible, figuring it would be safer to hide there for the rest of the day.

A herd of cows was grazing in the meadow beside the tracks. We had eaten all the sausage and bread the previous day, and I certainly felt hungry. Perhaps the cows were an opportunity. We decided to risk being seen in the daylight for the possible reward of some fresh milk from one of those cows. Hunger pangs are a powerful motivator. As with many similar situations, it is easy to become careless if things go too well for a while, and things had gone very well for us since our escape. We decided to try to corner one of the cows and milk her.

We left the tracks and headed through grasses and weeds growing on the sides of the railway embankment which were almost a metre high. Suddenly, two Russian soldiers stood up right in front of us. They were armed with rifles and definitely too close for us to try to run away. For a few moments nobody moved. We just stared at each other. The young soldiers appeared as surprised to see us as we were to see them. My mind raced to devise some clever ploy to convince them that we were actually supposed to be there. We tried to talk to them, but they just ignored what we said, or more likely they did not understand German. Then the agonizing realization sunk in that I was a prisoner once again. I felt so stupid. I should have known that where there were cows, there would be cow tenders. How could I have let myself be lulled into travelling during daylight, let alone chasing a cow like some silly schoolboy?

One of the soldiers motioned with his rifle for us to get moving and escorted us to the woodlot we had seen in the distance, the same woodlot we had decided to spend the day hiding inside. When we reached it I was surprised to find it was occupied by an entire company of Russian soldiers. There must have been over a hundred troops, and it was obvious that they had been camped there for days. There were tents, a mess kitchen, and rough-hewn camp tables. I could not understand why they would camp here in the woods rather than occupy some of the houses in the nearby villages, especially since the war was over and the woodlot could not possibly have had any strategic significance.

At one of the wooden tables there sat four Russian soldiers, including one officer who motioned for us to sit down across from him. The officer was probably in his mid-thirties, tall and clean-shaven. He sent one of his men away to fetch another soldier who spoke German. My two companions looked old enough that they could have passed for civilians, especially since they were unshaven, dirty, and dressed in shabby civilian clothes. But I was twenty-seven years old and, in spite of my appearance, they must have known that I was a soldier.

I immediately went into my dysfunctional hand routine that may have saved my hide in Döberitz. When the interpreter arrived and asked me what we were doing here, I repeated much the same story I had used in Döberitz. The officer listened politely and acted casual and friendly, more like we were fellow travellers than escaped prisoners. He asked each of us who we were and where we were going. We introduced ourselves and told him we were heading for our homes now that the war was over. None of us carried identification papers and, to my surprise, he did not ask for any. I gently removed the picture of my wife from my vest pocket and showed it to the officer. The officer looked at the picture and smiled. The interpreter explained that the officer was also married and had a family with two young children waiting for him back home in Russia. He then called over one of his men and gave him some instructions. The man then walked toward a tent in the woods.

The interpreter said that we had no need to worry. I was still suspicious that his congenial manner might be a trick. I asked him if we could have something to drink and, ironically, he gave us some milk.

When the officer's man came back I thought we were done for. He was carrying a spade and two shovels. Not knowing what the Russians would be thinking or what orders the officer had to contend with, or if he had just changed his mind, I had no idea what to expect from them. When he handed each of us a shovel a horrifying image of us digging our own graves flashed through my mind!

The interpreter must have noticed my anxiety. He laughed and then explained that we should carry the shovels with us to make it look like we were on a work detail. If we were to be stopped by any authorities we could tell them we are on an assignment to bury some dead cattle. When we got up to leave the officer wished us luck on our way home.

I was quite sure those Russians had not believed our stories about being discharged, but perhaps he had felt sorry for us, or perhaps he knew that they already had too many German prisoners, or he just thought it was unnecessary to detain three more fugitives when the war was already over. Whatever his reasons, I was grateful and unbelievably happy to be released. That act of kindness left a lasting impression on me. That chance meeting with that decent man reaffirmed my faith in human nature, and left me with a sense of respect for Russians that has remained to this day.

We again walked westward along the tracks and after a few kilometres saw people in the distance. We immediately went into hiding again until nightfall, not wanting to take any more chances. Next time we might not be so lucky. I promised myself never again to be so stupid and careless. We slept the rest of the day in the tall weeds beside the railway embankment and were on our way again when it was dark enough to avoid being seen.

It was probably close to four in the morning when we saw the outline of the railway bridge across the Elbe River in the pale moonlight, perhaps a hundred metres distant. We left the tracks and headed across the field toward the flood-control dyke that ran along the riverbank, downstream from the bridge. The dyke was simply a long, grass-covered, earthen dam that ran parallel to the river, about four or five metres high on average. It was just like the dyke I had helped to construct along the Danube six years earlier.

The silhouette of the railway bridge crossing the river could be seen from where we were. The bridge was collapsed in half, with the broken ends of the central sections resting on the bottom of the river. The steel trusses and support beams along the sides and top of the bridge were bent but still connected, so it might have been possible to cross the river by walking along the top of the beams along the sides of the bridge. That was not an option though, as there had to be sentries guarding it. Sure enough, as we got a little closer soldiers could be seen moving about in a lighted wooden shack near the end of the bridge. They made no attempt to conceal their presence. I suspected that the sentry post was too conspicuous, and may have been a deliberate strategy to lull would-be escapees into thinking they were the only guards around. There could be sentries posted along the dyke itself, perhaps stationed every few hundred metres, assigned to watch out for Germans trying to escape across the river. If we could cross the dyke and reach the river's edge without being spotted, odds were good that we could swim safely across to freedom.

We reached a farm fence running roughly parallel to the dyke and followed it away from the sentries on the bridge. A few hundred metres downstream we turned toward the river and cautiously approached the dyke. Even though there were no signs of them, I was convinced that sentries would be hiding somewhere on the dyke. We crossed the fifty metres or so of potato field from the fence and then, fearing that our silhouettes could be spotted in the moonlight, we crawled on our hands and knees up the grass-covered slope to the top of the dyke. I moved slowly, trying not to breathe too loud, alert for any sign of danger.

From the top of the dyke the river was just barely visible about two hundred metres in front of us. The bank was dotted with the faint outlines of bushes and trees, which might provide some cover. Between the dyke and the river's edge was open meadow, with almost no opportunities for concealing our movements. There was nothing else for us to do but crawl across the top of the dyke. When I figured we could not be seen from the other side I stood up, and we three then walked quickly and steadily across the grass, as if we had a purpose for being there. I could feel my heart beating in my chest as we reached the river.

The water was calm and black. I knew the current in the Elbe was slow-moving, slow enough that there was no danger of being swept away. It was probably two hundred metres across to the other shore from where we stood, but it was difficult to judge the distance in the darkness. It was still dark enough to swim across without being noticed, so I suggested to my two companions that it would be easier to swim if we took our heavy clothes off. We would meet on the other side of the river.

A voice entered my head, which at first did not register, or perhaps I subconsciously tried to ignore it. It sounded like, "I can't swim."

"What?" I turned to face the voice.

"I can't either," another voice said. "At least not strong enough to cross such a wide river."

This was unbelievable! What a time to tell me! How were these two idiots expecting to get across the river? I was furious, but I kept my feelings to myself. Here was a situation similar to many I had experienced before. I was in command again and my two subordinates were depending on me to see them through this predicament. I was a good swimmer and knew I could make it easily across the river on my own, but the sense of comradeship that had been instilled in me as a soldier made it impossible for me to abandon my mates. Compassion and assistance to any comrade in need is an inviolable obligation, as a soldier unquestioningly shares dangers with a fellow soldier, even at the risk of his own safety. So we walked along the shoreline searching for a boat, a timber, or anything that would float enough to enable them to make the crossing. We must have searched about three hundred metres of shoreline with no success.

I was still under the assumption that the Russians, besides guarding the bridge, would have posted sentries along the dyke itself but not along the river's edge. As we approached one of the many clumps of trees and bushes that grew along the water's edge, two Russian soldiers emerged, both armed with rifles. My two companions did not move, but I immediately bolted along the riverbank in the direction of the bridge as fast as my soccer player legs could carry me. I did not dare to run toward the dyke, since that would have meant crossing open terrain.

As I ran I glanced behind me a few times and did not see anyone chasing me. Perhaps they had not even seen me turn and run? I noticed with some alarm that visibility was rapidly improving with the coming dawn. I stopped running when I reached the bushes where we had originally intended to cross the river, quickly tore off my jacket, shirt, and shoes, and stepped off the bank into the water. Suddenly, I felt something hard and cold strike the top of my shoulder and heard a Russian voice right behind me yell, "*Rooki wehr!*"

I hesitated for a moment. I was so close! Alternative courses of action flashed through my mind in a blinding flurry. Part of me wanted to just go for it, jump into the water and take my chances. The more sensible part decided the risk of being killed at such close range was too great, especially since it was now light enough to see clearly. I turned around slowly and looked straight into the barrel of a rifle. A young soldier was standing right behind me on the shore, pointing his rifle at my head. With the little bit of Russian I knew I implored him with "*Nyet, Tovarish!*" (No, friend!) and lifted my hands high over my head. He looked very shaky with that rifle in his hands. He could have shot me on the spot. He motioned for me to get out of the water.

I was annoyed with myself for not having heard him approach. Perhaps my heart had been beating so hard it had drowned out his footsteps, or perhaps he had been hiding in the bushes near my intended departure spot and had just stood up to catch me. Whatever, he had me.

This was the fourth time I had been captured, and each time I had come out of it. This time I figured my luck had run out. Feeling absolutely dejected, I was headed back into Russian bondage.

32 *Gulag Hohengöhren*

VERY SLOWLY I CLIMBED OUT OF THE WATER. The Russian soldier did not let me put my other clothes and shoes on, or even pick them up. He just said something in Russian and motioned for me to move. A rough prod from the end of his rifle underscored the immediacy of his orders. At gunpoint he escorted me back to the sentry post in the bushes. My former fellow fugitives would not look me in the eye and just kept their heads down. They knew it was their fault we were prisoners again. It was no use being angry; the opportunity to escape had passed.

One of the sentries escorted the three of us across fields and along the road to a nearby village. I was shivering in the morning cold, wearing nothing but my wet pants, and craved for the sun to rise high enough in the hope it would warm me.

Still freezing cold, we reached the village of Hohengöhren very early in the morning. As we entered the village we saw Russian soldiers about, many gathered in the street in front of one of the houses. We were hustled through the iron gate of the yard wall and up to the house. Two Russian sentries stood at the door. We were shoved inside, pushed against the far wall of the foyer, and left to wait. Our guard went into what I guessed was the commanding officer's quarters. Through the open door I could hear Russian voices.

After a brief wait our guard came out and waved us inside. There were half a dozen Russian soldiers in the room standing in front of a table at the far side. An officer was sitting behind the table, attended by other soldiers, all engaged in an animated discussion. The officer looked up and gave us a cursory glance. He had a quick exchange with our guard, perhaps trying to decide what to do with us. I was worried we would end up in another prison camp, the unpleasant memories of Döberitz still fresh in my mind. The officer then gave an order to the guard, who turned and waved us outside into the front yard again.

Once outside we were handed over to another Russian soldier. He was strikingly ugly, with very short black hair, a wide bulbous nose with upturned nostrils, small dark eyes like a pig, and what looked like two warts on his forehead. He was sitting like a big lump on a huge brown horse. From his expression I knew immediately that we were now in the custody of someone not burdened by any humanitarian notions. He did not even bother to get off his horse; he just pointed toward the gate and motioned for us to get moving, emphasizing his intentions with a kick to the back of one of my fellow prisoners. He herded us out through the gate, down the cobblestone street, and out of the village.

Once again we were driven like cattle along the road. My bare feet were soon covered with cuts and bruises, and began to hurt terribly. My pants were still wet and I was shivering from the cold. Our escort was not the least bit bothered by my plight. Whenever we moved too slowly for him he would shove one of us in the back with his horse or his boot. I was so glad when the sun finally rose high enough that it began to warm me up.

He drove us to another village a few kilometres away. When we arrived we were brought to the Russian commandant's headquarters, which had previously been a pub. There were dozens of soldiers standing around outside. We stood and waited outside the door while our disagreeable guard went inside. Eventually an officer came out with our guard, who pointed a stubby finger toward us. We must have looked absolutely wretched. The officer hardly even looked at us, said something to our guard, and then waved the back of his hand toward us. With that he turned and went back into the building.

Our apocalyptic horseman got back on his mount, pointed toward the street, and we were on our way again. I was sure we were headed for a prison camp. He drove us back along the same route we had taken to get here, back toward Hohengöhren. This time the pain in my feet made the return trip seem much longer than the first. By the time we arrived both my feet were a bleeding mess. Despite the wretched condition of my feet, I was incredibly relieved not to have been marched directly to a prison camp.

Once again we were escorted to the commandant's house. This time we just waited in the front yard while our guard went inside. After a while he came out and once again pointed us toward the street. Not again. This time we turned the other way, toward what I assumed was the centre of Hohengöhren. By now it was probably about ten in the morning.

When we reached the town hall our Russian guard motioned for us to go inside, but did not follow us. Inside we were greeted by an elderly lady behind the counter in the hall.

"Are you here to see the mayor?" she asked.

"I'm not sure," I replied. "We were captured by the Russians and escorted here by an armed guard."

"You look terrible," she said to me. "Do you have any other clothes?"

"No," I replied, almost embarrassed.

"Where is your home?" she asked.

"Michelau, Oberfranken," I replied.

"May I ask your name?" she continued.

"Albin Gagel."

"Just a moment," she said, and went into the adjoining office.

She returned a few minutes later accompanied by a small man wearing thick glasses, who was probably in his sixties.

"This is the mayor." She introduced us very formally, as if we were delegates from Michelau here on official business. Perhaps she had not heard about the war?

He looked at my wretched condition, shook his head, and said, "You look dreadful."

"My apologies for bleeding on your floor," I said, suppressing any sarcastic tone in my voice as much as the pain in my feet allowed.

My most urgent need was to obtain new clothes and shoes, so I politely asked, "Is it possible to get some clothes and a pair of shoes?"

"I think we can help you," he said. He looked me up and down as if measuring my dimensions and then went into an adjoining room. I looked through the door opening and could see racks of clothes and shoes along the walls. I suspected they had been gathered from local homes that had been abandoned by civilians who had fled from the Russians.

The mayor came out with a pair of leather shoes, socks, a shirt, underpants, an undershirt, and a jacket. He was actually very helpful, and even expressed sympathy for my poor feet. I put the shirt on and, after satisfying myself that the rest of my new attire would fit reasonably well, thanked him very much.

"I can take you to your new quarters," the mayor said to the three of us, and went out the front door. "Follow me."

When we stepped outside I expected to be put back in the custody of the Russian horseman, but he was gone. As we walked along the street the mayor chatted with us as if we were long-lost friends. "The Russians appointed me mayor when they arrived a few days ago," he told us. "The former mayor fled across the Elbe before the Russians got here."

I was trying to remain interested in what he was saying, as my common sense kept telling me I might need information to help me escape, but the pain in my feet was so distracting that I probably missed most of what he said.

"Where are the Russian guards?" one of my companions asked.

"Oh, somewhere about. They keep mainly to themselves. They allow us some freedom and normally do not prevent us from walking about, such as to and from the town hall, as long as we don't try to leave the village. The Russian commandant has his office right next to mine."

After a few minutes we approached a large two-storey brick house on the side of the main street of Hohengöhren. "This is the house where you can stay. It used to be the parish minister's residence," the mayor explained, "but he abandoned it as soon as he heard the Russians were approaching Hohengöhren."

"How did he escape?" one of my companions asked.

"A division of German troops went through here just as the war ended and fled westward over the Elbe, across the railway bridge. They took him with them. Him and the mayor. More than half the people in the village are now gone."

"Why did you not leave?"

"I am too old to worry about the Russians. Where would I go anyway? This is my home." As we turned to go through the gate the mayor said, "There are a few German soldiers living here already."

Living? I wondered what that meant.

"Most of them were rounded up by the Russians just recently," he continued. "Make yourself comfortable in your temporary quarters. I don't think you will be here for long. This damn war is finally over and very soon everyone will go home."

That was his opinion.

On the opposite side of the street, behind and slightly to the right of a large iron gate in the wall, I recognized another large old house. It was the Russian commanding officer's residence, where we had already been twice that morning. Two sentries were posted beside the iron gate. Coincidentally, or perhaps deliberately, our "living" quarters were situated right across the street.

When we entered the former parish minister's house it was deserted. "The men are away on work detail," said the mayor. "Find yourself a place to sleep." With that he left us. I got the impression he thought of that house as a hostel and that we were there as guests.

The first thing I did was to look for a place to wash and attend to my bleeding feet. It was too painful to put socks and shoes on. I took my pants off, washed myself and especially my feet in the bathroom sink, and then carefully dressed my feet. After that I found a razor and shaving soap. I was sure whoever owned them would not mind if I shaved. I put on my new clothes and then rejoined my companions. They had found some bread and jars of preserved fruits and vegetables in the pantry. It occurred to me that we three had not eaten in almost two days. Although I was momentarily reluctant to eat food that did not belong to me, the pangs in my stomach overcame any sense of propriety that may have been left over from my pre-war upbringing in social protocol. We wolfed down whatever we found until our hunger was satisfied and then cleaned up after ourselves. I lay down on the couch and put my still throbbing feet up.

My wallet was still in the back pocket of my pants. I took it out and opened it, worried that the picture Gisela had given me in Brandenburg had been ruined by the river. Luckily, it was only slightly water-stained at the top. I cherished that picture, as it was my only memento of my wife. I also thought of it as a good luck charm, convinced it had reminded the Russian officer in the woodlot of our shared humanity and persuaded him to let us continue our journey.

The house had a big flower and vegetable garden in the backyard. Downstairs on the main floor there was a spacious kitchen, a living room, a large dining room containing a big wooden table and chairs, a cosy study with walls covered in bookshelves with hundreds of books, and a clean bathroom with running water and a flush toilet. Upstairs were four bedrooms and a small room containing a wash basin. About a dozen mattresses had been placed throughout the house, including the downstairs living room and study, as well as the upstairs bedrooms.

Late that afternoon the rest of the parish house inmates returned from their work detail, accompanied by two Russian guards on

The picture with the water stain

horseback. There were at least two dozen men, and they did not look like a happy bunch. One man acknowledged our presence. "Welcome to Guesthouse Hohengöhren," he said. The rest of the men just filed in, some flopped onto chairs, beds, or mattresses on the floor, obviously tired. The men got water from the pump in the backyard for the wash basins and washed their hands and faces. One man cooked a big pot of potatoes; others just scrounged around for other food. Most gathered at the table and ate. As the sun set all of them just went to bed. Apparently it was every man for himself at Guesthouse Hohengöhren.

Each of us three newcomers had to find our own space to sleep. As there were so many incumbent prisoners living in a house that had only six beds, every room was already occupied. Most of the men slept on mattresses on the floor. I made myself a bed out of straw stuffed into sacks, and found an unoccupied spot in the corner of one of the upstairs bedrooms. A cloth bag filled with rags served as a pillow. There were blankets enough for warmth at night. Considering some of the places I had slept during the last five years, it was comparatively comfortable.

Since no Russian soldiers had hindered our walk from the mayor's office to our residence, I assumed we were permitted some freedom of movement inside the village. Talking with other "guests" in the minister's house, I learned there was a strictly enforced dusk-to-dawn curfew. There were armed guards posted at the ends of every street leaving the built-up area and a guard outside our front door all night. During the day it would have been impossible to leave the village without being seen by at least one of those guards. So Hohengöhren was a prison camp after all, a *gulag*, as the Russians called them.

During my first night in Hohengöhren I was awakened by the sound of a woman's frightful screaming coming from another house. The image of the fat-faced, ugly guard on the big horse violating some poor woman came to mind. The screaming and crying were repeated a few more times during the night. A terrible rage welled up inside me listening to those screams, as well as a painful frustration at being powerless to do anything about it. It was inexcusable for anyone to prey on the defenceless. What is it in a man's nature that allows him to victimize a woman, to abandon all decency and suppress his normally protective instincts towards women? In my entire experience as a soldier I had never witnessed or even heard of anyone being raped. There had always been an unspoken code among the troops with which I had served and fought that civilians were not combatants, and that innocent women and children deserved all the protection that soldiers could give them. How strange that rules of conduct could be so lax in the Russian army. That heinous torment only happened that first night. It may have been that the Russian commander disapproved and ordered it stopped.

The next morning we newcomers were told we would be kept busy on work detail every day. One man suggested I find a large bag to carry my lunch, gloves, a hat, and whatever else I might need for my work assignments.

"Where do I get these?" I asked.

"In abandoned houses," he answered. "That's where we found most of our food, and the bedding. The previous owners are now refugees and will never need them again."

I carefully wrapped new bandages around my still lacerated feet, hoping we would not have to walk too far. We were assembled outside our front door in a straight line. Two Russian guards arrived on horseback, and one of them counted us before leading us out of the yard. The other guard followed behind. We were led toward the railway bridge I had seen the night before last.

For at least a kilometre along both sides of the road leading from Hohengöhren to the railway bridge on the Elbe, and scattered over a wide area of the surrounding countryside between the road, the tracks, and the flood-control dyke, the ground was littered with the discarded detritus of war. Broken supply wagons, two-wheeled carts, broken field kitchens, many hundreds of various infantry weapons, including mortars and *Panzerfaust*, boxes and boxes of munitions, crates and bags of military supplies, and other assorted derelict debris were lying strewn about. There were even a dozen of the stubby 150mm howitzers, standard German army infantry close-support weapons, near the sides of the road, along with their ammunition limbers. A great many 150mm shells lay on the ground near the guns. Some of the horses that had towed those howitzers were lying dead on the ground, still hitched to their harnesses.

Judging by the sheer volume of abandoned war materiel, an entire division of retreating German soldiers had been pushed to the Elbe by the advancing Russians. They had converged on the railway bridge to cross to the western side. The collapsed bridge would have forced them to cross the river on top of the beams connecting the support trusses along either side of the bridge. There was no way to get wagons, horses, or any heavy weapons or supply materials across the bridge. Not only that, but the German soldiers must have reckoned that they would no longer have any use for their weapons on the other side of the Elbe, so everything that was not essential for survival was left behind. There must have been a desperate skirmish near the bridge before the German troops eventually escaped or were captured. Many of the wagons were wrecked, and the telltale craters left by exploding shells pockmarked the area. Even though there were dead horses, I was happy to see that there were no dead soldiers, although there must have been casualties. The look on my fellow labourers' faces told me the dead had already been buried.

Our first work assignment was to bury the dead horses as quickly as possible, as they were bloated from rot and emitted a disgusting smell. We dug a large pit for each horse, then tied two ropes to its legs, trying to fight off the swarms of flies infesting the carcass and the feeling of nausea from the stench. At least half a dozen men were needed to pull the carcass into the pit. Amazing how huge and heavy a horse really is. A man then climbed into the pit to remove the rope in order to use it again. That was the hardest task to stomach. We then sprinkled lime over the carcass and shovelled dirt over it as fast as possible and packed it down. It was exhausting work under the hot May sun.

When we returned to our quarters we were spent. What was worse was that we smelled of rotting horseflesh. The odour clung to our clothes and seemed to seep into the walls and floors of the house, like a living thing. The stench seemed to permeate the whole house, so that even after washing thoroughly it was impossible to feel clean. It took days for me to get rid of repeated feelings of nausea. I am not sure if the smell ever actually dissipated or we eventually just got used to it. We spent two days on that gruelling task.

After all the dead horses had been buried we were assigned a new chore. If burying rotting horseflesh had been distasteful, our new assignment was downright dangerous. We were ordered to collect the many thousands of munitions left behind by the fleeing army and bring them back to be stockpiled in Hohengöhren. All of the discarded munitions were potentially deadly. Much of it was still in boxes, some stacked in abandoned supply wagons or two-wheeled carts. Many hundreds of mortar projectiles were still in their containers, as well as the familiar metal cases containing belts of machine-gun bullets. We discovered crates containing land mines in some of the supply wagons, and more had been spilled from wagons onto the ground. Most disconcerting were the empty crates we found. The terrifying thought occurred to me that the area, or at least the perimeter of the battlefield, had been mined. There was no indication from the Russians that there was any danger, so we just set to work.

The debris field was concentrated along and near the sides of the main road out of town, but much of the munitions were strewn about in the cultivated fields adjoining the road near the railway bridge as well as in pastures near the dyke. I knew how to handle most of that ordnance, but some of the other men did not. I made sure the men with me knew what they were doing before I let them touch any live munitions; not just for their sake, but mine too.

The collected munitions were put onto wagons and carted back to Hohengöhren. To my amazement, we were ordered to stockpile everything behind the brick wall in the Russian commandant's front yard, just past the gate, about twenty metres away from the commandant's house and right across the street from our quarters! I could not understand why the Russians decided to store that highly dangerous explosive material in the middle of the village, among residences, and especially so close to the commandant's sleeping quarters. We just did what we were told, something we former soldiers were all used to doing.

We took our time, not so much to observe all of the precautions, which were obviously necessary, but because no one felt any enthusiasm for such dangerous enforced labour.

That stressful task took three or four days to complete, during which time the stockpile in the front yard of the commandant's house became larger and larger. When we were finished it was well over a metre high in places, three metres wide, and about fifteen metres long.

When most of the larger munitions and battlefield detritus had been cleaned up, the Russians gathered us up and one of them told us in broken German that anti-personnel mines had been planted on the site, and it was now our task to find those mines and remove them. Just imagine the thrill that news sent through me. Presumably one of the Russian officers had been astute enough to notice the empty mine crates among the debris field.

I tried to remember the lesson about disarming land mines during my initial military training in Grafenwöhr, but it had dealt with a theoretical situation about clearing a Russian minefield in preparation for an attack. That was also years ago, and I knew nothing about finding and disarming the type of mines we might find here, which I assumed were all of German manufacture. Luckily one of the men in our group knew how to disarm land mines. He gave the rest of us a quick lesson on how to find, dig up, and handle them safely, if anything about land mines could be considered safe.

We had no idea how many mines had been buried in the area or their extent, and neither did the Russians. We searched a very wide area, beginning near the road leading from the village to a railway siding inland from the bridge. We had no metal detectors, so we lined up about two metres apart and moved forward on our hands and knees, very slowly, each one using a sharpened steel rod to probe the ground in front of us. One false move and a mine could blow up right in your face. Meanwhile, the Russian guards judiciously kept their distance.

Cleaning up munitions had been dangerous, but removing buried land mines was truly tense and terrifying. We moved forward very slowly, and I soon began to sweat. At first there were false alarms where the inexperienced men thought they had discovered a mine, but it turned out to be a buried stone, or root, or some other harmless item. After a few hours I was beginning to feel hopeful that there were no mines, when one of the men found one. From then on each call of "mine!" brought everyone to a hold-your-breath halt. We quickly decided it was safest to let our expert verify and disarm the mines, rather than try to do it ourselves. He was brought over to every mine we found to defuse it before it was carried away.

After two days of nerve-wracking, sweaty, and painfully slow work on our hands and knees, we had cleared a swath running from the dyke to the other side of the main road leading to the village. Eventually we spent an entire day searching and found no more mines. Our task was complete. I was exhausted from the tension.

Perhaps due to patience and meticulous attention to detail, or just plain luck, no mines were set off and no one was injured. The hundreds of mines we dug up were put into crates and added to the huge munitions pile in front of the commandant's quarters.

It crossed my mind that we three fugitives had only a few nights ago passed through part of that minefield during our failed escape attempt at the dyke. Any of us could easily have blundered onto a hidden mine and been blown to pieces. We had been incredibly lucky.

A few more soldiers arrived after we did, so by the end of my second week in Gulag Hohengöhren, there were thirty-three prisoners living together in the former minister's residence. That meant sleeping four or five men per room.

We were able to get enough bread and potatoes to sustain us reasonably well, which we supplemented with preserved vegetables from local larders and unripe gooseberries from the garden in the backyard. At first we went on foraging trips into abandoned houses where we scrounged for food, but after a while every larder was picked clean. We did our own cooking in our well-equipped kitchen. The horses that had been killed had been butchered and put into salted storage by the Russians. There was so much horsemeat available that the Russians shared it with us. Seasoned with salt and pepper, it was a veritable delicatessen delight.

We even had dessert, made from the unripe gooseberries, mixed with lots of sugar. The Russians had confiscated a barge in the Elbe

River that was transporting tons of sugar in one of its cargo holds, so we were able to get as much sugar as we wanted. One of my more imaginative comrades discovered an innovative use for it. Gooseberries soaked in water with plenty of sugar and left to ferment for a while made a savoury and potent punch, which we were careful to keep hidden from our Russian guards. Although I did not care for alcohol, I tried that concoction anyway. It was sweet and surprisingly tasty.

We quickly learned that eating unripe gooseberries caused serious diarrhoea. Dysentery was universally feared by all soldiers. However, as uncomfortable, distressful, and debilitating as it was, there was a positive side to being afflicted with serious diarrhoea—it allowed a man to take a break from work detail.

After the battlefield detritus had all been cleared away, our next assignment was to cultivate the potato fields. Hohengöhren was a typical rural German village, with the farmhouses grouped around a village centre containing the municipal offices, a church, and most of the commercial establishments, including the pub. The entire community was built in a relatively compact urban form and was surrounded by dozens of small fields that were separated by oxcart trails. Most of the fields were growing potatoes, while others contained wheat, rye, or oat crops. There were some pasture fields for cattle, which were fenced, and a few vegetable plots near the village growing mostly cabbages and carrots. The fields where we worked were all situated well within a kilometre of the Elbe River flood-control dyke.

Early each morning we were led out of the village along an ox trail to the potato fields by our mounted guards, where we worked until late in the afternoon. Each of us took a hoe for cutting the roots of the weeds between the rows of growing potatoes, as well as a canvas pouch or bag with a shoulder strap in which to carry our lunch, and a tin can for retrieving water. We stopped work at noon to eat whatever we had brought in our pouches. After work we returned to our quarters and mostly remained inside the house, or at least inside the yard. We were allowed out to search for food or provisions until dusk. Once a night two guards would come into our house and inspect our quarters, probably just to make sure we were all still there.

Every morning before we left the house for work and again when we returned, the same Russian guard invariably pointed his finger at each of us in turn and made nodding motions with his head, as if counting us. After a few days I noticed that he never asked where anyone was if there were less than thirty-three men, which was often the case. Sometimes one, two, or three men were assigned to work details somewhere other than the potato fields, or they missed work altogether because they were too sick. I suspected our guard did not know how to count. Either that or he just went through the motions, not really caring how many men left and returned with him each day.

I discussed that supposition with some of my companions in the house, partly to confirm my own observations and partly to find out if any of them had any brilliant ideas for a plan of escape. To my amazement, most of them seemed completely uninterested. Because the war was over, most believed that it would only be a matter of time before they would be released to return home. That might be true, but I thought it unlikely. I started thinking about my own escape plan.

If I succeeded in getting out of there I would need some identification papers, so I went to the mayor's office to ask for his advice. Surely there must have been other men in a similar predicament before me? The mayor was sympathetic; he went into his office and sat down in front of an ancient typewriter. With slow, deliberate and faltering fingers, he typed a note on a half page of paper and handed it to me. That typed "document" was entitled *Bescheinigung* (certificate), and stated that I was on my way home to Michelau and that any authorities I might encounter should give me assistance to reach my home. He signed it under the title of "The Mayor," and stamped it with an official-looking stamp.

Reading the *Bescheinigung*, I had serious doubts he had any idea what an official document should look like. That little page looked like no other identification paper I had ever seen before. I politely asked, "Will this be recognized as official identification papers by the Russian authorities?"

He thought for a moment, took back the document, and went into the adjoining office. He returned after about thirty minutes with the *Bescheinigung* and handed it back to me. "There," he said, "that should do it."

Unbelievably, or perhaps cynically, the Russian commandant had made a handwritten translation of the mayor's message on the back of the paper, and signed it. I am sure the commandant had no idea where Michelau was. Considering the circumstances it was probably immaterial

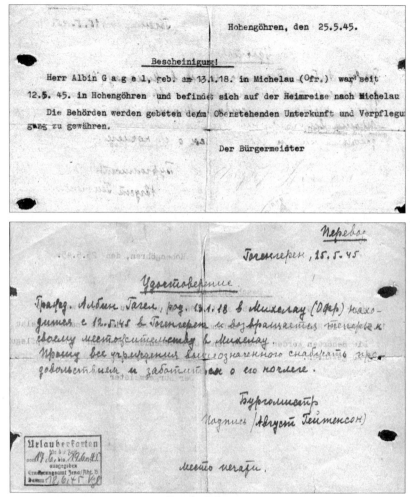

Bescheinigung

anyway, because we were not allowed to leave Hohengöhren, even if we only wanted to travel inside Russian-occupied territory. Whatever, that *Bescheinigung* would have to do. At least I now had a paper in my possession with the signatures of both a German mayor and a Russian commandant. Although I had my doubts, it may be of some future use, especially since the Nazi regime no longer existed.

The daily routine of working in the fields and sleeping in our crowded quarters continued for another week after receiving my *Bescheinigung*. During that time I found it difficult to sustain any efforts to look for a means to escape. There was no sense of urgency, especially since the hard work left me very tired at the end of each day. That, and perhaps the routine, contributed to making me somewhat complacent. Perhaps it was just too much mental effort to devise and implement a plan, especially with the lack of enthusiasm for an escape from my housemates. Perhaps I subconsciously tried to convince myself that we actually would be allowed to return home soon.

It was early June when, one night, a huge clap of thunder startled me out of my sleep. It was close to midnight. A short while later it started to rain and quickly developed into a very severe storm, with repeated brilliant lightning, closely followed by very loud thunderclaps coming at short intervals. I rolled onto my back and tried to fall back to sleep. Suddenly, there was a tremendously loud and protracted explosion! Before I had a chance to react, the roof above my head lifted into the air and crashed back onto the house, farther toward the rear, leaving a metre-wide gap between the wall and the roof! Then the rain pelted down on top of me.

My battlefield instincts immediately took over and I leaped out of my makeshift bed and dove for cover. When no more explosions followed I stood up to look around, feeling slightly dazed for a few moments, my ears ringing from that loud detonation. There was broken glass and pieces of window frame all over the floor of my room. As I went downstairs I was joined by other men who had also been roused out of their sleep. The crash had obviously startled the daylights out of everyone. Every window in the house had been shattered, and there were glass shards, pieces of wood and plaster, furniture, and household items strewn about. We milled about in confusion as we tried to figure out what had happened and what to do next. It occurred to me that the unthinkable had happened. Lightning must have struck the munitions pile we had so neatly stacked behind the wall across the street.

Well! It didn't take long for the Russians to react. A commotion bordering on hysteria broke loose as a dozen armed soldiers rushed into our house and very brusquely ordered us out, pushing and shoving us to hurry along. We were not even given time to get dressed. We soldiers and the rest of the German civilians in Hohengöhren were rounded up and herded into the village square. I could hear a Russian soldier shouting "Sabotage! Sabotage!" We were all lined up in the square alongside one wall. Groups of Russian soldiers rushed into the square and set up three machine-gun crews, their guns pointing at us in the rain.

The scene was surrealistic. It was as if I had been transported into a horror movie, with poor lighting and strange camera angles. Everything seemed out of focus. The light from the telephone pole in the corner of the square illuminated only one side of the faces of the soldiers behind the machine guns, giving them an eerie and menacing appearance, almost inhuman. Everything was bathed in rain, washing out distinct shapes. As the wind shifted, the interplay of light and dark, along with the intermittent flashes of lightning, created a confused and dazzling spectacle that made the scene all the more dramatic.

The far edge of the square was hidden in darkness, to appear suddenly with each flash of lightning, only to flicker out into oblivion. Each time the shapes of the men and machine guns in the square assumed grotesquely magnified proportions. Even the noise of the rain and the thunder could not match my heart pounding in my ears. Each thunderclap exploded in a heart-stopping shock as I thought the machine guns had fired.

After having spent countless days in battle, facing an enemy intent on killing me, it appeared I was going to die because of falsely induced hysteria, after the war was over! That predicament was more terrifying than any enemy attack at the Eastern Front had ever been. Here was a dilemma I had never before experienced during six years of war. I was unarmed, unable to fight or flee from men intent on murdering me, totally powerless to do anything to save myself from imminent death.

For what seemed like hours, but was probably less than one hour, we stood in the pouring rain while heated arguments took place between the Russians and some Germans. Even some of the Russians were arguing among themselves. Then I saw the commandant, which was momentarily heartening, as I assumed he had been killed. He was talking with one of his soldiers who gestured toward the blast site and then toward the sky. He must have realized that it was lightning and not German sabotage that had caused that unfortunate and unbelievable explosion. The situation finally began to calm down. Eventually the guards herded us out of the square and back to our quarters. Soaking wet, but immensely relieved, we returned to our houses.

The terror of that moment, standing helpless in the rain, facing three machine guns and expecting to be shot dead, left an indelible impression in my mind.

Back at our quarters we cleaned up as best we could. The rain was still coming in through the windows, and especially into the upstairs bedrooms through the metre-wide gash in the front of the roof. So much water came in that it was running down the stairs into the front hall, through the kitchen, and out the rear door. We shovelled and swept up the wet debris on the floors, pouring out buckets and boxes of glass shards, wood splinters, wet plaster pieces, and sundry material into a heap in the front yard. We retrieved whatever of our household items we could. Those of us who had slept in the two front bedrooms upstairs tried to find sheltered sleeping areas in other rooms. I moved my soaked sack mattress downstairs to the living room, realizing it could not be dried until morning. None of us slept any more that night. It was not until just before dawn that the rainstorm finally abated.

In the morning we discovered that the two guards who had been posted beside the gate were nowhere to be found. They had been blown to bits. Where the munitions stack had been there was a huge crater half full of muddy water. Fragments of twisted and burned metal, as well as bricks from the former courtyard wall, were scattered about the yard, the street, and the vicinity. Beyond and to the right of the crater, the front of the commandant's farmhouse was completely wrecked. The entire front and one side wall had been blown inward and the roof had been blown right off. The Russians who had been sleeping in the rooms near the front of the farmhouse were injured when they were buried by the collapsed walls, but the room at the rear where the Russian commandant slept had withstood the blast intact. The fact that he had escaped unhurt might have been at least part of the reason our lives were spared.

We spent the rest of the day cleaning up debris in the street and re-pairing our house. One of the men made sure that none of the rafters and construction material in the roof would come crashing down on us. I expected that we would be assigned to repair the roof or even construct a new one as quickly as possible, but after that brief cleanup no one seemed to care any further about the condition of our house. None of the windows that had been shattered upstairs were replaced. Living conditions in the house now became uncomfortable and even more crowded. I slept on the floor of the living room that night. I assumed the Russian commandant procured himself a new residence, in a better neighbourhood.

The following morning everyone was ushered to the town hall where we were registered with the Russian authorities. We had to give our family name, first name, first name of our father, date of birth, home address, and occupation. This cataloguing carried with it a connotation of permanence, which made me feel very uncomfortable. I began to worry that we might yet end up in a Siberian labour camp. Even if I did not end up rotting in a prison, I was well aware that the Russian empire was a totalitarian state and its citizens were not free to live as they pleased or leave if they wanted. I had lived long enough under Hitler's dictatorship to recognize that freedom under the Russian communists would be just as much of an illusion as service in the *Wehrmacht*. I would still be a slave of the state; just the ownership would have changed.

I wanted to get away from a society where armed men had the power to shoot me at their discretion. I wanted to see my wife and home again and was not willing to wait for the Russians to decide my fate. The registration incident made me focus on escaping again. I needed to devise a plan to leave as soon as possible.

There had to be a way to get across the Elbe. Seeing that gateway to liberty so tantalizingly close every day made me certain that it could be done. I would need some kind of flotation device large enough to keep my clothes dry while swimming across the river.

At every possible occasion I looked for an inner tube. Near the mayor's office there was an abandoned mechanic's garage. Although there were no cars being serviced anymore, the garage still had lots of automotive parts lying about, as well as a small derelict truck with no wheels. I made a deliberate effort to investigate the place thoroughly, looking for an inner tube. That evening I had the opportunity to snoop through the junk at the back. As luck would have it, I found an inner tube from a truck tire. Although it was completely deflated, there did not appear to be any holes in it. Perfect. I hid that treasure in my satchel and returned to my quarters, stashing it under my mattress.

The next step was to get an air pump. I asked around among the men in the house, and the following day one of them approached me and quietly said, "I hear you need an air pump."

"Yes," I replied with anticipation.

"I saw a bicycle pump earlier this week, in one of the houses just around the corner. I'll try to find it."

Later that evening he came in with a pump. It worked perfectly. He had a questioning look on his face when he handed it to me. I thanked him profusely, then quietly asked him if he was willing to try to escape with me. He was somewhat hesitant at first. "What do you think our chances are?" he asked.

"I'm sure we can do it," I answered. "What have we got to lose?"

"You're right," he said. "I want to go with you."

"Can you swim?"

"Yes."

"Good." We shook hands. His name was Hans.

I now had two treasures under my mattress.

Now all I needed was a piece of rope to tie to the inner tube so that it could be pulled along in the water. I retrieved a curtain cord from one of the nearby abandoned houses. Perfect once more.

For a while I questioned my own judgement in having someone else along on my escape attempt, especially considering what had happened the last time. Weighing the potential consequences of trying it alone or with others, I decided it was best if others came along in case something went wrong. If I were to be killed trying to escape and one or more of the other fugitives were to survive, he could inform my wife.

I discreetly asked around if anybody else in our house would be inclined to join us and eventually found another man willing to take the risk. He was from Hamburg. He was about thirty years old, and he seemed a very sensible person. His name was Manfred, but preferred to be called Manie. He shared my suspicions about the good will of the Russian administration. Two was enough, as I did not want a massive escape, as every man added meant another opportunity for a mistake. The others in the house appeared convinced that they would soon be allowed to go home anyway. I made up my mind to attempt our escape the next day.

The three of us would-be runaways sat together in the kitchen late that evening, as I explained my plan. By chance our current work detail was in a potato field, adjoining a large wheat field where the grain had already grown to about a metre high. I would hide the inner tube in my satchel, Hans would hide the air pump and rope, and Manie would carry extra food. Toward the end of our workday we would watch for an opportune moment when the Russian guards would not be looking to slip into the wheat field and hide until it was completely dark. We would then crawl over the dyke to the water's edge, inflate the inner tube with the pump, tie one end of the rope to it and the other end to me, pile our clothes on the inner tube, and silently swim across the river.

We assumed we would again be guarded by the same two soldiers, who usually sat in the shade of a tree while we worked. If my assessment of our guard's ability to count was correct, we would not be missed right away. Once we got to the dyke we would have to be on the lookout for guards. I knew about the soldiers that would be manning the railway bridge, as well as possibly guards near the water's edge. We agreed that it was not likely there would be guards on the dyke itself, as we had never seen any guards there during our workdays. It was risky, but a good enough plan to be worth the risk.

The morning dawned bright and sunny. By now it was the middle of June and the weather was warm and pleasant. We stashed our escape tools and lunches into our bags, all according to the plan. The flattened inner tube folded up nicely. As usual, when we were assembled in front of our house the Russian guard counted us before marching us off to work. I watched him carefully and was sure that each nod of his pointed finger was just him going through the motions. I was betting my welfare and the welfare of my two accomplices on the assumption that he could not count.

All day we cultivated that potato field. Hans, Manie, and I stayed reasonably close to each other; not so close as to arouse suspicion, but close enough that we could easily pass a signal to scurry into the wheat field at the appropriate time. I thought it best to wait until late in the afternoon before attempting our move.

Near the end of that workday I gave discreet signals to Hans and Manie that the time was rapidly approaching and pointed toward the wheat field. We nonchalantly worked our way closer and closer to the westerly edge of the potato field. Our guard was sitting on a crate at the edge of the oxcart trail that separated our potato field from the adjoining fields, watching his horse eat grass at the side of the trail. The oxcart trail was raised slightly above the surface of the fields, allowing him to see us easily. The other guard was a long distance away, tending to his horse, perhaps already preparing for the ride back to the village.

The time for our return to Hohengöhren was rapidly approaching. Our guard got up, and I thought he was going to order us to line up. We were not yet in position. He began slowly pacing back and forth along the trail. That was exactly the opportunity we needed. I waited until the second time he turned his back to us and signalled my two comrades to move, now. We walked quickly across the trail and into the wheat field. Twenty seconds later we lay down flat among the tall wheat, about thirty metres from the trail. I looked at the sky and held my breath.

Minutes passed. There was no sign of any commotion from the potato field. More time passed. The sun sank lower in the western sky. Finally, I heard the guard summon the work party to return to the village. We did not move. I waited another half hour before daring to raise my head to check out the situation. In the evening light the three of us were alone. I quickly laid my head down again. It was not yet dark enough and there was no point risking being spotted now. In the middle of June daylight lasted about as long as it can get. I quietly told the other two to stay hidden until it was completely dark. For a while I worried that the guard may actually have counted the men upon the return to our house, but my guess that he did not or could not count appeared to have been correct, as no one came back for us.

After it was totally dark I decided it was about as safe as it could be to leave our hiding place. I stood up. Hans and Manie quickly followed, and we headed for where I figured we would be least likely to encounter any guards while crossing the dyke. We made sure to take our hoes with us, not wanting to leave any evidence of our departure. There was no moonlight to expose us in our flight, or perhaps it may have just been cloudy, which was good. We walked steadily and as quietly as we could up to the dyke, alert for any sounds.

When we reached the base of the dyke, I carefully crawled up to the top and tried to see what lay ahead of us. The light from the window of the sentry post on the bridge slightly illuminated part of the flood plain, so it was possible to see only a few dozen metres ahead. Hopefully the Russian guards could not see well across the flood plain either.

Nothing for it but to head for the river. We went over the top and across the flood plain at a deliberately slow but steady pace. On the off chance we were noticed, three men running would look much more suspicious than three men walking. We crouched low behind some bushes and tried to be as quiet as we could. I pumped up the inner tube and laid some twigs across the tube. We then took off our shoes and clothes and placed them on the twigs. I tied one end of the rope securely around my chest, from right shoulder to left armpit, and the other end around the inner tube. Hans and I then placed the inner tube gently onto the water, being careful not to make any splashing noises and not to spill its precious cargo. It floated perfectly, keeping our clothes high and dry. I suggested that we drop our hoes in deeper water, so that the Russians would not immediately find any evidence of our escape. The longer we were not missed by the Russians, the better the chances of preventing any negative repercussions for the prisoners left behind.

With the rope securely tied to me, I silently slipped into the water and began to swim for the far bank. Hans and Manie followed. I swam straight across with a sidestroke, easily pulling the inner tube behind me. The water was cold at first, but felt better and better the closer I came to the far bank. I oriented myself by keeping the light from the sentry post at about the same angle over my shoulder.

It may have taken ten minutes to swim across the river. I reached the far bank, waded out of the water, pulled the inner tube onto the shore, and untied myself. Taking my clothes from the inner tube, I quickly got dressed. My two companions were nowhere to be seen. They may not have been strong swimmers, so the current could have taken them farther downstream. I headed along the bank in that direction, carrying their clothes and shoes. The sound of splashes and whispers led me to where they came out of the water, each wearing nothing but a great big grin.

We had made it! We were free! Joyous smiles and hearty handshakes all around as we congratulated each other on our artful escape. Just then the church bell in a nearby village rang twelve times . . . midnight. "A lucky omen," Hans declared.

We headed off in the direction of the church bell, then turned south and soon came upon railway tracks. We knew they would eventually lead us to a city, so once again we used the familiar tactic of following the tracks. I was not certain where we were, but assumed we were heading for Magdeburg, which I knew was west of Brandenburg.

After about an hour we approached the outskirts of a city. The first sign we saw read "Stendal." So, it turned out we were actually north of where I had estimated. No matter, we were on the west side of the Elbe, which we all assumed was still American- or British-occupied territory.

We looked for a house with some lights on in the hope of finding someone still awake, but soon gave up. We came upon an open-sided storage shed full of hay in a large yard and decided that would be as good a place as any to spend the night. Now that we were back in civilized society we did not want to disturb anyone so late at night.

As I lay down to sleep I felt elated. For the first time in a long time I felt genuinely optimistic about my future. It was also the first time in almost six years that I felt like a free man, in charge of my own destiny.

33 *The Road Home*

IN THE MORNING, THE OWNER of the house came out to find us sleeping in his storage shed. He looked at us as if perplexed, then asked us if we wanted some food. We accepted eagerly and gratefully. He brought us out some bread with cottage cheese, which was absolutely wonderful.

Having accomplished our common goal of gaining freedom, we escapees now wanted to return to our own homes. Hans would continue westward to a village in Westphalia near the Ruhr. Manie's destination was Hamburg, to the north. He had not been home for almost two years. He had heard about the fearsome bombings that had devastated Hamburg and was worried about his family. I would of course head south to Michelau. We shook hands, wished each other heartfelt good luck, and went our separate ways.

Michelau is at least four hundred kilometres from Stendal, so I knew it would be a long walk. The best possible break would be to find a bicycle; however, I soon discovered that there were no abandoned houses or discarded bicycles on this side of the Elbe. It was British-occupied territory, and the local inhabitants had remained in their homes. After walking a few kilometres I decided to try to beg a ride from a passing motorist heading south.

I eventually heard a vehicle approaching from behind me. By the rattling sound of the motor and the raspy exhaust note, I recognized it as a Volkswagen, the "People's Car" that Hitler had employed Ferdinand Porsche to design as the answer to everyone's automotive transportation needs. I waved my arms to flag it down. To my delight, the car slowed and pulled up right beside me. To my horror, there were three officers inside, British officers. My initial instinct was to run for the woods. As those thoughts raced through my mind the young officer in the front seat leaned partway out the window and said in impeccable German, "I am very sorry, but we are not permitted to take Germans with us."

Astounded by his courtesy, I nodded politely and they drove off. Perhaps only the English would have been so civil. They had not even asked to see my identification papers. The country was destroyed, but apparently civilized society still functioned. Relieved that I would not be detained, I resumed my walk.

As night fell that first day on the road I approached a farmhouse to ask if I could sleep in the barn. The elderly couple who answered the door must have realized the state I was in. As I turned to go to the barn, the lady asked, "Are you hungry?"

Almost apologetically, I said, "Yes." I had not eaten since that morning.

"I can bring you something," she said.

As I piled up some straw to make a bed in the barn, she came in with some boiled potatoes and a cup of milk. I thanked her for her kindness and asked about her family.

"I have two sons. We received a letter from one back in February, but that was the last time we heard anything. I am so worried about them. Why don't they come home? The war is over." Tears were welling in her eyes.

"I was held by the Russians for two months after being captured. There were still thousands of German soldiers in camps."

"The Russians might send them to Siberia, or kill them," she said.

"No, they treated us fine. Your sons are probably in a camp waiting to be sent home. I am sure they will return soon." Perhaps they would? I hoped for her sake they would.

I awoke with a start, frantically searching for my rifle, crouching low to keep from being seen by Russian machine-gunners. As my eyes focused I recognized that it was just a dream. My heart was pounding in my chest. Since that night in the rain in Hohengöhren, terrifying dreams about machine-gunners hunting me in the night had been especially vivid and intense. As I recognized where I was, my terror was replaced with elation. I was free! The dawn was bright and beautiful. I was eager to resume my journey homeward.

I joined up with another traveller also heading south. He was very rough-looking and was still wearing army-issue trousers and his military greatcoat over a newly acquired civilian shirt. He looked a few years older than I and was not a talkative fellow. He had that familiar wary disposition of an experienced soldier. His destination was Magdeburg.

We walked along mostly rural roads, trying to keep our bearing generally southward, for most of the day. We kept looking for anything that might hold some promise of food; however, it may have been too early in the year for ripe fruit or vegetables. My companion gathered some chestnuts from under a tree and peeled one. Most were rotten and impossible to eat. I felt like a wild animal foraging for food.

We made slow progress. He suggested our best strategy would be to follow the railway heading south. Even if we could not ride a train, the tracks would provide the most direct route south, especially through urban areas.

Eventually we came upon a railway siding in the outskirts of a small city, which may have been Tangerhütte, where a locomotive was being hooked to a freight train. We walked along the edge of the yard to reconnoitre the situation from a distance. There were many workers in the yard, and I walked up to a middle-aged man who looked like a railway employee.

"Is that train heading south?" I asked, as if checking the service schedule.

"Where do you want to go?" he asked, seemingly unconcerned about my presence in the siding yard, or my welfare.

"Michelau, Oberfranken, near Coburg."

"Ah, that train will be going south all right, but only as far as the next station. Most of the railway bridges have been destroyed, so you won't get far."

"Is it ready to leave?" I asked.

"In about fifteen minutes," he replied. "Just watch yourself."

My companion joined me and we searched for an open boxcar. There were about two dozen wagons on the train, but all of them had their doors closed. We kept trying each door until the train started to move. Both of us immediately jumped onto two wagons and hung on, being careful not to let the two huge bumpers on the ends of each wagon crush our legs or feet. We clung precariously to the hardware between the wagons.

The train moved slowly and made frequent stops in small towns along our route. Other travellers joined us for short distances, also clinging to handholds on the wagons. We watched the countryside roll by until we eventually reached a town where the train could go no farther, as the railway tracks had been destroyed.

We continued our journey on foot and came upon a canal. We detoured until we reached a pontoon bridge that had been installed across the canal. We could see two British soldiers manning the far end of the pontoon bridge. I was reluctant to cross the bridge, thinking the British guards might detain me because I had no official papers. I did not want to spend any more time in a prison camp, anybody's prison camp.

After nightfall we went back to the pontoon bridge. My companion approached the guard post as stealthily as a cat. No one there. So we just walked across the bridge. We did not see any sentries on the other side. We continued on foot until we reached the city of Magdeburg, where my companion and I parted company.

I travelled along whatever thoroughfare offered the most direct route south—railway tracks or rural roads—stopping at nightfall to beg for food and find whatever sleeping accommodations were available, usually in barns or hay storage sheds. I met many travellers on the roads and sometimes walked a few kilometres with others who were also heading in the same direction.

I had no reason to fear being apprehended while travelling within the British-occupied part of Germany.

Toward evening of perhaps the sixth day of my journey homeward, I approached another of the many small groups of travellers—former German soldiers—coming the other way. As they passed by, one of them said, "You better watch out, there is a checkpoint about a kilometre ahead."

From his demeanour it was obvious the checkpoint was something to be avoided. "Is there trouble?" I asked.

"Over there starts the American occupation zone. American military police arrest everyone they suspect was in the *Wehrmacht* and take them away."

"Where to?" I asked.

"I don't know," he replied. "Probably to a camp."

That was disconcerting. I had not expected any problems in American-occupied Germany. Still, I heeded his warning and decided not to take any unnecessary chances.

"That's good to know," I replied. "Which way do I go now?"

"Go around the checkpoint, through the fields and woods, until you get past the village," he said as he waved his arm toward the south.

"You should not travel alone," he added. "There are many guest workers about who now think they own the country."

The "guest workers," of course referred to the millions of foreign workers in the country, most of whom were former Russian prisoners of war who had been used as labourers in factories, farms, coal mines, and other work camps. The end of the war meant the end of their enforced labour. It was understandable that former prisoners of war might harbour animosity toward their captors now that the war was over and the Nazi authorities were no longer in control.

I carefully circumnavigated the checkpoint, which turned out to be a jeep parked in the middle of the road at the edge of a village, manned by armed American soldiers wearing white armbands and a white stripe on their helmets. It was difficult to believe that the Americans, those champions of freedom and free enterprise, would be rounding up people after the war was over. What reasons would they have to send former soldiers to a prison camp? Until then I was convinced they did not even have camps. Still, it was wise to be cautious. Perhaps I had just deluded myself into thinking, or hoping, that the *Amis* would be friendlier governors than the Russians.

As I continued south the groups of travellers on the roads were constantly changing, as one or another companion took his own route and others joined us. Everyone had the same goal—to get home. People everywhere were kind and helpful. I was almost constantly hungry, but always received just enough food, usually potatoes, to keep me going. By each evening we always made sure there were not more than three travellers seeking sleeping accommodations in one place, as those would be more difficult to find for a large group of rough-looking travellers. It would also be unrealistic to expect a farmer to feed a large group when we begged for food.

I kept a watchful eye ahead and stayed off the main roads, choosing instead to keep to less travelled routes that led through small, out-of-the-way villages. I was always ready to bolt for the nearest woods at the first sign of danger. That could lengthen the duration of my journey considerably, but there was no need to be reckless. I had ended up in trouble every time I let myself become complacent.

We were repeatedly warned by passing travellers about the next American checkpoint. Sometimes we avoided detection because of instinctive knowledge born of experience. That is not easy in Germany, mainly because all roads, including country roads, are an incessant series of curves, often making it impossible to see more than a few hundred metres down any road. However, we often sensed that certain sites ahead would make a likely location for a checkpoint and avoided walking to it. An ideal spot for a checkpoint was usually on the main road near the edge of a town or at bridges. Frequent large detours made it difficult to make much progress. If anyone of our group spotted a uniform everyone immediately scattered for cover. We were constantly wary for signs of what we termed *Ami Bonzen* along the roads, especially when approaching towns and villages, and there is a town or village every few kilometres in rural Germany.

I passed by the city of Halle, and a day later passed a sign that read "Naumburg an Der Saale—4 km," familiar territory. Eventually I reached the hilly and more wooded countryside of Thüringen, which lifted my spirits, as it was beginning to feel like home.

One morning I approached the outskirts of the city of Jena. It was evident that Jena was some kind of headquarters for the American occupation forces, as there was considerable military truck traffic along the roads into and out of the city. A circuitous detour around the city would cost me an extra day on the road. I could wait until night when darkness would help conceal my movements, but there was still a dusk-to-dawn curfew in effect that could be enforced more stringently in cities than in rural areas, so travelling through town at night would be risky. I decided to go through Jena during the day, hoping to become invisible or at least inconspicuous among the crowds. By noon I was in the heart of the city. American jeeps were everywhere. All that activity made me nervous, but by then gnawing hunger pangs began to preoccupy my consciousness. Where to get some food?

"You look lost," I heard a voice beside me say.

Turning, I saw an older man standing beside me on the sidewalk. "Yes, I am, sort of," I replied. "And hungry."

"If you follow me, there is a soup kitchen in the town square, beside the *Rathaus*."

"Gladly," I replied.

We lined up in a long queue at a mobile field kitchen parked at the edge of a cobblestoned square. It was a former army field kitchen, now operated by civilians. After waiting almost an hour we were given a bowl of soup and a piece of bread. Just as we handed back our bowls, a jeep came around the corner and approached the kitchen. Two American soldiers got out and started walking among the patrons. Time to make a discreet exit. My dining companion and I walked as casually as we could toward the nearest door, the entrance to the *Rathaus*.

Inside the entrance hall there were people sitting on benches along the walls, obviously waiting. We sat down. A lady sitting behind a huge desk asked politely, "Can I help you?"

"I'm not sure," answered my companion, completely unruffled. "I seem to have lost my identification papers," he said as if surprised.

"Just a moment," she said, and plugged in the telephone jack.

After a few words into the telephone she politely said to both of us, "Please go up to the second floor."

There we were greeted by a middle-aged gentlemen in a suit, who walked with a pronounced limp. "I'm the city clerk," he introduced himself. "How can I assist you?"

"There are military police outside checking papers, and I have none," my companion told the clerk.

"And you?" he asked, looking at me.

"All I have with me is this *Bescheinigung* I received from the Russian authorities and the mayor of Hohengöhren."

"Very well," he said. "Wait a moment." He called an assistant over who took my companion into another office. "Let me see the *Bescheinigung*. Where are you heading?" he asked as he looked at it.

"Michelau, Oberfranken," I replied.

"You don't have much farther to go, then."

"Why are there so many checkpoints?" I asked. "The war is over."

"They are looking for war criminals." Noticing the perplexed look on my face, he added, "Generals, SS men, anyone who associated with the Nazis, and any former Gestapo. All are now considered war criminals."

That was the first time I ever heard the term "war criminals." What were they going to do? Arrest everyone in our former government and everyone who supported them? All who had a hand in starting the war were criminals. Making war is criminal. Both sides committed terrible crimes during the war, but of course Germany lost the war. I felt no sympathy for members of the Gestapo, and hoped they would all be apprehended and prosecuted as criminals. They had been feared and despised by every citizen in Hitler's Germany.

"I just want to get home and put the war behind me," I said.

"If you're carrying nothing but your *Bescheinigung*, you could be in trouble if they catch you. It will probably take weeks to get you new papers," he said.

"I really don't want to wait that long," I said sincerely.

"That's understandable," he replied. "Perhaps a stamp that says you are on vacation might help." He stamped the Russian side of my *Bescheinigung* with a rubber stamp, then signed and dated it. I doubted a stamp would make the slightest difference to the American authorities if I had to show them my papers; however, I had nothing else.

"Good luck," he said as I left.

After leaving Jena the necessity of avoiding checkpoints along my route had forced my footsteps farther eastward than I had originally wanted to go, so that I was now more east than north of Michelau, somewhere in the Frankenwald region. No matter, I was still free and felt better every day as I came closer to my destination.

I was at an intersection on the outskirts of the town of Kronach, when a truck pulled up right beside me and stopped. I stepped up to the passenger door and asked the driver, "Are you by any chance heading towards Michelau?"

"I'm going to Bamberg, but first I have to stop in Kulmbach."

Perfect, I thought, as Bamberg is on the far side of Michelau. "Could I ride with you as far as Michelau?"

"Why not," he replied. "Get in."

He was a powerfully built man, probably in his late twenties, friendly, talkative, and quick to smile. He was taking a load of lumber to Bamberg. Perhaps he liked company on his long drive. We talked as he drove, mainly about the state of the country.

"What do you think will happen now?" he asked. "Is there any hope for Germany after this terrible war?"

"There's always hope," I replied. "As long as we're still alive, we can rebuild."

"So much has been destroyed."

That was obvious. "It will take time and a lot of work," I said. That, too, was obvious. "Maybe the *Amis* will help Germany recover."

"The Americans?" he said with disdain in his voice. "I doubt we can expect much help from them. I heard a rumour that the *Amis* captured lots of German soldiers who had crossed the Elbe fleeing from the Russians and handed them back to the Russians."

"Really?" I replied. "I was warned to stay away from American checkpoints. Maybe I was lucky not to get caught."

Actually, that news shocked me. Those rumours raised my suspicions about the *Amis* even more. Apparently I could not relax my vigilance, even now when I was so close to home.

We talked mainly about the future, not the past. I had no interest in discussing the war or even thinking about my recent experiences any more, and I sensed he felt the same way.

"I'm just happy to be alive," I said, with heartfelt sincerity.

We rounded a corner coming into the town of Kulmbach and came upon an American checkpoint. There was no time to get out of the truck or to change course. I suddenly felt trapped. The driver stopped the truck. "Good day," he said politely.

The American soldier leaned into the driver's window and asked, in English, what I assumed was, "Where are you going?"

The driver acted as if he did not understand.

"Where are you going?" the guard asked in stilted German.

"Bamberg," the driver replied.

"Papers," he said matter-of-factly.

My companion reached into his vest pocket and showed him his papers right away. My heart started beating faster, as I had no papers, other than the *Bescheinigung*. Not only that, but there was Russian writing on it, so perhaps the American soldier would think I was an escaped prisoner from Russian territory and send me back. My mind raced trying to figure out what to do as I fumbled in my pants pocket as if looking for papers. Do I bolt out the door and run for the nearest alley, hoping to find a temporary hiding place, or just stay calm and hope that the good fortune that had been with me throughout the war had not deserted me?

My companion sensed my agitation. He turned to the guard and casually said, "My mate here left his papers back at the shop."

The American looked sceptical and then said, "Get out!"

To my amazement the truck driver did not move and became downright cocky. "Come on, we don't have all day. We have a job to do. This is my assistant, and I can't unload the damn truck by myself! So let us get on with our job."

My unshaven and dishevelled appearance must have made it obvious that I was not a civilian worker. My fate was once more in someone else's hands. The discussion continued while I sat there looking as dumb and innocent as I possibly could.

"I must see his papers," the guard insisted. "Everyone has to carry his papers with him at all times. I can't let anyone pass without papers."

"We know you are just doing your job," the truck driver said in a charming voice. "We have to get this truck unloaded, so let us do our job. Come on . . ."

The guard paused, then said, "Get outa here," in English and waved us on.

As we drove away I looked in amazement and amusement at the driver. "How did you manage that?"

"I insisted," he laughed out loud.

"That was amazing, quick thinking," I said, also laughing. "Many thanks."

"Americans are people, too," he replied.

What an excellent human being. He really did not know me and had never met me before this morning, yet he risked getting into trouble by covering for me. Adversity seems to breed compassion and assistance for men sharing a common plight, even out of uniform.

Eventually we approached Michelau. I became filled with feelings of anticipation and apprehension. Anticipation for a happy reunion with my family, especially my wife, and apprehension about the safety and health of everyone I loved. "This is it," I told my truck-driving benefactor as we reached the intersection leading to Michelau. He stopped the truck. I thanked him for his kindness and stepped out.

As he drove away, I could see Michelau before me — home! I crossed the railway overpass and headed toward Bahnhof Strasse, toward my father's house. By now my steps were swift and sure, my body feeling as light as air. My spirits soared. It was a beautiful, sunny June day. The flowers in the meadows beside the road appeared more lovely than I had ever seen them before. Birds were singing in the trees. How good it felt to be alive!

My father's house is on the south side of the Main River. The majority of Michelau is on the north side. As I approached the house it looked like the bridge over the Main, just past the house, had been wrecked. So the war had reached Michelau after all. Hopefully that was the worst of it.

When I showed up at the door the first person to see me was Anna, Hermann's wife. Instead of greeting me warmly, she seemed distressed. She blurted out that I should go see my wife and promptly slammed the door shut. Perhaps I had committed the unpardonable sin of returning home before my older brother? No matter, my wife was in Michelau! My most fervent wish had come true.

Tante Gustel screamed for joy at seeing me. She gave me a great big hug and cried. Dear lady. Anna's two boys, Adolf and Richard, politely said hello to their uncle. Turko was overjoyed. He had not heard from me for so long that he was not sure if I was still alive. I immediately asked about Gisela.

"She is here, and well," Turko said. "You better wait here for her; the *Amis* are manning the bridge." He sent Richard to fetch Gisela.

Turko explained that the American occupation troops had arrested all men of military age and taken them away somewhere. They had already taken Hermann, shortly after he had returned home in March. That explained Anna's reaction. I was happy to hear that Hermann had at least survived the war. The last letter Turko had received from Edwin was from a hospital in Jena. There had been no news about Oskar or Karl for months. I was surprised to hear Karl was in the army, as he was only sixteen.

I washed, shaved, combed my hair, and straightened my clothes to make myself look as presentable as I could, then waited. Gustel made me something to eat. "You must be hungry," she said as she hugged me again. She was so right.

"You are a treasure," I said as I wolfed down the plate of potatoes and pickles.

Gisela arrived at Turko's house about twenty minutes later. A wave of joy came over me. I kissed and hugged her with a joy I had never felt before. She had tears in her eyes. She had not heard any news about me for over three months. "When you didn't return right after the end of the war I was afraid you had ended up in a labour camp in Siberia," she said.

"No," I said, "Siberia didn't appeal to me. I had to come back to you."

We spent hours talking in Turko's kitchen. After the euphoria of my return subsided, the happy reunion became tempered by my brothers' absence. Hermann had been the first to return, but after he was taken away by the *Amis*, Turko suspected he had been sent to a prison camp. When he had gone to visit Edwin in Jena, he was no longer in the hospital, so he had no idea where he was now. Karl had joined an anti-aircraft battery in Augsburg. Turko had not heard from him since April. There had been no news from Oskar for many months. Turko was obviously worried about his sons. Gustel was especially worried about Karl, and in my presence made a point of letting Turko know he should never have let him go off to war.

I was astonished when Gisela told me about meeting my messenger in Wittenberg. Had I stayed with Armin on his journey, I would have joined up with Gisela in Wittenberg and possibly could have avoided two months of incarceration. On the other hand, something else and perhaps worse might have happened, so it was better to just be grateful that I had made it home intact.

When Gisela told me she already had an apartment for us, I was surprised and pleased, but I could not accompany her home just yet. The Main River separated my father's house from our apartment in the village on the north side, and the only bridge, thirty metres away from my father's house, had been blasted by the retreating German soldiers just before the end of the war. The Americans had built a pontoon bridge across the river beside the wrecked bridge, big enough to carry trucks, with a checkpoint in the middle.

I still did not have any official civilian papers, so had to avoid the checkpoint. Richard said that it was not always manned. There was a curfew in effect from 9 p.m. until dawn every day, so Gisela returned to the apartment before then. I waited until midnight, when it was very dark. Richard had also said the guard would often leave his post at night because there was no one about. One small checkpoint was not going to thwart me now. I would swim across the Main if I had to.

I approached the bridge very cautiously, stepped down the slope onto the pontoon section, and walked up to the checkpoint as silently as my front-line training had taught me. No one there, so I just continued my walk to the apartment.

When I reached our new home I held Gisela as if for the first time. How good it felt. Her warmth penetrated my entire being, healing the scars inflicted on my psyche by the traumas of the last months and filling my starving soul with love.

I marvelled at how cosy and homelike she had made the place. To my astonishment, lo and behold, there was our furniture, the furniture we had bought in Nürnberg. Gisela took great delight in telling me the saga of the furniture. When she had moved into the apartment she did her best to set up house, but she had practically no possessions, other than what she had carried from Brandenburg in her bag and what we had stored at Turko's house. The only piece of furniture in the apartment was one very old sofa. Fortunately, Gisela found a friend in Aneliese Neckwehr. She had married an SS soldier during the war, Georg Neckwehr, who was one of the most sociable and charming persons you could ever meet. He was not originally from Michelau. Because he was six feet tall and in excellent health, he had been drafted into the *Waffen SS*.

When Georg was apprehended by the Americans near the end of the war he was assigned to an internment camp, processing and discharging German soldiers. Perhaps through his contacts, he had learned of a container stored beside the *Turnhalle*, which had a waybill that included a list of furniture for a "*Leutnant* Gagel." Gisela had repeatedly passed that container but had not taken any notice of it. The waybill was so old it could hardly be read, but the date—July something, 1944—was still visible. That meant it had been sitting unmolested in Michelau for almost ten months. The members of my family knew nothing about it.

Gisela was as much astounded as surprised, as she had assumed that the furniture had been lost or destroyed on the way to Brandenburg. The last instructions the furniture dealer had been given was to deliver it to our home in Brandenburg. That was in August 1944. It had never occurred to her that they would deliver it to Michelau and just leave it there.

There was no key to the lock on the container, so Gisela and Aneliese borrowed a four-wheeled handcart from the neighbour and forced the container open with a crowbar. They unloaded the furniture pieces and carted them one at a time the two blocks to the apartment—two beds, a chest of drawers, two night tables, a clothes cabinet, a kitchen cupboard/cabinet, and a kitchen table with four chairs, completely undamaged and exactly as beautiful as they were when purchased in Nürnberg just after our wedding.

Our little farmhouse apartment was near the centre of the village, not far from the *Turnhalle*. It was across the river from Turko's house, across the street from the post office, about half a block from the church, and just around the corner from the Krone pub. A great location! It had a relatively large kitchen/living area off the entrance hall on the ground floor. At the back, behind the kitchen, was a small bedroom, just large enough for two single beds and a night table. It had been a storage room, with the ceiling only about a metre-and-a-half above the floor,

The author and Albin in front of the farmhouse where we lived in 1945.
Photo taken August 1996.

Gagel Family Faterhaus, *Bahnhof Strasse, Michelau*

so it was impossible to stand up straight. Our mattresses were stuffed with straw.

The toilet was just outside the back door—a two-seater privy, positioned on a porch over the farmer's manure pit. The right side of the privy was reserved for the tenants living in the two right-side apartments of the semi-detached house, and the left for the residents living in the two left-side apartments. It was primitive, but effective; however, it took Gisela a while to get used to the ever-present aroma of fresh cow manure wafting up from the backyard.

All things considered, we were very comfortable. I was ecstatic. After the places I had slept during the past few months, and indeed during the last few years, our tiny apartment was the lap of luxury to me. I never forgot what it was like to sleep in a foxhole at the front, so I appreciated a warm bed for the rest of my life.

I was so pleased that Gisela's flight to Michelau had such a happy ending. Best of all, we were both alive and well, and together again, which was what truly mattered.

It felt wonderful to be home. After so many years away, so many years a prisoner of the *Wehrmacht*, after months as a prisoner of the Russians, and the long road home; after so many hardships, so much strife and toil, it was overwhelming to be somewhere that I could truly call our home. I almost cried with joy and relief. Up until then I had not dared to believe it was real. That modest two-room flat was heaven. For the first time in almost seven years I was free from the demands of warfare. I hardly dared to believe my most ardent dream could actually come true—that Gisela and I could now begin to build a life together.

34 *"The Peace Will Be Worse"*

THE FIRST DAY IN OUR NEW HOME I learned that the American occupation troops had turned the schoolhouse into a garrison and the officers were living in the larger homes of some of Michelau's formerly wealthy businessmen. Still, none of Michelau's residents had been evicted from their homes or confined to their quarters, and there were no work crews labouring under the watchful eye of armed guards. Other than the American soldiers guarding the bridge, the checkpoints on roads leading out of the village, and the ubiquitous jeeps that scurried about, the occupation troops generally kept to themselves. Gisela said she felt quite safe in Michelau.

I did not feel safe. I feared being picked up by the American military police, and for good reason. When American troops had first arrived in Michelau they commanded all German soldiers to convene in the village square for debriefing and to be discharged. Those that went were taken away in trucks and, almost two months later, had not returned. That included my brother Hermann. Radio broadcasts aired nothing informative and there were no reports in the newspapers. The most reliable source of information was the "grapevine." Suspicion born of experience had convinced me that my freedom was still at risk from people representing authority, only the nationality of that authority had changed.

Regardless, a formal discharge was necessary; otherwise, I would continue to be a soldier in the *Wehrmacht* with no official identity as a civilian. No identification papers meant I could not get any ration stamps, which meant no food.

Gisela's friend, Aneliese, told us that her husband, Georg, was one of the staff at the American camp in nearby Frauendorf. He agreed to help me with my discharge. Still sceptical and wary, I crossed the Main after dark and spent the night in my father's house, close to the train station. In civilian clothes, I took the first train to Frauendorf very early Friday morning.

The camp was crowded with thousands of German soldiers waiting to be discharged. Although the American soldiers in the camp were

CERTIFICATE OF DISCHARGE

ALL ENTRIES WILL BE MADE IN BLOCK LATIN CAPITALS AND WILL BE MADE IN INK OR TYPE* SCRIPT.	PERSONAL PARTICULARS	

SURNAME OF HOLDER___ GAGEL

CHRISTIAN NAME___ ALBIN

CIVIL OCCUPATION___ ARBEITER

HOME ADDRESS___ MICHELAU / OBERFRANKEN

DATE OF BIRTH___ 13. JANUAR 1918
DAY, MONTH, YEAR

PLACE OF BIRTH___ MICHELAU / OBERFRANKEN

FAMILY STATUS – SINGLE – Ø
MARRIED
WIDOW(ER)
DIVORCED

NUMBER OF CHILDREN WHO ARE MINORS___

I HEREBY CERTIFY THAT TO THE BEST OF MY KNOWLEDGE AND BELIEF THE PARTICULARS GIVEN ABOVE ARE TRUE.
I ALSO CERTIFY THAT I HAVE READ AND UNDERSTOOD THE "INSTRUCTIONS TO PERSONNEL ON DISCHARGE"(CONTROL FORM D.1)
SIGNATURE OF HOLDER...... *Albin Gagel*

NAME OF HOLDER IN BLOCK LATIN CAPITALS___ ALBIN GAGEL

II
MEDICAL CERTIFICATE

DISTINGUISHING MARKS___ SCARS ON RIGHT LOWER BELLY, RIGHT ELBOW-JOINT

DISABILITY, WITH DESCRIPTION___ PARALYSIS NERVI RADIALIS RIGHT AFTER INJURY

MEDICAL CATEGORY___ POOR

I CERTIFY THAT TO THE BEST OF MY KNOWLEDGE AND BELIEF THE ABOVE PARTICULARS RELATING TO THE HOLDER ARE TRUE AND THAT HE IS NOT VERMINOUS OR SUFFERING FROM ANY INFECTIOUS CONTAGIOUS DISEASE.

SIGNATURE OF MEDICAL OFFICER *Charles J. Mock*
NAME AND RANK OF MEDICAL OFFICER IN BLOCK LATIN CAPITALS___ CHARLES J. MOCK CAPTAIN M C SURGEON

III

THE PERSON TO WHOM THE ABOVE PARTICULARS REFER WAS DISCHARGED ON___ 30 JUN 1945
(DATE OF DISCHARGE)

FROM THE X___ ARMY

RIGHT THUMBPRINT

OFFICIAL IMPRESSED SEAL

CERTIFIED BY
NAME, RANK AND APPOINTMENT OF ALLIED DISCHARGING OFFICER___

Max D. McLaughlin
Capt. Inf.
Adjutant

Ø DELETE THAT WHICH IS INAPPLICABLE
X INSERT "ARMY" "NAVY" "AIR FORCE" "VOLKSSTURM", OR PARA MILITARY ORGANIZATION, e.g. "RAD", "SPK", etc.

IN BLOCK LATIN CAPITALS

(WHEN PRINTED THIS FORM WILL BE IN ENGLISH AND GERMAN)

Discharge paper

carrying sidearms, it was not a prison. After a lengthy wait I was shown into Georg's office. He told me it would take some time to prepare my new papers. I asked him how he got the job of discharging soldiers. He was not sure, but rumour had it that General George Patton had ordered his commanders to use the existing German overseers, notwithstanding that they were former Nazi bureaucrats or even SS soldiers, to do the everyday occupation duties. As military governor of Bavaria,

Patton must have realized that some common sense had to be introduced into governing post-war Germany. So Germans did the work, while the Americans rubber-stamped the papers.

"I like this assignment a lot," Georg said with a grin. "As employees of the American army they feed us very well."

I knew what a crucial benefit that was.

My discharge could not be processed before late Saturday. Once again I slept in barracks that reminded me of my days in the *Arbeitsdienst*, which now seemed so very long ago. True to Georg's comment regarding food, our meals were splendidly filling.

On Saturday afternoon I underwent a medical examination, after which I received my discharge paper. The American doctor had recorded "poor" in the medical category blank. I was thin and had an impaired arm, but certainly did not consider myself in poor condition.

Free at last! Finally, I could officially resume my life as a legal German citizen, a civilian. What a great day. I thought about my future. I had spent the last seven years as a soldier, obeying orders in the enforced service of my country. I would have to get used to being a civilian again, which meant learning to make my own decisions, chart my own path, and follow my own destiny. But what opportunities were there for me in post-war Germany? The country's economy was in chaos, all of Germany's large cities were reduced to rubble, most of the industries had been destroyed or dismantled, and much of the country's institutional infrastructure was not functioning. On top of that, there was the very pragmatic necessity of finding enough food to stay alive long enough to realize any kind of ambitions for the future.

Armed with my precious discharge paper, I went to the *Rathaus* to tell the German authorities I had returned and to get my ration stamps. There I met Michelau's new mayor, Herr Bayer. He had been a member of the Social Democratic Party before the war, which was at the opposite end of the political spectrum from the Nazis. He told me he had spent time in one of Hitler's concentration camps, and that may be why the *Amis* appointed him mayor.

He recorded me in the municipal registry and issued me a month's worth of ration cards. "Yes. That's it," he said in reply to my questioning look after reviewing the stamps. "I know it's not much, but that's the best the government can do under the circumstances. We are all going to have to tighten our belts a little more."

I asked the mayor if he knew of any opportunities for me to find work in Michelau. My father's basket-making business was all but non-existent. Bayer was a kind-hearted man, but all he could do was welcome me back to my hometown and wish me luck.

Eventually I found a job working for F.D. Burkhardt. Before and during the war Burkhardt had sold fruit baskets, clothes hampers, baby carriages, wicker chests, and other assorted utility containers. Now his business was also suffering, mainly because customers were not able to pay with anything of value. He paid me, but not in anything we could eat. We still had to find a way to keep from starving.

The war was over, but the battle for survival was not. There was one more enemy to fight—starvation. Everyone in Germany had considered wartime rationing to be barely adequate, but that was nothing compared to conditions imposed after the war. Germany's food-producing capacity had been severely crippled in the last months of the war, not only because vast armies had swept across the country, but also because large portions of German territory and their agricultural production had been taken away. To make matters worse, huge numbers of refugees had fled into non-Russian-occupied Germany from the eastern parts of the former Reich. Germany was still as dependent upon food supplies from overseas as before the war, but no food aid from overseas came into post-war Germany. Consequently food of any kind was extremely scarce.

Each person was issued ration stamps for what he or she could purchase in one month. Rationing applied to almost everything, including meat, lard, dairy products, flour, rice, sugar, potatoes, baby formula, coal, gasoline, clothing, and shoes. Goods not rationed, such as furniture, appliances, household kitchen equipment and utensils, and practically all other manufactured goods, were virtually unavailable. Prices for consumer goods were strictly regulated, and price hikes were illegal. Money was used to pay for the items, but only if you had the requisite stamps. Money was also used to pay for things not rationed, such as employee wages, rent, taxes, hydro, movies and other such non-necessities, or dire necessities such as beer or wine. When making a purchase, the shop clerk would cut off the stamps allotted for that purchase, then send them to the government in order to be resupplied with the amount sold. Once your month's allotment was used up there was no way you could legally obtain any more before the next month.

Government rations could not provide even a subsistence existence. Each person was allowed, per month: 450 grams (about half a pound) meat, including sausages and other meat by-products; 250 grams butter; 62 grams cheese (one small, wrapped wedge about the size of a man's thumb); 170 grams fat; 1,000 grams sugar; 1,400 grams flour; 125 grams ersatz coffee; and one litre milk. Even simple staple foods like bread and potatoes were rationed, at 8,250 grams and 9,000 grams (about 20 pounds) respectively, per month. The only food items not rationed were vegetables such as cabbages, carrots, beets, and onions, which could be grown in small private garden plots, making them impractical to control.

To overcome the worthlessness of the German currency the *Schwarzmarkt* soon emerged and continued to flourish for years after the war. What you could buy with money was strictly limited by your ration stamps, but if you had something to trade, you just might do all right through discreet bartering. Craftsmen and tradesmen who had stuff or services to trade for food from farmers fared best. However, if you were caught trading without the proper stamps you were fined and jailed.

All farmers in Germany had to deliver almost all of their crops, livestock, and meat products to the government ration agency. That included pigs, cows, goats, and chickens, as well as milk, butter, cheese, eggs, and all cereal crops. These would be collected, apportioned, and doled out by the government distribution centres. The government set strict quotas for each farmer, mainly according to the size of his farm. For example, if a farmer produced eight beef cattle he had to give seven to the government-regulated market. He could keep one cow to do with as he pleased, for his own consumption or to trade for consumer goods. It was illegal for farmers to sell, trade, or give away any government-quota products to anyone else. Violators could have all their property confiscated. Government inspectors rigorously enforced these regulations, and that included frequent inspections of farm operations.

Such seemingly harsh regulations were the only means by which the government could control farm products and distribute them so that everyone received a share. If the government had not been so strict, many millions more would surely have starved to death after the war than did. People in the larger cities felt the shortages most acutely, as they had less access to farmers and therefore fewer opportunities to acquire food on the black market.

Some farmers tried to circumvent the regulation with such tactics as building a false wall in a stable to hide one or two cows, or keeping an animal in the basement of a building not usually used for animals. It required nerve to function in the black market. Anybody who knew about your underground dealings could turn you in. That could be someone who held a grudge against you, was jealous of your possessions, or self-righteously felt obliged to protect the "welfare of the people."

The post-war rationing and food distribution rules were set into effect by what became known as the new West German government in Bonn. It was not the work of the Allied military occupation governors. It was soon apparent that the American officials in charge of our sector, which included all of Bavaria, were not concerned with the plight of the people, as they did nothing to alleviate the starvation conditions.

Considering the circumstances, the German government's efforts at organizing the post-war economy were nothing short of miraculous, an amazing example of organization, skill, and discipline. It was a demonstration of the old adage by which most Germans were taught to live: *Ordnung muss sein* (there must be order).

All of the refugees now living in West Germany also had to be housed. Most of the refugees were German citizens who had been forcibly evicted from their homes in East Prussia, Silesia, and the Sudetenland. There were also refugees from the Baltic States, Hungary, Romania, and the Ukraine. They had been forced to leave with only what they could carry. Their lands, their homes, and the possessions they left behind were all confiscated.

The government ordered every city, town, and village to take its share of refugees. Government inspectors had the authority to look through anyone's home, and they were very thorough in ensuring that every room was occupied. A quota was set, requiring two people per room, including living room, dining room, study, and den. Every room, except kitchens and bathrooms, was included in the quota. The big cities had been largely destroyed by the Allied bombing campaign, aggravating the already desperate housing shortage. It really was amazing that the displaced people were assimilated into the smaller towns and villages in West Germany after the war. Bavaria had to accept a disproportionately large number of refugees, because it had not been as severely bombed as the cities in the north or in the industrialized Ruhr region.

By the time I returned to Michelau in June 1945, there were already many refugees living there. Two refugee families were living in my father's house, occupying two rooms each on the second floor. The situation eventually normalized somewhat, if that is the right way to say it, as the displaced persons became integrated and gradually accepted by the locals.

Ironically, Gisela's little joke was turning out to be grimly prophetic after all. "Enjoy the war. The peace will be worse."

As the weeks passed I became increasingly worried about my brothers. By August the war had been over for three months, and they had not yet returned home. We heard rumours through the grapevine that there were still hundreds of thousands of German soldiers interned in Allied prisoner-of-war camps. We did not make any concerted attempt to verify those rumours, as we had no idea where the camps were. Even if I had known, I certainly would not have gone to look for them. That would be gambling with my own freedom.

Late in the afternoon of August 27 there was a knock on our door. Heinrich Schmidt stood there. "Albin, I came to tell you that Hermann and Edwin have come home."

I felt huge relief and joy, and immediately rushed to my father's house to see them, anticipating a joyous reunion. When Anna opened the door, however, I sensed that something was wrong. She said nothing and just motioned for me to enter. Thus forewarned, I expected to see Hermann with some terrible wound, yet nothing could have prepared me for the shock of seeing him.

He was sitting on a chair in the corner of the kitchen, staring at the floor, swaying back and forth. When I came near I could hear him mumbling, "Potatoes, I need potatoes," over and over again. He smelled terrible, of earth and old excrement, combined with the distinctive, pungent odour of delousing powder. His breath had a sickly, sewer smell. His hair was filthy, the growth of beard on his chin indicated he had not shaved in months. There was a blob of flesh in the middle of his face where his nose had been. His eyes were two dark sockets in his gaunt face.

Turko could hardly speak. Anna tried to feed Hermann some potato soup. He fumbled desperately to eat but any more than a few sips and he would gag and throw up. After repeated tries he finally managed to keep some soup down. He was so weak we had to help get his grimy uniform off so we could wash him.

I felt a pain grip my being when I saw the condition of his body. His bones were clearly visible under his skin. Every rib was distinctly outlined. His pelvic bone was visible even from the back, as there were just shallow cavities where his buttocks had been. The hip joints were visible, and a wide gap separated his legs, which were as thin as my arms. His skin was sallow and dry, like parchment, with dark grey patches that may have started as bruises. His belly was hideously swollen, as if he had swallowed a ball. When I pressed my finger into the swelling it left a depression that took some minutes to disappear. He could not have weighed more than a hundred pounds. He had been starved.

How could this have happened, so long after the war was over? The story that unfolded was as horrific as anything I had experienced.

In February 1945, Hermann had been serving in a *Pioneer* unit somewhere on the Eastern Front when he was struck in the nose by a piece of shrapnel, completely removing his nose except for the tip around his nostrils. He was taken to Würzburg, where he was operated on. To rebuild the nose the doctors cut open the skin on the inside of his forearm and stitched the flesh to the opening in his face, so that it would grow over the space where his nose had been. The living tissue of the arm provided a live piece of flesh for the new nose. The scar on his forearm healed quickly, but he was left with a grim-looking lump in the middle of his face, which would require at least one more operation to turn it into a reasonable-looking and functional nose. He was waiting at home for the second operation when the American occupation troops arrived in Michelau and assembled all men of military age in front of Die Krone pub and took them away. All of them ended up in a prison camp near Bad Kreuznach.

Edwin had also been wounded while on the Eastern Front, shot in the hand by a Russian sniper, near the end of March. He was recuperating in a *Lazarett* in Banz, near Lichtenfels, when the Americans arrived sometime in April, capturing him along with hundreds of other invalids. Some of the soldiers were not even allowed to take their greatcoats with them and consequently suffered terribly from the cold. None of them was given any medical treatment by their captors, and some died of blood poisoning or gangrene before they even reached the prison camp.

Edwin and Hermann met by chance at the Bad Kreuznach camp. That was an incredible coincidence, as it was a huge internment camp, consisting of a series of fenced enclosures in open fields near the city of Mainz in the Rhineland.

Conditions were nightmarish. Edwin later described how thousands of captured German soldiers were kept inside a chain-link fence and barbed-wire compound, completely in the open, and just left there. There were no buildings, shacks, or shelters, and only those soldiers that had managed to bring their *Zeltplan* capes with them had any kind of protection from the elements. The prisoners slept in holes in the ground, which turned into deadly, muddy pits with the cold spring rains. Many of them were hardly more than boys, and some were too old to have been soldiers. There were others like himself who had been wrested from hospital beds, some with horrible-looking wounds. There was no medical treatment for the injured or sick, and no sanitation facilities other than planks laid across open pits. Many prisoners died of diseases brought on by exposure and the horrible unsanitary conditions, aggravated by malnutrition. Disease symptoms he recognized included pneumonia, scabies, scurvy, gangrene, and dysentery, all of which could have been prevented with even the most rudimentary medical attention. Like Hermann, most of the men suffered from the bloated belly condition called edema. Edwin saw emaciated corpses dragged to the gates every morning, thrown onto trucks, and hauled away. He did not know where they were buried.

Edwin had expected to see Red Cross representatives in the camp, bringing medical supplies and food packages, but no kind of aid ever arrived. Edwin never saw anyone other than armed American guards in the camp. One incident was particularly appalling. German civilians brought food to the camp, because they could see that the imprisoned soldiers were starving. The American jailers took the food and threw it onto the ground just outside the barbed-wire fence, where the prisoners could see it, but not reach it, and watched it rot.

Of all people, why would Americans do that, and after the war was over? Perhaps the captured soldiers had been deliberately starved as punishment for the war, or perhaps as retaliation for the concentration camps discovered by the Allies near the end of the war? It is probably inherent in the nature of war that the losers are made to suffer, but ordinary soldiers had had nothing to do with concentration camps. Like most people in Germany, I knew nothing about those camps. Considering their gruesome purpose, the Nazis had deliberately kept them a guarded secret from German citizens.

Edwin had lost almost as much weight as Hermann. Even though he had been apprehended about the same time, he was younger and somewhat stronger. When they were finally released the two of them returned home together. Edwin told me Hermann would not have made it alone.

Hermann had been driven temporarily insane by his ordeal. For days after his arrival he would stand in a corner of the living room for hours at a time, mumbling about potatoes. He had to be fed with soft food—mushy soup, cream of wheat, or mashed potatoes—for weeks to restore his strength. It took Hermann months before he could be considered healthy again.

I felt terrible for my brothers. I also knew that fate may again have been kind to me. If I had gone straight to Michelau after escaping from the Russians that first time near Görlitz, rather than trying to fetch Gisela in Brandenburg, I too might have been captured by the Americans. At the time, who would have thought that being captured by the Russians was better than being captured by the Americans?

There were other stories told by veterans, where German prisoners of war were repeatedly beaten, fed terrible food, and kept in appalling conditions with little or no medical treatment. Many of those men brought with them deep psychological scars that remained for the rest of their lives.[15]

On September 9, 1945, my brother Oskar came home. He looked fit and healthy. His return really was a joyful reunion. He had no horror stories to tell of his internment. In fact, he was the only one of us brothers eager to tell the rest of the family the story of his wartime adventures as a cook with the *Kriegsmarine* in the Black Sea. He had been captured by Allied troops in northern Germany at the beginning of May 1945 and

---

15 Inquiries by independent investigators have corroborated these personal accounts. Appalling numbers of German and other Axis soldiers died in American and French prison camps after the war, most of whom were starved to death or died of diseases brought on by malnutrition. Many more former soldiers died in Russian *gulags*. Recorded evidence indicates that more German soldiers died in Allied prison camps (American, French, and Russian) after the war than were killed in action during the war.

spent about three months in a prisoner-of-war camp run by what he at first assumed were Americans, but turned out to be Canadians. He said they talked like *Amis*, but looked like Tommies (British). He did not have any stories of inhumane treatment by his captors. His work crew spent most days cultivating local farm fields and picking peas. That was hot and dirty work, but not debilitating. The prisoners supplemented their rations by whatever they gleaned from the fields. Their food was not lavish fare, but not starvation rations either.

Sometime in late July he and some other former seamen were turned over to the Royal Navy and sent to the North Sea, where he was assigned to a former German minesweeper. The way Oskar told it, they removed the same mines that the *Kriegsmarine* might have laid in the first place. How efficient and resourceful of the British to have Germans clean up their own detritus of war. After the mine-clearing assignment was completed the British returned him to Witmundhaven, where he was discharged. With discharge papers in hand he did not have to worry about being detained or apprehended at some checkpoint.

Oskar had nothing but praise for his former Canadian and British captors. They had treated him well and fed and clothed him better than the *Kriegsmarine* had during at least the last year of the war. He had heard rumours that the German prisoners were to be kept in fighting shape as they might have to again take up arms against the Russians. It was common knowledge that Churchill did not trust Stalin, and the Western Allies might have to rescue Poland and Czechoslovakia from Russian domination. After all, those two countries had been allies against Germany from the start, and it was England's promise to aid Poland that had precipitated England's entry into the war in the first place.

I, like other Michelauers, tried to adjust to living conditions after the war as best as we could. I started going to Die Krone or Zum Schärfner's pub on Friday evenings, playing cards with some of the men. Beer was not rationed and it was relatively cheap. Gisela and I made new friends, mainly with displaced persons from Hamburg, and especially with Germans from the Sudetenland who had been relocated to Michelau. Gisela eventually learned to understand, if not speak, the Michelau dialect. We occasionally went to a dance at the Turnhalle on weekends and visited with friends for cards or just some lively conversation. After more than a decade of living under a very serious government, including six years of war, everyone was starving for some lighthearted enjoyment in life. It felt almost too good to be true to be able to have some fun.

Those good feelings were frequently tempered by sad realities. Everywhere I went in Michelau there were poignant reminders that a great many of Michelau's sons were not coming home again. Almost every day I would meet sad-faced mothers, fathers, brothers, or sisters of men who had fallen. The highest casualty rate was apparently among the infantry. Michelau sent ten infantry officers that I knew of, all of whom had served in Russia. Only myself and Edwin Schardt survived that ordeal. What a terrible waste of young lives, the very best of a generation. During my service in Russia the full meaning of the deaths I witnessed at the front made less of an impact on my consciousness than the aftermath that confronted me now. These deaths were a tragedy in the lives of the family members they left behind, a loss that could not be replaced or alleviated with any amount of comforting.

I also experienced deep feelings of remorse—more like guilt, actually—knowing that I had survived when so many had not. I would grope for words to apologize for living when another's son did not, to make some excuse that it was the fault of fate, not mine, that I had lived. I kept telling myself that life goes on regardless, but could not help feeling like a condemned man who had somehow, undeservedly, escaped the gallows when more deserving friends had not. I was often profoundly aware of walking among ghosts.

By the end of September the annual potato harvest had begun, and we approached local farmers to try to buy potatoes. We had saved much of my officer's pay, so we had money, but offering money turned out to be a waste of time. The farmers knew the value of their crops and guarded their fields, especially the potato fields, to prevent looters from taking anything.

A 9 p.m. curfew was still being imposed by the occupation forces, and I decided to use it to my advantage. Desperation influences moral values and personal codes of conduct, and the spectre of starvation was a powerful motivator. One evening just before nine, I hid my knapsack under my suit coat and casually walked into a woodlot that bordered a potato field near the village. After it was dark I went into the field and dug up as many potatoes as could be stuffed into my little knapsack. After digging up each potato I spread the soil around to cover the holes to make the theft look less obvious. I then spent the rest of the night in the woods. Early the next morning I walked out of the woods and back home with my precious knapsack full of potatoes.

I did the same thing a few more times during the two-week potato harvest. Those potatoes fed us for a few weeks that fall. Eventually I realized that we did not have enough to sustain us through the coming winter, so we scrounged around for something of value that could be traded for more food. I remembered a bolt of cloth my brother Hermann had obtained from a freight train that had been bombed near the end of the war. Sure enough, in the basement of my father's house, that bolt of heavy wool material was still there, approximately four metres of which was my share. Perhaps we could trade it for food?

After the war German men were not permitted to wear military uniforms. I had no suit to call my own, except my lieutenant's dress uniform. My brothers had worn the clothes I left behind when I had left home to go to the *Arbeitsdienst*. My resourceful wife took the epaulettes and flaps off my uniform, sewed some red cloth patches onto the inside of the pockets, some green bands onto the outside edges of the pockets, and produced a suit that looked like a traditional Bavarian *Jaeger* (hunter) outfit. The original had been a grey-green officer's uniform and the colour suited my newly styled *Jaeger* suit very well.

I had intended to use the bolt of cloth to have a suit made for myself, but did not need the cloth as much as we needed food. So I knocked on doors and finally found a farmer in Schnei, about ten kilometres away, who agreed to trade six hundred pounds of potatoes for my cloth. The farmer even transported that precious load to our home in his wagon. We stored the potatoes in our storage stall in the cellar.

From October 1945 to early summer 1946, we ate boiled potatoes, mashed potatoes, potato dumplings, potato pancakes, potato salad, and potato soup. There were no fried potatoes—fat was just too scarce—although we occasionally supplemented the main course with carrots or onions from our garden. Sometimes we could add a spice cube to make a watery gravy. Our meat ration was almost always six pork sausages for each of us per month.

When I became an officer in Potsdam in December 1942 the army issued me a ceremonial dagger. It was beautifully crafted, with a fine blade and an ivory handle. I had left it in Michelau when I was sent to the front. After the war the Americans announced that all weapons of war and other German army paraphernalia, including the ceremonial daggers carried by officers, had to be turned in to occupation head-quarters. Gisela told me she had seen American soldiers confiscate the daggers, pack them in boxes, and ship them home to their families as souvenirs. Regardless, I did not want to risk being caught with that dagger in my possession, so I traded it to a friend everyone called *Der Doctor* in exchange for a pregnant rabbit. He said he could use it as a butcher knife. He removed the swastika on the handle, discarded the scabbard and chain, and was left with a useful tool.

We kept the rabbit he traded to us as an investment in our future food supplies. I constructed a rabbit hutch against the side wall of the stable behind our house out of wood and wire. Shortly afterward we had a few baby rabbits, which grew quickly. They required little main-tenance, and we fed them grass and weeds gathered from the nearby Main River flood plain. The efficient little critters even ate potato peel-ings.

Late one evening sometime near the end of October, Gisela's mother showed up at our door. Julchen had somehow managed to make it to Michelau by herself, leaving behind everything she could not fit into a handbag. Apparently in the fall of 1945 it was still possible to leave the Russian-occupied zone. Since there was no other place available, she moved in with us. She adapted better to life in Michelau than Gisela did, even though she must have had a difficult time adjusting to the dialect. Eventually she obtained a job as a waitress at Die Krone pub.

Thinking back, I believe Julchen was quite resilient and more than a little tough, in the most flattering sense of the word. Her generation had seen war disrupt their lives twice. She had also seen the economy crash and the value of money evaporate twice. She accepted her chang-ing fortunes with aplomb. She always tried to make the best of circum-stances, no matter how dire they appeared. "As long as nobody dies," she used to say, "everything else will be all right."

Now there was only one member of the family still missing—Karl, my youngest brother. Turko had granted permission for Karl to join the armed forces in 1945, when he turned sixteen. Apparently Karl had been bored at home and wanted to contribute his part to the war effort. I will never understand why Turko granted him permission.

Karl was assigned to a *Flak Abwehr* (anti-aircraft) battery in Augs-burg, just west of München. When he had not returned home by the fall of 1945 we really started to worry. It was inconceivable that he would have had a long and dangerous journey home. Our best hope was that Karl was being detained in some distant prisoner-of-war camp in France, or that he had joined the French Foreign Legion, as other German soldiers had been coerced into doing.

Even though no one mentioned it, eventually we thought it a vain hope that Karl would ever be coming home again. Except Gustel; she would not accept the possibility of Karl being dead. Gustel had raised Karl since he was nine, after our mother died. She never had children of her own and Karl was very special to her. The anguish in her face was painfully obvious every time Karl's name was mentioned.

Shortly after Christmas we received a letter postmarked in Stuttgart, which I recognized right away as Wolfgang Schwarz's home town, and eagerly opened it. It was from Wolfgang's sister. My heart sank as I read that Wolfgang had been killed in Russia. I could only imagine what his family must be feeling. Who knows what great things Wolfgang might have accomplished if his life had not been cut short by the war. I wrote back to his sister and tried to express my sincere feelings of sadness and loss, saying I had always admired Wolfgang and considered him my closest friend. How unfair that such an excellent person had been killed.

One of the best ways we found to help quell hunger was sleep. Sleeping not only burns minimal energy, but also keeps you from thinking about hunger pangs. We slept a lot. Julchen commented that she thought Gisela and I were crazy to sleep so much!

In May 1946 Gisela told me she was pregnant. I was thrilled. We had both worried that we could not have children. Even though times were tough, I was optimistic that the future would be better for us. We were pleased and relieved to find out that the government issued pregnant women extra food rations, especially for milk.

The main reason that living conditions remained so harsh for Germans after the war was that leaders of the Allied occupation forces devised and instituted a deliberate strategy to turn occupied Germany into an agrarian nation, "a goat pasture," as Gisela put it. There were no jobs available in the factories, as all the machinery had been dismantled and shipped out of the country by the occupation forces. A friend of the family, Udo Lauer, had seen rows of large industrial machinery sitting at a railway station, left to rust, possibly near Moscow, on his way back to Germany from a Russian prison camp in 1948. The German lettering was still legible. That strategy had a name that every German knew very well—the Morgenthau Plan.

The lean times were hard on everyone, but affected the old and sick the most. Many of them did not survive those years.

One day late in the summer of 1946 I saw Turko walking across the bridge to the village. He was thin as a rake. Oskar and I went to visit him at his house. Turko looked gaunt and pale, drawing shallow breaths through his mouth and staring blankly at the floor. I looked at my father as if seeing him for the first time. He had deep lines in his face, his hair was not only white, but thin and straggly, and his weather-worn hands showed the distinctive yellow-brown stains from years of smoking cigarettes. His demeanour was strangely detached, as if alone in his mind.

"You have to take better care of yourself," I said, knowing what my father's reaction would likely be. It was not my place to oversee his life or make decisions for him.

With a nod of his head he said, "You're right," which was his way of telling me there was nothing that could be done to change things. He looked up at me, then said very seriously, "There's no more enjoyment in living."

The conviction in his voice made me suspect that he had lost his will to live. I decided to fetch the doctor.

Dr. Meyer examined Turko. "It doesn't look good for him," he said, "but there's nothing else I can do here. He should go to the hospital in Lichtenfels."

"No hospital," Turko said in a weak but determined voice. Oskar and I just looked at each other, powerless to do anything, resigned to accept whatever fate had decided. Then I heard Turko say, "This is no life. What's the use of living like this anymore? I'm going to lie down and die."

And he did.

He was sixty-three, although he looked much older. All his life he had been a strong man, in every sense of that word. Now he looked so frail and tiny. It surprised me that watching my father die did not produce the stabbing pain that had accompanied seeing many of my comrades die in battle. Perhaps I had been preparing for his death for a long time and his actual dying was just the inevitable conclusion. I grieved over his loss, but felt relieved that his suffering was over.

There were over a hundred people in the procession to the graveyard. If a man's legacy can be measured by the friends he made in his life, then Turko was a wealthy man. I believe the formal ceremony and associated personal interactions help people cope with their grief, as well as provide reassurance that there is support for those left behind. Thinking back, it is ironic that with all the tragic deaths of excellent people I had witnessed because of the war, Turko's death was the only one marked with such ceremony.

Shortly after Turko died, so did our landlord, Der Alte Heiner. Gisela went to the Housing Authority to find out what was to be done with the vacant upstairs apartment, because we could certainly use the room after our child was born. My pregnant wife was very persuasive, so we were permitted to move upstairs. The big room had a ceramic tile oven, which was nice and cosy in the wintertime. Our furniture fit well. Julchen got her own bedroom. Best of all, the bedrooms both had a full-height ceiling, so that we could stand up straight, something we had not been able to do in our alcove bedroom downstairs. There was also enough room for a crib.

My brothers had become specialists at operating on the black market, trading mostly chinaware, mainly Hummel figurines that they acquired from employees of the local Hummel factory, to the American occupation troops and especially their wives, for cigarettes or other items of value. From 1945 until 1948 the only means of obtaining extra food was to barter some commodity of value for it, and that commodity increasingly became American cigarettes. For example, one small or medium-sized Hummel figurine could be traded for two to four packs of American cigarettes, which in turn could be traded to farmers for food, or to merchants for household commodities or luxury items such as nylons, makeup, toiletries, or other contraband. In effect, cigarettes took the place of currency.

The "market area" for my brothers covered a huge part of Oberfranken, from Bamberg south to Nürnberg and west to Würzburg. The most profitable locations were cities that contained large American military garrisons. The entire operation depended on the co-operation, or at least the tacit support, of the local community.

Edwin and Oskar were identical twins, and it was difficult for anyone except family members and close friends to tell them apart, which they used to their advantage. One brother was always conspicuously present in some public place while the other was off wheeling and dealing with his suitcase full of contraband. When the police suspected one of illegal activity, there were always witnesses willing to testify that whichever one they suspected had actually been with them the entire time of the alleged infraction. Since the courthouse and local police headquarters were in Lichtenfels and not in Michelau, that ruse worked well on several occasions. A network of family and friends also helped warn them of inspectors or potential police interventions that could have curtailed their exploits.

In early summer of 1946 Gisela and I tried our hand at black marketeering. We went knocking on doors where the families of American officers were living, trying to sell our own Hummel figurines. In most cases the German maid opened the door and politely said something like, "No thank you, they already have far too many."

After a few hours Gisela stopped and said, "I feel like a beggar. And they treat me like a beggar. I've had enough of this degrading venture. There has to be another way."

I was not going to put my pregnant wife through that ordeal again. I approached my boss, F.D. Burkhardt, with an idea. I would try to trade some of Burkhardt's wicker wares to local farmers for farm produce. He agreed it was worth a try. I had been stationed in Forchheim after returning from France, so I knew some of the farmers in that area.

Carrying our wicker goods on the trains was not a problem, as they were not contraband. The trick was to bring farm goods back to Michelau without getting caught by the police. The German police had the authority to detain and search anyone they suspected and, not only could they make arrests, they could also confiscate all our goods.

On my first trip I got on the train with as many of Burkhardt's fancy fruit baskets and ornamental bowls as I could carry in a canvas duffle bag. In Forchheim I searched out a farmer I knew from 1940. When I knocked on the door he recognized me and invited me in. He seemed genuinely pleased to see I had survived the war intact. I explained my mission and showed him my wares. We bartered and soon exchanged some of my items for eggs and butter. He told me of other farmers who might be interested. By the time I finished calling on the third farmhouse, everything I brought with me had been exchanged for food items, including some bacon. I stuffed those treasures into my duffle bag and headed back to Michelau. By pure good fortune, the police on the train did not ask to look in my bag and I was not searched at the station. I returned triumphant from that trip.

Buoyed by success, I convinced Gisela to accompany me on subsequent "business" trips. Because she was pregnant, bringing Gisela along may actually have helped, as the farmers and especially their wives must have sympathized with her. She might also have helped avoid our being detained; after all, how could anyone be callous enough to search a pregnant lady? We always split the farm foods with Burkhardt, half and half. That precious bounty supplemented our diet, and we ate comparatively well for quite a while.

Eventually I became convinced that the black market could not be relied upon to support my family for much longer; eventually I would have to find a decent job. Gisela had made it clear that she did not want me to be a basket-maker, carrying on my father's business. She also disliked the parochial attitudes and antiquated customs of Michelau's small-town society, where adults and their grown children worked together at home all day, after which the men went to the local pub to play cards and drink with their buddies, while the women stayed home and did housework. Even though I had grown up with it, I realized that if I wanted to preserve my marriage, we would eventually have to leave Michelau, and the sooner the better.

There were few opportunities for a career in Michelau, or for any kind of job outside the wicker industry. A friend suggested I apply for a job like his at the *Finanzamt*, the internal revenue department for the West German government, in Lichtenfels. Gisela encouraged that idea. A government job might be just the thing, as sooner or later the German economy would recover and such recovery would surely be administered by the government. I went to Lichtenfels to apply for work, but there were no openings available there at the time; however, while in Lichtenfels I learned that there might be an opening at the *Finanzamt* in Coburg.

At the end of October I took the train to Coburg and filled out an application for employment at the *Finanzamt*. The clerk explained it would take some time to process my application, as there were many applicants for only a few openings, but the office was becoming increasingly busy and I should call back in a week. That sounded encouraging.

Gisela went into labour on the morning of November 8, 1946. I fetched the local midwife to help with the birth. In Michelau, and probably throughout most of Germany at the time, children were usually born at home with the assistance of a midwife. Gisela and I had little concept of what to expect. At first we thought everything was going well, but after almost an entire day of stressful labour the midwife sent me to fetch Dr. Meyer.

Dr. Meyer concluded that she was not making substantial progress. "I don't want to be responsible for her. She needs special help that she can only get at a hospital." We quickly bundled Gisela into his car and drove to the nearest hospital, in Lichtenfels.

After thirty-two hours of labour, the doctors took her into the operating room and used forceps to pull the baby out. Those were some of the most anxious moments of my life. The baby was born in the evening of November 9—a son, eight pounds. When I first looked at our new baby boy, I was startled by his appearance. His head looked deformed, long and thin, with bruises on the upper part of the forehead and under part of his chin.

"Is he all right?" I asked in dismay.

The doctor explained that it was normal for the head to be squeezed by the birth canal, and that the bruises were caused by the forceps. "Not to worry," he said. "He'll be fine in a while." And he was—my very personal, amazing miracle of a new life. After a few days everything about him looked normal and healthy.

Giving birth had completely exhausted Gisela. Shortly afterwards she developed a fever, which was caused by an infection during delivery. I worried again, but Gisela was strong and received medication that quickly cured her. A week later we returned triumphant to Michelau with our marvellous new addition to our family. He was a tremendous hit with the family members. Everyone agreed he was beautiful.

We named him Wolfgang Oskar Gagel. I liked the name Wolfgang for very personal reasons, as a memorial to the memory of my friend Wolfgang Schwarz, that very fine person who had been killed in Russia.

The middle name was bestowed by my brother Oskar, who would be Wolfgang's godfather.

Our son was born during the midst of tough times, and from then on his welfare was foremost in our minds. In the beginning we were very concerned that he would starve. For some reason Gisela could not nurse. Thankfully the government provided extra rations for infant formula, which was a lifesaver that helped keep our son healthy. After 1945 children under the age of fifteen also got extra rations of milk and sugar. In those days we did not have the luxury of considering sugar as the scourge of the obesity-conscious that it is today.

Shortly after Wolfgang was born we ran out of coal and wood to heat our home and cook our food. I scrounged around as best I could but could not gather enough fuel to sustain us through the winter. Once again, desperate times called for desperate measures. I went into the nearby woods late at night and cut up some dead trees for firewood. That was illegal, not only because the woods belonged to the owner of the property, but because coal and firewood were still rationed. I went deep into the woods so the sound of my chopping would not be heard. At first I tried to hide the bundle in my pack, but after a few trips I became bolder, until I eventually carted out as much wood as I could strap to my back and carry in a sack under my arm. That pilfering of small bundles of wood worked reasonably well until all the easily cut and gathered pieces had been gleaned.

One night I might have worked too hard and made too much noise. When I emerged from the woods there was a policeman standing in my way. "You will have to put that wood back, my friend," he said in an almost cordial manner, "and come with me. You know the rules."

I stood steadfast for a moment, weighing my options. Do I give my bundle up and spend some time in jail? Not a comforting thought. Do I try to bribe my way out of this? What did I have of value? Money was no good and I had nothing else. Not only that, but trying to bribe him might have made the situation worse. Do I dare test his resolve? He may be bluffing, but what if he is adamant? Then I heard myself saying, "I have a wife and infant son at home who could freeze to death if I don't bring home this wood. So you can try to stop me if you want, but I am taking this wood home."

He slowly stepped aside and did not take his eyes off me. "I must give you a fine."

"Go ahead," I said and stepped past him. I continued my walk home without looking back, carrying my precious bundle of wood.

Gisela must have sensed my agitation when I came in the door. "What happened?"

"Nothing to worry about," I answered. "I might have to pay for this wood." I explained the little escapade at the woodlot.

"What are we going to do now?"

"I'm not going to let you freeze."

The next day we received a fine from the police, 40 Marks. The wood was worth much more than the money. I paid it and nothing was ever mentioned again. That woodlot, and others, continued to supply my family with precious firewood during that winter, but I was much more careful from then on.

I was so preoccupied with looking after my wife and new son that I forgot to go back to Coburg about the *Finanzamt* job until December. During the interview the clerk asked if I had any accounting experience.

"Keeping books for my father's wicker business," I replied.

"You will go to businesses in the district to check their books and make sure they are following all the government regulations and laws, particularly about paying business taxes. The job carries a lot of responsibility."

"I'm sure I can do it," I said, positive that I could quickly learn whatever was necessary. I got the job and started work on December 16, 1946. The pay was 160 Marks a month, during a time when one package of American cigarettes cost 100 Marks on the black market. My brothers thought it foolish of me to work for so little money, but I believed that sooner or later the money would regain real buying power.

I commuted by train to and from work every day. At first my duties all felt alien, but I learned quickly. I was sent to the *Finanzschule* (school of accounting) in Coburg, where I studied formal accounting. Upon graduation I was promoted to auditor and given additional duties and responsibilities. I was given a bicycle with a carrier on the back—a government vehicle—to carry my briefcase as I went from company to company inspecting their books. Everyone was aware of their responsibility to work together to assist the country's economic recovery.

My job included a major perk—the office provided one meal a day to its employees, at noon, which freed up one meal of rations for me at home every weekday.

Family portrait, 1948

In June 1948, the government implemented the *Währungsreform* (currency reform). All the money in West Germany was exchanged: ten old Reichsmark for one new Deutschmark. This was made possible because of what the Americans called the Marshall Plan, an incentive revitalization plan designed to help the country recover economically. That happened shortly after Churchill's famous "Iron Curtain" speech, in which he portrayed Stalin as the new menace to western civilization. Recognizing the implications of that speech, I believe the leaders of the former Western Allies realized that there was now only West Germany standing between Stalin's Soviet Empire and the rest of Western Europe; therefore, what remained of Germany would need to be made healthy again as a western ally in order to be able to resist potential expansionist designs by the Soviets. As a result of the Marshall Plan, tons of food aid and substantial financial assistance poured into West Germany. Consumer goods suddenly became available again, food quickly became adequate and then plentiful enough that rationing could be abandoned. The black market ceased operating virtually overnight.

After the *Währungsreform* life quickly became noticeably better for us. My pay became quite attractive, as those 160 Deutschmarks now had real buying power. During the summer of 1948 conditions all over West Germany improved greatly. It had been three years of struggle to rebuild our lives; for most Germans much of that striving had been concerned with the need to survive. A renewed sense of optimism swept the country, along with a determined effort to rebuild their lives and their communities.

It felt like the war was finally over.

In November 1948 we received a letter from the Red Cross, postmarked Berlin. The authorities had uncovered a mass grave in one of the suburbs of Augsburg containing the remains of those killed during a bombing attack. One of the items found in that mass grave was Karl's dog tag.

It is ironic that the youngest of the family had been killed, the one with the most life ahead of him, the most innocent of all of us. He was also the only one who had volunteered for military service. Along with a terrible grief, I could not help feeling resentment toward my father for having granted Karl permission to join the army. Perhaps it may have been impossible for Turko to have prevented Karl from joining. I remembered being sixteen, when dying had no real meaning, when I had been convinced, as Karl may have been, that death could not possibly claim me. Regardless, I suspected Turko may not have done everything in his power to prevent Karl from enlisting.

Even though the family had been expecting it, the reality of Karl's death was a dreadful shock. For years afterwards I felt a painful sinking feeling in my heart every time I thought of him. Gustel took it very badly. She had steadfastly refused to accept that Karl could be dead. She had kept his possessions just the way he had left them for the past three years. "My Karla, my Karla," she would say under her breath, "everything will be here for you when you return." The reality almost killed her. She did not eat for days. She spent hours in her room by herself. She went about her rounds in the village in a daze, doing her chores by rote. I visited her often, but nothing anyone could say or do comforted her. I doubt she was ever really happy again.

The true meaning of the war had hit home with brutal clarity. Karl's death was an irreversible tragedy which our family would have to live with for the rest of our lives. Whenever I remember his bright blue eyes, his cheerful smile, and his indomitable enthusiasm for life, I feel an upwelling of painful emotion. Karl's death was a terrible lesson about what is truly important. To this day I feel somewhat indifferent toward material possessions. If a thing is broken or lost it can be fixed or replaced with something the same or at least similar. If you lose the life of a loved one it leaves a permanent hole in your heart. So I cherish my family. None of them can ever be replaced.

I also cherish life. I appreciate the good times with my family and friends, and all the other precious gifts that life has to offer. I will never again take anything for granted, for I have experienced difficult times, when life was cheap, when human rights were non-existent, when personal freedom was unattainable, and even survival was just a matter of luck. I impart to all who will listen, as my father had imparted to me, "No matter how bad you think things are, remember they can always get worse; so treasure what you have while you can."

An old adage says, "Constant vigilance is the price of freedom," and that is as true now as it was then. Warfare is an excuse for taking away personal freedoms, for enslaving a nation's own citizens. Warfare dehumanizes people, removing their individual identities, and enables persons in power to treat people as objects to be used and disposed of without punitive consequences for those in charge. Hardest to understand may be that a nation's own leaders can be their people's worst enemy. Beware when your government proposes to take away civil rights in order to protect its people from "enemies of the nation," no matter who those enemies are purported to be. Be suspicious of patriotism, as it is a convenient tool of tyranny. Do not be fooled by the media's support for militaristic actions, no matter how righteous it sounds; rather, weigh the costs with common sense, question the motives of those who stand to gain from those actions, and listen to your conscience. Remember your responsibility to keep political leaders honest, to guard against your government eroding personal rights and freedoms, and to resist any and all self-serving clamour for war. Exercising that responsibility can involve personal effort, risk, and even hardship, but history has repeatedly demonstrated that the consequences of doing nothing are far worse.

"Lest we forget" has meaning, for it can happen again.

Epilogue *Never Again*

THOUGH LIFE IN GERMANY quickly became much better after the Marshall Plan, it continued to be plagued by the ghosts of war.

Events were again making us apprehensive: the Czechs had staged public demonstrations against Russian control that were put down by Russian tanks in the streets of Prague; the Russians closed the *autobahn* route into Berlin, forcing the Berlin airlift—the Iron Curtain had been raised across Europe, dividing East from West. Leaders on both sides blustered and bellowed belligerence at each other.

I had enough of Europe's seemingly never-ending political crises. I would look at my infant son and worry about the world he would grow up in. I was not willing to raise him in a country where I could one day be forced to watch him sent off to war.

Gisela and I spoke often about the political situation unfolding in Europe. We started looking for another place on the planet where we could be free from the spectre of the draft. At first we had contemplated moving to America, the "land of the free," where everyone was undoubtedly rich. However, there was still conscription in the United States, where every young man had to serve two years in the military; so, America was not for us. After doing some research, only two countries emerged as reasonable choices.

The first was Australia, which one of our friends had described as incredibly beautiful. Gisela's father had travelled to Australia on many occasions while working on ships for Norddeutscher Lloyd, and he had described it as a very attractive country, clean and unspoiled, with vast open spaces where a family could put down roots. It did not have conscription, which was good. One drawback was that we did not know anybody living in Australia who could help us move there or give us more information. Another drawback was that it lay on the other side of the planet and getting there would be expensive. Gisela had a tendency to get very seasick, so a four-week sea voyage could possibly kill her.

The second was Canada, a country we also knew very little about, except that it was a big northern land, reputedly cold and sparsely populated. Most of what we had heard from friends or had seen in news-reels or movies indicated that it was rugged and relatively primitive. My brother Oskar and my friend Kurt Raabe described the Canadian soldiers they had met while in detention near the end of the war as really decent chaps. Best of all, it had no mandatory military service. Canada sounded like the best opportunity for a new life.

Gisela and I were well aware that life in Canada could be challeng-ing. I was sure that, as an immigrant, opportunities for a white-collar job like the accountant position I held with Revenue Germany may not even be possible in Canada. Also, in the early 1950s Germans were still considered undesirable aliens by the Canadian government. We would not be permitted to immigrate to Canada without a sponsor who would guarantee my employment. No matter, the spectre of my son in a uniform at a new Russian front was a powerful motivation for abandoning the "Fatherland." We had to make the effort.

By a twist of fate, one day I was reading the newspaper when I hap-pened to spot an ad placed by someone looking for a female pen pal, with the idea of establishing a relationship that could eventually lead to marriage. The ad was by an Eric Rasche, from a place named Pickle Crow, Ontario. I recognized his name as being German and so wrote to him, saying that I was not keen on marrying him but would like for me and my family to emigrate to Canada. I sent my letter off not really ex-pecting anything to come of it. To my great surprise and joy, he replied. He offered to sponsor me, a fellow German, to acquire a work permit that would allow me to come to Canada to work with him in a gold mine. I had no idea what working in a gold mine would be like, but the prospect of being able to leave Germany for Canada was irresistible.

I discussed this plan of moving to Pickle Crow with Gisela, who agreed it was a gamble worth taking. So I eagerly accepted Eric Rasche's offer. Gisela and I went to the Canadian consulate in Frankfurt to make the necessary arrangements. Eric Rasche had Pickle Crow Gold Mines send me a formal offer of employment so I could get a work permit.

It turned out to be a major undertaking to obtain all the necessary approvals. I had to leave for Canada first, after which Gisela and our son would be allowed to follow. I sold my share in my father's house to my brothers to purchase the steamship fare. By the time all the forms had been filled out, signed and approved, and the associated government pa-perwork was completed, it was 1952.

So we left Germany behind. We turned our back on Europe, never again wanting to experience its nationalistic anxieties, military obsessions, and political turmoil. We emigrated to start a new life in Canada, one rooted in peace and freedom.

But that is another story.

Appendix

Glossary of German Terminology

Abteilungsführer	unit leader
Altstadt	Old City as opposed to New City (*Neustadt*)
Amis	German slang for Americans
Arbeitsamt	Labour Bureau
Arbeitsdienst	Compulsory Labour Service
Artillerie	artillery
Bauernhof	farmyard enclosed by buildings and walls
Bescheinigung	certificate
Blitzkrieg	Lightning War (fast-moving, coordinated attack tactics)
Burgermeister	Mayor
Bonzen	derogatory slang for Nazi government officials
Eintopf	stew
Eisernes Kreuz	Iron Cross
Ersatz	substitute
Feind	enemy
Feldgendarmerie	military police
Feldwebel	sergeant
Feldgeschirr	soldier's field dishes
Feldflasche	canteen
Finanzamt	Internal Revenue Bureau
Flak	anti-aircraft weapon
Fliegende Kommando	derogatory slang for military police
Führer	leader
Fussball	soccer
Gaststätte	restaurant
Gefreiter	private, first class
Gestapo	short for *Geheim Staatspolizei,* Secret State Police
Gauleiter	district administrator, similar to county reeve
Granatwerfer	mortar
Handelsschule	trade school

Hauptmann	captain
Hitler Jugend	Hitler Youth
Hoch Deutsch	High German, the formal language
Im Felde	at the front, literally "in the field"
Kanonier	gunner
Kirchweih	Michelau church fair, held in summer
Kommisbrot	heavy, dark rye bread
Korbmacher	basket maker
Krapfen	Bavarian donut-like pastry
Krieg	war
Kriegsmarine	German navy
Kübelwagen	Volkswagen-built military scout car similar to jeep
Lagerführer	camp leader
Lazarett	military hospital
Leberwurst	liver sausage
Lederhosen	deer-leather shorts
Leutnant	lieutenant
Luftwaffe	German air force
Makhorka	Russian tobacco
Malzkaffee	barley malt coffee
Mannschaft	team
Mettwurst	a type of sausage paté or spread
Musterung	military muster, i.e. call to arms
Nazi	abbreviation of National Socialist
Oberleutnant	first lieutenant
Ofenrohr	stove pipe, slang for Panzerschreck
Ordnung	order, as in organizational order
Paate	godfather
Panzer	armour, also tank
Panzerfaust	hand-held infantry anti-tank weapon
Panzerschreck	bazooka-like anti-tank weapon
Pionier	army engineers
Rathaus	city or town hall municipal offices
Realschule	high school
Regierung	governing regime
Reich	state or empire

Reichsmark	German currency during the Hitler regime
Reichswehr	100,000-man German army permitted by the Treaty of Versailles
Reiter	cavalry, literally "rider"
Rollbahn	road
Schutzstaffel (SS)	Guard Corps, National Socialist Army/Police
Skat	German card game, a little like bridge
Sturm Abteilung (SA)	Storm Unit, Nazi brown shirts private militia
Schwarzmarkt	black market
Soldbuch	soldier's pay book
Soldat	soldier
Sparkasse	bank
Sportplatz	soccer stadium, literally "sport place"
Stalin Orgel	Stalin's pipe organ, slang for Russian rocket artillery
Sudetenland	that part of western and northern Czechoslovakia predominantly populated by ethnic Germans before and during the war
Sudetendeutsche	ethnic Germans from Sudetenland
Truppenführer	squad leader
Turnhalle	community centre gym
Unteroffizier	Corporal
Untersee Boot	submarine
Vaterhaus	family home, literally "father house"
Waffen SS	Nazi Special Forces, literally "Armed Guard Corps"
Währungsreform	monetary reform (10:1) under the Marshall Plan, 1948
Wirtshaus	Bavarian pub
Wehrmacht	German Armed Forces of 1936 to 1945
Wochenschau	weekly newsreels shown in theatres
Wohnungsamt	housing bureau
Weib	slang for woman or wife
Zeltplan	soldier's cape (technically Zeltbahn)
Zug	platoon
Zugführer	platoon leader

To order more copies,
please contact the author at

261 Ferndale Avenue,
London, Ontario N6C 5L1

Email: d.gagel@delcan.com
Telephone: 519-680-3484